ROUTLEDGE LIBRARY EDITIONS:
LANDMARKS IN THE HISTORY OF
ECONOMIC THOUGHT

Volume 9

HISTORY OF MONETARY AND CREDIT THEORY

HISTORY OF MONETARY AND CREDIT THEORY

From John Law to the Present Day

CHARLES RIST

TRANSLATED BY JANE DEGRAS

Routledge
Taylor & Francis Group
LONDON AND NEW YORK

First published in English in 1940 by George Allen & Unwin Ltd

This edition first published in 2017
by Routledge
2 Park Square, Milton Park, Abingdon, Oxon OX14 4RN

and by Routledge
711 Third Avenue, New York, NY 10017

Routledge is an imprint of the Taylor & Francis Group, an informa business

British Library Cataloguing in Publication Data
A catalogue record for this book is available from the British Library

ISBN: 978-1-138-21086-8 (Set)
ISBN: 978-1-315-40933-7 (Set) (ebk)
ISBN: 978-1-138-21729-4 (Volume 9) (hbk)
ISBN: 978-1-138-21731-7 (Volume 9) (pbk)
ISBN: 978-1-315-44096-5 (Volume 9) (ebk)

HISTORY OF MONETARY AND CREDIT THEORY

FROM JOHN LAW TO THE PRESENT DAY

BY

CHARLES RIST

PROFESSEUR HONORAIRE
A LA FACULTÉ DE DROIT DE PARIS
MEMBRE DE L'INSTITUT

TRANSLATED BY JANE DEGRAS

LONDON
GEORGE ALLEN & UNWIN LTD

The French original, "Histoire des Doctrines relatives au Crédit et à la Monnaie," was first published in Paris in 1938

FIRST PUBLISHED IN ENGLISH IN 1940

TO

MY WIFE

"Ces connaissances sont trop négligées par les hommes d'Etat qui tournent tous leurs regards vers des parties plus brillantes mais moins grandes et moins utiles. Il en est de même des hommes littéraires, dont l'érudition grecque et latine n'est d'aucun secours, ni pour le commerce, ni pour la finance."

Melon, *Essai politique sur le Commerce* (1734).

"Si les mots d'*impôt*, de *monnaie*, de *banque*, de *crédit*, de *commerce*, de *propriété* viennent souvent se placer sous ma plume, je n'ai assurément pas la prétention de résoudre les questions dont ils peuvent fournir le sujet; je me permettrais tout au plus de regretter qu'ils aient été si rarement l'objet des premières études de ceux qui ont pris part aux affaires publiques."

Mollien, *Mémoires* (1845).

"Mr. Bagehot, than whom there is no higher authority on such a matter, says that there never was, since the world began, so high and massive a brain-power applied to any one question as is applied to financial problems in England."

Marshall, Evidence before the Indian Currency Commission (1899).

PREFACE

This is not a work of erudition. I have tried to give the history, not of books or of men, but of ideas. At all times the problems of credit and of money have excited controversies in which there have been apparent, from the first, the same theoretical conflicts. It is this permanence of the problems and of the points of view that it is interesting to bring into prominence; and, with the lapse of time, it is worth while to attempt once again to check the answers given at different periods by the facts relating to the matters at issue.

Credit and money are human institutions. Like all human institutions, they may be regarded in different ways. Experience alone indicates the practical results to which these different conceptions lead. But neither the public nor even statesmen are familiar with more than a small part of that experience. In France, for example, it has no place in the teaching of history. It is not, therefore, inappropriate to bring it back to mind, and at the same time to remember that in such a subject there is neither "orthodoxy" nor "heresy." The effects which the various methods employed have had on the well-being of nations will in the last resort be judged by the nations themselves. If to be orthodox means to favour those methods which have been hallowed by success, I accept the qualification.

But let us beware of forgetting that in these matters nothing is simple. The truth of this will, I hope, be apparent to those who read this book. It would be a most serious error to believe that it is possible to summarise in a few brief precepts the totality of experience relating to credit, and to apply those precepts to daily life and politics. Man can never dispense with thought, but thought unsupported by experience is futile. And the experiences examined here are complex in their nature.

"Whatever the activity under consideration," wrote Marshal Foch, "whether it be history, literature, poetry, the novel, the study of social questions, arts of all kinds (including the art of war), nobody can approach it without a body of knowledge, that is to say, without the knowledge of what has been done in the past, without having analysed, discussed and reflected upon it, without having elucidated the principles that governed and constituted different schools of thought at different times."

In our subject the difficulty arises from the fact that the normal functioning of credit and money is constantly disturbed by wars and crises. The complex and delicate monetary mechanism of modern countries is periodically thrown out of gear by the extraordinary requirements of war, or by the abuses arising in times of peace from the collective psychosis born of economic booms and depressions. A great deal of ingenuity and courage is necessary to re-establish a workable monetary system. Equally great ingenuity and courage are required to recall to minds agitated by the monstrous consequences of paper money or by the exaggerations of credit, the few essential ideas in the absence of which no monetary system can function. Rigidity is not less dangerous than the reckless pursuit of so-called originality. Monetary systems are always undergoing adaptation; but to adapt is not to destroy.

I have sought, above all, to be clear. Indeed I have at times sacrificed brevity to clarity. With the same end in view I have grouped the principal theories discussed here around certain particularly representative writers. The penalty of this method—the only method that does not distract the attention of the reader—is the impossibility of quoting a large number of writers of distinction, who have frequently made important corrections and additions to fundamental theories. I apologise in advance to those of my contemporaries in Europe and America, and even in Asia, who are at the present time devoting so much ability and skill to the solution of these problems, and whose ideas it was practically impossible for me to present or to analyse in detail. It was not without regret that I was compelled to omit many names justly held in high esteem, and even famous. In Chapter VIII, I have tried, more briefly than I would have wished, to do justice to the indisputable contributions they have made to the advance of monetary theory since the nineteenth century.

The reader will, however, find in the footnotes references to special books or articles containing detailed bibliographies. He will only have to consult them to discover the latest theories concerning one or another aspect of this vast subject.[1]

[1] I should like to refer here to the excellent and comprehensive book by M. Valentin Wagner, of Basel: *Geschichte der Kredittheorien*, and to M. Baudin's *La Monnaie et la Formation des Prix*. Both provide a masterly treatment of the problems dealt with in this book.

It will be seen that I have not used history as a means of evasion. In no instance have I concealed my views regarding the essence of the problems treated in this book. I have tried to justify my opinion by arguments whose value will be judged by the reader. But history is itself a critical instrument of the highest order. To bring back to mind the opinions expressed by the great thinkers of other times, the mistakes that they made, and the circumstances in which their views originated, is of great value in placing in their true perspective many theories of to-day, which their authors sincerely believe to be wholly new. It is well to remember that history repeats itself; but it should be added that it never repeats itself in exactly the same way. It is these variations which constitute the difficulty of the problems confronting the intelligence and the courage of the governments of to-day.

CONTENTS

CHAPTER ONE

Confusion between Credit and Money in the Political Economy of the Eighteenth Century

PAGE

CHAPTER TWO

Eighteenth-Century Theories of the Action of the Precious Metals on the Price Level and on the Rate of Interest

CHAPTER THREE

Thornton, Ricardo, and the Bullion Report

CHAPTER FIVE

Tooke, Creator of the Credit Theory. The Currency and Banking Principles Controversy

CHAPTER SEVEN

The Action of Gold and of the Discount Rate on Prices

CHAPTER EIGHT

The General Theory of Money at the Beginning of the Twentieth Century

CHAPTER ONE

Confusion between Credit and Money in the Political Economy of the Eighteenth Century

INTRODUCTION.—§ I. DISTINCTION BETWEEN MONEY AND CIRCULATING CREDITS.—§ II. JOHN LAW.—§ III. RICHARD CANTILLON.—§ IV. ADAM SMITH.—§ V. COUNT MOLLIEN.

Introduction

In monetary matters the experience of the eighteenth century was of the most varied kind. It witnessed money functioning in times of peace and times of war. It was familiar with the difficulties of the double standard, with those arising from worn and clipped coins, with those created by excessive seigniorage charges, or by the refusal of the State to bear the costs of reforming the coinage. For the greater part of the century metallic money was in use, gold, silver and copper. England gradually took to gold. In France silver was more common. In the American colonies paper money was in use, and "necessity moneys," as Galiani called them, were frequently used in Europe. Above all, the eighteenth century escaped none of the problems arising from the prohibition of the export of money, from the "augmentations" and "diminutions" which, by changing the metallic value of the money of account, were used by rulers to lighten the burden of their debts or to give temporary satisfaction to creditors. With the exception of England, the coining of money was everywhere used by the State as a means of securing revenue.

The publicists of the time discussed all these questions with cogency and understanding. Their knowledge of the subject was at least equal to that which their nineteenth century successors were to display. Their comments were based upon prolonged observation of the mischievous administration of the currency on the part of almost all governments, and on their knowledge of the effects on

European economy of the influx of gold and silver from America from the sixteenth century onwards.

In this they were only continuing, though with more insight and ease, the work of a long succession of writers who, in the sixteenth and seventeenth centuries, discussed the same problems.[1]

In one particular, however, the eighteenth century witnessed a new phenomenon, that of the bank-note—"this new invention of paper," as Hume called it.[2]

The eighteenth century was familiar with a number of credit instruments, from the money-notes or interest-bearing Government bills, which vitiated the end of Louis XIV's reign and the beginning of the Regency, to the registered receipts used by the banks of Amsterdam and Venice.

Their nature was perfectly well understood; the former were claims representing part of the floating debt, the latter simple acknowledgments of moneys received. But neither represented bank credits, as did the notes issued by the Bank of England or the Bank of Scotland, both founded in the last years of the seventeenth century, or by the constantly growing number of private banks of issue established, first in Scotland and then in England, throughout the eighteenth century.

This idea of *bank* credit as distinct, on the one hand, from the paper money issued by the State and from deposits in public banks, and, on the other, from the commercial drafts and bills of exchange circulating among merchants, made its way slowly. The lines of demarcation between these different instruments of payment were not well defined. Galiani regretted being unable to devote an entire book to this subject which, he says, by reason of its importance no less than by "the mysterious obscurity in which it is enfolded" deserves to be called "very great." [3]

Thus, in the eighteenth century, in the ever-widening stream of monetary theory, it is the ideas relating to credit which

[1] A convenient survey of the ideas of the seventeenth and eighteenth centuries on these different subjects is to be found in Monroe's *Monetary Theory Before Adam Smith*, published by the Harvard University Press, 1923, 312 pp.

[2] Hume: *Essay XXVII, Of the Balance of Trade.*

[3] *Della Moneta*, Bk. IV, Chap. IV. It will be seen that the "mysteries of credit," so called by those who delight in obscuring rather than illuminating economic phenomena, are not a modern invention.

display the greatest originality. We shall begin by examining them.

The first observation to be made is that the majority of writers did not distinguish either between paper money and bank-notes, or between bank-notes and money. They did not differentiate clearly between credit instruments and money properly so-called. Cantillon is the single exception. In Law the confusion is partly deliberate and partly unconscious, in Adam Smith and Mollien unconscious but unmistakable, in Ricardo systematic. Apart from these fine distinctions, the confusion between money and credit is general. It was not terminated until the controversies aroused by Tooke, and then only for a short time. For the same confusion is clearly manifest, toned down it is true, after the world war, among English writers who thought it possible to apply to paper money theories valid only with regard to credit instruments. From the very outset we note the striking continuity of ideas on these matters, whether the ideas are true or false. In tracing the history of all the subjects considered in this book, we shall note the persistence of two great parallel streams carrying truth and error side by side, without either ever running dry or mingling with the other.

Everybody in the eighteenth century was familiar with metallic money. It circulated freely from hand to hand, usually in a fairly bad condition. Everybody had to take precautions against worn or clipped coins. Everybody, too, was familiar with bills of exchange, which facilitated transactions between merchants in one and the same country, and merchants operating in different countries. Nobody thought of calling them money; they were commercial credit instruments, not final means of payment. Finally, everybody knew about the paper money issued by governments when they were in difficulties, credit bills, sometimes bearing interest, or forced paper currency, the loss on whose depreciation was always borne by the last bearer.

On the other hand, when bank money came to be used, there was doubt.

"Bank money" takes two forms. In the first it is a simple receipt certificate, transferable by a mutual clearing arrangement, as was the custom at the Bank of Amsterdam. For each receipt there was in the repositories of the bank an exactly equivalent amount of metal (at least in theory, for Law accuses the Bank of Amsterdam of having sometimes lent its funds, and there is truth in the accusation).[1]

Secondly, it takes the form of a bank-note in the modern sense of the word, a circulating credit; in this case the bank undertakes to exchange it on sight for coin, but does not undertake to keep always in hand an equivalent amount of metal; this was true of the Bank of England and the Scottish banks.

It is here that doubt enters. Is this "money" in the true sense of the word? Is it credit? Do these notes have the same effect as metallic money? Will their multiplication raise the price level or not? Is this bank money an *addition* to ordinary money, or is it merely a means of making previously existing money *circulate*? We shall have a better understanding of the perplexities of the writers to be dealt with in the following pages if we first of all survey briefly the mechanism by which the note is brought into circulation. Even to-day that mechanism is frequently misunderstood, despite its simplicity, and we shall therefore open this historical chapter with a short theoretical dissertation.

§ 1. *Distinction between Money and Circulating Credits*

In essence, the function of commercial credit is to *make commodities circulate.* When a wholesaler sells goods to a retailer on credit, commodities are circulated more rapidly than they would have been by a cash sale. There is no loan of money, there is deferred payment,[2] thanks to which a sale is made which would not have

[1] This is confirmed by the notable study recently published by M. Van Dillen on the origins of the Bank of Amsterdam, in a most important volume which he edited in 1934, published at the Hague under the title: *History of the Principal Public Banks accompanied by an Extensive Bibliography of the History of Banking and Credit of Eleven European Countries.* This volume contains the latest researches into the Bank of Venice, the Saint-Georges Bank of Genoa, the Bank of England, the Banks of Sweden, Hamburg, etc. The very full bibliography on the origins of banks makes it superfluous to refer here to any other special books.

[2] Credit operations have sometimes been presented as transactions in which the buyer pays the seller and receives the same sum back again immediately as a loan, or as transactions in which the seller lends the purchaser the sum concerned for the period of the credit. Neither of these conceptions corresponds to the economic reality: the first thing is to know exactly where the money is that is used in the operation and not to imagine what *could* have happened, but what in fact does not happen.

been concluded without this postponement. The bill drawn on the debtor records the sale. The payment of the price by the final purchaser of the goods will provide the retailer with the money with which to pay, when it falls due, the bill drawn on him by the wholesaler. If the latter has in the meantime made the bill over to another in payment for goods purchased, and this second man to a third, the final payment of the bill, which has been endorsed at each transaction, will liquidate all these sales at one stroke, like the "trace" on the exchanges. The goods will have changed hands without money having circulated. The bill of exchange is, therefore, a means, not of making money circulate, but of *dispensing with it.*

All commercial credit operations registered by bills that can be endorsed and used as means of payment have the effect of making *commodities circulate more rapidly, without the use of money.* Yet nobody has ever thought of calling bills of exchange money.

What is added to this process by the intervention of the banker? The important thing about a banker is that he has at his disposal his own money-capital, or better still, deposits received from his clients, composed originally of coin. The existence of these deposits introduces a new element into the process. Instead of using a bill to make payments, the merchant can take it to the banker and have it discounted, that is to say, receive the amount in money. From that point, a *bank* credit is added to the purely commercial credit. The bill of exchange is created and circulated without the intervention of money. Its discounting by the banker has a twofold effect: in the first place, the banker takes the place of the industrialist or merchant as creditor of the person on whom the bill is drawn; in the second place, the drawer of the bill is put in immediate possession of the sum which he had agreed to collect later. A sum of money which was not involved in the first example, enters the process.

The bank advance may be given—as in the case of discount—on a credit *already granted*; or it may be given (as in advances on securities or open credits) in relation to a transaction that has yet *to be carried out*, or a debt to be settled. The difference is unimportant, for the bank advance always consists in the banker *utilising sums which belong to him, or which he has received on deposit from the public, and putting these sums into circulation* by a credit operation.

Now what happens if the person to whom the recipient of the credit has given the cash deposits it again in the same bank? The bank's liabilities will be increased by one deposit, and its cash in hand restored to its former level. If the banker repeats this operation a great number of times, and on each occasion his cash in hand is made up to its former figure, the amount of deposits will increase with each advance, and the difference between the amount of cash in hand, which remains the same throughout, and that of deposits, which increases on each occasion, will be represented on the asset side by the figure of advances made (bills in hand), this figure being equal to the amount of money he has put into circulation.

For in this case it *really is money that is circulating*. The deposits received by the banker are lent by him to merchants and manufacturers who employ them in making new purchases and new payments. The coin thus put into circulation may be deposited in a bank by those who receive it—the bank which originally granted the credit, or another bank, which will in its turn lend it again, and so on.

Bank credit only takes on large dimensions if the habit of making deposits in the bank is widespread; in the eighteenth century this habit was confined to merchants, but more than one writer (Turgot, for example[1]) realised its great potentialities once the banks concentrated the innumerable small sums that individuals keep in their own possession. (Turgot remarks that this is done by dairy and poultry farmers with regard to milk and eggs.)

So long as cash in hand equals deposits, the bank's *credit margin* is intact; but to the extent that the gap between deposit liabilities and cash in hand widens, the bank is in danger of being unable to meet cash demands on sight. The credit margin is narrowed. If it is completely obliterated, if, in other words, demands by depositors for repayment of their deposits come to exceed the repayment of advances by borrowers, the bank, unless it obtains emergency credits or receives further deposits, runs the risk of crashing.

It should be observed here, although its importance will appear later in relation to the theory of crises, that in the case both of the credit usually granted in the form of a bill, and of the bank credit which takes the form of a money advance, the initiative in the operation may come either from the one that grants the credit or the one that requests it. The retailer who believes that consumption

[1] Cf. *Réflexions sur la Formation et la Distribution des Richesses*. The edition used is the *Œuvres Complètes*, published by G. Schelle. English edition, 1793, *Reflections on the Formation and Distribution of Wealth*.

is increasing may urge the manufacturer to supply him with more goods on credit, or, on the other hand, the manufacturer, wishing to stimulate consumption, may urge the retailer to take more goods. In the same way, the banker may encourage the manufacturer to ask for credit (by offering favourable terms), or, on the other hand, wait until the manufacturer or merchant considers that conditions are favourable for borrowing. The economic forces which speed up or slow down the credit mechanism are distinct from the mechanism itself, which acts with greater slowness or rapidity according to circumstances. But it *is usually set in motion by external factors.*

All this remained quite clear so long as the banks were limited to granting credits *in money*, that is to say, with the same coin that they received. Except in England, this was the case with the majority of banks in the eighteenth century. "The Paris bankers," said Cantillon, "have often observed that the same bag of money has come back to them four or five times in the same day when they had a good deal to pay out and receive." [1]

This early clarity was lost when the banks began to issue notes, or authorised their clients to make use of cheques. Historically, payments by transfer, in purely commercial transactions, precede the use of the bank-note. But the cheque as a *generalised* means of payment is subsequent to it. It can hardly be said to have taken root before the beginning of the nineteenth century. The formula: "The bank-note was the forerunner of the cheque" is well known. For the moment, therefore, we shall confine ourselves to the former, and leave discussion of the cheque for a later occasion.

Until the bank-note came into use, *metallic money* alone was used for ordinary transactions, payment by bills being as a general rule confined to merchants. Then *bank money* came into circulation, which, apart from the fact that it was made of paper, was similar in all respects to ordinary money; it was divisible into equal units and transferable from hand to hand without endorsement. Was this not a new but genuine kind of money added to metallic money?

Actually, the bank-note too is only a means of making real money circulate, real money alone finally discharging indebtedness and being an object of desire for its own sake.

For the note is never more than a certificate of deposit; issued originally against coin brought in by the client, it is still a certificate

[1] *Essai sur la Nature du Commerce*, Higgs edition, 1931, p. 312.

when the coin given by the banker in exchange for a bill is at the very same moment re-deposited by the borrower. In the credit operation, the banker receives a bill of exchange and pays its price in coin, *thus making money circulate*. But if the client finds the coin heavy and cumbersome, what more natural than to *re-deposit* it immediately at the bank and ask for notes, that is to say, for new deposit certificates? That is in fact what happens. Thus the bank-note becomes a means of making money circulate *without actually moving it*.

As this habit became general, the banker, when giving credit, no longer expected his client to object to the coin and to re-deposit it; he gave him notes straight away. This practice, however, was not adopted without outside aid. Just after the Bank of France had established a branch at Rouen, Napoleon wrote to Mollien: "Above all, see that they discount in notes"—proof that the borrower still frequently asked for coin. That perhaps is the origin of the expression "from loan to circulation" used by many writers to describe the issue of the note. It is an ambiguous expression, for the banker, properly speaking, does not lend: he receives *a deposit* in coin, in exchange for which he gives a note confirming his obligation to refund the sum to the depositor. This is so both when he himself has just provided by way of discount the coin which the client deposits, and when it is brought to him from elsewhere. In both cases the note represents a deposit of coin. The only difference is that the coin is of different origin.

The limits which determined the maximum of the bank's credit margin before it issued notes are not however changed by the fact that the deposits are now represented by notes in circulation, instead of being registered by entry in the bank's books. The only difference between this and the former situation is found in the headings of the balance sheet, where the item "deposits" is replaced by the item "notes in circulation." The real credit operations are identical before and after the use of the note. The conditions for their security have not changed; the form alone is different. As before, the bank puts into circulation the coin which it has in its repositories, but, thanks to the bank-note, it does not need to make this money circulate *physically*. The number of notes not covered by cash in hand, sometimes small, sometimes large, measures the extent of the credits given, the greater or less intensity with which the bank is making money circulate. But this circulation has become nominal.[1] It is kept within narrow limits by the risk which the bank runs of having its notes presented for redemption more quickly than the credits which it has advanced are repaid. The bank is debtor in coin for the sum total of its notes, and the term "circulating credit" is the only correct description of the bank-note.

Once a new device is introduced into a given social system, however, it is not without effect on the system as a whole. Before the bank-note the bank's clients *used coin in their dealings with one another.*[2] To make their payments they had to go to the bank for coin and transfer it physically, although the sum might be immediately re-deposited in the bank by the new owner. With the note, this became unnecessary. Granted that there is confidence in the bank issuing them, *the clients make their payments to each other in notes*, and the coin deposited at the bank ceases to circulate. *Among the clients of the bank* the circulation of notes supplants that of coin, as it has already done in *transactions between the bank and those who borrow from it.* That does not mean that there is a more active circulation of money among the clients. On the other hand it does mean that, since there is now less likelihood of cash demands on the bank, *its margin of credit is extended*: it can manage with a smaller cash reserve for the same number of notes. The use of the bank-note, as later that of the cheque, increases the credit capacity of banks by weaning the public from the habit of using coin. Thanks to this ingenious social device a large part of the sums deposited with the banker is used by him to grant credits to borrowers, while at the same time it remains at the disposal of its owners for making payments to each other. That is the entire "mystery" of credit.

But in all this there is no increase in *money*, there is merely a more rapid circulation of *existing money*. Thornton, whose perceptions were very sharp, saw this quite clearly: If at any given moment an inventory were made of the wealth of a society, the notes issued by the bank, included among the bearer's assets, are counterbalanced by commercial drafts among the liabilities of the signatory; credit and debit equal each other and cancel each other out. "The case of

[1] This term is used by Knut Wicksell in his *Lectures*, p. 76. The German translation of this book was published by Fischer at Jena, under the title *Vorlesungen über Nationalökonomie*, in 1928. The Swedish edition was published in 1906.

[2] Except, of course, in those transactions settled by transfer arrangements.

gold, on the other hand, differs from that of paper inasmuch as the possessor of gold takes credit for that for which no man debits himself." [1]

Let us put the thing a little differently. A man has in his cashbox a certain sum of money which he will need in a month's time to make some payments. He can let this sum go for a month, but not for longer. A friend borrows it from him on condition that he will return it at the end of the month, and gives the owner a written promise to pay it back on that date. In the owner's cashbox the money is represented by an acknowledgment of the debt signed by the borrower. During the term of the loan the money is circulating among the public. Has there been any increase in money? None whatever. There has been put back into circulation a sum which otherwise would have remained inactive. Now let us bring a banker into the process. Suppose that many owners entrust him with their surplus funds. He can make these sums circulate by lending them, *but, theoretically, only for the same period of time as the owners themselves would have had them at their command.* The only difference arises from the circumstance that, since he does business with a number of depositors, the banker's cash in hand is being continually renewed: as one depositor makes a withdrawal, another makes a payment; thus the banker can constantly *renew* his credits.

Taken all together, the bank-notes representing advances constitute what the statisticians call a "renewable aggregate," similar to the population of a country at any moment. A given population is constantly diminishing as a result of deaths, and increasing as a result of births. At any moment, the figure of population is the result of this twofold process. In the same way the number of uncovered notes (that is, the credits given in bank-notes) is being constantly diminished by the repayment of loans, and constantly increased by their renewal. The banks have only to restrict their credits for the number of notes in circulation to decrease, if repayments continue at the same rate, and conversely. It is easy to imagine a very great reduction in the number of notes during a period of crisis when the banks suspend credits and retain repayments. Such deliberate reductions are impossible in the case of money, for the amount of metallic money in a country (and the same is true of

[1] Thornton: *An Enquiry into the Nature and Effects of the Paper Credit of Great Britain* (1802), p. 21.

paper money) is usually increased in a steady and regular fashion. Normally there is no birth and death of money; once introduced into circulation, money stays there; there is no normal means (apart from wear and tear, which is of little practical significance) by which money once introduced can be made to disappear. For hoarding is not the death of money. The importance of this distinction between the way in which money increases, and the way in which bank-notes, which enter into circulation through bank advances, increase, will be seen later. For the moment it is enough to shew that the volume of bank-notes in circulation is essentially elastic.

One last observation on the meaning to be given to the term, velocity of circulation. The establishment of banks of issue (and later that of banks issuing cheques) increases the rate at which the money in a country circulates. After their establishment, there is normally a certain amount of credit below which, so to speak, the banks never descend. This minimum velocity of circulation that the banks impart to money becomes one of the normal factors in the monetary system of the country.

But this velocity is not constant. It can increase or diminish, and that in two ways: either the minimum to which I have just referred is raised, as the practice of resorting to credit becomes more widespread; here it is the velocity of circulation of the *cash deposited with the banks* that increases—or, the velocity of circulation remaining the same for each unit of money delivered to the banks, *the number of these units* is increased, as the public resort more and more to the practice of concentrating their monetary resources at the banks. Here there is an increase in the *velocity of circulation, not of the money placed in the banks, but of the total stock of money within the country.* The two phenomena may occur simultaneously, may strengthen each other, cancel each other out, or act in contrary directions. But they do not arise from the same causes. The second phenomenon is slow and steady in its working, the first displays rapid alternations of growth and decline, corresponding to phases of boom and slump, or to a prolonged rise or fall in prices. It is by far the more important. The second is of interest because, *up to a certain point*, it can compensate for an inadequate supply of the precious metals.

An increase in the precious metals in a country usually increases the number of monetary units received on deposit by the banks, and which they can put into circulation. As a result the *total volume of credits*, apart from any change in the velocity of circulation of these units, may be greater. On the other hand, according as to whether the new addition to the stock of precious metals is distributed between the banks and the public in the same proportion as the previous stock, or a greater or lesser proportion is acquired by the banks, the velocity of circulation of the *total volume of money within the country* remains the same, or becomes greater, or diminishes.[1]

The expression velocity of circulation, a favourite term among English writers, is, it is evident, full of ambiguities in its application to banking phenomena. It would be better to restrict its use to the movement of the monetary units deposited at the banks, and to use the expression "concentration of coin in the banks" for what has here been called the *velocity of circulation of the total stock of money within the country.*

It is possible to go still further, and to call the changes in the velocity given by the banks to the cash deposited with them simply an *increase or decrease of banking credit*. This is done by certain writers, for example Irving Fisher, who reserves the expression velocity of circulation for payments made *among themselves* by the holders of the instruments of payment (whether coin, notes, or current credit accounts).

It is not our task here to prescribe certain definitions but to specify the phenomena indicated in the current definitions, and above all to make it clear, firstly, that the credit operations of banks are in reality operations by which the cash deposited with the banks is put into circulation, and secondly, that what is called the creation of notes or current accounts is only the ingenious form given to this act of putting deposits into circulation.

These explanations were necessary in order to understand the theories that we are about to discuss. We shall deal first of all with those of John Law, whose famous experiment left its mark on all the theories of the century. The wise and sound ideas of the banker Cantillon will serve as contrast. In comparison with those of Cantillon, Adam Smith's theories appear dubious. The confusion between credit and money stands out very clearly, and this confusion was to dominate all the ideas enunciated at the close of the century.

[1] This, of course, assumes that the velocity of circulation imparted by the banks to the cash deposited with them remains constant.

Despite his sound common sense, Mollien was not free of it. In this chapter we shall try to shew the connection between these ideas, to explain their significance and to discuss the practical consequences drawn from them.

§ II. *John Law*[1]

The failure of John Law's unfortunate attempt to establish a bank of issue in France dominated the ideas of the eighteenth century about credit. His contention that to create money is to create wealth was vigorously rejected by all his contemporaries. The efforts made in the course of the century by so many writers, including Smith, Hume and Turgot, to reduce the role of money in the national economy to nothing or to insignificance, were directed against Law rather than against mercantilist ideas about money, which had already worn thin. Had not Law announced that an increase in the quantity of money was the only way of stimulating the national economy?

The failure of the *Banque Royale* made a great stir. Nobody had a good word to say for the System. Dutot, Law's former collaborator, took up his defence in vain.[2] Hume, referring to Dutot's

[1] No bibliography relating to Law and his system will be given here. Everything useful that can be said on this subject has been said by M. Harsin, either in his valuable work *Les Doctrines Monétaires et financières en France du XVIe au XVIIIe siècle*, Paris, 1928, or in his preface to the three volumes of the *Œuvres Complètes* of John Law, published in 1934 by Sirey. Nobody can hope to add anything, with regard either to the accuracy of the texts (of which a few are here published for the first time) or to the fulness and reliability of the information that M. Harsin has collected about our author. It is a matter of great regret that these volumes reached me too late for me to use the text as the source of my quotations. I have used the old Daire edition, in the Great Economists Series, but I have followed M. Harsin as to the dates of the different writings. On the other hand, I cannot agree with him in many of his appreciations, not of the man, whose eloquence and sincerity I have no wish to deny, but of his ideas; M. Harsin has, like so many others, allowed himself to be too easily seduced by Law, in particular in regard to the workability of the System. But all those who have made a study of John Law owe too much to M. Harsin not to express their grateful recognition and admiration for his work before undertaking an explanation of the theories of the extraordinary visionary.

[2] M. Harsin has recently prepared a new edition of Dutot's *Réflexions politiques sur les Finances et le Commerce*, together with Dutot's reply to Pâris-Duverney's criticism of his first book, now published for the first time. Published by G. Droz, Paris, 1935, two vols.

Réflexions politiques, accuses him of frequently adducing facts and arguments of doubtful authenticity.[1] Galiani calls the System "one of the strangest productions of the human intelligence."[2] As for Adam Smith, he does not even discuss Law's ideas, but is content to write of his first book:

> "The splendid but visionary ideas which are set forth in that and some other works upon the same principles, still continue to make an impression upon many people, and have perhaps, in part, contributed to that excess of banking, which has of late been complained of both in Scotland and in other places."

He calls the System "the most extravagant project both of banking and stockjobbing that, perhaps, the world ever saw."[3]

The nineteenth and twentieth centuries have at times been less critical of Law.[4] Certain passages written in a restrained and reasonable manner are quoted as expressing the real essence of Law's thoughts. Actually, they are tactical concessions to the necessities of the moment. It has also been said that he was an unrecognised forerunner, because certain bankers to-day have taken up some of his most debatable formulas. It would be more correct to regard these belated disciples as backsliders. The eighteenth century was not mistaken in its attitude. It saw through the fundamental confusion between credit and money that Law deliberately and persistently maintained throughout all the vicissitudes of his tormented career. I would go further: credit had no interest for him except as a means of making the public familiar with paper money. He was, it is true, influenced by banking experiences which are to-day completely forgotten, but to which he constantly refers, and which were bound to maintain that confusion. This has not been sufficiently stressed; but unless these experiences are borne in mind, there is a danger of not understanding his real thoughts.

Law visited Amsterdam and Venice; he was familiar with the workings of the banks of Naples, and particularly with the workings of the Bank of England and the Bank of Scotland. Now, at Amster-

[1] Hume, *Essays. On Money*, note.

[2] Galiani, *Della Moneta*, Bk. IV, Chap. IV.

[3] Smith, *Wealth of Nations*, Bk. II, Chap. II. Cannan edition, Vol. I, p. 301.

[4] I would mention, *inter alia*, the sympathetic study devoted to Law by Olinde Rodriguez in 1827, which appeared in the Saint-Simonian review *Le Producteur.*

dam and Venice, there was a curious custom rarely mentioned when these banks are spoken of: the *obligation* to make use of transfers, that is, of cheques, for commercial payments above a certain amount. A merchant could not withdraw in coin the sums deposited by him, once he had been credited in the bank's books with a sum corresponding to the effective silver or gold content of that coin; in the same way, when he handed over a bill of exchange to the bank, he could no longer dispose of his credit except by transfer. This rule arose because the purpose of "bank money," at Amsterdam and Venice as well as at Hamburg, was precisely to protect merchants from the losses of wear and tear, or from falsification of coin; these banks, it will be seen, were not credit banks: they were purely "monetary" institutions. But this prohibition on withdrawals in coin gave rise to ambiguity concerning the nature of bank deposits.

Melon and Galiani quote a saying that was current at the beginning of the century; it was calculated to appeal to adventurers in finance, and was not unknown to Law: "The good bank is the bank that does not pay."[1] The banks that did not pay were "good," it was thought, because, not giving credits, they always retained the funds deposited with them, and thus the depositors ran no risk.

But this saying should not be taken too literally, for, in addition to its inconvertible money, the banks of Amsterdam and Venice had *convertible* bank money; at Amsterdam this was the case in regard to the certificates given in exchange for bullion,[2] and Galiani explains that at Venice also there was a supply of ready cash "which far from diminishing wealth, increased it and strengthened confidence in the bank." With his usual insight he adds: "It was recognised that trade would suffer if the withdrawal of deposits were

[1] "At the time that Law's bank suspended payment," wrote Melon (Daire edition, p. 804), "a number of broadsheets appeared, in one of which it was written that *the good bank is the one which pays nothing*. The occasion was used to make a joke of a principle which, rightly understood, is correct and sound. The Amsterdam Bank pays nothing because it has a good use for the money." Galiani, Bk. IV, Chap. IV, explaining the working of the Bank of Amsterdam, adds that it was this bank "which gave rise to the saying that *the good bank is the bank that does not pay.*" It seems quite clear that the witticism was not coined in regard to Law's system, but was a common saying applied ironically to the *Banque Royale*.

[2] Cf. the description by Adam Smith of the fairly complicated mechanism of these certificates.

forbidden, and that, even if it were true that the good bank is the bank that does not pay, it is also true that the bank which has credit is the bank which does not refuse to pay." [1]

If we turn from the "monetary" banks to the real "credit" banks, the Bank of England and the Bank of Scotland, we find that at times they were unable to convert their notes—the former during the war of succession in Spain,[2] and the latter in 1695; but they recovered after the crisis, without their notes suffering anything more than a temporary loss in value.

Among those given to generalisations (*in generalibus latet error* said the Schoolmen) this was bound to give rise to the idea that invariable "convertibility" of the note was not, after all, a condition *sine qua non* of the good functioning of a bank, and that one could, without risk, slightly increase the issue at the cost of "convertibility."

"The certain good it [i.e. the establishment of a bank] does," Law remarks, "will more than ballance the hazard, tho once in two or three years it failed in payment; providing the Sums lent be well secured." [3]

Do not the statutes of the best banks to-day contain restrictions on convertibility which are peculiarly liable to ambiguity? The Bank of France, in its early days, would only convert its notes at Paris, the Reichsbank only at Berlin. When England returned to the gold standard after the War the first clause of the law passed in 1925 to effect this change proclaimed that notes were not exchangeable against specie. In the same way, when the French currency was stabilised in 1928, it was stipulated that the Bank of France would convert its notes only if they were presented at Paris, and then only for a minimum sum which was fixed very high. Thus it can still be said to-day: "The best bank is the bank that does not pay." When these facts are considered by ill-informed or superficial persons, is it surprising that they should reach the conclusion that paper money, not convertible into specie, is as trustworthy as any other?

This was the conclusion that Law instantly drew from the

[1] Galiani, *loc. cit.*, p. 328: quoted from the first edition, 1750.

[2] See Andréadès, *History of the Bank of England*, p. 120.

[3] John Law, *Money and Trade considered, with a Proposal for Supplying the Nation with Money*. Edinburgh, 1705, pp. 37–38.

examples that he had himself witnessed, and which strengthened the fundamental confusion that, with greater or less Machiavellianism (for this brilliant writer, this accomplished man of the world, this passionate gambler, had nothing of the simpleton about him[1]), he never ceased to create between credit and money.

The confusion is manifest in his first memorandum, addressed in 1705 to the Scottish Parliament. There, without any disguise, he reveals the kernel of his idea: to make a country wealthy it is necessary to increase the quantity of money. It is by the quantity of money that wealthy countries are distinguished from poor countries. In his opinion an abundance of money is not a symptom but a source of wealth. Obviously he was inspired in this by the sight of Dutch prosperity, with its great trade and abundance of coin. Law did not stop to think that real money—money that costs something to produce and has a value in itself—that is to say, metallic money, enters a country only as a result of goods or services that it has provided for others; that it is, like all other products which it imports, merely the recompense for its labour, the abundance of its resources, or the security which it offers for the employment of funds from abroad. To infer from the abundance of metallic money in a prosperous country that it is enough to "create" paper money (for that is the only kind that is "created" and not acquired) in a poor country in order to develop industry or natural resources in which it is lacking, is an idea that affronts common sense, notwithstanding all the ingenious arguments advanced by Law.[2] Scotland, a country of shepherds and fishermen, mountainous and poor in raw materials, situated, moreover, off the great trade routes, could have increased its currency, but it would have given the country neither industry, nor trade, nor agriculture, nor a prosperous

[1] In Vol. III of Law's *Œuvres Complètes*, in the long *Mémoire Justificatif* that M. Harsin has rediscovered, there is an amusing portrait of Law by himself, in which the following occurs: "If at times he used specious arguments when he considered them a necessary road to the truth, it was with so fine an art that one found oneself brought suddenly into brilliant light, without noticing that one had passed through darkness to get there."

[2] Among Law's writings there can be found a number of hypothetical instances, such as have been frequently portrayed since his time, in which money created and spent by one section, then comes into the possession of certain groups who, in spending it, bring prosperity to another part of the population, which in its turn, by using the money for purchases, enriches still others, etc., etc. Cf. the passage (Law, *loc. cit.*, p. 97) beginning: "Suppose an island belonging to one man . . ."

shipping industry.[1] That could be attained only by the labour and frugality of its inhabitants.

This, however, was the proposal submitted by Law in 1705 to the Scottish Parliament (which very wisely rejected it). An account of this proposal was published in the same year under the title *Money and Trade considered with a Proposal for Supplying the Nation with Money.*[2]

It is a regular treatise on money, and contains Law's basic ideas. First of all, the introductory statement that abundant money is necessary to increase wealth.[3]

"Considering how small a share we [i.e. Scotland] have of the Money of Europe, and how much Trade depends on Money: It will not be found very practicable to better our Condition, but by an addition to our Money. Or if it is practicable without it, it is much more so with it. . . . National Power and Wealth Consists in numbers of people, and Magazines of Home and Foreign Goods. These depend on Trade, and Trade depends on Money. So to be Powerful and Wealthy in proportion to other Nations, we should have Money in proportion with them; for the best Laws without Money cannot employ the People, Improve the Product, or advance Manufacture and Trade . . ." [4]

Foreign trade and home trade, he continues, depend on the abundance of money.

"Good Laws may bring the Money to the full Circulation 'tis Capable of, and force it to those Employments that are most profitable to the Country; but no Laws can make it go furder, nor can more People be set to Work, without more Money to circulate so as to pay the Wages of a greater number." [5]

That is the foundation of the structure, the fundamental postulate. It is followed by an account of all the processes by which the quantity of money can be increased; to-day this is called "increasing

[1] It is frequently contended that Law confused money with capital, or saving. He did nothing of the kind. He knew quite well what he was saying: he knew that saving is a slow process, and he wanted things to move quickly.

[2] A French translation appeared in 1720 under the title *Considérations sur le Commerce et sur l'Argent*; it was published by Daire in the *Recueil des Economistes financiers du XVIIIe Siècle* (Guillaumin, 1843).

[3] Law did not confuse money with wealth, but considered the former the essential means of creating the latter.

[4] Law, *loc. cit.*, pp. 57–60.

[5] *Ibid.*, p. 13.

purchasing power" by his offspring (and there are many) unaware of their descent from the great financial wizard.

These processes, almost all of which still have their advocates to-day, are: (1) to prohibit the export of coin and to impose on merchants engaged in foreign trade the obligation of bringing money in; (2) "augmentation" of the coinage, or, as we should say to-day, "devaluation"; (3) credit through the mediation of the banks; (4) finally, paper money based upon the security of land.

Like all the enlightened mercantilists of his time, Law is opposed to the first method—prohibition on the export of coin and obligation on the part of exporters of goods to bring in bullion. He considered it ineffective. It is, however, the method which the majority of countries that are in a weak monetary position have to-day re-installed in the place of honour: exchange control everywhere consists in compelling exporters to give up their foreign currency and in forbidding individuals to export capital.

Law is also firmly opposed to the "augmentation" of the coinage, which is in the nature of both devaluation and inflation.[1] In this he knew what he was about. The money of account at the time was the livre, and it was decided that a piece of silver, e.g. the écu, was to be worth so many livres more (augmentation) or less (diminution). This was one of the expedients dictated by the distress of the times, and after an interval of nearly two centuries we have again resumed the sad tradition. Our money of account is the paper franc, the only money circulating among the public. Devaluation consists in diminishing by law the quantity of metal which the bank is obliged to refund to the bearer. This was the device employed in the eighteenth century, as Galiani tells us, by countries having banks (as at Venice); in other countries it was necessary to re-mint the coins, or to stamp them with a special mark. The results—always

[1] Augmentation (also called raising) consisting in diminishing the silver content of the livre, it follows that the same coin, e.g. an écu, which was worth five livres before reduction, is now worth six. There are thus more livres in circulation. The man owing thirty livres, who would formerly have had to pay six écus, need now pay only five écus to settle his debt, each of these being worth six livres under the new law. In the same way, devaluation diminishes the quantity of metal by which the value of the franc is defined, and automatically the cash held by the bank represents a greater number of francs. On this question of the augmentation and diminution of coins, see Landry's *Essai sur les Mutations de Monnaie dans l'Ancienne France*, Paris, 1910. "Augmentation" or "raising" is contrasted with "diminution" or "lowering" in the terminology of the time.

the same in principle—varied however in intensity and therefore in harmfulness, according to circumstances. The advantages and disadvantages of debasement were a favourite topic of discussion among eighteenth century writers. They brought to bear on it a great deal of passion and rather less honesty, but in their writings there can be found all the arguments so often repeated in Europe and America since the world crisis.

Law (and there is something diverting in this attitude on the part of the great inflationist) was strongly and unambiguously opposed to devaluation: "But as it is unjust to raise or allay Money . . . and as it has bad Effects on home or Foreign Trade, so no Nation practises it, that has regard to Justice, or understands the Nature of Trade and Money."[1] In fact, augmentation "is laying a Tax on the People, which is sooner pay'd and thought to be less felt, than a Tax laid on any other way."[2] This is a double-edged argument which the advocates of devaluation use to-day to support their case. "This Tax," he continues, "falls heavy on the poorer sort of the People."[3] As to foreign trade, Law does not deny that it might be stimulated, but he would prefer a subsidy for exports to any tampering with the currency. He realises that augmentation will encourage foreigners to make purchases, and describes in the following terms the phenomena that was to be called "loss of substance" during the post-war inflation: "If we could be suppos'd to be without any Commerce with other Nations, a 100 *lib.* may be allay'd and rais'd to have the same effect on Trade as a Million: But, if a Stranger were suffer'd to come to *Scotland*, he might purchase a great part of the Land or Goods with a small Sum. And a rich Man here would make a very small Figure abroad."[4] Finally, he sees clearly that the mere possibility of augmentation drives coin out of the country, or, as we should say to-day, causes a "flight of capital," with the object, once the reduction or devaluation has been effected, of making a profit from converting the metal exported into the national currency.

After more than a century of stable money, we have rediscovered all these consequences of inflation; one after the other they have made their appearance since the World War, following inevitably from the policy of reckless expenditure on the part of the belligerent governments.

[1] Law, *loc. cit.*, p. 36. [2] *Ibid.*, p. 51. [3] *Ibid.*, p. 51. [4] *Ibid.*, p. 48.

Law's severity is rather astonishing. In this he had few followers in the eighteenth century, but they included Forbonnais, d'Aguesseau (a violent antagonist of Law, whose treatise did not however appear until much later), and Dutot, Law's friend and collaborator, who took up his defence on every point. Melon, on the other hand, in his short and weighty book published in 1734, recommends devaluation as the only way of coming to the assistance of the people when "debts can no longer be recovered without the use of military force"; this device, he says, "is in accordance with the natural disposition of the French nation, because it will be quickly and easily brought to a successful conclusion."[1] Galiani in his turn supports Melon, whom he calls *uomo d'ingegno grandissimo et d'animo veramente onesto e virtuoso.* In two chapters, astonishing for their liveliness, wit, and good sense, he discusses all the arguments for and against devaluation and concludes, in opposition to the contention of the Parlement of Paris and its president Le Camus,[2] that the devaluation of 1718 was inevitable and necessary to liquidate the costs of former wars: "War is the luxury of Monarchies," he writes, "and in peace it is impossible to get rid of the effects of war except by economy and frugality. On the other hand the French may be pardoned for their outcry against augmentations, for the sick man always shouts and screams when he takes medicine, but not when he is taking his sickness by living too well; that is why war is full of joyous songs and celebrations and gaiety, while monetary changes are lugubrious and sad."[3] He freely admits that such measures are repugnant to popular feeling, but, he adds, what is to be done, "since nobody has anything else to propose"?[4]

David Hume was not opposed to a slow and steady reduction in the metallic content of money. He contended that in France reductions were not followed by proportionate price increases (an extremely interesting observation, which appears to be confirmed by

[1] The quotation from Melon is taken from Daire's edition, p. 833. The same contention is made to-day by M. Despaux in his book, *Les Dévaluations Monétaires dans l'Histoire*, Marcel Rivière, 1936.

[2] The arguments put forward resemble so clearly those advanced by the Chancellor in his *Considérations sur les Monnaies* that it is permissible to wonder whether they were drawn up by d'Aguesseau; M. Harsin shows that the *Considérations* was written about 1717–1718, although not published until 1777, at a time when these problems no longer interested the public.

[3] Galiani, *op. cit.*, p. 263. Here already is what M. Caillaux has called in our day "la grande pénitence."

[4] *Ibid.*, p. 267.

the evidence of contemporaries) and did not prevent the price of wheat from remaining at the same level between 1683 and 1740. He therefore proposed a periodical recoining at which, on each occasion, the shilling was to be reduced by one penny-worth of metal. "Were all our money recoined, and a penny's worth of silver taken from every shilling, the new shilling would probably purchase every thing that could have been bought by the old; the prices of every thing would thereby be insensibly diminished; foreign trade enlivened, and domestic industry, by the circulation of a great number of pounds and shillings, would receive some encrease and encouragement."[1]

Although he was opposed to augmentation Law was in favour of the diminution of coins, that is, of a reduction in their nominal value while retaining the same weight of metal. To-day we would call this "deflation" or "revaluation." The reasons he gives are extremely curious, and enable us to recognise the real character of the wizard in finance and the specialist in banking operations. Nothing more clearly reveals the essence of his thought.

Law had in mind an incident that occurred in the very first years of the Bank of Scotland, an incident that he witnessed, and to which he returned on more than one occasion.[2]

Trade shewing an unfavourable balance, gold left the bank. The bank then printed pound sterling notes to meet small payments (as Law himself was to do later when he printed convertible ten-livre notes) and would without doubt have been able to check the panic if the unfortunate announcement of an *augmentation* of money had not brought the citizens of Edinburgh to the bank demanding coin. The notes were marked in pounds sterling and shillings, while the coin held by the bank consisted of crowns worth 5s. 6d. If the bank decided to make these crowns pass for 6s. instead of 5s. 6d., that would mean for each note-bearer a diminution of the gold content of his note, while the cash held by the bank would be "revalued." There was therefore a run on the banks by people who wished to have their notes converted at the old rate while there was still time. The bank itself provoked the demand for conversion.

[1] Hume, *Essays*, *On Money*.

[2] In *Money and Trade Considered*, 1705, and in the *Mémoire sur les Banques*, 1715 (Daire, p. 573).

Law was of the opinion that it would have been wiser to announce a *diminution* of the coin by declaring that the crown was to be worth only 5s. instead of 5s. 6d., "If the Privy Council had lower'd the English Crown to 5s. . . . to take place 2d. per crown in 3 Days, and the other 3d. in a Month, in all appearance money would have been return'd to the Bank."[1] Everybody would have hastened to bring their crowns to the bank while they could still exchange them for notes at the rate of 5s. 6d.

This provides us with a clue to many of Law's operations. For this episode in the history of the Bank of Scotland made a lasting impression on him. The account he gives of it throws a bright light on his views. *The diminution of the coinage is a convenient method of attracting specie to a bank of issue when it is in difficulties:* that is why he does not condemn the expedient. Augmentation, on the other hand, makes for the redemption of notes and the loss of gold.

Law remembered this in 1720 at a critical moment for the System. Public anxiety had been aroused by an unlimited note issue, and people flocked to the *Banque Royale* to demand coin for their notes. Law's policy at that moment has in general been misunderstood. But the idea behind it will be readily grasped when this account of the Bank of Scotland is borne in mind.

To stop the panic Law took a number of steps making the use of the note compulsory in settling bills of exchange, and for all sums in excess of 300 livres (reminiscent of the methods of the Bank of Amsterdam). But his most remarkable action—and the one which historians in general neglect—was to announce a series of *diminutions of the coinage* (a step which he had already taken in July 1719, to counter a presentation *en masse* of notes by his opponents).[2] These diminutions were intended to reduce the silver mark by degrees from eighty livres, its rate on the day of the announcement (March 11, 1720), to twenty-seven on December 1st, an enormous and monstrous diminution. "All these operations," says Dutot, "had no other object but to attract coin and bullion to the bank, where but little remained . . . the results corresponded fairly well to the intention."[3] It was the accident at the Bank of Scotland that prompted him to employ this method.

[1] *Money and Trade Considered*, p. 33.

[2] Harsin, *Les Doctrines Monétaires et financières en France du XVIe au XVIIIe Siècle*, p. 164.

[3] Dutot, Daire edition, p. 915.

The reader will note that he would not have been able to use this method if the notes, instead of being marked in *livres tournois* (i.e. in money of account) as they had been since the transformation of the General Bank into the Royal Bank, had been marked in gold écus,[1] as had been compulsory in the early stages of the System. For in that case there would have been no advantage in exchanging notes against coin, or coin against notes; the note would have appreciated or depreciated concurrently with the coin which it represented. This change in the marking of the notes (of whose import Law was perfectly well aware) provides one of the strongest reasons for allowing us to doubt his good faith from the outset, at the time when he put forward his ideas as prudence itself. In changing the marking of the notes from gold écus to livres tournois, he knew perfectly well with what an effective lever it would eventually provide him for making the note preferable to gold. Moreover, as we have seen above, in his mind diminution did not exclude the possibility of subsequent augmentation, once the desired result had been obtained. What banks of issue to-day try to accomplish by raising or lowering the discount rate, Law claimed to accomplish by the announcement of a diminution or augmentation of the coinage in relation to notes marked in money of account. It was a conjuring trick excellently designed to discredit a bank of issue, and one which his contemporaries—particularly the bankers, among whom failures increased—did not forgive him.[2]

[1] M. Harsin is mistaken in saying, on p. 159 of his book, that "the bank was empowered to conduct all its operations in a money of account, *stable by definition*(?)." In fact the opposite was true, as can be seen from the accounts of the *Banque Royale* published on p. 303 of his book. At first Law presented his proposal as a sort of new Bank of Amsterdam, where each note would represent a fixed weight of gold. This is clear from Law's memorandum published by M. Harsin on p. 24 of the second volume of the *Œuvres Complètes*, where it is said that the Director of the Bank will make *bank-notes for five franc pieces to be called bank écus, by which is meant écus of the same weight and fineness as at present*, that is to say, *the very opposite of a money of account*. When the bank was changed to the *Banque Royale*, the notes were marked in livres. Contemporaries were not mistaken as to the importance of the change, and Dutot explains its consequences in full (pp. 915 *et seq.*). Dutot maintains that it was against Law's wishes that the note was made fixed and invariable, but it is quite impossible to believe him in this, the more so as it was not the edict of 1719 (as Dutot says) which allowed the notes to be marked in livres; this was done when the *Banque Générale* was changed to the *Banque Royale*.

[2] In the middle of the eighteenth century the English economist, Postlethwayt, asserted that of the two hundred bankers in Paris all but four went bankrupt. Cf. Cantillon, Higgs edition, p. 370.

Nevertheless, two centuries later, an identical operation carried out by the least imaginative and the most popular of statesmen, was to be wholly successful. It is true that in the grave crisis of 1926, when M. Poincaré decided that the Bank of France was to buy gold and silver coins at the market price, that is, at a price corresponding to the rate of exchange against the pound sterling (gold currency), he did not suspect that he was closely imitating a device for which John Law had been so severely condemned. At that time (in September 1926) the gold value of the bank-note marked in paper francs was rising from day to day, the rate of the pound sterling in francs on the foreign exchanges falling steadily. From more than 200 francs to the pound it had fallen to 170, and consequently the gold louis, like the pound sterling itself, exchanged against an ever smaller number of paper francs. Apart from the fact that in 1720 the reduction in the price of the silver écu reckoned in paper livres was a result of the arbitrary decision of the sovereign, whereas in 1926 the appreciation of the gold louis in paper francs was the effect of a spontaneous rise on the exchange (and the difference is important) the situations are identical. M. Poincaré took the opportunity of publicly offering to buy for notes gold and silver at the market rate. And as his desire to "revalorise" the franc was known, the public hurried to bring in their gold coins, in fear of seeing their price, in notes, diminish from week to week. Which was in fact what happened. But the cash at the Bank increased by several hundred millions, not indeed without some danger to the Bank, for the gold louis for which it paid at the rate of 170 in September was worth no more than 140 in November. The Bank, on the resumption of specie payments, might have to pay more gold in exchange for each note than it had actually received from the bearers. But the stabilisation of the franc effected in December 1926 put an end to this danger. M. Poincaré would have avoided this imitation (though it had fortunate results) of John Law's machinations if, as was advised by the Committee of Experts which he strongly criticised, he had in advance fixed once and for all the new value of the franc, before proceeding to the purchase of gold on which he was so strongly bent.

But let us return to John Law and to the means of increasing the currency in a country. Having rejected some, he advocates first of all, credit, and if that is not enough, paper money.

Here we are at the heart of the problem. What were Law's ideas about credit? He thought that as a means of increasing monetary tokens it was too slow and demanded too much patience. "It is true that credit is both necessary and useful. It has the same effect as if the quantity of money were increased, and is as good for trade." It is a formula which appears quite obvious but is in fact dangerously ambiguous. For the money which credit puts into circulation enters it only to leave it again as soon as its task is accomplished. The bank-note returns to the issuer when the bill discounted is paid as it falls due. On the other hand when paper money is used in payment it continues to circulate indefinitely. That is what Law failed to see clearly. For him a note is money, distinguishable from other kinds of money only because its issue is strictly limited. And that precisely is what he has against it.[1] "Credit that promises a Payment of Money, cannot well be extended beyond a certain proportion it ought to have with the Money. And we have so little Money, that any credit could be given upon it, would be inconsiderable."[2] "For as Credit is voluntary, it depends on the Quantity of Money in the Country, and Increases or Decreases with it."[3]

In other words, Law thought that convertible notes were an instance of credit issue. But that convertibility was a nuisance; and a system had to be devised which, while conferring on paper the same public confidence as the convertible note, was not limited in the same way. The problem consisted in increasing the quantity of money by means of notes which would have all the qualities of bank-notes with the exception of convertibility, while the public could not see what was happening. Law was not unaware that sound credit increases the means of payment only by slow degrees. The bank must be given time to win the confidence of the public, to get them accustomed to its notes, to develop its business slowly. But it was precisely this delay which the revolutionary financier was unwilling to tolerate. He wanted to see money increase immediately. And thus he arrived at the sole remaining method of increasing money—paper money. In Scotland in 1705 he suggested issuing paper money secured on land; later, in France, when the number of

[1] The phrase "the good which the bank does by increasing the quantity of money" is constantly used by Law. Cf. *Mémoire sur les Banques*, pp. 559–560. It is a most dangerous phrase, which was to be taken up by Smith and Ricardo.

[2] Law, *loc. cit.*, p. 60.

[3] *Ibid.*, p. 39.

notes had been increased beyond the capacity of the public to absorb them, he simply advised forced currency and compulsory acceptance.

All the arguments produced since that time by the avowed or unavowed advocates of forced paper currency, all the sophisms by which they attempt to dissuade a public whom they characterise as reactionary or fetishistic from demanding in payment, instead of a simple circulating credit, a metal which has value in itself, are to be found in the writings of Law; there they are presented with a vigour, a sparkle, an eloquence and indeed a note of sincerity which are almost convincing, if one did not hesitate to admit that a man of such high intelligence could for an instant be deceived as to the true bearing of his schemes. Granted that his memorandum of 1705 was a youthful mistake. In his letters of 1720, and later in his *Mémoire justificatif* of 1725, discovered and published by M. Harsin, there is apparent, at the best, nothing more than the desperate attempts of a man who feels that his undertaking is doomed and who demands from public authority what he knows he is no longer able to obtain from those whose confidence in the notes has been destroyed.

In summarising Law's ideas, let us pause for a moment over two of them which, persisting in the most recent theories, have had a fatal effect on currency systems, without, however, thereby discouraging their advocates.

First, Law criticised silver as a standard of value because it was always fluctuating and falling in value; gold, on the other hand, although it fell less, was little better. A hundred and fifty years too soon he announced the demonetisation of silver. Two hundred years after Law the League of Nations Gold Committee was to be little more satisfied with the yellow metal, with this difference, that their complaint against gold was that it was not plentiful enough and rose in value. That, obviously, is a defect which cannot be attributed to paper money. In paper money (so long as its quantity is regulated according to demand) Law found a much more stable measure of value. It is objected that paper money cannot be exported? The objection is invalid, for trade is nothing but the exchange of commodities against commodities, and is it not all to the good that an exporter should be able to import only the exact equivalent of what he has exported, and no more? There already is the theory of bilateral trade—"I buy from him who buys from me"

—so dear to the Europe of to-day. Law saw that in the absence of a common currency the nations would be compelled to regulate trade.[1]

But let us tackle the essential argument, the argument in which Law is a real forerunner, the crushing argument which, since his time, has been used by all the currency cranks and by all plundering states. What is money but a simple exchange voucher conferring the right to a certain quantity of goods? And if that is its function, what is the point of using a costly metal?

Here we reach the cardinal point of Law's theory. Money is only a voucher for buying goods. It is a formula which has provided the starting point for all currency cranks, an apparently self-evident axiom on which have been based all systems which deny the citizen the right to a means of storing value. Money is made only to purchase with. Money is not the durable and indestructible good, of stable value and unlimited acceptability, with the help of which man has been able to put by the product of his labour, the instrument for saving by means of which a bridge is built between the present and the future and without which all provision for the future would become impossible. No!

"Money," says Law in a famous passage, "is not the value *for* which Goods are exchanged, but the Value *by* which they are Exchanged: The use of Money is to buy Goods, and Silver while Money is of no other use."[2]

And elsewhere: "I consider an écu itself merely as a note drawn up in

[1] Cf. *Mémoire pour prouver qu'une Nouvelle Espèce de Monnaie peut être meilleure que l'Or et l'Argent* (1707), in the *Œuvres Complètes*, Vol. I, p. 195. This memoir, found by M. Harsin in the Bibliothèque de l'Arsenal, is not included in the Daire edition. Cf. *Money and Trade Considered*, p. 102. "If a money is establish't that has no intrinsick Value, and its extrinsick Value to be such, as it will not be Exported; nor will not be less than the Demand for it within the Country: Wealth and Power will be attained, and be less precarious. . . ." "No Nation keeps to Silver because it is used in other Countries, it is because they can find nothing so safe and convenient. Trade betwixt Nations is carried on by Exchange of Goods, and if one Merchant sends out Goods of a less Value, than he brings Home; he has Money furnish't him Abroad, by another who brings Home for a less Value than he sent out: If there is no Money due Abroad, then the Merchant who designed to Import for a greater Value than he Exported, is restricted; and can only Import equal to his Export, which is all the many Laws to regulate Trade have been endeavouring," p. 104. Thus the return to international barter (as Law realised well), in the absence of an international currency, limits trade, just as exchange between individuals, without the use of money, reduces the extent of their transactions. In our own time we have achieved this object by the collapse of currencies.

[2] Law, p. 100.

these terms: 'Any seller whatsoever will give to the bearer the goods or merchandise which he needs up to the value of three livres, as for other goods or merchandise,' and bearing as signature the portrait of the prince or another public mark." [1] (Daire, p. 674.)

The function of money is and should be confined to this task. But then, what is the point of using metallic money? Any sort of paper could be used in the same way and much more cheaply.

"That is my chief contention. Gold and silver are of course commodities like any other. The part of them used for money has always been affected by this use, and goldsmiths have always been forbidden to buy gold and silver louis and use them for their craft. Thus all this part has been withdrawn from ordinary commerce by a law for which there were reasons under the old government, but which is a disadvantage in itself. It is as if a part of the wool or silk in the kingdom were set aside to make exchange tokens: would it not be more commodious if these were given over to their natural use, and the exchange tokens made of materials which in themselves serve no useful purpose? But the greatest advantage of having exchange tokens made of such materials is that there would never be any temptation to divert them from their proper purpose, which is to circulate." [2]

Are there really people so malevolent, and so ignorant of the most elementary economic truths, as to give way to such a temptation and divert money from its proper destiny, which is to circulate? That cannot be borne. The fatal temptation must be removed. Hoarding—that is the unpardonable sin. It was not necessary to wait until the present time to see that.

"The prince has direct power over those who lock away and conceal coin, for this coin is the property of individuals only as a means of circulation, and they have no right to make it their own in any other sense; I am pleased to repeat and to explain this proposition as you tell me my previous letter astonished and wounded some persons, although there is no truer proposition of policy. . . . All the coin of the Kingdom belongs to the State, represented in France by the King; it belongs to him in precisely the same way as the high roads do, not that he may appropriate them as his own property, but in order to prevent others doing so; and as it is one of the rights of the King, and of the King alone,

[1] This is from his third *Lettre sur le Nouveau Système des Finances*, 1720, in which Law defends the System that had by then broken down. But the precedent is in the *Considerations* of 1705. It is the same Law.

[2] *Ibid.*, Daire, p. 675.

to make changes in the highways for the benefit of the public, of which he (or his officers) is the sole judge, so it is also one of his rights to change the gold or silver coin into other exchange tokens, of greater benefit to the public, which he himself will accept as he accepted the others; that is the position of the present government. However, as the coin of gold or silver bears the image of the prince or some other public mark, and as those who keep this coin under lock and key regard it as exchange tokens, the prince has every right to compel them to surrender it, as failing to put this good to its proper use. The prince has this right even over goods which are your own property, and he can compel you to sow your land and repair your houses on pain of losing them; because, at bottom, your goods are yours only on condition that you use them in a manner advantageous to the community. But, in order to avoid the searches and the confiscations of money, it would be better to go at once to the source of evil, and to give men only that kind of money which they will not be tempted to hoard."[1]

Never in the age-old struggle between the State, bent on making counterfeit money, and individuals defending their fortune against its exactions, have the implications of a tyrannical idea been followed up with greater logic. The right to the ownership of money has never been denied with a more thorough cynicism, nor the rights of the State over the goods of its subjects affirmed with less hypocrisy. Is it necessary to point out the similarity between these formulas and some of those advocated in our own day?

Unfortunately, they fitted in only too well with what the French people in the eighteenth century were wont to expect from the State in financial affairs. Something quite different would have been required to reconcile them to the idea of a bank directed by the Government. Law on one occasion expresses indignation that individuals should have greater credit than the State. But the State of the seventeenth and eighteenth centuries had done all and more than was necessary to ruin its own credit, and Law was well aware of it.

In 1715, in the Memoirs addressed respectively to Desmarets while Louis XIV was still alive, and to the Regent, in which he pleads for his Scheme, Law devotes whole pages to shewing—

[1] *Mémoires sur les Banques*, pp. 574–575. In Volume III of M. Harsin's edition of Law's *Œuvres Complètes* containing the *Histoire des Finances pendant la Régence*, a number of passages in a similar vein will be found. Cf. in particular, pp. 80, 91–92, 365–366. This memoir as a whole is extremely interesting.

What?—that the Government, that is to say the Regent himself, would have the strongest motives for not seizing the funds deposited at the new bank. It was the chief objection raised by his opponents, to which they returned time and again in order to prevent the establishment of the bank—the temptation that such a fund was bound to provide to governments that were short of money. It is a fact, alas, too well known, that French efforts to establish a bank of issue during the course of the century were all wrecked by that fear. The fear was to be justified in the case of the Discount Bank, established in 1776, which Necker himself ended by ruining. In 1717, when Law suggested changing the *Banque Générale* into a Royal Bank, the merchants of Lyons expressed their opinion in a very characteristic letter. They made it clear that the change in name alone would destroy confidence in the bank. "The mere name of the King arouses distrust. His Majesty it is true . . . is master by force in his kingdom, but as to confidence and credit, these he cannot create, however great his authority, except in the ways that individuals do, in order to maintain their credit, that is, by paying."[1]

Confidence, as Law himself said in one of his good moments, "is nothing but the certainty of being paid." This certainty was wholly lacking among the subjects of the King of France. Look through the volume in which M. Harsin has republished the numerous proposals for a bank drawn up in France in the course of the century, and it will be seen that one theme—and always the same theme—recurs in the statements in which these projects are set forth. Confidence is lacking; confidence must be re-established. At the very time when the English Government was establishing the credit of the State on firm foundations by displaying the most scrupulous respect for its obligations, the Government of France, by the deplorable administration of its finances, was itself creating the conditions which made it impossible for it to raise a loan. What contemporaries thought of its honesty can be gauged from the following passage from Montesquieu, which is the most damning criticism of the working of the *ancien régime*.

"In states that carry on an economical commerce, they have luckily established banks, which by their credit have formed a new species of wealth; but it would be quite wrong to introduce them into governments

[1] Vigne, *Histoire de la Banque à Lyon*, p. 230.

whose commerce is founded only on luxury.[1] The erecting of banks in countries governed by an absolute monarch supposes money on the one side, and on the other power: that is, on the one hand, the means of procuring everything, without any power; and on the other, the power, without any means of procuring at all. In a government of this kind none but the prince ever had, or can have, a treasure, and wherever there is one, it no sooner becomes great than it becomes the treasure of the prince." [2]

The tremendous crash which put an end to Law's system, and the arguments by which he had justified his methods, probably did more than anything else to destroy in the eighteenth century any liking for credit, and any desire to see banks established in France. The *assignats* were to play the same part of scarecrow throughout the early part of the nineteenth century.

One other of Law's ideas deserves our attention for a moment, that of securing money on land. It is an idea which recurs periodically among currency cranks. It played an important part at the time of the creation of *assignats*. It was revived after the World War in the creation of *Rentenmark*. But these two ideas should not be confused with Law's, however closely they resemble it. When they were first started, the *assignats* were intended only to anticipate the proceeds in money that the sale of national property was to bring in. The idea *would have been sound* if it had been possible to sell that property quickly and profitably enough in the midst of an intense political crisis; that was, in fact, a Utopian expectation, as Talleyrand clearly demonstrated. Law's scheme was more Utopian still. It consisted in giving notes to whoever was prepared to mortgage his land or to sell it to a public body created for that purpose. It is possible that a part of the bearers would be satisfied so long as the notes did not shew any marked fluctuations in value. But how could those bearers be reassured who were not satisfied and lost confidence? How to prevent them from getting rid of the paper at any price if in any case they have no use for the land represented by the paper? Dühring subjected this idea to thorough and devastating criticism.[3] But Law's formulas were not forgotten and their echo can be heard, magnified to the stature of the speaker, in certain phrases of Mira-

[1] Montesquieu is referring to France, in contrast to England.
[2] *Esprit des Lois*, English edition, trs. by T. Nugent, 1878, p. 347.
[3] Dühring, *Kritische Geschichte der Nationaloekonomie*, p. 94.

beau's speech to the Constituent Assembly in 1790.[1] As to the Rentenmark, the assertion that its stability was based on land is a pure fable. The Rentenmark was stable only because the mark against which it was exchangeable had itself been stabilised in the ordinary way.

Whatever may be said in favour of the contention that Law acted in good faith, there is no doubt that from the time of his first memorandum the essence of his thought is summed up in the idea of the creation of paper money. It is true that there was nothing alarming in the proposals he submitted in 1715 to the advisers of the Regent and in the two memoranda which he drew up on the banks,[2] for he was anxious to disarm formidable opponents—d'Aguesseau and the brothers Pâris.

The bank, he declared, was only to issue paper willingly accepted and always convertible. This paper was to be marked in gold écus like the money of the Bank of Amsterdam, marked in *marcs banco*. Even if the bank issued no paper in excess of its metallic cover, it would still be of great service because of the ease with which notes can be carried, their greater rapidity of circulation, and the use of the note instead of domestic bills of exchange.[3] Confidence in the note would be assured by its convertibility. "There is nothing better His Royal Highness can do to enhance the reputation of his regency than to hold money sacred." [4] Furthermore, Law himself would put all his fortune into the undertaking. What better guarantee of his good faith could be required?

But through the mild and cautious phrasing of these memoranda runs the idea that the essential thing is to introduce the bank-note in France and to accustom the public to its use. That done, con-

[1] On the subject of *assignats* see the second volume of M. Marion's excellent *Histoire financière de la France depuis 1715*, where all the relevant quotations can be found.

[2] The two memoranda are in places repetitive. The second is perhaps the more interesting because of the details Law gives of the speculations which the augmentation and diminution of the coinage induced foreigners to undertake. Diminution (i.e. greater weight, corresponding to what happened in France when the franc rose as against the dollar and the pound) led to the purchase of French money by foreigners for the purpose of changing it into foreign money at a more favourable rate.

[3] The idea that representative money, paper money, circulates more rapidly than coin, is absurd. Cantillon was to contradict it later, and Law's opponents—in particular the banker Hentsch—spoke in the same sense to the Regent. On all these points see M. Harsin's Introduction to Law's works.

[4] Daire edition, p. 607.

vertibility will always be enough, even if it is suspended from time to time (as it was in London and Edinburgh), even if (as Law was to suggest in 1720) the public were *compelled* to make payments in notes (as at Amsterdam and Venice commercial payments of sums in excess of a given amount had to be made by transfer). The important thing was to make a beginning. Having once begun, he would easily find ways of increasing the circulation beyond that dictated by the strict rules of credit which, as he had explained as early as 1705, never allow for more than a slight extension of currency.[1] In one place, Law compares his system with that of Descartes, which took forty years to gain recognition. But "a new financial arrangement demands greater speed. It was therefore necessary to support it. A system in existence only one year cannot be ten years old, and some assistance must be given it until it is able to stand on its own" (*Deuxième Lettre sur le Nouveau Système des Finances*, 1720).

That is precisely what put an end to the System, compromised as it was when the *Banque Générale* was changed into the *Banque Royale* by the rapid increase of its note issues, and finally ruined when the Bank was authorised to provide notes to allow capitalists without means to subscribe to the shares of the Compagnie des Indes.

At that moment, confronted by the demands for redemption, Law returned openly to his original idea: forced paper currency. In 1720, in his *Troisième Lettre sur le Nouveau Système des Finances*, Law explains why forced currency is preferable to free currency.[2] The John Law of 1720 returns openly to the ideas he always held. The passage merits quotation in full, as a warning to all who believe it possible, in matters of exchange, to substitute compulsion for agreement freely arrived at.

"The majority of men will surely say that the credit of a particular note is based on and is maintained by the freedom to accept or reject it; on the contrary, I am of the opinion that the credit of this note is in doubt

[1] M. Harsin's discovery and publication of the important memorandum on the *Finances de la Régence*, which forms Volume III of Law's *Œuvres Complètes*, fully confirms what has been said above. See in particular the passage on p. 378 which begins: "The objects of the system go beyond the establishment of a moderate credit which merely turns the wheels of business and trade. . . . In France widely extended credit was necessary," etc.

[2] Daire, pp. 673 and 675.

and its circulation limited, precisely because its acceptance is left free. The first man to reject the note, without even having an avowed reason for doing so, spreads the fear that the issuer of the note, an individual subject not merely to the obvious embarrassments of public affairs, but also to the secret embarrassments of his private affairs, will not be in a position to supply the sum marked on the note; in doing so he stops its circulation, and the note returns always to the issuer. On the other hand, if everybody were compelled to accept the note, it might never be returned at all, and the issuer would never be compelled to redeem it."

Law's writings, so numerous, so lively, so full of examples and information, already contain all the ideas which constitute the equipment of currency cranks—fluctuations in the value of the precious metals as an obstacle to their use as a standard, their probable abandonment as a result of too great abundance which will lower their value (later it was their scarcity that was presented as a drawback), the ease with which they can be replaced by paper money, money defined simply as an instrument of circulation (its function of serving as a store of value being ignored), and the conclusion drawn from this definition that any object can be used for such an instrument, the hoarding of money as an offence on the part of citizens, the right of the government to take legal action against such an offence, and to take charge of the money reserves of individuals as they do of the main roads, the costliness of the precious metals compared with the cheapness of paper money, the acceptance *in fact* by the public in certain given cases of inconvertible money as a proof that they will accept it in all cases and in all circumstances.

It would be absurd to deny that Law foresaw some of the effects of the bank-note as a means of unifying the currency and eliminating exchange within a large country, that he clearly understood the close similarity between the note and the commercial bill whose place it took, that he realised the advantages of a concentration of metallic money in a large central bank, that he had the most exact knowledge of the effects of appreciations and depreciations of money on international trade and speculations on the exchange, that, in brief, Law was a most intelligent crank, one of those cranks who do not create an ideal world all of a piece, to fit in with their own feelings, but who find the constituent parts of their Utopia in the real world, while deceiving themselves as to the relative importance of those parts by assuming that what was able to function for a moment in exceptional circumstances is bound to be workable at all times in normal circumstances.

But apart from that, he misunderstood the real character of metallic money, and it is this that makes him so representative of all the currency cranks. He ignored the function of money as a means of *storing value* in a world where men are so anxious to preserve the product of their labour and their saving from price fluctuations and vicissitudes of all kinds. It is that which ruined the System. That metallic money is not an ideal instrument of circulation, and that it can be conveniently replaced in this respect by all sorts of circulating credits has been known from the earliest times. But nobody has yet shewn that circulating credits can replace the precious metals in their function as a store of value. None of the monetary systems yet known to us, even the most advanced, has dispensed with the precious metals, that *ultima ratio* of trade. This is what Galiani, speaking of "representative money," wrote in *Della Moneta*, an astounding book from the pen of a young man of 25, which appeared a quarter of a century after the breakdown of the *System*, and which is striking both for the clarity of its style and the penetration of its thought:

"Representative moneys are nothing but the manifestations of debt. Their security rests in the difficulty of imitating them, their acceptability in the good faith and honesty of the debtor. Their value is therefore composed of the certainty of the debt, of the punctuality of the debtor, and of the authenticity of the representation. When these three requirements are fulfilled in the highest degree, the value of the representation is equal to that of the thing represented; since men value the present as much as a future which can be converted into a present at any moment by an act of will. That is why these representations, finding acceptance easily, become moneys which may be considered in all respects equal to real money, if there is no danger of their becoming counterfeit as the result of the loss of any of the three attributes noted above; for these attributes, not being intrinsic qualities, are not as firmly attached to them as are the attributes of the beauty and brightness of the metals of which real money is composed." [1]

Galiani did not confuse money and paper money. At the outset he gives the reasons why (as against the theory put forward later

[1] Galiani, p. 319.

by Ricardo) the value of paper money cannot be determined solely by its quantity.

Law did not understand the difference between increasing the quantity of money and increasing its rapidity of circulation, between money and bank-notes. We shall see this confusion prolonged throughout the eighteenth century, being as it were hallowed by the authority of Adam Smith and later Ricardo, and involving the most serious consequences for the entire credit organisation of modern times.

§ III. *Richard Cantillon*

Richard Cantillon, an Irishman (the name is Spanish in origin), was in all respects the opposite of the Scottish John Law. It is true that both wrote in French, and excellent French. It is true, too, that both set forth ideas formed by observation and experience at more or less the same period.[1]

To this was added, in the case of Cantillon, remarkable erudition. He was familiar with the monetary history of Greece and of Rome. He had read all the English economists from Locke to Petty. But what a difference there is between the two men in ideas and in temperament! Law allowed his dreams to carry him beyond the confines of reality. Cantillon analysed reality coldly, and having no financial panacea to propose, penetrated far more deeply than Law into the real relationship of phenomena. One hundred and fifty years later the same conflict between the practical financier and the idealist was renewed in the struggle between the Rothschilds and

[1] Cantillon's book, *Essai sur la Nature du Commerce en Général*, was *written* between 1730 and 1734, and was first *published in French* in 1755 and translated into English *for the first time* by Henry Higgs in 1931. The date is significant. It took two centuries before the work of one of their most eminent compatriots was made available to the English. The quotations here are taken from Mr. Higgs' edition, which was published together with the French text in one volume by Macmillan in 1931, and it is to Mr. Higgs that I owe all the biographical details mentioned in this book. All the relevant information concerning the discovery of Cantillon's book in 1880, and the great enthusiasm aroused in Jevons when reading it, can be found in Mr. Higgs' edition; Mr. Higgs himself is an eminent and profound authority on everything concerning the Physiocrats and the economic literature of the eighteenth century. He is a guide on whom one can fully rely, as M. Harsin is for John Law, and his work makes it unnecessary for me to give any other biographical or bibliographical references.

the brothers Péreire. In the *Crédit Mobilier*, the latter tried to put into operation, by doubtful methods, ideas which it is true were actually more sound and fruitful than those of Law; but they came to grief because of the opposition of practical men of affairs, for whom experience counts for more in business than imagination.

Cantillon, a Paris banker up to 1719, with funds deposited in all important European centres, engaged in speculation during the System, and even lent money to Law's brother, but he sold out his shares in time and used his profits to purchase foreign currency, as all large-scale speculators in depreciated currencies do to-day.[1] He was a man of the world and a great traveller; but he did not dream of making a kingdom wealthy. He was content to increase his own fortune. With penetrating curiosity he analysed the mechanism of money and the circulation of goods. Far from seeing in credit the mysterious source of boundless wealth, he was rather inclined to minimise its importance. What, for example, did the sums deposited at the Bank of Venice represent? Scarcely one-tenth of the specie in the Republic. That surely was not a great deal. "It may be said of national banks generally that their utility never corresponds to the tenth part of the current money circulating in a State."[2] Even in London, notes are used almost solely to transfer large capital sums. For current expenditure, coins are used. There should be no illusions as to the services which a national bank can render, particularly in great States. If metallic money is abundant, as in France, such a bank "does more harm than good."[3] This takes us far from the expectations of Law, who imagined all the coin of France concentrated in the vaults of his bank, a grandiose achievement that it took two centuries to realise, and then as a result of exceptional circumstances created by a frightful world war, with in any case as many disastrous as fortunate consequences.

If, moreover, argued Cantillon, the money put into circulation is "fictitious and imaginary" (here again it is Law he has in mind)

[1] He even speculated, if not with the money, at least with the shares of others. He granted loans on the security of shares in the System, foreseeing their fall. He sold the shares deposited with him as security (in itself an improper transaction) and transferred abroad the sums thus realised. This operation concluded, he repurchased shares on the market at a lower price, in order to return them to the borrower; he demanded the repayment of the loan he had made, and the coinage having in the meantime been "diminished," he received a larger number of écus for the livres he had lost. Thus he speculated on a fall in shares and a rise in money. Cf. Higgs, p. 369.

[2] Cantillon, Higgs edition, p. 308.

[3] *Ibid.*, p. 310.

"it causes the same disadvantages as an increase of real money in circulation, by raising the price of Land and Labour, or by making works and manufactures more expensive at the risk of subsequent loss. But this furtive abundance vanishes at the first gust of discredit and precipitates disorder." [1]

This is the opinion of Law's System expressed by one who saw its weaknesses from the beginning and earned the enmity of the Controller-General by making investments abroad.[2]

What useful purpose do banks then serve? It is to give greater rapidity of circulation, not to all the money in a country, but to that part of it which wealthy persons—great lords and land-owners, "economical gentlemen who put by every year money from their savings"—deposit at the bank "to avoid the trouble of keeping this money in their houses and the thefts which might be made of it." [3]

"In these circumstances the Banker will often be able to lend 90,000 ounces of the 100,000 he owes throughout the year and will only need to keep in hand 10,000 ounces to meet all the withdrawals. He has to do with wealthy and economical persons; as fast as one thousand ounces are demanded of him in one direction, a thousand are brought to him from another. It is enough as a rule for him to keep in hand the tenth part of his deposits. There have been examples and experiences of this in London. Instead of the individuals in question keeping in hand all the year round the greatest part of 100,000 ounces, the custom of depositing it with a Banker causes 90,000 ounces of the 100,000 to be put into circulation. This is primarily the idea one can form of the utility of Banks of this sort. The Bankers or Goldsmiths contribute to accelerate the circulation of money. They lend it out at interest at their own risk and peril, and yet they are or ought to be always ready to cash their notes when desired on demand." [4]

The amount of coin which the bankers should keep in hand varies, of course, with the needs and habits of their clients:

"If those who deposit money with the Banker are Undertakers and Merchants who pay in large sums daily and soon after draw them out, it will often happen that if the Banker divert more than one third of his cash he will find himself in difficulty to meet the demands . . . while we have seen Bankers who were safe with a cash reserve of one-tenth,

[1] *Ibid.*, p. 311.
[2] Cf. His conversation with Law given on p. 336 of Higgs.
[3] *Ibid.*, p. 299.
[4] *Ibid.*, pp. 298–300.

others can hardly keep less than one half or two-thirds, though their credit be as high as that of the first."[1]

That, then, is all credit can do—"accelerate the circulation of money." It is a modest function, and requires for its fulfilment that the banks repay regularly and on demand deposits received or notes issued. Of course, confidence in the banker reduces the demands for repayment.

"If he has a great flow of deposits and great credit this increases confidence in his notes, and makes people less eager to cash them, but only delays his payments a few days or weeks when the notes fall into the hands of persons who are not accustomed to deal with him, and he ought always to guide himself by those who are accustomed to entrust their money to him. If his notes come into the hands of those of his own business they will have nothing more pressing than to withdraw the money from him."[2]

That is precisely the action that the brothers Pâris had taken against Law in 1719; Cantillon was quite familiar with these "brotherly" practices, which continued long in England and elsewhere.

If the banker cannot meet the demands made on him, his notes fall into "discredit" and there is a "disorder" which he must put right as quickly as possible.

If a bank is in danger, there is nothing it will not do to save itself. Here, too, Cantillon describes a course of action that has been taken frequently since his time. During the period of speculation in the South Sea Company, the Bank of England, he said, did not overlook a single "refinement" that might help to conceal its position; it "set up a number of clerks to count out the money to those bringing notes, to pay out large amounts in sixpences and shillings to gain time, to pay some part to individual holders who had been waiting whole days to take their turn; but the most considerable sums were paid to friends who took them away and brought them back secretly to the Bank to repeat the same manœuvre the next day. In this way the Bank saved its appearance and gained time until the panic should abate. But when that did not suffice, the Bank opened a subscription, engaging trusty and solvent people

[1] *Ibid.*, p. 302.

[2] *Ibid.*, p. 302.

to join as guarantors of large amounts to maintain the credit and circulation of the Bank-notes. It was by this last refinement that the credit of the Bank was maintained in 1720 when the South Sea Company collapsed. As soon as it was publicly known that the subscription list was filled by wealthy and powerful people, the run on the Bank ceased and deposits were brought in as usual."[1]

These passages give some idea of the gulf that separates Law and Cantillon.

When the bank does not pay, it is for Cantillon a time of "discredit" and "disorder." In Law's eyes it is precisely these periods that are most suggestive and interesting, providing an example to be followed: do they not in fact shew that a note can go on circulating even when the bank does not pay? What does it matter if confidence is destroyed and repayment ceases, so long as the notes circulate?

Another and fundamental difference relates to the very conception of credit. The reader will have noted it already. For Law, the really useful banks are those that create the most money. For Cantillon, their power consists exclusively in *putting into circulation* money which would otherwise remain idle in the owners' cashboxes. He summarised his views on this question in a profound remark: "Banks," he writes, "prevent so much of it (money) from being hoarded as it would naturally be for several intervals." What does that mean, if not that the bankers do no more than put into circulation the *cash balances of individuals who do not for the time being require to use them*? Concentrated at a bank, these surplus funds can then be used for the granting of credit, without their owners being in fact deprived of them. It is the same definition of the money market as that given earlier in this book, and it follows, although Cantillon does not put it into so many words, that, just as an individual who is keeping certain sums of money in order to spend them on certain dates in the future cannot risk lending them unless he is sure that they will be returned to him in time, so a bank can only lend those sums whose repayment will cover the withdrawals of its depositors.

It will be seen that the effects of credit are not very great. Much more important are the effects that an increase or decrease in the quantity of real money can have in a given country. "Silver alone

[1] *Ibid.*, pp. 318–319.

is the true sinews of circulation."[1] "The establishment of a general Bank in a great kingdom where its utility would never correspond to the tenth part of the money in circulation when it is not hoarded, would be of no real and permanent advantage, and that considered in its intrinsic value it can only be regarded as an expedient for gaining time. But a real increase in the quantity of circulating money is of a different nature."[2]

Here again it is Law that the writer has in mind, Law who identified an increase in credit with an increase in money.

It should be noted in passing that Cantillon, like other eighteenth century writers, does not make a distinction between the bank-note and the registered receipt that is circulated by means of transfer.

"Bank money" (that is, bank deposits transferable by cheque), which certain writers to-day talk of as a novelty, was as we have seen well known in the seventeenth and eighteenth centuries. It even preceded the bank-note. The great deposit banks—Amsterdam, Venice, London—made use of it, and some made its use compulsory. The writers of that time, Law as well as Cantillon and Galiani, and later Thornton,[3] made no distinction between this money and bank-notes, in regard at least to their nature, if not to their convenience.

"If payments in a national bank are made by transfers or clearings there will be this advantage, that they are not subject to forgeries, but if the Bank gives notes false notes may be made and cause disorder. There will be also this disadvantage that those who are in the quarters of the city at a distance from the Bank will rather pay and receive in money than go thither, especially those in the country. But if the bank-notes are dispersed they can be used far and near. In the National Banks of Venice and Amsterdam payment is made only in book credit, but in that of London it is made in credit, in notes, and in money at the choice of the individuals, and it is to-day the strongest Bank."[4]

[1] *Ibid.*, p. 318.

[2] *Ibid.*, p. 314. On p. 160 he writes: "I have already remarked that an acceleration or greater rapidity in circulation of money in exchange, is equivalent to an increase of actual money up to a point." The reader will note this limitation, to which I shall return later (see below, p. 115).

[3] Cf. the passage in Chap. III of his book in which he points out that, in the absence of bank-notes, payments are made "either by bills of exchange, or by the transfer of debts of one merchant to another, in the books of the banker" (p. 54).

[4] Cantillon, p. 304.

It was the dogmatism of the Ricardian School and the false ideas imposed by the Currency School that created the preconception of an essential difference between the bank-note and current credit accounts. This distinction, vigorously contested by Tooke, Gilbart, MacLeod,[1] survived all controversies and persisted, particularly in France, up to the Great War. At the beginning of the twentieth century it was again denied by Withers in England and Ansiaux in Belgium. The eighteenth century, often so superior to the nineteenth in the clarity of its economic ideas, was consistent throughout in declaring the bank-note and the deposit identical.

To continue with the points on which Cantillon differs from Law: the contrast is so thorough that one might suppose Cantillon had wished to write a sort of "anti-System" when, following the downfall of Law, he formulated, for his own satisfaction alone, economic principles completely opposed to those of the great conjuror.

In Cantillon we find the absolute and emphatic denial that money is the source of wealth. The real sources of wealth are labour and land; even less can paper money be a cause of wealth. In the three extremely interesting chapters in which he describes the methods by which a country can acquire money, which constitute, as it were, an appendix to those devoted by Law to the same question in his *Considerations* of 1705,[2] he does not refer once to paper money. In itself this omission is significant. For Cantillon, money follows industry and does not create it.

One more contrast: Cantillon, like all the writers of his time,

[1] MacLeod, *Theory and Practice of Banking*, Vol. I, p. 330: "The student must, therefore, carefully observe that in the language of banking, a Deposit and an Issue are the same thing."

[2] The list of these methods is the same as that which we would give to-day. They are: the exploitation of mines, a favourable trade balance, subsidies from abroad, expenditure of travellers and ambassadors, the transfer of legacies (such as those caused by religious persecution), loans from abroad, and finally tribute imposed by force. On these two last points, in particular, Cantillon expressed opinions which could have been pondered with advantage after the war of 1914–1918. Of tribute, he says "all the Nations who have flourished in this way have not failed to decline." As to foreign loans, they are "a fire of straw"; "it most commonly happens that States loaded with these loans, who have paid heavy interest on them for many years, fall at length by bankruptcy into inability to pay the Capital" (p. 192). The eighteenth century, as well as the nineteenth, had some experience of this, but it was in the post-war world of the twentieth century that this process reached a magnitude previously unknown.

was concerned with the augmentation and diminution of the coinage. It will be remembered that Law, hostile to the former, was an advocate of the latter, and presents the amusing paradox (explained above) of an ardent inflationist being in favour of deflation. Cantillon is in favour, quite simply, of stable money. Diminution is as disastrous as augmentation. The chapter in which Cantillon discusses this question is well worth re-reading. In it he presents, with the brevity and force of a great writer, all the arguments for and against these changes: the hoarding of money when it is diminished, that is, in the case of deflation, the export of money abroad, the unfavourable balance of trade, "the circulation falling into convulsions":[1] and, in the case of augmentation the inverse phenomena, a favourable trade balance, the return (but to an insufficient extent) of coin; all of which is to the advantage of the King of France and harmful to her people. "France is all round the dupe of these operations. She pays very high prices for foreign goods during the diminutions, sells them back at very low prices at the time of the augmentation to the same foreigners."[2] And the conclusion which summarises his opinion: "It matters little or nothing what is the nominal value of coin provided it be permanent."[3]

Cantillon's book is one of the great works on money and credit. All those who read his simple and profound words, in which the acuteness of his insight is supported by a remarkably concise style, will understand the outburst of admiration from Jevons when, after the lapse of a hundred and fifty years, he rediscovered and

[1] Cantillon, p. 291. [2] *Ibid.*, p. 292.

[3] *Ibid.*, p. 296. In this chapter, which should be read carefully, Cantillon shews how the lowering of coin by the Government, if it is *announced well in advance*, does not always have the same effects as those which would have resulted had there been no such previous announcement; at first, diminutions sometimes provoke a rise in prices instead of the anticipated fall, which does not occur until much later. Conversely he recognises (as Hume did) that augmentations do not always raise prices as much as would seem reasonable; he explains this by the reduction in the currency due to former "diminution." "If I am told that what cost 20 livres or 5 ounces of silver before the lowering referred to does not even cost 4 ounces or 20 livres of the new money after the augmentation, I will assent to this without departing from my principles, because there is less money in circulation than there was before the diminutions" (p. 296). Clearly the purely logical reasoning applied by men like d'Aguesseau to these questions was contradicted by the facts, and Cantillon, an observant and experienced man, tries to discover the real process rather than the logical but unreal process. He found it by applying the quantity-theory.

published it. Cantillon will be quoted more than once in the chapters that follow; on questions relating to the rapidity of circulation, the effect of abundant money on the rate of interest, the mechanism of the action of the precious metals on prices, Cantillon gives evidence of the same penetration as he displays in his analysis of the role and function of banks.

There is nothing to add to what he has said on these questions. Standing between the adventurous ideas of Law and the narrow ideas of Adam Smith, he provides the only theory which, even to-day, really explains the phenomena of credit.

One objection, however, may be made. Penetrating in his analysis when the problem is to explain facts, he displays a certain smug conservatism on the question of the organisation of credit. Law dreamed of gigantic reforms; Cantillon, who consolidated and increased his fortune in the existing system, saw no need to modify the credit mechanism.

Nevertheless the French banking system left much to be desired. We can get a good picture of its organisation from Savary's *Parfait Négociant*, from the pages of Law and of Cantillon. At the base are cash payments. The transfer of bags of coin from banker to banker and from district to district is still very widespread.

"Inside the City of Paris the carriage of money from one house to another usually costs 5 sols per bag of 1,000 livres. If it were necessary to carry it from the Fauxbourg St. Antoine to the Invalides it would cost more than twice as much, and if there were not generally trustworthy porters of money it would cost still more. If there were often robbers on the road the money would be sent in large amounts, with an escort, at greater cost, and if someone charged himself with the transport at his own cost and risks he would require payment for it in proportion to those costs and risks. So it is that the expense of transport from Rouen to Paris and from Paris to Rouen amounts generally to 50 sols per bag of 1,000 livres which in Bank language is ¼ per cent. The Bankers generally send the money in strong kegs which robbers can hardly carry off because of the iron and the weight, and as there are always mail coaches on this route the costs are not considerable on the large sums sent between these two places."[1]

On the other hand, at the beginning of the eighteenth century, people had not yet lost the habit of accumulating considerable

[1] Cantillon, p. 244.

sums of money, as was general in the seventeenth century. At that time it was not unusual to find legacies of several hundreds of thousands of francs left in coin. Sainte-Beuve, in his *Port-Royal*, speaks of a certain M. de Chavigny, a great friend of Richelieu, who on his death left, in addition to 973,000 francs in securities, the sum of 300,000 francs in pistoles "which were in the coffer in his room."[1]

"The French," wrote Hume in 1741, "have no banks: [he means banks issuing notes; there were a large number of bankers in Paris] . . . so that many have large sums in their coffers."[2]

Coin was abundant in France, but widespread hoarding prevented this abundance from having its effect on prices.[3]

Thus bankers normally provided bills of exchange, receiving funds, at Paris for example, from those who had to send money to other towns in France, delivering to these latter persons drafts on those towns, and undertaking to transport the specie to cover the drafts. But the banker also made advances for which the borrower frequently gave a bill of exchange payable *on maturity at the Lyons fair*. Lyons had entirely lost its character of a fair where goods were bought and sold, and had become a great bankers' clearing centre, where at every quarter the bankers congregated, not only from France, but also from Switzerland, Holland, Germany and Italy, in such numbers that at a single fair, payments totalling 80 million livres were made with one million of cash.[4]

The bill of exchange payable at Lyons, the *billet de change* which Savary mentions, was a sort of bank-note that circulated, but an interest-bearing note, a promissory note. Gradually, however, as Paris came to be the centre of business and of expenditure, the bill of exchange *on Paris* took the place of the bill of exchange on Lyons.[5] The importance of Lyons as a financial centre declined steadily, as Paris became the most important centre of production and consumption in France. It should be noted that the cheque, or, to use the terminology of the time, the money-order was not wholly unknown in France, but it was used only in a few very large centres,

[1] *Port Royal*, Bk. II, Chap. V, note.

[2] Hume, *On the Balance of Trade*.

[3] *Ibid.* As a result of hoarding "provisions and labour still remain cheaper among them, than in nations that are not half so rich in gold and silver."

[4] Cantillon, p. 310.

[5] Cf. the studies by H. Sée, published in *Mémoires et Documents pour servir à l'Histoire du Commerce et de l'Industrie en France*, 10th series, pp. 61–128.

such as Marseilles. Money brokers had organised there, we are told by M. Masson in his *Commerce français dans le Levant*, a system of deposits which the owners transferred by money-orders issued by the brokers. It sometimes happened that the brokers issued more money-orders than they had received cash. In other words, they granted credits, and this was sometimes followed by local catastrophes if the credits were excessive.

Law's originality consisted in his having realised that the system of transferring and despatching funds could be greatly simplified by the concentration of coin in a single repository which would undertake to make these transfers; the depositors, so far as such operations were concerned, having to undertake only the far less costly and far less risky transfer of notes. In fact the notes of the Bank of France did eliminate domestic exchanges, replacing them by the costs of despatch by post. Such a concentration of funds would obviously have allowed the bank which managed it to grant credits and make advances on a scale impossible in its absence.

That is what Cantillon did not realise. A banker himself, he mistrusted banks and expressed this mistrust in more than one passage of his book.

At the end of the eighteenth century this organisation had not changed. When it is compared with the English money market as described in 1802 by Thornton, the enormous difference in the development of credit on the two sides of the Channel is seen. This difference will be dealt with later.

§ IV. *Adam Smith*

Cantillon's book, written about 1730, was not published until 1755, and then in French. He could not therefore have had much influence on English thought. In France, then as now, the number of those interested in credit questions was very limited. Moreover, Cantillon's book, known to a small circle, was plagiarised by many writers who as a rule did not acknowledge their debt. Two great writers of the time, one French, the other Scotch, did however do him justice: the first was Condillac, who reproduced entire chapters of the book, and the second was Adam Smith, who obviously had studied it. That would have been the extent of his fame, if he had not been rediscovered and recognised for what he was by one of the greatest economists of the nineteenth century, Stanley Jevons, and translated into English by Henry Higgs, an eminent authority on French and English economic literature. The passages in the *Wealth of Nations* dealing with money and banks give the reader a far better idea of Cantillon's importance, and of the great loss suffered by the development of economic thought because his name and his work were forgotten for nearly a hundred years after Adam Smith.

In the period which elapsed between the publication of Cantillon's book and the *Wealth of Nations*, banks of issue had become much more numerous in Scotland. These banks, which called forth praise from Hume although he had openly expressed his mistrust of paper money, grew up, according to Smith, in the twenty-five or thirty years preceding the publication of his book "almost in every important town of the country and even in some villages." They discounted commercial bills and also granted credits to individuals by opening cash credits guaranteed either by personal pledges or on the security of land.

Notes had almost wholly superseded coin in Scotland. "Silver very seldom appears except in the change of a twenty shillings bank-note, and gold still seldomer."[1] According to Thornton the numerous private banks of issue in England which existed at the end of the eighteenth century did not really start functioning until the outbreak of the War with America, that is to say, in the last quarter of the century. In any case, Smith does not refer to them. On the other hand, he was quite familiar with the different kinds of paper money issued by the American colonies throughout the eighteenth century, and distinguished clearly between the effects of non-convertible paper money and those of the notes convertible at sight issued by the private banks.

His familiarity with these two types of paper money, and his exact knowledge of the way in which the Banks of England and Amsterdam worked, provided him with the essential basis for his observations on credit and the bank-note.

In the *Wealth of Nations* there are a number of simple ideas which had by then become common property; captivated by their

[1] *Wealth of Nations*, Vol. I, p. 280. Edwin Cannan's excellent edition of 1904 is used throughout.

soundness and correctness, his contemporaries were led to accept *en bloc* the true and the false in those chapters in which, for the first time, credit and banking questions are treated with the fulness they deserved in a book on political economy.

Smith gives a perfect description of the mechanism of the banks in England and Scotland; he shews quite clearly that bank money, if its value is to be maintained, must always be convertible on demand, that without this convertibility its value in metallic money cannot be maintained,[1] and that a banker should always have sufficient metallic money in hand to meet possible withdrawals. In all this there is no conflict with Cantillon. He understood very well—much better than the economists of the nineteenth century with whom Tooke was to come in conflict—the difference between convertible bank paper and paper money. He set forth in detail all the reasons for which a prudent bank should not lend except on short term, and should restrict its credits as soon as it sees that a client does not pay back on the date due the advances he has received. He notes, without, it is true, being able to explain its mechanism (as Thornton very rightly points out), that with a too plentiful paper currency there is a danger of bullion leaving the country, and of the value of the paper money falling because the certainty of conversion into coin is lessened. He described, in terms which Count Mollien was content to copy almost word for word, the "inconveniences and difficulties" created by fictitious bills of exchange, "for which there is no real creditor but the bank which discounts them," an operation which the English have since named "pig on pork." He remarked also, as did Cantillon, but without drawing the conclusions which follow therefrom, that in fact the sums which the banks use to grant credit are only the cash surpluses which the public are for the moment not using.[2]

On the other hand, unlike Cantillon, Smith never stated explicitly that bank credit serves only to make existing money "circulate more rapidly." He regarded the bank-note as *another kind of money*, a much cheaper money which can be used with advantage instead of metallic money and enables the latter to be dispensed with. This reveals complete confusion between money and credit; he is indeed, as it were, frank about it, for he realises

[1] Ricardo held the opposite opinion, as will be seen later.

[2] Smith, Vol. I, p. 303.

that there is a difficulty,[1] although he is unable to overcome it, and, in spite of Thornton's criticism, nothing contributed more than certain famous passages of Smith's book to encourage the confusion made subsequently by Ricardo between inconvertible paper money and convertible bank money, between which he himself had so carefully distinguished.

Smith elaborated two ideas which had a great influence on the subsequent development of currency theory: first, that the chief function of notes is to economise the use of metallic money; second, that there cannot be more bank-notes in circulation in a country than there would be coin if the notes did not exist.

The first idea is closely bound up with the opinion frequently expressed by Smith, and held by many eighteenth-century writers, that fundamentally, metallic money is only of secondary importance in comparison with the consumable goods which alone constitute the wealth of a country. He develops this thesis with a great wealth of arguments in the first chapter of Book Two, which is given over to an attack on mercantilism. The argument is summarised in the following passage:

> "If, notwithstanding all this, gold and silver should at any time fall short in a country which has wherewithal to purchase them, there are more expedients for supplying their place, than that of almost any other commodity. If the provisions of manufacture are wanted, industry must stop. If provisions are wanted, the people must starve. But if money is wanted, barter will supply its place, though with a good deal of inconveniency. Buying and selling upon credit, and the different dealers compensating their credits with one another, once a month or once a year, will supply it with less inconveniency. A well-regulated paper money will supply it, not only without any inconveniency, but, in some cases, with some advantages. Upon every account, therefore, the attention of government never was so unnecessarily employed, as when directed to watch over the preservation or increase of the quantity of money in any country." [2]

Now, what is the function of the bank-note? It is precisely to economise money:

> "The substitution of paper in the room of gold and silver money, replaces a very expensive instrument of commerce with one much less

[1] As the passage quoted on the following page shews.

[2] Smith, Vol. I, p. 403.

costly, and sometimes equally convenient. Circulation comes to be carried on by a new wheel, which it costs less both to erect and to maintain than the old one. But in what manner this operation is performed, and in what manner it tends to increase the gross or the net revenue of the Society, is not altogether so obvious, and may therefore require some further explication." [1]

The way in which this replacement is effected has still to be explained; it is here that the difficulty arises, and the passages in which Smith attempts to surmount it, reflect the doubt he felt. He conceived of it briefly as follows: to the extent that paper is issued, the currency will be *overloaded*; the public, not knowing what to do with it, will keep the paper and export the metallic money; gold and silver will leave the country to purchase goods abroad; after this loss, there will be the same quantity of circulating media in the country, but in addition there will also be a quantity of useful objects, bought with the exported gold and silver. Thus the country's revenue will be increased, for metallic money does not constitute part of the income of society in Smith's well-known meaning of the word, and everything will be in order. The exact words in which he sets forth these ideas, which he was the first to enunciate, deserve quotation:

"Let us suppose, for example, that the whole circulating money of some particular country amounted, at a particular time, to one million sterling, that sum being then sufficient for circulating the whole annual produce of their land and labour. Let us suppose, too, that some time thereafter, different banks and bankers issued promissory notes, payable to the bearer, to the extent of one million, reserving in their different coffers two hundred thousand pounds for answering occasional demands. There would remain, therefore, eight hundred thousand pounds in gold and silver, and a million of bank-notes, or eighteen hundred thousand pounds of paper and money together. But the annual produce of the land and labour of the country had before required only one million to circulate and distribute it to its proper consumers, and that annual produce cannot be immediately augmented by these operations of banking. One million, therefore, will be sufficient to circulate it after them. The goods to be bought and sold being precisely the same as before, the same quantity of money will be sufficient for buying and selling them. The channel of circulation, if I may be allowed such an expression, will

[1] Smith, Vol. I, p. 275.

remain precisely the same as before. One million we have supposed sufficient to fill that channel. Whatever, therefore, is poured into it beyond this sum, cannot run in it, but must overflow. One million eight hundred thousand pounds are poured into it. Eight hundred thousand pounds, therefore, must overflow, that sum being over and above what can be employed in the circulation of the country. But though this sum cannot be employed at home, it is too valuable to be allowed to be idle. It will, therefore, be sent abroad, in order to seek that profitable employment which it cannot find at home. But the paper cannot go abroad; because at a distance from the banks which issue it, and from the country in which payment of it can be exacted by law, it will not be received in common payments. Gold and silver, therefore, to the amount of eight hundred thousand pounds, will be sent abroad, and the channel of home circulation will remain filled with a million of paper, instead of the million of those metals which filled it before."[1]

And he concludes:

"When paper is substituted in the room of gold and silver money, the quantity of the materials, tools, and maintenance, which the whole circulating capital can supply, may be increased by the whole value of gold and silver which used to be employed in purchasing them. The whole value of the great wheel of circulation and distribution, is added to the goods which are circulated and distributed by means of it. The operation, in some measure, resembles that of the undertaker of some great work, who, in consequence of some improvement in mechanics, takes down his

[1] Smith, Vol. I, p. 276. Cf. also Vol. I, p. 283: "The whole paper money of every kind which can easily circulate in any country never can exceed the value of the gold and silver, of which it supplies the place, or which (the commerce being supposed the same) would circulate there, if there was no paper money. If twenty shilling notes, for example, are the lowest paper money current in Scotland, the whole of that currency which can easily circulate there cannot exceed the sum of gold and silver which would be necessary for transacting the annual exchanges of twenty shillings value and upwards usually transacted within that country. Should the circulating paper at any time exceed that sum, as the excess could neither be sent abroad nor be employed in the circulation of the country, it must immediately return upon the banks to be exchanged for gold and silver. Many people would immediately perceive that they had more of this paper than was necessary for transacting their business at home, and as they could not send it abroad, they would immediately demand payment of it from the banks. When this superfluous paper was converted into gold and silver, they could easily find a use for it by sending it abroad; but they could find none while it remained in the shape of paper. There would immediately, therefore, be a run upon the banks to the whole extent of this superfluous paper, and, if they shewed any difficulty or backwardness in payment, to a much greater extent; the alarm which this would occasion necessarily increasing the run."

old machinery, and adds the difference between its price and that of the new to his circulating capital, to the fund from which he furnishes materials and wages to his workmen."[1]

This is followed by the famous comparison, so often quoted, in which the effects of the issue of notes are likened to those which would follow the substitution of aviation for land transport, as a result of which highways could come under the plough.

"The gold and silver money which circulates in any country may very properly be compared to a highway, which, while it circulates and carries to market all the grass and corn of the country, produces itself not a single pile of either. The judicious operations of banking, by providing, if I may be allowed so violent a metaphor, a sort of waggon-way through the air, enable the country to convert, as it were, a great part of its highways into good pastures and cornfields, and thereby to increase considerably the annual produce of its land and labour."[2]

It is difficult to imagine a more complete confusion of ideas. First, with regard to the mechanism by which the precious metals are exported when the note issue is excessive. Thornton later gave a detailed account of the process: the excess of bank-notes leads to a rise in prices on the home market, which in turn produces an unfavourable balance of trade that is met by the export of gold. Smith had nothing to say on this. He is content to affirm the demands for gold without explaining them, and Thornton was justified in saying that this passage in the *Wealth of Nations* is written "in a manner which is particularly defective and unsatisfactory."[3]

The idea that the total amount of paper money *cannot exceed the total amount of metallic money in the absence of banks* is more startling still. What are banks for? To make money circulate more rapidly, and this increase in the rapidity of circulation is represented by the issue of notes. When coin alone is used, it is impossible to distinguish the coins used in payment by their owners from those which the banks have put into circulation by credit. The result of the invention of the bank-note was precisely to embody publicly, as it were, this putting into circulation, by the increase in the number of notes issued. The bank-notes must be an *addition* to the

[1] Smith, Vol. I, p. 279.

[2] *Ibid.*, Vol. I, p. 304.

[3] Thornton, *An Inquiry . . .*, p. 203.

coin, and the total quantity of instruments of circulation must exceed that which existed before the establishment of the banks. Otherwise the banks would serve no purpose at all.

Equally odd is the idea that one of the advantages of notes is that they lead to the export of the precious metals. It is undoubtedly true that an *excess* of credit (and not only of notes) means that gold will leave the country, and Smith knew this very well. But to see in this the chief benefit arising from the establishment of banks of issue is to commit a strange error. The economic advantage in issuing notes is to *make better use of the existing precious metals* by making them circulate more rapidly, not by making them disappear. For this rapidity of circulation of money is the means of making *goods* and *labour* circulate more rapidly, which alone is of importance to the national economy. Credit makes it possible to utilise all the productive forces more fully. It is this extension of activity which constitutes the benefit accruing from credit, and not the alleged transference abroad of the precious metals imagined by Smith, which has no basis in fact, for the precious metals leave a country only when there is an *excess* of credit, and their loss constitutes the most visible indication of that excess. Smith himself noted that since the establishment of banks the trade of Glasgow had trebled. That indicates the real effect of credit, not the transference to foreign markets of the stock of unused coin.

This idea of a more economic use of the precious metals as the chief effect of the introduction of the bank-note ended by entirely dominating Smith's thought, and it did so because, in fact, he shared Law's ideas as to the nature of money, and believed that money is only a "voucher to purchase": "A guinea may be considered as a bill for a certain quantity of necessaries and conveniences upon all the tradesmen in the neighbourhood."[1] Is this not the equivalent of the quotation from Law given above? The identity of thought between Law and Smith has not been sufficiently noted. It is, however, fundamental, and explains many of the errors in English currency theory in the following century. Like Law, Smith does not regard money as a *durable good* whose chief function is to *store up for the future the value* of goods and services sold; he completely forgets its function of *saving*, as Walras was to call it (which becomes more important as commercial activity increases); he

[1] Smith, Vol. I, p. 274.

ignores its function of providing a bridge between the present and the future, which is the part it plays at all times, and the most important part; he can see in it only a voucher to purchase in the present, an instrument for distributing goods, not a means of conservation. For him it is, before all, "the great wheel of circulation." Hence that long and tedious chapter (Chap. II of Bk. II) in which he tries painfully to explain that money is part of the capital and not of the income of society, and which ends in the characteristic passage:

> "Money, therefore, the great wheel of circulation, the great instrument of commerce, like all other instruments of trade, though it makes a part and a very valuable part of the capital, makes no part of the revenue of the society to which it belongs; and though the metal pieces of which it is composed, in the course of their annual circulation, distribute to every man the revenue which properly belongs to him, they make themselves no part of that revenue." [1]

If, indeed, metallic money is not income, if it is only a costly "instrument," then obviously any economy in its use is of advantage. But it is precisely here that the mistake lies.

Nevertheless, this idea was seized upon with extraordinary alacrity and found high favour.[2] Taken up by Ricardo and adopted by Count Mollien and J.-B. Say, it dominated the thought of English writers in the nineteenth century. The belief that the use of metallic money is a retrograde and costly system, to be discouraged by all possible means, is firmly fixed in British thought on currency and banking. The use of the cheque and the banknote was for a long time regarded only from this point of view. These two instruments were considered merely as means of economising money; the idea was taken as the guide to the country's currency policy, and the most disastrous conclusions were drawn from it. It is, moreover, in harmony with the remarkable qualities displayed by the English as bankers. The art of utilising to the maximum the coin deposited with them, and of developing all methods of credit, has nowhere been carried so far as at London. But, admitting their ability in this, the application of Smith's idea,

[1] Smith, Vol. I, p. 275.

[2] It is criticised by the eminent American economist Sprague, and by the author, in the article *Banknote* in the *Encyclopaedia of Social Sciences*.

held by so many others after him, led the English to under-estimate the importance of a large stock of money to support a vast edifice of credit. Thornton understood this well, and Tooke still better. In conformity with this conception, the cash reserves of the central bank were reduced to the minimum, a state of affairs which the more prudent banks of issue criticised sharply. They built up strong reserves of bullion, whose importance was appreciated during the War, when England made great efforts to acquire gold. The same conception was responsible for serious mistakes in English monetary policy, mistakes which were frequently pointed out by such far-sighted writers as Thornton and Tooke, and later Hartley Withers. We shall refer to this again in the chapter dealing with central banks.

Taken up by Mollien and the First Consul, this idea was to give rise to the closely related conception that to issue bank-notes is to create money, and the right to issue a right to "mint money," which was a privilege that should be controlled by the State, whereas the issue of cheques remains outside its province.

This idea of an economy in the use of money is so pregnant with ambiguity that it deserves closer attention. In fact, it boils down to the idea held by Law and taken up by Smith, according to which an increase in the quantity of existing money and an increase in the rate of its circulation are one and the same thing.[1] As we have seen, this idea is wholly false.

It is true that the use of credit in a country enables greater use to be made of the money in circulation there. It is true that, as with wine or wheat or any other commodity, there is no point in acquiring metallic money indefinitely. It is useful only within certain limits, and to purchase gold by the export of other goods is not the object of foreign trade. It is true that a well-developed credit system enables a country, *where economic activity is at a certain level*, to import less money than it would have to, in the absence of that credit system, in order to maintain that level of activity or to raise it. Nor should it be forgotten that, if such a country grants large foreign credits, it must strengthen its metallic reserves in proportion to the demands for repayment that may be made from abroad. But, from whatever aspect credit is considered, it is absurd to measure its usefulness by the economy which it permits in the use of the

[1] Cf. Smith, Vol. I, p. 27.

precious metals, since it is impossible to say what quantity of the precious metals *would be necessary in the absence of credit.* Are the advantages obtained from the use of electricity for lighting measured by the number of candles which, because of electricity, we do not have to buy *to-day*? In the absence of electricity, we should obviously be satisfied with less light than that to which we have become accustomed by the use of electricity. Are the advantages of steam navigation measured by the number of sailing vessels *which we are saved* from building? Steamships make transport possible on a scale undreamed of when sailing vessels were in use, and it is fantastic to imagine that, by acquiring a sufficient number of sailing vessels, a country could do as much as another country using steamships. In short, Adam Smith did not realise that credit is one of the ways in which a country's activity is expressed, rather than a substitute for metallic money; this latter is a secondary result which cannot even be positively affirmed, since in a developing country money and credit increase concurrently. Even more important, he did not see that credit does not replace metallic money either as a store of value or as a mainstay for prices.

This brings us to another question discussed by Smith, to which, again, he does not give a really satisfactory answer, but which is too important to be overlooked here—*the effect of the bank-note on prices.*

Smith gives the following account. In the case of inconvertible paper money, or paper convertible only at the end of a certain period, more or less distant, such as the paper used in the American colonies, the value of the paper in relation to the precious metals will certainly fluctuate, either because of uncertainty as to its redemption, or, even if no such uncertainty exists, because the *present* value of a note convertible in, say, fifteen years time (and not bearing interest, which was the case with regard to the notes issued in the American colonies) is not the same as its value on the date of repayment. The depreciation in the value of this paper, adds Smith, proved the impossibility of maintaining it at parity in these conditions, in spite of all the legal regulations directed to that end.

This passage shews that Smith was well aware of the reasons which make the value of inconvertible paper money vary, much better, for example, than Ricardo, who was later to attribute fluctuations in the value of paper money solely to *changes in its quantity*. Smith was equally well aware of the part played by *demand* in these fluctuations—a factor which Ricardo, as we shall see, completely overlooked; he notes, for example, that the willingness of the colonial governments to accept these notes at par for the payment of taxes frequently gave them "additional value," and sometimes even sent paper up to a premium as against metal.[1]

In any case, depreciation of paper money will necessarily raise prices by the full extent of that depreciation in the country in which it circulates. On the other hand, if the paper is always convertible at sight, prices cannot rise.

> "A paper money consisting in bank-notes, issued by people of undoubted credit, payable upon demand without any condition, and in fact always readily paid as soon as presented, is, in every respect, equal in value to gold and silver money; since gold and silver money can at any time be had for it. Whatever is either bought or sold for such paper, must necessarily be bought or sold as cheap as it could have been for gold and silver."[2]

This brings us right into the Currency and Banking Principle controversy that was to break out later, and it is interesting to note that Smith in his time took up the position that was to be held by Tooke.

It is most important to bear in mind that the question is one of *long-term* effects. He compares prices in Scotland at the beginning and in the middle of the century, and states that the increase in the number of bank-notes during that period did not raise the price level. In this connexion he makes a clear distinction between the bank-note and paper money. In a country where the note is con-

[1] Smith, Vol. I, pp. 307–311. Colonial issues have been thoroughly examined by Mr. Curtis Nettle in an extremely interesting article published in the *Economic History Review* for January 1934. Speaking of the different explanations of the depreciation of paper money given by Smith and Ricardo, the writer displays a tendency (see p. 54) to agree with the conclusions reached by Ricardo. He argues that many issues of paper money were maintained at parity so long as the issue was not excessive. It is true that he hastens to add, very rightly, that there is a close connexion between an excessive issue and a decline in the value of the paper, so that, in this way, Smith's contention may be considered well-founded. Other American writers (Ely and Laughlin) incline on the other hand to agree with Smith. The truth is that, once paper money becomes inconvertible, and its value depends on the esteem in which it is held by those who demand or supply it, anything may happen, even that the paper money rises in value above par. Tooke realised this clearly.

[2] *Ibid.*, Vol. I, p. 307.

vertible, prices are at the level resulting from the given quantity of gold and silver. In countries using paper money its depreciation makes prices rise. It is the same position that Tooke was to take later, and it is interesting to note at this point that if there is confusion in Smith's mind about bank-notes and *metallic* money, since he regards one as a substitute for the other, he does not confuse bank-notes with paper money, as Ricardo did later. In the long-drawn controversy that divided Tooke from his opponents, in which the latter were to mix up all kinds of paper money, Smith chose his side, and chose well. He saw that *in the long run* credit does not affect prices. Their level depends at bottom on the long-period relationship between the quantity of goods and that of the precious metals.

But though Smith's answer is correct, the reasoning on which it is based is worthless. He argues from the theory, confuted earlier in this book, that the bank-note merely displaces metallic money, and that the amount of metallic money so displaced is equal to the sum of the notes issued, which do not increase the total amount of instruments of payment.[1] If this were so, it would mean that bank-notes could not affect prices *either over short periods or long periods*. But there is no doubt that bank-notes do have an effect on prices. The abundance or restriction of credit in all its forms undoubtedly affects short-term price movements, whether it accompanies these movements or gives rise to them. On the other hand its influence (which will be examined more closely when we come to deal with Tooke) does not last unless it is supported by a simultaneous increase in the quantity of metallic money. If that increase does not take place, or if there is a decrease in the amount of metallic money, the rise in prices occasioned by the increase in credit (represented by bank-notes or by the inflation of credit accounts) soon gives place to a fall. After a short period of expansion, credit is contracted. For credit influences prices in a different way from money. Smith did not understand this. He believed that an increase in credit had the same effect as an increase in money. The two phenomena are different, but, like Law, he was unable to distinguish between them.

There is one last point to be noted before concluding this

[1] Smith, Vol. I, p. 307. "As the quantity of gold and silver, which is taken from the Currency, is always equal to the quantity of paper which is added to it, paper money does not necessarily increase the quantity of the whole currency."

section. In saying that the value of the convertible bank-note is always equal to that of the metal it represents, Smith appears to be making an obvious remark. But it deserves rather closer examination than he himself gave it. It is wholly *true within a given country.* But within that country *the value of the metal itself may be affected by the issue of bank-notes*, and such modifications are reflected in the exchange rates. Gold, for example, may for a time be worth less in England than in France, or vice versa. That happens when credit inflation (shewn by an increase in bank-notes) *raises the price level in England* and consequently affects imports and exports. In this case the exchanges move against England. In Paris, bills of exchange on London fall below metallic parity, and provided that the gap is wide enough, it is profitable to bring gold coin from London to Paris; for that coin, sold at the French mint for French coin, or at the Bank of France for notes, will fetch a somewhat larger sum in gold francs than was spent to purchase the bill of exchange on London. In other words, gold in London paid out in francs is in this case worth slightly less than gold in Paris paid out in francs. What does this mean if not that English money—notes and coin—has lost some of its purchasing power as against foreign money, at the same time as it has lost some of its purchasing power as against English commodities? This is the normal effect of credit inflation in one place if there is not at the same time credit inflation in other places. The familiar result is that gold leaves the country where the inflation has occurred. The initial cause is an excess of credit, or, to go back to Smith's times, an increase in the number of bank-notes, *leading to a loss of purchasing power of both notes and coin.* The loss of gold is followed by credit restriction in England, which corrects the position.

Smith did not perceive the working of this process; Thornton, on the other hand, saw it clearly and his account is admirably lucid and useful.

Smith touched on all the important questions concerning credit and currency that were to be raised during the nineteenth century. The answers which he gave to these as to many other problems are fairly ambiguous. Certain important truths he enunciated very clearly, although frequently he gave the wrong reasons. Where argument was lacking, he brought sound common sense to bear, but he did not avoid certain confusions. The confusion between credit and money, the idea that one can be substituted for the other and that their effects are the same, was not the least serious in its effect on subsequent theory.

§ v. *Count Mollien*

French ideas about bank-notes were derived directly from Adam Smith. The only Frenchman who, at the beginning of the nineteenth century, entertained his own opinions on this subject,[1] Count Mollien, refers explicitly and all the time to the great Scotsman.[2] In his *Notes à l'Empereur*, he reproduced Smith's fundamental ideas, and tried to get them embodied in the statutes of the Bank of France.

If Mollien was thoroughly imbued with Smith's ideas and regarded the Scotsman as his guide, he was also a man who, from 1774 to 1791, that is to say for seventeen years, worked under fifteen different Finance Ministers,[3] who had known Turgot, Necker and Calonne, who had profited from the brilliant and provocative conversations of the Swiss banker Penschaud, Necker's great opponent and a warm admirer of all things English, in whose salon were to be found, at the close of the *ancien régime*, all who were interested in public and private finance. He lived through the dangers of the Terror and the *assignat* experiment. In 1798 he left France to make a study of the Bank of England, which had just suspended specie payments. He noted with astonishment the ease with which forced currency was established. He observed how "in that country of the world which has most payments to discharge, most wages to regulate, most exchanges to effect, the government, consumers, manufacturers, divers purveyors, were able to fulfil their engagements, keep their credit intact, preserve their mutual relations and maintain in all the details of their social activity their ordinary regularity." He had nothing but admiration for the way in which "the most important proceeding that a nation can have with the shareholders, administrators, and creditors of a bank, was concluded in two days, as though it were a transaction carried out within a family."[4] A century later, with the same admiration, the

[1] J.-B. Say and Sismondi were content to follow Smith.

[2] *Mémoires*, Vol. I, p. 15.

[3] *Ibid.*, p. 3.

[4] *Ibid.*, p. 187.

world was to witness England abandoning the gold standard in peace time, without the holders of her notes losing the least confidence in her currency.

Mollien brought back from his voyage an admiration for the economic and banking structure of England which he was never to lose. He fully appreciated the width of the gap between the rudimentary credit organisation of France and the highly developed credit system which already existed in London, and he was determined, not to imitate England, but to use her as an example. He began to give expression to his ideas in 1802, in a note to the First Consul.[1] Those ideas received encouragement from the banking crisis which preceded the Austerlitz campaign.

In 1810 he again set them forth in the famous Havre note, written at the time when the Emperor wished to grant credit, through the Bank, to the manufacturers who were in difficulties as a result of the continental blockade.[2]

It is not surprising to find in Mollien the same uncertainties as in Smith. In Mollien it is the practical and the positive which predominate, although he was willing to theorise when necessary. His chief object was that the Bank of France should escape the fate of its two predecessors, Law's *Banque Générale* and Turgot's *Caisse d'Escompte*.

Having dealt with the brilliant speculator John Law, the cautious and fortunate banker Cantillon, the professor and philosopher Adam Smith, we shall now consider the views concerning banknotes of an administrator and civil servant, who was trying to make a success of an institution which up till then had been unable to take root in France because of the special dangers to which it was exposed.

These dangers threatened from a government that was always

[1] Reproduced in his *Mémoires*, Vol. I, pp. 293 *et seq.*, and as an appendix to the same volume. It is in this note, rather than in that known as the Havre note, that Mollien's most important ideas can be found.

[2] The Havre note is summarised in the third volume of the *Mémoires*, pp. 144 *et seq.* The full text was published by Wolowski in his book on banks. Napoleon was so pleased by this note that he thought of having it printed, but in the end had copies of it sent to the governors of the Bank who, if Mollien is to be believed, did not understand it very well: "The great majority," he says (Vol. 3, p. 157), "after declaring that the Board should not reply to such questions without thorough preliminary deliberation, did in fact deliberate for a long time, and ended by not giving a reply."

short of money and anxious to subordinate everything to its political ends, and from the very men charged with the management of the Bank, who were too easily tempted to use it in their own interests. Mollien wanted to protect it from the one and the other. Smith's simple and practical maxims provided him with a theory admirably suited to this purpose.

A bank of issue should only discount good commercial paper; it will thus avoid the requests of a government always in search of treasury advances, and the cash facilities which the bank directors might ask for their personal affairs. "The fact that a man is a shareholder gives him no right to obtain discount at the bank." [1] Above all, the bank should avoid all speculative paper, all "friendly accommodation," all "fraudulent paper" or "collusive securities" which do not represent real commercial transactions, and the payment of which is not guaranteed by "the share in real money with which each consumer should directly or indirectly furnish it." [2] To make sure that bills accepted by the bank are of this character a third signature, that of an endorser, is indispensable. As to treasury advances, Mollien is firmly opposed to them, because all supplementary issues not arising out of the ordinary requirements of trade will undoubtedly return to the bank and thereby provoke demands for repayment.[3]

It should be noted that Mollien was not aware of the practice actually followed by the Bank of England throughout the eighteenth century. In fact the Bank did make Treasury advances; in contrast to the policy which Smith recommended for private banks of issue, the Bank of England usually discounted only Treasury bills and intervened in the commercial market only to a very limited extent. Thornton, in the book which he published in 1802, gives the reasons for this, to which we shall return in Chapter Nine. Thus (and apparently without Adam Smith's being aware of it) the Bank of England engaged in open market operations as a matter of course. It was only the Napoleonic wars which for a time changed the situation. Bearing Smith's principles in mind, Mollien applied to the Bank of France a doctrine which in England was considered

[1] It is characteristic of the time that, in a long letter to M. Perregaux, at that time president of the Board of Governors of the Bank, Mollien had to explain that shareholders should not have the privilege of getting paper discounted with only two signatures. *Mémoires*, Vol. I, pp. 341 *et seq.*

[2] *Ibid.*, Vol. I, p. 463.

[3] *Ibid.*, Vol. II, p. 46.

correct for private banks, but was by no means adopted by the Bank of England. This was one of the misunderstandings which made two utterly different institutions out of the externally similar Bank of France and Bank of England.

Mollien's somewhat elementary and over-simplified rules of banking conduct are derived from a conception of the bank-note which, like Smith's, lacks complete clarity.

His essential idea, and in this he was wholly right, was that the bank-note issued in the conditions which he stipulated, that is to say only against short-term commercial paper, merely substitutes one currency instrument for another already in existence. Mollien held firmly to the "quantity" theory of bank-notes. If the notes are too plentiful, they decline in value. He put this idea forward during the 1805 crisis, which served as an excuse for reorganising the bank according to his directions, and again when Napoleon selected him as Treasury Minister. If notes are issued against sound bills of exchange, they only substitute a more convenient paper, with all the characteristics of money, for maturities created in the course of trade. Like Smith, Mollien did not investigate the mechanism by which paper, when it is issued in excessive amounts, is returned to the bank for redemption. In Paris, at the time that Mollien was writing, this mechanism was extremely simple: when the notes became too numerous, confidence in their convertibility was shaken: the public, to reassure themselves, demanded coin. In London the process was more complex: there was no distrust of the bank-note, but the excess of credit, by raising prices, affected the trade balance and gold left the country. Thornton shews this clearly in his book, published in 1802, which Mollien had not seen.

The idea that the note is merely a substitute for commercial money spontaneously created in the course of trade is correct, though it does not tell the whole story; it dominated all Mollien's thought on this subject. The inference might be drawn that a bank of issue, so long as everything goes well, can dispense, if not with cash, at least with capital. The Havre note of 1810 develops this idea. He tried to persuade the Emperor that, far from requiring capital from him, the shareholders should pay him a capital sum in exchange for their privilege (as did the founders of the Bank of England). On the other hand, Mollien realised the necessity for a cash reserve to guarantee the convertibility of the notes. He makes this clear in the following interesting passage in which, it will be noted, he is thinking only of an internal crisis. In England, at the same time, Thornton regarded the Bank's cash in hand as a reserve for payments abroad; nothing indicates more clearly the superiority of English over French thought on the credit question.

"In the general opinion, and for ordinary purposes, what confers the value and the title of gold or silver coin on the money issued by a currency bank, that is to say on the bearer notes signed by the governor of the bank or his agents, is the certainty that they can be immediately converted into real money at the will of the bearer; in order to fulfil this condition a bank cannot limit the guarantee that it gives to the bearer of its notes to the value of the commercial bills in exchange for which it issued the notes, even though these bills represent, because of the profit on the discounting which the bank keeps, a larger sum than the value of the notes. The bank must in addition hold a quantity of coin always available for redeeming its notes, when redemption is demanded. Such a reserve in itself causes a void in the circulation which gives additional justification for the issue of notes, for the highest justification for any money is that there should be a need for it. But it would obviously be an exaggeration of caution to the point of absurdity to ask that the reserve of coin should be equal to the sum of the notes that a bank puts into circulation; if, in addition to the security for the bank-notes represented in the bills of exchange which the bank has discounted, it were to keep in its repositories a sum in coin equal to the notes, the bank's existence would be both impossible and useless, for it could only form this reserve by keeping in a state of stagnation at the very least the capital of its shareholders.[1]

"The reserve of coin which a bank holds should therefore be measured against the number and the nature of the causes which can make repayments more frequent. When the operations of the bank are proceeding in a regular fashion, and there is no disturbance in public affairs, the bank has recourse to its reserve only in order to meet the few demands for withdrawals that are made on it from day to day, and often enough each day sees an equal amount of coin enter the bank by another channel. In times of political crisis erroneous calculations, arising from the first wave of excitement, may for a time swell the volume of these demands, particularly if the crisis is of a kind to slow down commercial operations and to narrow the channel of circulation." [2]

[1] Mollien is here thinking of the arguments of Cretet, Governor of the Bank, who considered that the cash reserve should equal the note issue.

[2] Mollien, *Mémoires*, Vol. I, pp. 419–421.

It did not occur to Mollien that the note is only a means of making the coin deposited beforehand in the bank circulate. He considered the cash reserve as one way of guaranteeing the convertibility of the notes, not as the foundation on which the entire activity of the bank was erected. The note, which he regarded merely as a substitute for commercial paper, is nevertheless a kind of money, "artificial money" as he called it. The right to issue notes is a privilege, and a privilege for which, as he repeatedly pointed out to the First Consul, the bank had not paid enough. By its very nature, this privilege carries with it a monopoly. When, therefore, in 1802, the three institutions which issued notes were amalgamated into one, he accepted the change willingly. But he did not wish to see the monopoly extended beyond Paris, since he did not wish to depart from the English model. In London only one bank of issue was allowed; but, beyond a certain radius extending from the capital, private banks issuing their own notes locally were in existence. It should be the same in France. Lyons and Rouen had branches of the Bank. That was enough. He did not want any more. Any towns that were anxious to have notes should establish their own banks and take upon themselves the responsibility of discounting bills drawn on merchants in those towns. But they were not to place this responsibility on the Bank of Paris (as Mollien called it) which had enough to do to judge the trustworthiness of Parisian signatures.[1]

Faithful to Adam Smith, Mollien considered notes useful because they economised the use of money. But this idea does not square with other ideas held by him. He thought of the note as a substitute for *bills* held by the bank; but bills are an *addition* to metallic money; they are a commercial money spontaneously created to *supplement* the circulation of coin. In acting as a substitute for bills, notes play the same part as bills: they are an addition to, not a substitute for, the coin in circulation. In this case Mollien is constrained *jurare in verba magistri.*

Napoleon looked to the Bank for quite different services. He wanted to use it to lower the rate of interest, and, at a time when the continental blockade brought serious difficulties to French trade, to appease the discontent of the merchants by almost unlimited credit facilities. "What you should tell the governor of the

[1] *Mémoires*, Vol. III, pp. 145 *et seq.*

Bank and the board," he wrote to Mollien on May 15, 1810, "is that they should inscribe these words in letters of gold in their meeting-place: 'What is the object of the Bank of France? To discount the credits of all French commercial houses at four per cent.' "[1]

Mollien protests against this idea. Such a policy would encourage bad bills, increase the number of notes, and thus, by arousing the distrust of their bearers, give rise to demands for redemption which might bring on another crisis, such as occurred in 1805. He firmly refused to adopt this suggestion.

But although Mollien had an intuitive grasp of the difference between credit and money, he did not succeed in defining that difference clearly. He himself admits this inability on his own part, when he speaks of "the mysterious, I might even say the abstruse nature of the privilege which attributes to an association of private interests the creation and the issue, practically at their own discretion, of a money which not even the best placed government could with impunity make for purposes of expenditure on the public services."[2]

Like Smith and like Hume, Mollien admitted the difficulty of giving an exact definition of the role of the bank-note. In one curious passage he even emphasises the difficulty of differentiating between bank money, metallic money and *assignats*.[3] That is because for him notes are always money, but their issue has a natural limit in the sum of bills of exchange which they replace. Guided by a sort of instinct rather than by any precise theory, Mollien was anxious that this limit should not on any account be over-stepped.

At the time that Mollien was formulating his ideas about bank-

[1] *Mémoires*, Vol. III, p. 145. [2] *Ibid.*, Vol. III, p. 139.

[3] "As money is in fact everywhere but a means, an instrument between production and consumption, it always finds its limit in the use to which it is put. Thus the very necessity for it is its strongest claim, and that is true not only of the money created cheaply by a discount bank: the same condition is imposed on real money, that is to say on the precious metals made into money, with this difference only, that if this sort of money is of standard weight and fineness, its excess will mean that it loses only in its capacity as currency; its value is restored when it is made into metal again, apart from a deduction for the cost of the labour of making it into coin . . . the excess of bank-notes, as of all fiduciary money, has many other serious consequences, as was shewn by the *assignats. Signum numerarium (quale sit) non alias mensuram propriam habet quam in rebus numerandis ad transmissionem.*" *Mémoires*, Vol. III, p. 152.

notes for the Emperor, an English writer, Thornton, a director of the Bank of England, wrote a thesis on credit which treated the most varied aspects of the problem with a comprehensiveness previously unknown. This book was to play a decisive part in the discussions aroused by the forced currency given to Bank of England notes. Nothing reveals more clearly the gap between credit development in England and France than a comparison of Thornton's book with the brief and somewhat dry writings of Mollien.

But before analysing Thornton's ideas, which in fact belong to a new period in monetary theory ending with Ricardo and the Bullion Report, it is necessary to examine certain other aspects of eighteenth-century currency theory which have not so far been touched upon in this book.

CHAPTER TWO

Eighteenth-Century Theories of the Action of the Precious Metals on the Price Level and on the Rate of Interest

§ I. CONTRADICTORY VIEWS ON THE IMPORTANCE OF METALLIC MONEY.—§ II. GENERAL BELIEF IN THE ACTION OF THE PRECIOUS METALS ON THE PRICE LEVEL. THEORY OF THE VELOCITY OF CIRCULATION.—§ III. RELATION BETWEEN ABUNDANCE OF THE PRECIOUS METALS AND THE RATE OF INTEREST.

Credit, in the special form of the bank-note, provided the economists of the eighteenth century with their newest theories; but they were also preoccupied with other monetary questions. The most important of these were concerned with the effect of an influx of the precious metals on prices and on the rate of interest. The answer given to this twofold question in the eighteenth century was extremely clear; it provided the foundations of a theory which the nineteenth century had little more than to adopt, and to which it was frequently to add confusion rather than light.

There was, however, another problem confronting the economists, more universal and more difficult, that of the role and importance of the precious metals in the national economy. Were not these metals, which circulated freely among the public, which did not wear out, which, apart from their use as money, had scarcely any other use except in the manufacture of luxury articles, an expensive and unnecessary means of making goods circulate? Could they not be replaced by a more simple and less costly instrument? Did not the effect of gold on prices, and therefore on income and wealth, present an absurd paradox? Did the prosperity or poverty of nations really depend on its plenty or scarcity? Was there not a peculiar mystery in that? And was not the attachment of mankind to these pieces of gold and silver the outcome of a great illusion?

These questions are still being asked to-day by philosophers, by historians, and even by certain economists. The function of the precious metals appears unintelligible to many even well-educated people. The discovery of a gold mine immediately attracts labourers and speculators. But the armchair theorist remains surprised and sceptical. There is something shocking to him in the fact that economic progress or depression should be bound up with the discovery of new gold or silver mines. He feels that there is something humiliating in the standard of value and consequently the extent of economic activity being beyond the control of reason. His reason violently rejects passive acquiescence in a rising or falling price level, against which man is as powerless as he is against a succession of droughts or floods. Wicksell, who made a profound study of this subject, remarked in one place: "It is a thing unworthy of our generation that without pressing cause the most important economic factors are left to pure chance."[1] In truth, when it is a question of laying down which direction of price movements—upwards, downwards, or stability—is most in conformity with postulates of justice or utility, reason, always eager to criticise and slow to construct, has so far shewn itself powerless, and the most ardent reformers hesitate.[2]

Reason is no less disconcerted by the thought that the discovery of the most precious metal has up to now been scarcely more than the *result of chance*, and that geological science has found no means of regulating its quantity in proportion to the needs of mankind. A number of tales have been written about what would happen if gold could be produced at will. Nevertheless in our own day the periods when the production of the precious metals has accelerated or slackened seem to depend rather less than formerly on pure chance. As the methods of exploitation have improved, mining responds more rapidly to alternations of profit and loss, which correspond with periods of falling and rising prices. The devaluation of the pound sterling, by increasing the profits of the mines, stimulated the production of gold at the very moment when the world dreaded a shortage. This is a new factor in world economy which was not present during the eighteenth century. To a certain extent it modifies the workings of chance in a field which formerly

[1] K. Wicksell, *Interest and Prices*, London, 1936, p. 194. This is the English translation of the author's first work, *Geldzins und Güterpreis*, published in 1898.

[2] We shall deal with these hesitations in Chapters Eight and Nine.

seemed to depend wholly on accidental discoveries. But the impossibility, from the technical point of view, of adjusting gold output to requirements (supposing that these were known) still troubles many minds. Up to the present, man has not discovered a way of controlling the gold price level, any more than he has succeeded in regulating the amount of sunshine or rain that the different seasons bring to the earth. Fortunately he did not have to wait until he could exercise this impossible power before cultivating the soil and adapting his activity to the changing seasons. Nor did he wait until he knew how to control the price level before working, producing, inventing and saving. And no doubt it is better so. For the supreme power charged with fixing the amount of sunshine and rain would create as much discontent as satisfaction every time a decision was taken. Whatever body had the power of fixing the price level would, even if it were purely national, certainly excite the same disappointments and the same grievances; if that body were international, its decisions would be followed by wars.

Finding no way of controlling prices in the world, attention was turned to the general desire for gold, and the persistence of man's attachment to the metal was called "fetishism." Mr. Edison, an inventor of genius, asked in 1907: "Is it not absurd to have, as our standard of values, a substance the only real use of which is to gild picture frames and fill teeth?"[1] There is more wit than wisdom in these words, but they were eminently satisfactory to the prophets of new currencies. A President of the United States followed Edison in this respect, and the categorical expression of this idea, transmitted by cable, put an end in 1933 to one of the greatest international conferences ever convened.

Others insist on the "fiduciary" character of the value which we give to gold, as if by doing so they were reducing its importance. François Simiand said: "Gold was the first of the fiduciary moneys."[2] Though his words were immediately hailed as a discovery, it is an old saying. Marshall, Knut Wicksell, A. Wagner,[3]

[1] Quoted by Irving Fisher in *The Purchasing Power of Money*, p. 347, note.

[2] Cf. Simiand, in *Annales Sociologiques*, Paris, 1934.

[3] The idea that the value of the precious metals has a "fiduciary" character is in fact extremely old. A. Wagner, in his first and best work, *Beiträge zur Lehre von den Banken*, Leipzig, 1857, p. 38, observes that the use of gold rests in part on the confidence of people that it will always serve as a means of purchase. He adds: "It is therefore correct to say of every kind of money, and *consequently of metallic money*,

and many others had already used it. The words seem to imply a denunciation of something artificial or imaginary in the value given to gold by the public, and the "reasonable" man derives some satisfaction from them. A closer examination, however, will shew that *all values have a fiduciary character*, for they are all based on the belief that *the conditions which impart a value to a good will be perpetuated in the future*. What would happen to the value of land if to-morrow chemists were to discover a way of producing harvests two or three times as great as those of to-day in hothouses extending over one twentieth the space now given over to cultivation? What would happen to the value of a railway if automobiles could provide the same services, of a merchant marine if aircraft could take its place, of a copper mine if aluminium could be used for all the purposes for which copper is now used? The value of every constituent part of the wealth of mankind is contingent on the possibility of a discovery which would render it useless, and gold is no exception.

It is noteworthy that public confidence in gold is not impaired by these philosophical objurgations. Many economists express their disapproval, but the public apparently have their own reasons, and their affection for gold becomes stronger with every attempt to deprive them of it. The accumulation of the yellow metal in the central banks of issue—which in effect merely substitutes for the public's love of gold the passionate attachment of bank directors to their metallic reserves—has only strengthened the public's inclination to build up their own individual reserves. The hoarding of the last few years is proof of this. We shall enquire more closely into the reasons for this general attachment to gold when we come to the question of the "demand" for the precious metals; here we would state that they are based on the experience of the stability of the value of gold over a long period, and on the experience over an equally long period of the instability of moneys created by

that, as distinct from barter, it presupposes a certain development of public confidence, from which it follows that every money rests in part on credit." The same idea was expressed a little later by MacLeod. In his evidence before the *Committee on Indian Currency* in 1899 (see *Official Papers* by A. Marshall, p. 269), Marshall, trying to find those points in monetary theory on which economists are agreed, declared: "I think it is also agreed that there is something fiduciary in the value of gold and silver; that is, that part of their value depends upon the confidence with which people generally look forward to the maintenance and extension of the monetary demand for them."

governments. The attachment to gold is one aspect of the eternal struggle between the individual and the State, the former anxious to protect himself against the hazards of the future, the latter anxious to use money as an instrument of its power and to keep for itself the monopoly thereof.

§ 1. *Contradictory Views on the Importance of Metallic Money*

The perplexity of many people to-day concerning the importance to be given to the role of money was well known to the eighteenth century.

No other epoch has given more forcible expression to its disdain for metallic money, a mere medium of exchange and contemptible like all middlemen. Nor has any other epoch accorded such widespread and free recognition to the influence of the precious metals on prices and on world economy. The contradiction, to which we have just referred, between the philosophers' disregard for gold, and the passionate search, on the part both of governments and individuals, for means of acquiring as much of it as possible, is just as striking in the eighteenth century as it is in our own day.

The century opened with the experiments of Law, who was inspired by the idea that an abundance of money is the royal road to wealth. But after the collapse of the System it is difficult to say which of the enlightened men—from Cantillon to Hume, from Quesnay and Turgot to Adam Smith, and from Smith to Thornton and Ricardo—insisted most forcibly on the idea that money is nothing, and that the labour of man and natural resources are all.[1]

[1] Turgot: "Gold and silver are two species of merchandise, like others, and less valuable, because they are of no use for the real wants of life." *Réflexions*, English edition, p. 31. Thornton: "Mr. Hume himself has remarked, 'That want of money can never injure any state *within itself*; for that men and commodities are the real strength of any community.' He might have added, that want of money can never injure any state *in its transactions with foreign countries*, provided it sufficiently abounds with commodities which are in demand abroad, and which it can afford to sell at a bullion price lower than that for which foreign articles of a similar kind can be afforded. The power of manufacturing at a cheap rate is far more valuable than any stock of bullion." *An Enquiry* . . ., p. 318.

Smith, Vol. I, p. 404: "It would be too ridiculous to go about seriously to prove, that wealth does not consist in money, or in gold and silver; but in what money

For the disparagement of money was a reaction not only against the ideas of the common people, for whom money is synonymous with wealth, not only against the mercantilists, the majority of whom had by the eighteenth century ceased to worship money; it was chiefly a reaction against Law, who had made money the source of all wealth.

Some eighteenth-century writers go even farther and describe money as "fictitious." It is a "fictive" value, said Hume in his essay *Of Interest*.[1] Locke had called it "imaginary," a phrase which Law made use of. "Gold and silver are either a fictitious or a representative wealth," wrote Montesquieu.[2] It is difficult to understand the exact import of these expressions. But whatever their precise meaning, they were obviously intended to belittle the importance given to money, and to place it below that of other goods whose value is not "fictitious."

This explains the widespread idea that metallic money can easily be replaced by another kind of money, and that the more this is done the better. Adam Smith's entire theory of the bank-note is based on this conception. It was he, too, who provided what appears to be the strongest argument against the importance attached to gold or silver. "The most abundant mines either of the precious metals or of the precious stones could add little to the wealth of the world. A produce of which the value is principally derived from its scarcity, is necessarily degraded by its abundance."[3]

It is a somewhat naïf observation, and the argument might be applied to any commodity whatsoever. If it means merely that food and clothing, even in excess, still retain their attraction—in contrast to those goods which do not directly serve to sustain life—it is true only for a man living in isolation, or for mankind in the most primitive conditions. Gold, moreover, has certain qualities in the absence of which its scarcity would be a matter of indifference.

purchases, and is valuable only for purchasing. Money, no doubt, makes always a part of the national capital, but it has already been shewn that it generally makes but a small part, and always the most unprofitable part of it."

[1] "Money having chiefly a fictitious value, the greater or less plenty of it is of no consequence if we consider a nation within itself." Hume, *Essays, XXVI, Of Interest.*

[2] *Esprit des Lois*, I. XXI, Chap. XXII. Trs. Nugent, p. 45.

[3] *Wealth of Nations*, Vol. I, p. 174, quoted by Ricardo in *The High Price of Bullion*, p. 16. A few pages further on Smith, it is true, says the precious metals are very *useful*, more useful than any other metal.

Its resistance to deterioration is perhaps even more remarkable than its beauty.

Even while attempts were being made to belittle the importance attached throughout the world to the precious metals, recognition was given to the part which they had played, and still continued to play, as factors making for general prosperity. In his *Réflexions* Turgot devotes an entire chapter to the civilising influence exerted by the influx of the precious metals from America. "The use of money," he writes, "has prodigiously hastened the progress of society."[1] Hume, who referred to the "fictitious" value of metallic money, expresses with great vigour his distrust of credit money "which foreigners will not accept of in any payment, and which any great disorder in the State will reduce to nothing."[2] He charges paper money and banks with driving gold out of the countries which adopt them. He emphasises the benefits France derived from the national habit of hoarding and from her reserves of the precious metals. "The advantages of this situation, in point of trade as well as in great public emergencies, are too evident to be disputed."[3]

Again, it was Hume who noted the stimulating effect on economic activity of the influx of precious metals, although he restricts that effect to the transitional period between the original price level and the higher price level which follows the influx.[4] Cantillon, who was so emphatic on the point that labour and land alone are the source of wealth and who, more than any other writer, contested Law's ideas, writes, not without irony: "Mr. Locke says that the consent of mankind has given its value to Gold and Silver. This cannot be doubted since absolute Necessity had no share in it. It is the same consent which has given and does give every day a value to Lace, Linen, fine Cloths, Copper, and other Metals. Man could subsist without any of these things, but it must not be concluded that they have but an imaginary value."[5]

We have seen in the previous chapter what importance he attributes to them. Smith alone, in his anti-mercantilist ardour, remains unyielding. He maintains—and up to a certain point he is right—that the discovery of America was of far greater importance for Europe as a new outlet for trade than as a source of the precious

[1] *Réflexions*, XLVIII. English edition, p. 51.

[2] *Of Money*.

[3] *Of the Balance of Trade*.

[4] Quoted by Thornton, p. 262.

[5] Cantillon, p. 112.

metals. In similar fashion, a hundred years later, Marshall was to attribute the prosperity of the period from 1850 to 1870 to free trade rather than to the gold of California.[1] Intelligent men like Galiani and Turgot realised that even though gold and silver do not in themselves constitute welfare or prosperity, they are essential. It is true, wrote Galiani, that mankind itself is real wealth, but money "is extremely useful, as the blood in the body of the State,"[2] "it should be maintained within certain limits in proportion to the veins through which it circulates; exceeding or falling short of those limits, it becomes fatal to the body."[3]

If, from the theorists, we turn to the men of action, what do we find? The eighteenth century—a century in which Europe was ravaged by war—displayed a more profound faith in the advantages of metallic money than any other period. The stability and inviolability of the principal monetary standards was one of the most precious conquests of the age. England held on to its standard, and was proud of it. On two occasions, in 1695 and 1774, the Government undertook the re-minting of the coinage, giving their original weight and fineness to worn and clipped coins; this in fact amounted to heavy deflation, but the principle of maintaining the intrinsic value of the coins was considered sacred.[4] The essential thing, Cantillon said, is to keep money stable, at whatever level. "It matters little or nothing what is the nominal value of coins

[1] See below, Chap. VI.

[2] Galiani, *loc. cit.*, Bk. II, Chap. IV.

[3] Discussing a memoir written by Praslin, Turgot (Schelle edition, Vol. II, p. 636) wrote: "I will only say that the other is greatly mistaken in regarding money merely as a *conventional token of wealth*. It is not in virtue of a *convention* that money is exchanged against all other values; it is because money itself is an object of commerce, a part of wealth, because it itself has a value, and in trade all values are exchanged against equal values." In the *Réflexion* (English edition, p. 46) he writes: "They (the precious metals) are not, as many people imagine, signs of value; they have an intrinsic value in themselves, if they are capable of being the measure and the token of other values. This property they have in common with all other commodities which have a value in commerce." This phrase seems to me to be aimed directly at Montesquieu.

[4] Precise details of these two reforms, particularly of the former, are given in Andréadès' *History of the Bank of England*. It was also discussed by Law who—deflationist as ever—gives his approval and strongly criticises Lowndes, the Treasury official who wanted to reduce the weight of the shilling to the level to which it had been worn down in use. Cantillon for his part tells of a conversation he had with Newton on the subject of a later reform, when he would have preferred the market price of the coin to be taken.

provided it be permanent."[1] Thornton proudly points out that in this respect, England has never imitated the evil practices of the continent. In France, after the last "augmentation" of 1726, the value of the coinage was not changed until the Revolution. The livre became as fixed as the guinea. Scarcely had forced paper currency been established in England at the close of the century than everybody began to ponder ways and means of returning as quickly as possible to a metallic currency. Pitt was never tired of prophesying that the *assignats* would accomplish the defeat of France. On his side Napoleon saw in the suspension of specie payments by the Bank of England a portent of England's hoped-for ruin. For himself, he kept to metallic money. Imitating Frederick II, he did not scruple to build up metallic reserves wherever possible.[2] In 1810 he shewed one of his ministers the 400 million in gold which he had stored at the Tuileries to cover the cost of the Russian campaign.[3] Individuals, too, continued to hoard, a practice encouraged by memories of the period of *assignats*.

For the business community continued to believe in a metallic currency, although the theorists rose in arms against it. It is true that, looking at things from on high—from on very high—the only things that count in the advancement of wealth are, on one side, labour and man's inventions, on the other, the resources (mines and forests, fertile soil or desert) which nature provides for man's activity. But once this wide basic standpoint is accepted, it must be borne in mind that man lives in *society*, that social life implies *exchanges* of services and products, that the greater part of these exchanges can only be effected *after an interval of time*, and that the goods which offer the best possibility of guarding against the uncertainties of time, of taking precautions against its risks, of preserving, in order to provide against future misfortunes, the equivalent of the labour and the services provided, are precious, rare, durable and indestructible objects, such as gold. Thus such objects necessarily play a most important part in all human societies—at least in all those societies in which attention is not given exclusively to the present, but for which the *future is a reality*. The place taken by the future in economic activity is as a rule

[1] Cantillon, p. 296. This passage has been quoted on p. 74.
[2] On this see Mollien's *Mémoires*, Vol. III, pp. 458 *et seq.*, and Vol. II, p. 77.
[3] Caulaincourt, *Mémoires*, Vol. I, p. 302.

under-estimated. The thought of the future is always present in the mind of the industrialist, the merchant, the business man. He is above all concerned with an attempt to envisage the future as regards prices, outlets, sources of supply and possibilities of sale. Stable money, metallic money, is the *bridge between the present and the future*. It is because of stable money, or, in its absence, of other stable and precious objects, that, within the economic sphere, man can wait, can reserve his choice and calculate his chances. Without that, he would be completely at a loss.

The contrast between the persistence of this belief and the philosophic assertion that metallic money is superfluous, constitutes one of the many examples of how social life, by its own peculiar processes, gives the lie to the conclusions of superficial rationalism.

Galiani expresses this contrast in remarkably vigorous words. In this respect he occupies a place apart. He alone, it may be said—not counting Turgot, who on this as on so many other questions had the right idea, which he did not have time to elaborate—managed to define the role and importance of metallic money without falling into the exaggerations either of those who would belittle it or those (whom he considered more dangerous) who would exaggerate it. "Money has been exalted by many writers, it has been abused by a far greater number with atrocious invective; but I have encountered nobody who has shewn, in a comprehensible fashion, in what its utility and excellence consist."[1] "Money consists of pieces of metal divided by the public authority into parts which are either equal or which bear a fixed relation to each other; they are given and accepted in full security by all as a pledge and as a *perpetual* assurance of receiving from others, *no matter when*, an equivalent of that which was given in order to obtain these pieces of metal."[2]

The present writer has italicised the words "perpetual" and "no matter when." They shew that Galiani fully realised that these coins, or "vouchers for goods," should be able to serve *indefinitely*

[1] Galiani, Bk. II, Chap. I, p. 26.

[2] *Ibid.*, Bk. I, Chap. IV, p. 68. It should not however be forgotten that on p. 147, Bk. II, Chap. IV, Galiani says: "Money is not wealth but its reflection, the instrument which makes wealth circulate; if it happens that wealth does sometimes increase, it happens far more frequently that, because of this circulation, it *seems* to increase without in fact doing so."

and that he understood the function of metallic money as a foot-bridge between the present and the future. Only an object that is universally acceptable can fulfil this function, and in order to be universally acceptable—for that is the essential characteristic of money[1]—an object must, he says, possess the four following qualities: "1—It should have a real value in itself, and at any given time it should have the same value everywhere; 2—its real value should be easily recognisable; 3—it should be difficult to debase by fraud; 4—it should be *durable*."

The same characteristics are mentioned by the majority of writers in the eighteenth century, particularly by Adam Smith (following Hutcheson) although he is somewhat more vague, and insists rather on the function of money as "the great wheel of circulation" than on its durability. In Galiani's book they are formulated more precisely than in any other. In addition to his insistence on the function of money as a "stock" of value, he makes one particularly noteworthy point in his analysis of the reasons why the value of the precious metals is not "imaginary" or "conventional," but based, like all value, on their *scarcity* and *utility*, that is their correspondence to the tastes and desires of man; (he devotes several pages to deriding the idea of a "convention" by which mankind is supposed to have agreed to adopt gold and silver as money). It is a remarkable chapter in which, long before Condillac and far better than in Smith, are to be found all the elements of a true theory of value, leading to the conclusion that the metals, being scarce and useful, have a value in themselves apart from their use as money. "Ignoring all these considerations, offspring of superficial and imperfect reflection, let us agree once and for all that objects which make men respected, women beautiful, and children attractive, are useful and rightly held precious. From which the very important conclusion may be drawn, that gold and silver have a value as metals before they have a value as money."[2]

[1] Menger also emphasises this quality as fundamental to money.

[2] Galiani, Bk. I, Chap. II, pp. 37–38.

§ II. *General Belief in the Action of the Precious Metals on the Price Level. Theory of the Velocity of Circulation*

If we turn from the quite general ideas of the eighteenth-century economists about money to their more precise ideas about the role of the precious metals and the influence of an increase in their quantity on prices and on the rate of interest, we find both greater clarity and a larger measure of agreement.

In the first place, there is complete agreement among these writers in attributing a decisive action on the price level to an influx of the precious metals.

How indeed could it have been otherwise? The discovery of America had accomplished a tremendous revolution in all spheres of human activity and thought, and its vast consequences continued to dominate men's minds for a long time. In regard to the precious metals, its effects can be summarised in the following quotation from de Foville: "The ten centuries which preceded the discovery of America brought to light ten cubic metres of gold, less than one cubic metre a century."[1] The discovery of the mines of Mexico and South America brought into circulation, in little more than one century 2·6 milliards of francs, or 754·2 tons or 39·1 cubic metres. A hundred years later these figures were nearly doubled.

At the same time there is uncontested evidence that in the sixteenth century there was both an enormous rise in prices and an all round increase in economic activity in Europe.[2] Throughout the seventeenth century the extraction of the precious metals, silver particularly, continued uninterruptedly though more slowly. At the beginning of the eighteenth century the coincidence of rising prices and an increase in the precious metals appeared to be an uncontested and incontestable truth. Law points out, about the year 1700, the depreciation of silver in relation to goods; he takes it as his text for announcing the forthcoming demonetisation of the metal and suggesting the use of a more stable standard, such as a paper money secured on land. Cantillon in his turn wrote: "Everybody agrees that the abundance of money or its increase in exchange,

[1] *La Monnaie*, p. 115.

[2] Cf. Harsin, *Les Doctrines Monétaires et financières en France aux XVIe et XVIIe Siècles*, Paris, 1925.

raises the price of everything. The quantity of money brought from America to Europe for the last two centuries justifies this truth by experience."[1] Fifty years later, in the famous "digression on money" in Book One of the *Wealth of Nations*, Adam Smith was writing in the same sense:

"The discovery of the abundant mines of America, seems to have been the sole cause of this diminution in the value of silver in proportion to that of corn. It is accounted for accordingly in the same manner by everybody; and there never has been any dispute either about the fact, or about the cause of it. The greater part of Europe was, during this period, advancing in industry and improvement, and the demand for silver must consequently have been increasing. But the increase of the supply had, it seems, so far exceeded that of the demand, that the value of the metal sunk considerably."[2]

The thesis put forward by Bodin in his famous controversy with Malestroict held the field. "In the first half of the eighteenth century all monetary theories are as it were obsessed by the clearly affirmed relation between prices and the precious metals," writes M. Paul Harsin, who has studied the writings of this period with great care.

From then on, however, the thoroughgoing formulas affirming strict proportionality between the rise in prices and the increase in money (which were to be used later on by certain opponents of the so-called quantity theory, de Foville, for example, to simplify the theories of that time to the point of caricature), are made subject to numerous qualifications. Montesquieu himself, whom de Foville had specially in mind, writes:

"If, since the discovery of the Indies, gold and silver have increased in Europe in the proportion of 1 to 20, the price of provisions and merchandise must have been enhanced in the proportion of 1 to 20. But if, on the other hand, the quantity of merchandise has increased as 1 to 2—it necessarily follows that the price of this merchandise and provisions, having been raised in the proportion of 1 to 20, and fallen in the proportion of 1 to 2—it necessarily follows, I say, that the proportion is only as 1 to 10."[3]

Thus the increase in production prevents the influx of precious metals from having its full effect.

[1] Cantillon, p. 160. [2] Vol. I, p. 191.
[3] *The Spirit of Laws*, English edition, trs. by T. Nugent, London, 1878.

Smith devoted many pages to proving that the increase in wealth tends to limit the rise in prices due to the influx of the precious metals. In doing so, he in truth adduces facts which tend rather to the conclusion that the cost of living is high in very wealthy and highly developed countries, and that in consequence the precious metals have less value there; this runs contrary to his argument and he tries to explain it, rather laboriously, by other causes.[1]

Melon,[2] Dutot, Voltaire, are of the same opinion as Smith and Montesquieu. Current doctrine compared the production of goods with the output of the precious metals, and saw in the former a factor which modified the effects of the latter if it did not completely nullify them.

There is still another factor which modifies the action of the precious metals on prices, to which French writers do not as a rule refer, but which has a very important place among the English (with the exception of Smith): that is *the velocity of the circulation of money*. Thornton, who made a special study of this, criticises Montesquieu and Smith for ignoring it. The passage in Thornton which deals with this subject gives an excellent account of the ideas held at the end of the eighteenth and the beginning of the nineteenth century on this complicated question:

"Mr. de Montesquieu has represented, in the following manner, the principle which regulates the price of the precious metals. He 'compares the mass of gold and silver in the whole world with the quantity of merchandise therein contained,' and 'every commodity with a certain portion of the entire mass of gold and silver': and then observes that, 'since the property of mankind is not all at once in trade, and as the

[1] Smith, Vol. I, p. 188: "The quantity of the precious metals may increase in any country from two different causes: either, first, from the increased abundance of the mines which supply it; or, secondly, from the increased wealth of the people, from the increased produce of their annual labour. The first of these causes is no doubt necessarily connected with the diminution of the value of the precious metals; but the second is not."

[2] Melon, quoted by Harsin, p. 242: "The dearness caused by an increase in coin is a general dearness relating to everything which enters into trade, goods, merchandise, carriages, the labourer's working day, . . . etc.; on the established principle that money is the common measure of everything, and that there is no more reason to change this measure for merchandise than for a carriage or other good. . . . The quantity of gold and silver brought into Europe since the discovery of America would have had the same effect independently of the coinage if the enormous increase in commerce had not increased the need for tokens of exchange in proportion to the number of countries which became commercial."

metals or money also are not all in trade at the same time, the price is fixed in the compound ratio of the total of things with the total of signs, and that of the total of things in trade with the total of signs in trade also.' This theory, though not altogether to be rejected, is laid down in a manner which is very loose and fallacious.

"Not to mention the misconception of the subject which may arise from the silence of Mr. de Montesquieu respecting the state of the mines, it may be observed, first, that he alludes, in a manner so imperfect as to be scarcely intelligible, to those effects of the different degrees of rapidity in the circulation both of money and of goods, which it has been one object of this work to explain. It is on the degree of the rapidity of the circulation of each, combined with the consideration of quantity, and not on the quantity alone, that the value of the circulating medium of any country depends.

"Mr. de Montesquieu also leaves out of his consideration the custom of transacting payments by means of entries in books, and of other expedients. In proportion as contrivances of this sort prevail, and they must abound more and more as commercial knowledge advances in the world, the demand for bullion will be diminished.

"He also does not advert to that reserve of gold and silver in the coffers of the banks of various countries which merely forms a provision against contingencies. The amount of this reserve will depend on the opinion which the banks entertain respecting the extent of the sum likely to be suddenly drawn from them, in consequence either of fluctuation in the national balances of trade, or of temporary interruptions of credit among individuals. In proportion, therefore, as the variations in the national balances of trade, as well as in the state of commercial confidence, are greater or smaller, the fund of gold which is kept out of circulation will be more or less considerable. On the amount of this fund depends, in no inconsiderable degree, the price of bullion in the world.

"Mr. de Montesquieu likewise omits to take into his account that now immense and perpetually increasing influence in sparing the precious metals which arises from the use of paper credit. The false impression which he gives of this subject, may chiefly be referred to his not having contemplated the effects of the introduction of the banking system."[1]

There are many points of interest in this passage. In the first place it brings out clearly the deficiencies common to all Montesquieu's economic conceptions, of which the least one can say is that they lack clarity; secondly, and most important, it reveals the great difference between the English economy of the time, already based

[1] Thornton, *loc. cit.*, p. 306.

on credit, and the French, in which metallic money is the only instrument of circulation which the economists—even the philosopher-economists like Montesquieu—feel it necessary to discuss; and finally, it shews how old is the place taken in English theories of prices by the idea of the velocity of circulation, which is usually considered to be of much more recent origin.

For Thornton the price level does not depend solely on the relation between the quantity of money in circulation and the quantity of goods offered for sale; it depends also on the rapidity with which the money circulates, on methods of payment which economise the use of money, on the volume of credit and the amount of money hoarded by individuals and by banks. Elsewhere in his book Thornton takes great pains to shew that different means of payment (particularly bank-notes, commercial drafts and metallic money) usually have different velocities of circulation. Finally he notes (and this is perhaps his most original contribution) that the velocity of circulation of the same kind of money, for example bank-notes, varies considerably according to other factors: in periods of crisis they are hoarded, and practically cease to circulate, while in periods of rapid development they circulate with greater speed.

Practically nothing was added to this argument in the nineteenth century. The part played by the velocity of the circulation of money in the formation of the price level, was nowhere brought out more clearly than in Thornton's book. A more methodical and clearer account was not given until Irving Fisher dealt with this question in his *Purchasing Power of Money*.

Thornton himself merely adds observations suggested by his experience as a business man and banker to ideas which had been expressed early in the eighteenth century (Locke and Petty had written on the same subject in the seventeenth) by Cantillon in a number of chapters in which he discusses this problem in his usual masterly manner.

For the conception of the velocity of circulation is very old. It arose in connection with speculations as to the quantity of money that is useful or necessary to a State. All the commercial and monetary theories of the eighteenth century are haunted by this question, and all economists attempt to persuade the governments that it is not as important as they would believe. If it could be shewn that a given quantity of money can circulate more or less rapidly, that is to say, effect a greater or smaller number of payments in the same time, or (what amounts to the same thing) afford the basis for a larger or smaller income and thus allow for the levying of higher taxation, then it would follow that the quantity of money is a matter of indifference so long as its circulation is well organised. Velocity of circulation is thus regarded as an equivalent of the quantity of money, the one being able to take the place of the other, and exerting moreover the same influence on prices.

"Whether money be scarce or plenty in a State this proportion will not change much because where money is abundant Land is let at higher Rents, and where money is scarce at lower Rents. This will be found to be the case at all times, but it usually happens in States where money is scarcer that there is more Barter than in those where Money is plentiful, and circulation is more prompt and less sluggish than in those where Money is not so scarce. Thus it is always necessary in estimating the amount of money in circulation to take into account the rapidity of its circulation."

A little further on Cantillon adds:

"I have already remarked that an acceleration or greater rapidity in circulation of money in exchange, is equivalent to an increase of actual money up to a point." [1]

The methods of increasing the velocity of circulation enumerated by Cantillon are banking operations, payments in kind, or payments by compensation (which he calls exchange by evaluation), and the more frequent settlement of accounts; (for example if payments are made quarterly instead of twice a year, only half as much money will be required). In this connexion Cantillon tries, in words remarkable for their originality and insight, to trace what might be called the map of the roads traversed by money income from the country to the town, then from urban consumers to the farmers, and finally from the farmers to the landowners—the first sketch of what was later to become, with all sorts of embellishments and useless complications, Quesnay's Economic Table. Cantillon concludes that the monetary stock of a country should in general be equal to roughly one-third of the rent annually paid to the landowners. He estimates that the landowners' incomes

[1] Cantillon, pp. 130 and 160.

are equal to about one-third of the annual produce: "It follows that the money circulating in a State is equal in value to the ninth part of all the annual produce of the soil."[1] Galiani, dealing with the same question, reaches the conclusion that the eighteen million ducats existing in the Kingdom of Naples are sufficient to effect annual payments totalling 144 million: "The entire commercial turnover of the country can thus be effected if all the money passes through eight different hands for making payments in the course of the year."[2]

The origin of the conception of the velocity of circulation, which has played so great a part in all monetary theories, will be traced later. For the moment we shall refer only to one widespread confusion to which this presentation of the idea gave rise.

From the fact that changes in the velocity of circulation affect prices, and that, *as between one country and another*, a different quantity of money can render the same service, when the monetary stock of one country circulates more rapidly than the stock of the other, the conclusion was frequently drawn that velocity of circulation and stock of money are two factors which, in regard to the activity of *one and the same country* and to the maintenance of the price level, can be substituted for each other, the action of one tending naturally to *compensate* the action of the other.

The idea is analogous to Adam Smith's theory that the bank-note is only a substitute for money, and that after its introduction there is no change in the total stock of monetary instruments—coins being driven out by paper.

These ideas are wholly incorrect. The idea that velocity of circulation slows down when the amount of money increases, and vice versa, is not only unsupported, but directly contradicted by experience. History shews that the velocity of circulation increases when the quantity of money increases *rapidly*, and diminishes when the volume of goods offered for sale increases more rapidly than the stock of money. This is the case when a paper money is increased, as Say observed with regard to the *assignats*, and there have been a number of examples in the recent period of inflation in Germany and Austria.[3] It also happens in the case of metallic

[1] Cantillon, p. 130. [2] Galiani, Bk. IV, Chap. I.

[3] Cf. Say, *Traité*, Sixth edition, Paris, 1841, Vol. I, p. 150. Quoted by Holtrop in the Supplement to the *Economic Journal*, 1929, p. 50.

money: the rise of prices which results from an influx of gold is always followed by an increase in credit and in the velocity of circulation generally; falling prices have the opposite effects. This correlation between the velocity of the circulation of money and monetary abundance or scarcity was noted in the eighteenth century by Verri.[1] Cantillon also remarked on it: "I conceive that when a large surplus of money is brought into a State the new money gives a new turn to consumption and even a new speed to circulation. But it is not possible to say exactly to what extent."[2]

But do these statements in fact completely contradict the idea that greater rapidity of circulation can, to a certain extent, compensate for an inadequate supply of metallic money? So long as the different factors that are merged too loosely in the ambiguous term velocity of circulation are carefully distinguished, no.

[1] Actually, when Verri speaks of the increase in circulation resulting from the increased quantity of money, he means *greater business activity*, involving a more rapid transfer of money from hand to hand, as well as more frequent credit transactions. What he calls greater rapidity of circulation is thus a result and not a cause of greater circulation of goods, itself the result of a rise in prices. Verri draws the conclusion that this increase in circulation tends not to *raise*, but to *lower* prices, just as he argued that an increase in credit tends to lower and not to raise the price of goods. What he calls rapidity of circulation is called by others increase in production, and has nothing whatever to do with the phenomenon resulting from the flight from money provoked by paper money, which is referred to in the text above. This is one instance of the ambiguity to which, from the very first, the phrase "velocity of circulation" gave rise, and which has not yet been wholly cleared up. The passage in Verri runs as follows: "The arguments so far put forward lead to the conclusion that the increase of the universal commodity (money) and of its representations is always an advantage to the State when circulation increases proportionately; as the sellers increase in the same proportion as the buyers, which means an increase in the annual reproduction. To obtain a more precise idea of this truth, it is enough to consider that every seller, seeking to draw a given sum from his daily sales, can be satisfied with a smaller percentage of profit on each individual sale as the number of such sales increases (p. 155). . . . The increase of money alone tends to make prices more dear. The more rapid the circulation the greater the tendency to lower prices. These two quantities, according to the manner in which they are combined, may increase the price of things, or diminish them, or leave them the same." *Meditazioni sulla Economia Politica*, 1771 (translated into French, 1773, Lausanne, and into German, Dresden, 1774), pp. 163–164. The edition used here is Custodi's *Scrittori Classici italiani di Economia politica*, Vol. XV, Milan, 1804. Count Verri was an official of the Austrian government in Lombardy, and was associated with all the administrative reforms of that period. He is chiefly known as the author of the first trade returns ever issued, those of the State of Milan. These trade returns were recently published by M. Luigi Einaudi under the title *Bilanci del Commercio dello Stato di Milano*, Turin, *Riforma Sociale*, 1932.

[2] Cantillon, p. 180.

If the phrase refers to the *mechanism of payments, and its organisation*—the establishment of new banks, the habit of depositing coin there, the setting up of clearing houses, and the elaboration of methods for rapid settlement on the exchanges, then there is no doubt that these institutions "economise money" and that to that extent a smaller quantity of money will be needed to settle a larger number of transactions. But this is a *very slow process*; such changes are made only very gradually. Moreover, the economy which they permit in the use of money is frequently difficult to prove, since at the same time—as happened in the nineteenth century—the monetary stock is being constantly increased by fresh imports of the precious metals. In difficult times, when immediate remedies are sought, and in countries with an adequate supply of the precious metals, the difficulties created by an insufficient or diminishing quantity of metallic money have usually been met not by accelerating the velocity of the circulation of the existing stock, but by creating paper money. The most famous examples are provided by the American colonies in the eighteenth century and the South American countries in the nineteenth.

If, on the other hand, the phrase is meant to indicate an *increase in the credits* granted by existing banks and *greater rapidity in the rate at which money passes from hand to hand in a given time*, then there is no doubt, as we have said above, that the velocity of circulation increases parallel with the increase in the stock of money, and slows down with its decrease, especially if the change in the stock of money occurs over a relatively short period. Far from the one compensating the other, the quantity of money factor is reinforced by the rapidity of circulation factor. This truth, forgotten like so many others in the nineteenth century, was realised in the eighteenth by Cantillon and Verri. The results were sometimes serious, as, for example, when attempts were made to counteract a prolonged fall in prices by an injection of credit, it being overlooked that the effect of such a fall is precisely to diminish the need for credit and to curtail its use.

Summarising the argument, it will be seen that the quantity theory, or rather the theory of the action of the precious metals on the price level, was fully worked out in the eighteenth century. It takes into account changes in the quantity of the precious metals, in the volume of goods, and in the rate at which money circulates, including in this latter conception not merely the number of times that instruments of circulation pass from hand to hand, but also the multiplication of such instruments by means of credit. This second factor was later excluded by Irving Fisher from his definition of the velocity of circulation.[1]

Once that theory was worked out, it would have been possible to express the relationship between the price level, the volume of transactions, the quantity of money and its rate of circulation by an algebraic formula of the kind later made famous by Irving Fisher, following his teacher Newcomb.

Another aspect of the quantity theory was worked out in the eighteenth century; this dealt with the movements of the precious metals from one country to another. The theory of the world distribution of the precious metals, the formulation of which is generally attributed to Ricardo, was worked out with the utmost precision first by Hume and later, in a much more detailed manner, by Thornton.

Hume's analysis is famous enough to merit quotation in full:

> "Suppose four-fifths of all the money in Great Britain to be annihilated in one night, and the nation reduced to the same condition, with regard to specie, as in the reigns of the Harrys and Edwards; what would be the consequence? Must not the price of all labour and commodities sink in proportion, and everything be sold as cheap as they were in those ages? What nation would then dispute with us in any foreign market; or pretend to navigate or to sell manufactures at the same price which to us would afford a sufficient profit? In how little time, therefore, must this bring back the money which we had lost, and raise us to the level of all the neighbouring nations; where, after we have arrived, we immediately lose the advantage of the cheapness of labour and commodities; and the farther flowing in of money is stopped by our fulness and repletion." [2]

Actually this passage is not, as has been said, a summary of the quantity theory and does not ignore the factor of rapidity of circulation. Hume was trying to make it clear that it is impossible to imagine a country losing its money over a long period without reactions being set up which would intervene to stop the outflow, and that there is a tendency for every country to keep the quantity of money required for its industry. The idea is rather optimistic,

[1] Cf. *Purchasing Power of Money*, pp. 13 and 453.

[2] Quoted by Thornton, p. 311.

for in recent years we have seen countries such as Germany lose practically all their money.

It is interesting to place alongside this passage from Hume, which was written in 1740, the passage from Thornton in which he discusses the same question in relation not only to metallic money, but also to bank money and paper money:

"The principle which I would lay down on the subject now under consideration, is, I think, simple and intelligible, and it applies itself to all periods of time, and to every kind of circulating medium which may happen to be in use. I would be understood to say, that in a country in which *coin alone* circulates, if, through any accident, the quantity should become greater in proportion to the goods which it has to transfer than it is in other countries, the coin becomes cheap as compared with goods, or, in other words, that goods become dear as compared with coin, and that a profit on the exportation of coin arises. This profit, indeed, soon ceases through the actual exportation of the article which is excessive.

"I would say again, that in a country in which *coin and paper* circulate at the same time, if the two taken together should, in like manner, become, in the same sense of the term, excessive, a similar effect will follow. There will, I mean, be a profit on sending away the coin, and a consequent exportation of it.

"I would say, thirdly, that in a country in which *paper alone* circulates, if the quantity be in the same sense excessive, supposing the credit of the banks which issued it to be perfect, the paper will fall in value in proportion to the excess, on an exactly similar principle; or, in other words, that goods will rise; and that a necessity will exist for granting, in the shape of exchange, a bounty on the exportation of them equal to that which would have been afforded in the two former suppositions, assuming the quantity of circulating medium to be excessive in an equal degree in all the three cases.

"It thus appears that 'the coming and going of gold' does not (as Mr. Locke expresses it, and as was supposed in the objection at the beginning of this Chapter) 'depend wholly on the balance of trade.' It depends on the quantity of circulating medium issued; or it depends, as I will allow, on the balance of trade, if that balance is admitted to depend on the quantity of circulating medium issued."[1]

Here, long before Ricardo, is the formulation of the entire theory of the equilibrium of international prices and of gold exports from one country to another; at the same time, this analysis in-

[1] Thornton, p. 277.

dicates the component parts of an old controversy which has always divided economists, and which was to break out again with new bitterness on the morrow of the World War: Is it the trade balance which determines the rate of exchange of a paper currency, or is it the quantity of money? The dispute is an old one, and, as will be shewn in the next chapter, the solution lies in recognising that a complex equilibrium is established between all the factors involved—quantity of money, the value placed on that money in foreign markets, domestic prices, and balance of trade. Here we shall only note the antiquity of the controversy without attempting to examine it. In doing so we are not giving way to the facile temptation of reminding the economists once again that there are many problems which they have failed to solve, or the non-economists that the problems which they unearth as novelties are in fact many centuries old; our object is rather to suggest that in controversies of this kind the only scientific way of extricating oneself from the deadlock is not by opposing to each other incorrigibly contradictory points of view, but by seeking the larger solution which will take into account the aggregate of all conditions affecting the problem.

One last observation before leaving this subject. The eighteenth century, which was so deeply concerned with the influence of an influx of precious metals on prices, paid no attention whatever to the inverse problem—an *insufficiency of the precious metals* for the maintenance of the price level reached by the national economy. This fear, which was acutely felt in the nineteenth century, when the bimetallist controversy raged, and in the twentieth century after the World War, was unknown to the authors whom we have so far considered. The only fear they express is that of an excess of money, as we saw in regard to Law. In the course of the eighteenth century, however, the rate at which the precious metals were increasing slowed down, particularly the rate for silver. In his curious "digression on money" (taken as the model for all subsequent studies of prices and the precious metals), Adam Smith admits that the value of silver increased slightly in the course of the first two thirds of the century, but he displays no anxiety on this score. Hume is the only author to concern himself with these long period movements; he suggests that the weight of the pound sterling should be slowly and gradually lessened in order to counteract the rise in the value of the precious metals. Nobody else took up this suggestion, particularly as, at the close of the century—in fact from about 1776, when Adam Smith published his book—there was again a rapid rise in prices, notably the price of wheat. This rise corresponded with an extremely rapid increase in the output both of silver and gold, the output of the Mexican mines in particular being doubled between 1750 and 1790. The interpretations put upon these movements differ, even in our own day, and many writers resolutely refuse to attribute them to the production of the metals, although they offer no other plausible explanation.[1] For the moment we shall not discuss this controversy, but merely accept as an undisputed fact that in the eighteenth, as in the sixteenth century, there was a general tendency for prices to rise.

It is, therefore, not surprising that the writers of the time did not raise the question that was to be raised on two occasions by the economists of the following century, influenced by fear of an inadequate supply of gold: How can the adjustment of the national economy to a steep and prolonged fall in prices be facilitated? Devaluation as a means of counteracting the effects of a "temporary insufficiency" of the precious metals is something new. Hume recommended the experiment, but its practical application was an invention of the twentieth century. Let us hasten to add that had it not been for the war, and the monetary dislocations which it brought in its train, the question would never have arisen. In the eighteenth century appreciation and depreciation of the currency were fiscal devices and nothing more. Since then we have used them as methods of economic adjustment.

[1] The most recent historian of prices in the eighteenth century, M. Labrousse, who refrains from seeking the origin of the rise in prices, which he accepts as a datum, observes that the price of wheat rose over 84 years, from 1734 to 1817, the longest period of an uninterrupted rise in wheat prices known to history (Cf. Labrousse, *Esquisse du Mouvement des Prix et des Revenus en France au XVIIIe Siècle*, Paris, 1933). M. Labrousse's book is a monument of erudition, containing an unrivalled wealth of information on this subject.

§ III. *Relation Between Abundance of the Precious Metals and the Rate of Interest*

The eighteenth century was particularly preoccupied with the problem of interest, both from the theoretical and the practical point of view. In the latter respect the question was to decide whether the legal limitations on the rate of interest should or should not be maintained. There was a good deal of thought on this subject in France and in England. The repeal of the prohibition of interest was one of the demands put forward by liberals. On the other hand not all writers were opposed to the legal determination of the rate, provided that it was not fixed too low. Smith is in favour of it, while Turgot advocated complete freedom, although he admitted that it could not be established immediately.

But, for us, the theoretical problem of fixing the rate of interest on the market, and particularly of the influence of the influx of precious metals on that rate, is of far greater interest than the practical problem, which has already been solved.

It is true that eighteenth-century writers were inclined to simplify this, as so many other economic problems. Their theories consequently have an ease and coherence that mislead us, but they fall short of their purpose of explaining the processes at work. To-day we distinguish between the long-term market for savings and the money market, the reward of saving and the discount rate, and there may often be a wide gap between these two rates. Elsewhere I have discussed the distinction between reserve saving and creative saving.[1] It is well known that the money market is in fact composed of distinct markets where the rates—although as a rule they vary simultaneously—frequently differ widely. The economists of the eighteenth century did not make these distinctions, and they were for a long time ignored by those of the nineteenth century, who treated the discount rate and the rate of interest on gilt edged securities as identical. That was to a large extent a result of the fact that until the middle of the century the money market and the capital market were not fully developed and had therefore not attained their present complexity.

Apart from these reservations, eighteenth-century thought on

[1] See my study *L'Epargne* in *Essais économiques et monétaires* (1933).

this subject was particularly penetrating and provided the foundation for all subsequent studies of the rate of interest.

The prevailing idea at the beginning of the century was that an abundance of the precious metals tends to lower the rate of interest. Locke expresses this idea in his work on the rate of interest;[1] on this point Law agrees with Locke.[2] A little later, Montesquieu[3] and even Turgot[4] (who, however, as we shall see, distinguished more clearly than anyone else between the *purchasing power* of money and the *price of money*), attribute the general fall in the rate of interest in Europe to the discovery of America. It is a well-established fact that mobile capital and saving increased in Europe under the influence of the greater output of gold and silver, and that as this happened the rate of interest fell. On the other hand the word "money" in English and the word "argent" in France are used to designate both the coin in circulation and the savings loaned in the money market. This twofold meaning helped to create confusion between the effects of an abundance of money which influenced the prices of commodities, and an abundance of money which influenced the return on saving. It seems that the "value of money" should fall in both senses, and that this fall should be reflected, in the one case in rising prices, in the other in a lower rate of interest. It is the superficial conclusion drawn from purely logical reasoning, which leaves out of account the mechanism of social phenomena and the entire complex of actions and reactions involved.

On this subject, as on so many others, Cantillon, the banker in close touch with the money market, is the first to introduce the necessary precision into his terms and to make a clear distinction between the purchasing power of money and the price of savings. The rate at which the income saved is lent and borrowed and the value of money in exchange for goods (what we would to-day call its purchasing power) are for him two wholly different conceptions.

"It is a common idea, received of all those who have written on Trade, that the increased quantity of currency in a State brings down the price of Interest there, because when Money is plentiful it is more easy to find

[1] Locke, *Some Considerations*, etc., London, 1696, pp. 6, 10, 11, 81.

[2] Law, *Considérations sur le Numéraire*, pp. 475 and 479.

[3] Montesquieu, *Esprit des Lois*, Bk. XXII, Chap. VI.

[4] *Mémoire sur les Prêts d'Argent*, §§ 30 and 39, and *Réflexions*, § 69.

some to borrow. This idea is not always true or accurate. For proof it needs only to be recalled that in 1720, nearly all the money in England was brought to London and over and above this the number of notes put out accelerated the movement of money extraordinarily. [Cantillon is here referring to the South Sea speculations.] Yet this abundance of money and currency instead of lowering the current rate of interest which was before at 5 per cent and under, served only to increase the rate which was carried up to 50 and 60 per cent. It is easy to account for this increased rate of interest by the principles and the causes of Interest laid down in the preceding Chapter."[1]

In the chapter to which Cantillon refers he says:

"Just as the Prices of things are fixed in the altercations of the Market by the quantity of things offered for sale in proportion to the quantity of money offered for them, or, what comes to the same thing, by the proportionate number of Sellers and Buyers, so in the same way the Interest of Money in a State is settled by the proportionate number of Lenders and Borrowers."[2]

In this passage he defines in the simplest way the difference between the purchasing power of money and the price of savings, which is fixed on a special market where lenders and borrowers meet. It is true that Cantillon does not distinguish, as we do to-day, between the market for long-term savings and the money market; nor does he distinguish between the various component parts of the money market and the different rates obtaining there. He saw but one market where we see several different markets closely associated with one another. But in his book he makes a clear distinction between *income lent* and *money spent* in the purchase of goods. The economist is astonished to find that even to-day many publicists and practical men seem to be unaware of that distinction.

The same distinction was strongly emphasised by Hume in one of his *Essays*, by Turgot in his admirable *Réflexions*, which contains the first thorough discussion of the idea of saving,[3] and

[1] Cantillon, p. 212. Two centuries later, in 1928, the same phenomena were witnessed in New York. [2] *Ibid.*, p. 198.

[3] "Now the silver which is carried to market is not to be lent; it is money which is hoarded up, which forms the accumulated capital for lending; and the augmentation of the money in the market, or the diminution of its price in comparison with commodities in the ordinary course of trade, are very far from causing infallibly, or by a necessary consequence, a decrease of the interest of money; on the contrary,

then by Smith, who in fact scarcely does more than repeat in practically the same words, what his predecessors and teachers had said before him.

The fact of the existence of a special market for income saved once established, two problems remain to be answered: first, how is the rate of interest on this market fixed? Second, what is the influence of an influx of the precious metals or, inversely, of a relative restriction of their output, on the price of savings?

The eighteenth-century writers answered these two questions with considerable clarity.

The rate of interest will fluctuate—like any price on any market—according to fluctuations in supply and demand. On this Cantillon, Turgot and Smith are in complete agreement. Savings are *supplied* in the form of money, since income is realised in money, and the part of the income saved will necessarily be offered in the form of money (this is a point on which they all insist[1]) and will of course depend on the amount of the net income saved. But they are chiefly interested in the *demand* for savings. The price at which this demand is made will depend essentially, Cantillon and Smith point out, on the *profit* which the entrepreneurs hope to make by using the sums borrowed. This anticipates the useful distinction made by Walras between the *savers* on one side, and the entrepreneurs on the other, between the market for savings and the market where the "services of capital" are sold. The function of the entrepreneur, in his words, is to *transform savings into capital* (land, houses, factories, etc.), the anticipated yield of this capital or, as Walras said, the price at which these services of capital will be sold, marking the maximum which the entrepreneur can offer to the saver as the reward of his saving.

"If there were in a State no Undertakers who could make a Profit on the Money or Goods which they borrow, the use of Interest would probably be less frequent than it is. Only extravagant and prodigal people

it may happen that the cause which augments the quantity of money in the market, and which consequently increases the price of other commodities by lowering the value of silver, is precisely the same cause which augments the hire of money, or the rate of interest" (*Réflexions*, English edition, p. 78). To this should be added the curious footnote to this paragraph written by Dupont de Nemours, in which he demonstrates that saving is an "expenditure."

[1] Cf. Turgot, *Réflexions*, last chapter, and Smith, Vol. I, p. 334.

would contract Loans. But accustomed as every one is to make use of Undertakers there is a constant source for Loans and therefore for Interest."[1]

What Cantillon calls "the current rate of interest" is, he says, that which will be paid in the class of "Merchants who are rich and reputed solvent. The interest demanded in this class is called the current rate of interest in the State and differs little from interest on the Mortgage of Land."

Turgot makes some reservations on the point that the rate of profit is the essential factor in fixing the rate of interest. There are, he says, many borrowers besides entrepreneurs (States and individuals borrow for purposes of consumption) who also exert some influence on the market.[2] This point, taken up later by Tooke, does not invalidate, but supplements the theory as enunciated by Cantillon. It is a warning against the tendency to neglect the entire complex of factors determining the price for the hire of savings, or any price on any market, in favour of one single factor.

The second question concerns the effect of a marked increase in the quantity of money on the rate of interest, and, conversely, the effect on the money market of a slowing down in the output of the precious metals. How will the rate of interest respond in the two cases?

The answer given in the eighteenth century was forgotten at the close of the nineteenth, and as a result a problem which is in fact rather simple, but of great practical importance, was rendered obscure and difficult: in the first case the rate of interest tends, not to fall, but to *rise* after a certain interval; in the second case it tends to fall, and not to rise.

Again it is Cantillon who shews the most profound insight into this question, which he analyses with his customary precision and brevity:

"If the abundance of money in the State comes from the hands of money-lenders it will doubtless bring down the current rate of interest by increasing the number of money-lenders: but if it comes from the intervention of spenders it will have just the opposite effect and will raise the rate of interest by increasing the number of Undertakers who

[1] Cantillon, p. 210.

[2] See Turgot *Réflexions*, § 72.

will have employment from this increased expense, and will need to borrow to equip their business in all classes of interest."[1]

The meaning of this extremely important passage, which we shall return to later in the chapter dealing with the mechanism of the action of the precious metals on prices, is as follows: an influx of precious metals can act in two ways (and, we would add, it must act in these two ways *at one and the same time*): the output of the mines may be *lent*, which will tend to lower the rate of interest; secondly, *and at the same time*, it may be directly spent, which will stimulate production, increase the demand for loans in the hope of making profit, and raise *the rate* that people will be willing to pay for such loans. What has in fact happened in such cases? When the output of the mines is large and the metal is brought to the banks, the short-term rate of interest *at first* falls, and even the long-term rate falls (although the influence of the precious metals is felt on the *money market* much more than on the market for long-term savings); but *very soon after* the rate of interest begins to rise, whether because the gold directly spent makes prices rise and thus stimulates production, or because the loans made themselves tend to increase production and profits.[2] Thus the influx of the precious metals involves, after the lapse of a certain time, not a fall but a rise in the rate of interest.[3]

This is exactly what happened in 1850 and in 1895, after the influx of gold from California and the Transvaal. The same phenomenon was witnessed in the eighteenth century, and Turgot devotes a long paragraph to it in his *Réflexions*. Irving Fisher has shewn that in the American colonies it was quite well known: there the increase in money was not of gold, but of paper, and brought with it not a fall but a rise in the rate of interest.[4]

This apparent paradox, to which we shall have to return later,

[1] Cantillon, p. 214.

[2] The relative importance of these two factors is discussed in Chap. VI.

[3] It can always be argued, as John Stuart Mill pointed out, that when money appears on the money market and in currency circulation *simultaneously*, the rise produced by the latter is compensated by the fall produced by the former. But this must be demonstrated by *the facts*. Up to the present, when gold has been mined in large quantities, this compensating process has not made itself felt. That does not mean that in certain circumstances it cannot occur. Logical reasoning is not enough when it is a question of *measuring* the influence of two economic factors working in contrary directions.

[4] Cf. Fisher, *The Rate of Interest*, Appendix V.

still intrigues certain economists to-day. Knut Wicksell devoted an entire book to explaining it. The writers of the eighteenth century were equally perplexed, but they could not interpret the facts because they lacked an adequately clear idea of what really happens on the money market when there is an influx of gold. As a result of the development of banks of issue and deposit banks, the mechanism is nowadays easy to understand. The gold brought from the mines is sold to the central banks against notes or current accounts. It can therefore be used, *at one and the same time*, both *by the bank* to grant new credits, and *by the depositors* in the form of notes or of cheques which they use for their direct expenditure. Thus the new gold exerts its influence *simultaneously* on the discount rate, which it lowers, and on commodity prices, which it raises. In fact, the same twofold influence was at work in the eighteenth century, but not so clearly. The gold *spent* increased incomes and thus increased *savings*. The gold *lent* also increased the expenditure of those who borrowed it for productive purposes. Cantillon and Turgot saw this quite clearly.

Now take the contrary hypothesis: abundant production of goods *without any increase in money* (or with only a slight increase). What happens to the rate of interest? Adam Smith has this to say about it:

"Any increase in the quantity of commodities annually circulated within the country, while that of the money which circulated them remained the same, would, on the contrary, produce many other important effects, besides that of raising the value of the money. The capital of the country, though it might nominally be the same, would really be augmented. It might continue to be expressed by the same quantity of money, but it would command a greater quantity of labour. The quantity of productive labour which it could maintain and employ would be increased, and consequently the demand for that labour. Its wages would naturally rise with the demand, and yet might appear to sink. They might be paid with a smaller quantity of money, but that smaller quantity might purchase a greater quantity of goods than a greater had done before. The profits of stock would be diminished both really and in appearance. The whole capital of the country being augmented, the competition between the different capitals of which it was composed would naturally be augmented along with it. The owners of those particular capitals would be obliged to content themselves with a smaller proportion of the produce of that labour which their respective capital employed. The interest of money, keeping pace always with the profits of stock, might, in this manner, be greatly diminished, though the value of money, or the quantity of goods which any particular sum would purchase, was greatly augmented."[1]

This passage is particularly interesting if the reader bears in mind all the controversies excited by the fall of prices from 1873 to 1895, and the peculiar currency theories to which it gave rise. At that time writers adduced the fall in the rate of interest as proof that the supply of money, far from being inadequate, was in excess of requirements. They forgot the fundamental distinctions made by eighteenth-century writers on this question: a fall in the rate of interest is no more an indication of a "sufficiency" of the precious metals than a rise is an indication of their "insufficiency." When prices fall, the profits of entrepreneurs fall, and with them the demand for capital; above all there is a fall in the rate of interest which entrepreneurs are prepared to pay for borrowed money. *Far from proving a superfluity of money, a continued fall in the rate of interest, accompanying a steady decline in prices, indicates that the new money extracted from the mines is not enough to compensate for the fall in prices consequent upon greater productivity.* A steady fall in the rate of interest confirms and does not invalidate the contention of those who attribute to the precious metals a preponderant influence on price movements. The passage quoted from Smith should be compared with the formulas advanced by Marshall before the 1887 Commission on gold and silver. But when these controversies were at their height nobody quoted Smith. The passage we have just given shews that the same fundamental problems arise in spite of changes in the economic environment, and have the same solutions.

This question, which will arise again later, is one of many which were rendered most obscure by the controversies at the close of the nineteenth century.

[1] Smith, Vol. I, p. 337.

CHAPTER THREE

Thornton, Ricardo, and the Bullion Report

§ I. PECULIAR CHARACTERISTICS OF FORCED CURRENCY IN ENGLAND.—§ II. THORNTON'S BOOK.—§ III. RICARDO AND THE IDENTIFICATION OF BANK NOTES AND PAPER MONEY.—§ IV. THEORY OF PURCHASING POWER PARITY.—§ V. THE 1810 BULLION REPORT.—§ VI. MECHANISM OF THE WORLD DISTRIBUTION OF THE PRECIOUS METALS.—§ VII. RICARDIAN CONCEPTION OF CREDIT.—APPENDIX.

§ I. *Peculiar Characteristics of Forced Currency in England*

During the first fifty years of the nineteenth century credit theories were dominated by the experiment of forced paper currency in England.

Large-scale wars, with the currency troubles that they bring in their train, have a profound effect on normal price and credit conditions. The World War provided the most striking proof; before that the American Civil War offered a notable instance; earlier still, the Napoleonic Wars and the suspension of payment in specie in England from 1797 to 1819 constituted a still more famous example. Reference has already been made to the strong impression made on Mollien by the establishment of a forced currency in England, and the extraordinary calm with which so serious a step was accepted.

We do not intend to give here an account of the important financial events of that time. That has been done often enough, and quite recently in a masterly manner by Mr. Hawtrey.[1] We are concerned merely to bring into prominence those circumstances which exercised a decisive influence on subsequent theoretical development.

First of all, forced currency and paper money were not unknown to Europe at the time when they were introduced in England. The

[1] In his *Currency and Credit*.

most recent case had been that of the *assignats*, which had made a profound impression. But all such paper moneys had had one common characteristic; they had been created by governments to meet their own financial requirements; thus the idea of paper money was closely associated with that of the financial standing of the State.

This time, however, England provided an example of paper money which was not issued by the State, but retained all the externals of bank credit. Although the advances demanded of the Bank of England by Pitt in 1797 might be regarded as the cause of the suspension of specie payments and the depreciation of the notes, the non-redeemable Bank of England notes issued during the first decade of the nineteenth century were put out primarily to meet the credit requirements of manufacturers and merchants. What the Bank of England discounted was commercial bills, and it was because of the increase in their number that the notes were issued in greater quantities. It was only in the very last years of the war, from 1812 to 1814, that "government bills' reached a high figure in the Bank's balance sheet. This fact is more remarkable in that the Bank's holdings of commercial paper in peace time were, in contrast, always considerably smaller than the total of advances to the government.

This use of forced paper currency, so different (at least externally) from the use to which it had been put up to that time by European and American governments, is the origin of all the ambiguities and controversies in the years following the Napoleonic wars. The confusion between bank-notes and money, between credit instruments and standard money, which, as we have seen, was characteristic of many eighteenth-century writers, was considerably strengthened. All the efforts which Tooke was to make twenty years later to distinguish between paper money and bank-notes were met by the affirmation that the forced paper currency issued by the Bank of England differed from the ordinary bank-note in one respect only; its non-convertibility into bullion. The misunderstanding arose out of the special conditions in which forced currency was operated in England; that is probably the chief reason why the correct theory of bank-notes and credit encountered so many obstacles in that country.

It is, I believe, impossible to exaggerate the importance of this fact. For many years confusion reigned concerning the different forms of paper money, simply because, for twenty years, Bank of England inconvertible notes had continued to play their part in banking and commercial credit, government expenditure being covered by taxation and loans.

When a bank is no longer obliged to redeem its notes the number of notes issued will henceforth be decided on a *new principle*, either to meet the financial requirements of the State, or to accommodate individuals whose credit requirements cannot be met by the normal note issue. Notes cease to be what in essence they are—*a simple means of making existing metallic currency circulate*—and become purchasing power created directly by the bank, no longer bound to the previously existing sum of metallic currency.

If this purchasing power is created to meet government requirements for expenditure that cannot be covered by ordinary revenue, the paper money is incorporated into the currency; it circulates freely among the public, like coin, and does not as a rule return to its starting point. If this purchasing power is created by the bank when granting credits to private individuals, the increase in the amount of paper money may be more slow; it may not even occur at all, if the repayment of credits compensates for the new issues. But this difference does not imply a difference in the nature of the notes thus issued. Their quantity is determined by the arbitrary decisions of the bank, and their value in relation to commodities is fixed, both for domestic and foreign transactions, on a market where their fluctuations encounter no barrier. Henceforth metallic currency plays no part, or only indirectly. In fact it disappears from circulation and is used only for hoarding or for making payments abroad.

It will be seen that the introduction of paper money represents more than a slight modification of what existed before; it is a new money, exercising its own specific influence on the national economy and the price level. Those who witnessed the period of forced currency in England do not seem to have realised this.

To understand the origins of the great controversy excited by the *Bullion Report* it is necessary to give a brief account of the legal conditions in which forced currency functioned.[1]

[1] We shall not discuss here the facts on which the Bullion Committee based their Report. Excellent studies on the controversial points have been published in recent

When the suspension of specie payments was announced there existed in England, in addition to the Bank's notes, a large number of notes issued by private banks. These banks redeemed their own notes either in gold or in Bank of England notes. After the announcement they redeemed them only in Bank of England notes, which thus became the normal instrument of payment in the United Kingdom. At first, however, they were not made legal tender. The notes were only made legal tender in 1811,[1] as the result of an incident which occurred after the publication of the *Bullion Report*; Lord King demanded that his tenants pay him in coin, claiming that coin alone was legal tender; Parliament then issued a proclamation making paper legal tender along with coin. Up till then Bank of England notes had been accepted in settlement of all debts by voluntary general agreement. An old law was invoked to prevent the export of coin, but the export of bullion was free, except such bullion as was obtained by melting down coin. Coin was, therefore, hoarded, and there was a premium not on coin, which was forbidden, but on bullion. This premium on bullion, which reflected the loss of value of paper in relation to gold, aroused discussions which ended in the *Bullion Report* of 1810. It was maintained by one section of opinion that gold had risen in price; the authors of the *Report*, on the other hand, shewed that paper had depreciated. The question of the bullion premium over money

years. The influence of governmental finance, of provincial bank issues and of the continental currency situation on the issue of paper money, on prices and exchanges in England during the period in question, has been dealt with in a most instructive fashion by Mr. James Angell in his *Theory of International Price* (Harvard University Press, 1926), particularly in Appendix II; by R. G. Hawtrey, in the book already referred to, and by Andréadès in his book on the Bank of England. The first two give comparative tables covering the most important statistical material, and the reader will also find there a complete bibliography of the works on which these authors have based their studies. The rise in prices seems to have been chiefly due to government expenditure and to the notes issued by the provincial banks. Exchange fluctuations were strongly affected by the subsidies paid by the British Government to their allies. The famous "St. George's Cavalry" cost Great Britain the stability of the pound, and the need of gold on the continent also played its part. The *Bullion Report*, as republished by Cannan (*The Paper Pound of 1797–1821*, London, 1921), gives tables of prices, paper money issued, budgets, Bank of England discount totals, etc., from 1797 to 1821. Lastly, the sections of Tooke's great *History of Prices* devoted to this subject are well worth re-reading.

[1] See Cannan's *Paper Pound*: In 1811 notes were made legal tender not directly, but as it were by implication. In 1819 payments in specie were resumed, and it was not in fact until 1833 that notes were explicitly made legal tender.

was not in any case new to England. As a result of the bad state of the coinage, bullion had on many occasions been of greater value on the market than the price of £3 17*s.* 10½*d.* an ounce paid at the Mint. As coins of a nominal value of £3 17*s.* 10½*d.* weighed less, when they had been used, than an ounce of gold, gold bars were exchanged for a little more than £3 17*s.* 10½*d.* *in coin.* When it was seen that bullion was at a premium as against paper, people naturally recalled these earlier instances, and did not attribute the premium to variations in the rate of exchange which that premium in fact reflected. A further complication clouding the issue was introduced by the fact that silver was the standard at Hamburg, which was at that time taken as the centre for exchange rates, and consequently the variable relation between gold and silver had to be taken into account in determining exchange fluctuations.

These few facts sufficiently indicate the complexity of the discussions aroused by the premium on bullion. At this distance of time the details relating to the special circumstances of the period have ceased to be of interest, but the facts themselves are still of great importance to an understanding of the first theories formulated about paper money and its relation to bank-notes.

§ II. *Thornton's Book*

At the time when the great controversy began, English theories concerning credit had attained a high degree of maturity; all the elements of a complete theory of bank-notes and paper money were present. Adam Smith had dealt with the effect on prices of convertible notes and of paper money, distinguishing clearly between the two. Hume had sketched the first outlines of a theory of the distribution of the precious metals. Above all, in his book entitled *An Enquiry into the Nature and Effects of the Paper Credit of Great Britain*, published in 1802, Thornton, supplementing and correcting the work of his predecessors, had drawn on his experience as a business man and a Member of Parliament, to provide the first analysis of the English money market that was worthy of so great a subject. His book deserves attention if only to note the difference between the flexibility and breadth of his ideas and the narrow and elementary theories with which, eight years later, Ricardo was to saddle English economic theory.

Thornton's book was published in 1802, during the brief truce in the war between England and France that was marked by the Peace of Amiens. Forced paper currency had been in operation for five years but had scarcely produced any noticeable effects. The premium on bullion and the fall on the exchange hardly exceeded 9 per cent. The number of notes in circulation was not much greater than it had been in 1797, if the one pound notes, the issue of which had been authorised at the time when forced currency was established, are left out of account. Nevertheless a certain amount of criticism was making itself heard. The wisdom of suspending payment in specie was at times questioned. Thornton took up his pen to defend that step.

His book has a double purpose: in the first place it is a defence of the measure adopted in 1797 which saved the country from disastrous credit restriction; in the second place, it is a warning against an excessive issue of notes, which would be bound to depreciate if the number issued were not limited.

With this twofold object in mind, Thornton appears at times to vacillate in his argument; nevertheless, on all controversial or doubtful points in the theory of bank-notes, the opinions which he expresses are infinitely more comprehensive and sounder than those of his predecessors. He is the first (after Cantillon) to present a satisfactory theory of the velocity of currency circulation, the first to describe the mechanism by which an excessive note issue, by leading to an unfavourable trade balance, provokes a demand for redemption; the first again in this, that, while recognising the effect of the balance of trade on the exchanges, he shews how an excessive number of notes in circulation is itself a source of disequilibrium in the trade balance; finally, he was the first to explain in detail the working of the London money market and the relations between the central and provincial banks. All the theories for which credit is usually given to Ricardo, but which in fact were formulated in the last quarter of the eighteenth century, are presented in Thornton's book with a lucidity and fulness that are not to be found in the work of his great contemporary. In short, it is to Thornton, and not to Ricardo, that we must look for an exposition of classical English credit and banking theory as it had been shaped by a century of experience and thought. Those who read his *Inquiry* will be the more astonished at the oblivion into which the book and its author fell; in many dictionaries of political economy they are not even mentioned.

Here we shall deal with two features of his theory in which it anticipates Ricardo. Like Smith and Ricardo, Thornton fails to see the essential difference between paper money and bank-notes. The clear distinction drawn by Cantillon between "fictitious money" and notes which "make coin circulate" is not to be found in Thornton. What he calls the "paper credit of Great Britain" refers both to the convertible note and to forced currency. He does not appear even to suspect that the suspension of cash payments created a difference between these two forms of credit; he does nothing to dispel the confusion between credit and money which characterises English economic thought from the time that the bank-note was first introduced.

One other extremely curious feature of his theory should be mentioned, which partly explains his attitude on this point: Thornton refused to recognise any similarity between the forced paper currency in England and the paper money issued on the continent. Continental paper money had often fallen in value because of well-founded fears as to its ultimate redemption. *Such doubts*, says Thornton, *have no foundation in England.* Unshakable confidence in the ultimate redemption of Bank of England notes is an important characteristic of English theory. It was in evidence both during and after the World War, and to a large extent explains the attitude of the economists of that time towards forced currency; unless due importance is given to this factor many of their ideas will be misunderstood. The following quotation from Thornton is very characteristic of an attitude of mind which was passed on unshaken from one century to another:

"The government of Great Britain is under little or no temptation either to dictate to the Bank of England, or to lean upon it in any way which is inconvenient or dangerous to the bank itself. The minister has been able to raise annually, without the smallest difficulty, by means of our funding system, the sum of no less than between twenty and thirty millions. The government, therefore, is always able to lessen, by a loan from the public, if it should be deemed necessary, the amount of its debt running with the bank. To suppose that bank-notes are issued to excess, with a view to furnish means of lending money to the minister, is, in a high degree, unreasonable. The utmost sum which he could hope to gain in the way of loan from the bank, by means of an extraordinary issue of bank-notes, could hardly be more than four or five millions; and it is not easy to believe, that a government which can raise at once twenty or thirty millions, will be likely, for the sake of only four or five millions (for the loan of which it must pay nearly the same interest as for a loan from the public), to derange the system, distress the credit, or endanger the safety of the Bank of England. This banking company differs in this most important point from every one of those national banks, which issue paper, on the continent. I understand that the banks of Petersburgh, Copenhagen, Stockholm, Vienna, Madrid, and Lisbon, each of which issues circulating notes, which pass as current payment, are all in the most direct and strict sense government banks. It is also well known that the governments residing in these several places have not those easy means of raising money, by a loan from the people, which the minister of Great Britain so remarkably possesses. Those governments, therefore, have, in times even of moderate difficulty, no other resource than that of extending the issue of the paper of their own banks; which extension of issue naturally produces a nearly correspondent depreciation of the value of the notes, and a fall in the exchange with other countries, if computed at the paper price. The notes, moreover, being once thus depreciated, the government, even supposing its embarrassment to cease, is seldom disposed to bring them back to their former limits, to do which implies some sacrifice on their part at the time of effecting the reduction; but it contents itself, perhaps, with either a little lessening, or with not further adding to, the evil. The expectation of the people on the continent, therefore, generally is, that the paper, which is falling in value, will, in better times, only cease to fall, or, if it rises, will experience only an immaterial rise, and this expectation serves of course to accelerate its fall. Hence it has happened, that in all the places of Europe, of which mention has been made, there exists a great and established, and, generally, an increasing discount or agio between the current coin and the paper money of the kingdom. Nor, indeed, is this all: several of the governments of Europe have not only extended their paper in the manner which has been described, but have, besides this, depreciated, from time to time, their very coin; and thus there has been a two-fold cause for a rise in the nominal price of their commodities when exchanged with the current paper. There is, therefore, a fundamental difference between the nature of the paper of the Bank of England, and that of all the national or government banks on the continent. No one supposes that the English guinea contains less and less gold than heretofore, through frauds practised by government in the coinage; and as little is it to be suspected that the Bank of England paper is about to be depreciated by an excessive issue either ordered or needed by the government."[1]

This brings home the immense difference between the English financial system, based on monetary stability and vast commercial wealth, and the financial system of other countries. It makes intelligible the pride with which it filled the English, the admiration with which it filled Mollien. This very illuminating passage also helps us to understand how the war was financed. In its main outlines the method resembles that used in 1914: the government first of all borrows from the Bank (for the Bank, as was noted above, carried more Treasury bills than commercial paper); its increased expenditure raises prices, and then it appeals to the public (whose incomes have increased as a result of government expenditure) to subscribe the loans with which it will repay the Bank. The Bank in its turn by means of discounts provides business men with the advances they need to take advantage of the rise in prices and the profits which it brings.[2] While the item "public securities" in the

[1] Thornton, *An Inquiry, etc.*, pp. 61 *et seq.* Thornton, however, is exaggerating. The historians who have studied this period most carefully are agreed that, in fact, the suspension of payments in specie in 1797 was brought about by excessive State expenditure and State loans from the Bank of England; Thornton hotly denies this, and attributes the fall on the exchanges to irrational continental fears, as Ricardo does in his *Proposals* and in his *Political Economy*, p. 346. (Cf. Andréadès, *History of the Bank of England*, Hawtrey, *Currency and Credit*, and Cannan, *The Paper Pound.*) In the four years from 1793 to 1797 the Bank advanced nearly £10 million to the government (Andréadès, p. 190). The Bank's anxiety about the loss of gold to foreign countries (partly, it seems, the effect of the English government's subsidies to its allies) and about the crisis which was then beginning, induced it to set limits to the discounts it was prepared to make. At that time the laws concerning usury prohibited a rate higher than 5 per cent. The fixing of a limit increased the demand for gold at the Bank, as the public (and particularly the provincial banks) wished to protect themselves against a possible scarcity of coin. On February 25, 1797, the Bank, which had a note circulation of £8,640,000 and a gold reserve of £1,272,000, requested the government to authorise it to suspend payment in specie. The law which gave force to this request is the Bank Restriction Act of May 3, 1797; it limited the total advances which the Bank could make to the government to £600,000, but it did not explicitly make the notes legal tender. But the British Government (since Pitt was convinced of his mistake and feared a repetition in England of the *assignats*) was extraordinarily moderate in its requests for advances from the Bank. Up to 1810—as Tooke shews—they never exceeded 4 or 5 million pounds. On the other hand the Bank's commercial advances mounted rapidly.

[2] From the outbreak of the war in 1793 the government issued loans annually, and at frequent intervals "consolidated" Exchequer bills and Admiralty bills, so that the public debt, which had stood at £238 million in 1793, reached one milliard in 1816. Cf. Hollander, *David Ricardo*, p. 17. Hollander's book was published in the Johns Hopkins series in 1910.

Bank's balance sheet only rose from £10 million to £13.3 million between 1792 and 1802, the item "private securities" jumped in the same years from £3.1 to £13.6 million. It was to reach £23.8 million in 1810, when the *Bullion Report* was published, whereas public securities at that date stood at £17.2 million.

But even if the moderation of the government's loans from the Bank and its undoubted willingness to repay them enable a clear line of demarcation to be drawn between the English forced paper currency and the notes of other countries, how can the fall on the exchanges be accounted for? If the argument of lack of confidence is rejected, one explanation alone remains: an excessive *quantity* of the notes issued by the Bank itself in granting credit. It was on this explanation that Ricardo pounced with all his dialectical ardour.

§ III. *Ricardo and the Identification of Bank Notes and Paper Money*

How did it happen that it was Ricardo's striking simplifications rather than Thornton's work which held the attention, not only of contemporaries, but of later generations?

It cannot be said that he made an original major contribution to currency theory. His idea of the mechanism by which paper money affects the exchanges is taken straight from Thornton. His theory of the distribution of the precious metals is no more than a simple repetition of Hume's theory. What is peculiar to Ricardo is the talent of the polemist. Political economy, in order, as it were, to give to later generations a clear picture of the question at issue, has always preserved those pamphlets which reproduce some of the heat and vitality of the controversies of a bygone age. Henry George, Proudhon, and many others, to whom the future will add Maynard Keynes, have shared in this privilege. When the pamphleteer is Ricardo, that is to say a writer whose general theories—even apart from his currency doctrine—exercised a profound influence on political economy as a whole, it is natural that he should come to be regarded as the most representative figure of an age in which works concerning money and banking abounded.[1]

[1] For an analysis of the writings of Boyd, Lord King, Lord Liverpool, and others, the reader is referred to Andréadès' excellent book, and to Angell and Hollander, cited above.

Ricardo was a great controversialist. His biting phrases strike at his opponents' weakest points, and remain firmly fixed in the memory of the reader. His explanation of the premium on bullion and the depreciation of paper was first set forth in three letters to the *Morning Chronicle*, published in August 1809.[1] In 1811, shortly after the Committee set up in 1810 by the House of Commons—the famous Bullion Committee—had issued its Report, Ricardo wrote his first pamphlet *On the High Price of Bullion*, designed to defend the conclusions reached by the Committee. When Bosanquet, Governor of the South Sea Company, criticised this pamphlet, Ricardo followed it up with his *Reply to Mr. Bosanquet*, and later (in 1816) with his *Proposals for an Economical and Secure Currency*.[2] All these writings have one practical and definite object: to persuade the government and the Bank to adopt a new policy: to re-establish the exchanges and return to the gold standard by restricting the note circulation. Ricardo was not concerned with elaborating a general theory of paper money valid for all circumstances. He was concerned only with the triumph of a particular currency policy at an exceptional moment in English history. General formulas are to be found in plenty in his writings, but they are there only to give added strength to his practical proposals, to specifically English solutions for specifically English problems.

The mistake made has been to take these pamphlets not for what they are, that is to say models of opportunist argumentation on a controversial point of the financial policy of the time, but for definite treatises on questions of general theory. That mistake was made not only by the English, but also by many continental and American economists.

It is however easy to understand the authority won by Ricardo's pamphlets, even outside England. The period in which he wrote was one of the most brilliant in English economic literature. The superiority of her writers over those of other countries was so striking that their pre-eminence in this field can be traced to those years. Even to-day their works are singularly pleasing to read. At that time England alone enjoyed a well-developed credit system;

[1] Republished in 1903 by Harvard University.

[2] All these pamphlets were published in one volume in 1926 by Mr. Gonner under the title *Economic Essays by David Ricardo*; the present writer has used this edition.

England alone had a bank of issue which dominated the money market and presented all the features of a "national" bank (the adjective is used by Thornton on many occasions); England alone had survived the test of paper money without final injury to the gold standard; only in England did public opinion regard credit problems with real interest, which was manifested in the enquiries of Parliamentary Commissions, in discussions in the press and articles in magazines, in pamphlets signed by names both famous and obscure; only in England did the government enjoy a public credit unsullied by bankruptcy. If to these considerations are added the unique prestige gained by English merchants and bankers throughout the world, the commercial and financial power which England had won in the course of the eighteenth century and which made her the clearing house of the whole world—a prestige and power which continued to grow during and after the Napoleonic wars—it is not difficult to understand the profound impression made throughout Europe and America by the controversies in which such men as Ricardo and Thornton, and later Tooke, took part; men whose names were closely associated with business and politics, and who illuminated their practical experience with a remarkable gift of exposition.

Nevertheless these controversies are disfigured by preconceptions and confusions which burdened all subsequent discussions. It is worth while pointing these out once again; but it should be remembered that in dealing (perhaps at somewhat too great length) with Ricardo's ideas, we are in fact concerned with the essential elements of the entire body of so-called "classical" theory which was to dominate the nineteenth century. Ricardo's ideas, which at a superficial glance appear so logical, do in fact conceal inconsistencies, and it is in noting these that we shall discover the flaws in his theory.

In the first place Ricardo does not distinguish between forced paper currency and convertible bank-notes. Secondly, in so far as they affect prices, he does not distinguish between paper money and metallic money; finally, these three means of payment—bank-notes, inconvertible paper money, and coin—seem to Ricardo to be three slightly different types of one single species, and the way in which it functions in these three different forms presents wholly negligible differences. By this arbitrary simplification Ricardo, as it were, diverted the course of English (and to some extent of continental) theory into a narrower channel than that along which it had, before he wrote, been developing. It was Tooke and his followers who redirected it into broader and more comprehensive channels.

It is unnecessary to spend much time on Ricardo's identification of bank-notes and paper money, for that misconception was common to all his predecessors except Cantillon; on this point, however, Ricardo's attitude was so paradoxical that nobody else dared to adopt it. It is not, he maintains, the convertibility of bank-notes which keeps their value equal to that of the coin; it is the limitation of their quantity. It is not necessary that paper money should be payable in specie to secure its value; it is only necessary that its quantity should be regulated according to the value of the metal which is declared to be the standard."[1]

A forced paper currency, if its quantity is kept within sufficiently narrow limits, will be as stable in value as convertible notes. Convertibility is merely a practical method of ensuring limitation of quantity. Obsessed by the idea of quantity, Ricardo ignored the difference between a claim on a clearly defined sum and a claim on an indeterminate amount. Neither Adam Smith nor Galiani would have agreed to this, and it was to be emphatically denied a hundred years later by Marshall, the most classical of the modern English economists: "I think it is agreed that, if the credit of a currency falls, its value falls relatively to commodities, even when there is no change in its volume. I think it is agreed that the history of the *assignats* and the American currency during the time of the forced paper currency shows that."[2]

Between these two generations of economists, those of the eighteenth century and those of the early twentieth, Ricardo stands out as an isolated doctrinaire.[3]

[1] *Principles of Political Economy*, Chap. XXVIII.

[2] Marshall: *Evidence before the Committee on Indian Currency*, 1899, in *Official Papers*, by Alfred Marshall, London, 1926, p. 269.

[3] Consider some of his most striking formulas: "Though it has no intrinsic value, yet, by limiting its quantity, its value in exchange is as great as an equal denomination of coin, or of bullion in that coin. On the same principle, too, namely, by a limitation of its quantity, a debased coin would circulate at the value it should bear, if it were of the legal weight and fineness, and not at the value of the quantity of metal which it actually contained. . . . There is no point more important in issuing paper money, than to be fully impressed with the effects which follow from

Another fundamental confusion vitiates all Ricardo's conclusions—his failure to distinguish between the working of paper money and the working of metallic money. For him what was true of the one was true of the other, and propositions in regard to one are equally valid for the other.

He has a pretty low opinion of metallic currency. The scorn expressed by eighteenth-century writers is really felt by Ricardo.

> "Money," he writes, "is precisely that article which till it is re-exchanged never adds to the wealth of a country: accordingly, we find, that to increase its amount is never the voluntary act of any country any more than it is that of any individual. Money is forced upon them only in consequence of the relatively less value which it possesses in those countries with which they have intercourse." [1]

How clear it is that at the time he was writing there were no gold mines within the territories of Great Britain and her colonies, and that the treasures of South Africa had not yet been discovered! He continues:

> "Whilst a country employs the precious metals for money, and has no mines of its own, it is a conceivable case that it may greatly augment the amount of the productions of its land and labour without adding to its wealth, because at the same time those countries which are in possession of the mines may possibly have obtained so enormous a supply of the precious metals as to have forced an increase of currency on the industrious country, equal in value to the whole of its increased pro-

the principle of limitation of quantity . . . it is not necessary that paper money should be payable in specie to secure its value; it is only necessary that its value should be regulated according to the value of the metal which is declared to be the standard. . . . Dr. Smith appears to have forgotten his own principle, in his argument on colony currency. Instead of ascribing the depreciation of that money to its too great abundance, he asks whether, allowing the colony security to be perfectly good, a hundred pounds, payable fifteen years hence, would be equally valuable with a hundred pounds to be paid immediately? I answer yes, if it be not too abundant. . . . Experience, however, shows, that neither a State nor a Bank ever have had the unrestricted power of issuing paper money, without abusing that power; in all States, therefore, the issue of paper money ought to be under some check and control; and none seems so proper for that purpose, as that of subjecting the issuers of paper money to the obligation of paying their notes, either in gold or bullion." *Principles of Political Economy*, Chap. XXVII, §§ 125–127. This is Ricardo's sole concession to his adversaries; the weakness of governments is the only thing which justifies compulsory convertibility. Never has the failure to distinguish between bank-notes and money been more complete.

[1] *High Price of Bullion*, etc. Appendix.

ductions. But by so doing the augmented currency, added to that which was before employed, will be of no more real value than the original amount of currency. Thus then will this industrious nation become tributary to those nations which are in possesion of the mines, and will carry on a trade in which it gains nothing, and loses everything."[1]

Bear in mind this last phrase, which is the conclusion of the Ricardian paradox. An increase in the amount of metallic money in a country does nothing except raise prices. The given quantity of money performs identical services whatever its magnitude; the price level is automatically adjusted to that quantity. As far as the national economy is concerned, there is no difference between a gold coin, a wooden token, or a paper note. Quantity is the only thing that counts.

"Now, a paper circulation, not convertible into specie, differs in its effects in no respect from a metallic currency, with the law against exportation strictly executed."[2]

This expresses the well-known idea of money as a voucher to purchase held by John Law and Adam Smith; it is at the bottom of all Ricardo's doctrines.

In this Ricardo overlooks one essential point, which is that inconvertible paper money is simply an "ersatz" (and a very bad "ersatz") for gold coin. Paper money is not, as Ricardo, following Adam Smith, constantly says, money which is *added* to the existing metallic money, thus making its quantity excessive; it is money which, by acting as the standard, *replaces* metallic money.[3]

When paper money becomes the standard, which it does as forced currency, metallic money has no longer any part to play in the currency, and disappears rapidly from circulation. Another money has taken its place.[4] Ricardo himself states that during periods of forced currency, paper money is the real standard of value and that therefore coin and bullion automatically become "merchan-

[1] *High Price of Bullion*, etc.

[2] *Reply to Bosanquet*, § 21.

[3] Cf. particularly *Proposals*, etc., § 4.

[4] Cf. Cassel, *The Theory of Social Economy*, p. 396: "The moment the bank is relieved of its liability to redeem its notes in gold the bank-notes become real money. A country then has a paper-money system; the inconvertible notes which are recognised in it as legal tender have a 'forced currency.' These bank-notes no longer represent money-claims, but are themselves money; though we must notice that, as long as there is any prospect of returning to cash-payments, the notes in a sense retain the latent character of money-claims."

dise" (a very debatable term, as we shall soon shew). He makes this statement in two places,[1] but he refuses to see that once paper money has become the standard of value, it responds to other influences than those which determine the fluctuations in the value of gold when gold is the standard. For gold and paper are *two different moneys used for different purposes*; consequently the *demand* for them arises in different ways.

To mention one essential difference only: while *any* quantity of gold offered at any moment meets with an equivalent demand on the markets of the world, paper money is not always in demand, and frequently its holders are anxious to get rid of it. The *assignats* shewed this clearly, and J.-B. Say was emphatic on the point. But Ricardo is unwilling to consider these two moneys except from the point of view of *supply*, and therefore of quantity. According to him the demand for money is always equal to the total supply, which is true of gold but wholly false in regard to paper money.[2] From this follows his conclusion that in order to re-establish the old rate of paper money in relation to bullion (and to foreign currencies) it is only necessary—assuming that paper has depreciated—to decrease the *quantity* of money within the country. Whether the paper money is convertible or not (for we have seen that Ricardo confused bank-notes with paper money) a reduction in the quantity of money in circulation will immediately raise the value of the paper.[3]

[1] "At present gold coin is only a commodity, and bank-notes are the standard measure of value. That gold is no longer in practice the standard by which our currency is regulated, is a truth." Ricardo, *Economic Essays*, pp. 25 and 148.

[2] It would, however, be an exaggeration to say that Ricardo completely ignored the part which may be played by the demand for money. He refers to it, for example, when he wishes to point out that in the absence of free coinage of bullion, the greater demand for coin can give it a greater value than gold bullion of the same weight and fineness. Compare § 3 in his *Proposals for an Economical and Secure Currency*. But Ricardo is apt to forget facts and circumstances which do not fit in with the argument that he is at any moment putting forward. It should always be borne in mind that the demand for money is inverse to its rapidity of circulation, as Wicksell later pointed out. From this angle, it might be said that Ricardo took demand into account, but into how little account!

[3] "Parliament," he writes, "by restricting the Bank from paying in specie, have enabled the conductors of that concern to increase or decrease at pleasure the quantity and amount of their notes; and the previously existing checks against an over-issue having been thereby removed, those conductors have acquired the power of increasing or decreasing the value of the paper currency." Ricardo, *Economic Essays*, p. 21.

On many occasions worn coins had in England been exchanged for bullion at a higher rate than was actually justified by the amount of metal which they contained, because of the need for currency and the inadequate supply of coins. Ricardo bears this in mind when dealing with the value of paper money. He argues that at any moment a country requires a certain quantity, or, as he says, a certain "proportion" of money to effect all its transactions. This quantity, he says, "must depend on three things: first, on its value; secondly, on the amount or value of the payments to be made; and, thirdly, on the degree of economy practised in effecting those payments." [1]

"No increase or decrease of its quantity," he says elsewhere, "whether consisting of gold, silver, or paper money (as always he lumps the different kinds of money together), can increase or decrease its value above or below this proportion" [2] . . . "for by diminishing its value, in the same proportion you will increase its quantity, and by increasing its value, diminish its quantity." [3]

To recapitulate: "The circulation can never be over full. If it be one of gold and silver, any increase in its quantity will be spread over the world. If it be one of paper, it will diffuse itself only in the country where it is issued. Its effects on prices will then be only local and nominal, as a compensation by means of the exchange will be made to foreign purchasers." [4]

[1] *Proposals*, § 2. Cf. also *High Price*, § 34.

[2] *Principles of Political Economy*, Chap. XXVIII. Elsewhere he writes: "We may, therefore, fairly conclude, that this difference in the relative value, or in other words, that this depreciation in the actual value of bank-notes has been caused by the too abundant quantity which the Bank sent into circulation. The same cause which has produced a difference of from 15 to 20 per cent in bank-notes when compared with gold bullion, may increase it to 50 per cent. There can be no limit to the depreciation which may arise from a constantly increasing quantity of paper. . . . We have paper money only in circulation, which is necessarily confined to ourselves. Every increase in its quantity degrades it below the value of gold and silver bullion, below the value of the currencies of other countries. The effect is the same as that which would have been produced from clipping our coins" (p. 24). He also says: "If the Bank were restricted from paying their notes in specie, and all the coin had been exported, any excess of their notes would depreciate the value of the circulating medium in proportion to the excess. If 20 millions had been the circulation of England before the restriction, and 4 millions were added to it, the 24 millions would be of no more value than the 20 were before, provided commodities had remained the same, and there had been no corresponding exportation of coins; and if the Bank were successively to increase it to 50 or 100 millions, the increased quantity would be all absorbed in the circulation of England, but would be, in all cases, depreciated to the value of the 20 millions" (p. 35).

[3] *Political Economy*, § 124.

[4] *High Price*, etc., § 22.

Thus a "proportion" corresponding to currency requirements is always re-established by means of the price level, whatever the quantity issued, and whatever the currency medium. If the quantity increases, prices rise; if it decreases, prices fall. If there is a more economical use of monetary instruments as a result of what, following Adam Smith, he calls elsewhere "the judicious operation of banks"[1] by which he means primarily the use of cheques, the quantity of money is restricted, and the converse is also true.

This is the strict formulation of the quantity theory applied both to metallic money and to convertible and inconvertible bank-notes (cheques are not taken into account); the three moneys being regarded merely as vouchers to purchase, their greater or lesser quantity will determine their value in relation to the commodities which they are designed to circulate, the demand for these vouchers being always unlimited.

This theory overlooks two factors, of equal importance; both concern the *demand for money*:

1. Convertible paper and inconvertible paper are merely legal claims; metallic money is a *good* desirable in itself. It is itself a part of wealth, as Turgot says. Being legal claims, paper money, like all claims, has only the value of the objects in which it is redeemed. Convertible paper can at any moment be exchanged against gold; it therefore has the value of the gold for which it can be exchanged, that value being fixed on the world market, where gold is always in demand. As regards inconvertible paper, it is a claim on something *which is not specified*; and it therefore fluctuates in value, as do all claims of which the redemption is uncertain either as regards the date of repayment or the amount. To the extent that it is used for the circulation of commodities (or, to put it in another way, to the extent that it is directly redeemable in goods), its value is fixed at any given moment on the market by the quantity of goods or services that it buys. It is clear that in this respect an increase in the quantity of paper money brings about a rise in prices if it is not at the same time accompanied by an increase in the volume of commodities. But if it is not used for the immediate purchase of goods, if, like all money, it is kept for a longer or shorter time, its value will fluctuate according to the holder's calculation of *what the paper will be able to buy at the end of the indeterminate period*

[1] *High Price*, etc., § 34.

during which he means to keep it. And if that estimate is too low it may be, as was the case with the *assignats*, that the holders will get rid of the paper at any price and that its value will fall to zero.

2. For—and this is the second consideration which Ricardo overlooks, and which is frequently ignored to-day—when a monetary standard itself fluctuates rapidly, one of the consequences is that the holders of the money *change the distribution of their expenditure as between the present and the future.* When the standard is stable, that is to say when the general price level remains constant or changes only slightly, individuals distribute their expenditure, as regards time, according to the normal time sequence of their consumption requirements, their debts and their investments. But when the standard varies rapidly, this distribution is as quickly changed. If the standard falls (that is to say if prices rise) the purchase of goods and the placing of investments are pushed forward, while the payment of debts is slowed down. Conversely if the standard rises (if the general price level declines) the purchase of goods and investments is slowed down and the payment of debts pushed forward. In the first case money is spent more quickly, in the second case more slowly; this itself immediately affects domestic prices, accelerating their rise in the first case, their fall in the second. In short, fluctuations in the standard, whether it is a metal or a paper standard, give rise to speculation—the general term used for the distribution of purchases and sales between the present and the future—which immediately reacts on prices. This speculation is, as a rule, much more intense with paper money, where the conditions of issue are uncertain. Such speculation, moreover, does not merely affect the internal distribution of expenditure, but also external expenditure by the holders of the currency in other countries: in other words it reacts on the balance of payments and on the exchanges. This brings us to an examination of the Ricardian theory of the exchanges.

§ IV. *Theory of Purchasing Power Parity*

Ricardo's theory of the exchanges cannot be understood unless the comparison which he makes throughout his writings between the depreciation of paper money and the depreciation of worn or clipped coins is constantly borne in mind. Many instances of such depreciation had been known in England. It had been observed that bullion automatically rose to a premium over coin of the same metal, and that at the same time the exchanges moved against the currency in proportion to the wear and tear of the coinage.[1] As a result, English prices rose; the depreciation of the pound on the home and foreign markets was exactly equal to the loss of weight of the English coinage.

In all these cases the origin of the unfavourable exchange rates and of the premium on bullion in relation to worn coins was to be found solely in the *internal* conditions of the English currency. It was the bad state of the coinage to which the results observed were due. To explain the changes caused by paper money, it was only necessary to liken the issue of paper to the wear of coins or, as Ricardo sometimes said, to rising coinage charges, or again to an "augmentation" of the coinage such as had occurred in France in the early eighteenth century. Nominal prices in England rose in proportion to the increase in the quantity of money. But as at the same time the paper depreciated against the currencies of countries with a metallic standard, real prices, that is to say prices expressed in metal, remained the same and the premium on gold over paper was, in Ricardo's view, the reflexion or even the *measure* of the "superabundance" of paper.

Ricardo thus treats an *analogy* as an *identity* and he is therefore able to give the quantity theory a precision which at the first glance makes a most satisfactory impression. This is the origin of a theory which has since become famous as the theory of purchasing power parity. According to this the rise in domestic prices consequent upon a greater quantity of paper money is an exact reflexion of the depreciation of that money. This depreciation is also expressed in a falling rate of exchange against the currencies of countries with a metallic standard. The rise in domestic prices and the fall on the exchanges are two manifestations of one phenomenon—an increase in the quantity of paper. The gap between the price levels of the country with paper money and of the other countries measures the depreciation of the paper money. The same theory is to be found in

[1] This was the case with the gold coin before the reminting of 1774, and with the silver coin in the reign of William III, before the coinage reform advocated by Locke and Newton.

the *Bullion Report* which contains a very precise account of what is called the "real" par of exchange based on the respective weights of the national currencies. The wear and tear of the coinage in one country affects the exchange rate of its currency; in the same way an increase in the quantity of paper money brings about a similar change:

"But this real Par will be altered if any change takes place in the currency of one of the two countries, whether that change consists in the wear or debasement of a metallic currency below its standard, or in the discredit of a forced paper currency, or in the excess of a paper currency not convertible into specie; a fall having taken place in the intrinsic value of a given portion of one currency, that portion will no longer be equal to the same portions as before, of the other currency."[1]

In both cases the "intrinsic" value is changed, in one case by the bad state of the coinage, in the other by the excessive quantity of paper (or, according to the *Report*, though this is not mentioned by Ricardo, by the discredit into which the paper money has fallen).[2]

After the war of 1914–1918, M. Cassel put forward a brilliant defence of the theory that the respective rates at which the par of exchange should be established as between countries with paper currencies could be calculated by the differences in their price levels.[3]

This is a simple repetition of the theory enunciated by Ricardo and expressed in the Report of the Bullion Committee, and the objections made against the one can be applied to the other. By paying attention only to the quantity of paper money, and to the fall in exchange rates as a direct result and a measure of an excessive issue of paper within the country, Ricardo fails to indicate any means of discovering the *amount of surplus* paper and entirely

[1] *Bullion Report*, p. 22. Reproduced in *The Paper Pound of 1797–1821*, E. Cannan, London, 1925.

[2] Cf. p. 17 of the *Report* where this theory is formulated even more precisely.

[3] Having explained the method of calculating variations in the purchasing power of money in different countries, starting from a given state of equilibrium, M. Cassel states: "I still regard, therefore, the purchasing power parities calculated on the above-mentioned grounds as the normal exchange rate. If the actual rate for a country's money is lower, then I say that the money of that country is undervalued. If the rate is higher, then the money is overvalued." *Money and Foreign Exchange after 1914*, London, 1922.

ignores exchange fluctuations due to other causes, firstly, to the balance of trade, and secondly, and more important, to the estimates made on foreign markets of the value of the paper money.

A fall on the exchange, even when it is the result of circumstances other than an increased quantity of paper, *leads to a rise in prices in the country with paper money at least as often as a rise in prices causes a fall on the exchange*. This action of the exchanges on domestic prices in countries with paper money has as a rule been misunderstood by the writers of Ricardo's school of thought. It had been observed by eighteenth-century writers, and it is of the greatest importance. It had been noted that a rise or fall on the exchanges exerted a powerful influence, by means of changes in the cost of imports, on the domestic price level, irrespective of any change in the quantity of paper money issued. Numerous instances had been recorded in which distrust of paper money had sent its value down below the level warranted by its quantity; conversely, expectation of a subsequent rise frequently sends its value above that level. To substitute for this factor the factor of quantity alone, to see in the appreciation or depreciation of paper on the exchanges the *measure* of its "excess" and in the rise or fall of the price level the mathematical expression of that excess, to believe that it is only necessary to reduce the quantity of paper to bring about a proportionate appreciation, or on the other hand, to increase the quantity to bring about a depreciation—this is an illusion without any foundation in actual history, and the *assignat* experiment had just demonstrated once again that it was an illusion. That is why, when the convertibility of paper has to be re-established and the exchanges stabilised, sound finance and a balanced budget count far more than limitation of the quantity of paper. The important thing in such a case is to reassure foreign holders of securities or currency as to the ultimate value of the paper, and this can only be done by convincing them that the financial stability of the State has been re-established. That is why, in 1819, the repayment by the English Government to the Bank of £10 million sterling did more to bring the pound back to par than the insignificant reduction in the number of notes which was effected at the same time.

Mention has just been made of the *assignats*. Why does no

reference to this striking experiment occur in Ricardo's writings? To answer this question we shall have to say something about the *Bullion Report*, which served as a pretext for Ricardo's pamphlets, published as commentaries on that Report.

§ v. *The* 1810 *Bullion Report*

In the opening years of the nineteenth century the forced currency had led to only a slight increase in the English note circulation, and exchange rates had not moved far from parity. It was only in 1808 that the increase in the currency began to make itself felt, as prices rose higher and higher and exchange rates fell. An ounce of gold rose in price from £3 17*s*. 10½*d*. to £4 10*s*. in 1909, and the pound was worth only 107 grains of gold instead of 123¼. Certain sections of the public expressed their anxiety, and early in 1810 Francis Horner, Member of Parliament, proposed in the House of Commons that a Committee be appointed to "enquire into the cause of the high price of bullion." After numerous witnesses had been heard, the Report, drawn up largely by Horner, Huskisson and Thornton, was laid before the House in June; it was not debated until April 1811 and its conclusions were rejected.

The ideas enunciated in the Report (in the writing of which Ricardo had no direct part, since he was not a member of Parliament) have often been identified with the ideas of the famous economist. In fact there are numerous divergences between his ideas and those of the Committee which on all points approximate far more closely to those of Thornton. The divergences are significant enough to deserve our attention.

On the question of determining what was the real standard of value in England since the suspension of payment in specie, the Report is not so definite as Ricardo. He explicitly declares that paper is the standard, although he does not draw all the conclusions which follow from this fact. The Report leaves the question open. Is it always gold which is the standard, or is it paper?[1] This, says

[1] "It may indeed be doubted, whether, since the new system of Bank of England payments has been fully established, Gold has in truth continued to be our measure of value; and whether we have any other standard of prices than that circulating medium, issued primarily by the Bank of England and in a secondary manner by

the Report, is open to discussion. On the other hand, there is no doubt that "it is, in either case, most desirable for the public that our circulating medium should again be conformed, as speedily as circumstances will permit, to its real and legal standard, Gold Bullion."

This hesitation on an essential theoretical point is significant. It undoubtedly reflects a divergence of views within the Committee, and an inadequate understanding on the part of certain of its members of the radical change made in the country's monetary standard by the introduction of forced currency. They found it difficult to believe that a simple claim of unstable value could serve as a standard of value. On this point, at any rate, Ricardo's attitude is both more candid and more correct.

Secondly—and this is a more important point—the Report does not deny that "a want of confidence in the sufficiency of those funds upon which the paper has been issued" may also cause it to depreciate. It adds, however, that this consideration "*plays no part in our present situation.*" It had done so in other countries using paper money, but not in England. In England the excess of currency alone was the cause of depreciation: "In the instances which are most familiar in the history of Foreign Countries, the excess of paper has been usually accompanied by another circumstance, which has no place in our situation at present, a want of confidence in the sufficiency of those funds upon which the paper had been issued."[1] In another passage enumerating the causes which may bring about a rise of foreign currencies, the Report mentions "the wear or debasement of a metallic currency below its standard . . . the discredit of a forced paper currency . . . the excess of a paper currency not convertible into specie."[2]

the country Banks, the variations of which in relative value may be as indefinite as the possible excess of that circulating medium. But whether our present measure of value, and standard of prices, be this paper currency thus variable in its relative value, or continues still to be Gold, but Gold rendered more variable than it was before in consequence of being interchangeable for a paper currency which is not at will convertible into Gold, it is, in either case, most desirable for the public that our circulating medium should again be conformed, as speedily as circumstances will permit, to its real and legal standard, Gold Bullion." Cannan, *The Paper Pound*, p. 16.

[1] *Ibid.*, p. 36.

[2] *Ibid.*, p. 22.

Thus, at the time that Ricardo was writing, it was admitted in England that lack of confidence, and not merely an excessive quantity, could influence the value of paper money. Indeed, it was impossible to do otherwise after the *assignat* experiment and the fate of colonial currencies, and after that significant evidence submitted to the Bullion Committee (by a "personage" who is described sometimes as a "most eminent continental merchant," sometimes as "very closely associated with the trade between this country and the continent," and who was in fact none other than Nathan Rothschild) in which it was stated that on the continent "it is only a matter of opinion what rate a pound sterling is there to be valued at, not being able to obtain what it is meant to represent." [1]

Forgetting their earlier caution, the Committee no longer hesitate to say, at the end of their Report, that the return to convertibility is the only way "that can effectively restore general confidence in the value of the circulating medium of the kingdom"; which implies that confidence had been shaken.[2]

Thornton had taken up a similar position in his book published in 1802. In it he affirms that there is a radical difference between paper money as it was known on the continent, in particular in France under John Law and during the *assignat* period, and paper money as it was known in England. In France, he says, the value of the *assignats* was maintained for a time because of the value placed by their bearers on the land on which the paper was secured, and because they trusted the French Government to redeem their pledges.

"It is, therefore, not at all surprising that French assignats should, for a time, have borne a price which was proportionate not so much to their quantity as to their credit. Their quantity, however, after a certain period, operated on their credit, and became a very powerful cause of their depreciation. Bank of England notes are exactly the converse to assignats in the points which have been mentioned; and their value, on that account, will be found to depend not so properly on their credit as on their quantity. . . . By saying, therefore, that the value of bank-notes depends not on their credit, but on their quantity, I mean to affirm that their credit, so far as it affects their value, is always good, and that the common fluctuations of their price, in exchange both for goods and bullion, are not, in the smallest degree, to be referred to variations in the

[1] *The Paper Pound*, p. 20.

[2] *Ibid.*, p. 70.

degree of confidence placed by Englishmen in the good faith or the solidity of the Bank of England."[1]

As proof he adduces the decisive fact that sterling improved on the exchanges in the months which followed the suspension of cash payments.

The *Bullion Report* follows Thornton in affirming complete confidence in the English currency. It is impossible to say whether this was a sincerely held belief, or whether it was a necessary precaution in a report that was to be made public, and whose authors were naturally concerned with the effect it might have on public opinion. In any case it followed from this that in the Report the depreciation of sterling was attributed solely to the *quantity* of paper issued.[2]

Finally, it is freely admitted in the Report that certain fluctuations in the rate of exchange had occurred without, as far as the authors could discover, any corresponding change in the quantity of notes; they were ascribed to movements in trade or to political causes. "Your Committee however, on the whole, are not of opinion that a material depression of the Exchanges has been manifestly to be traced in its amount and degree to an augmentation of notes corresponding in point of time. They conceive, that the more minute and ordinary fluctuations of Exchange are generally referable to the course of our commerce; that political events, operating upon the state of trade, may often have contributed as well to the rise as to the fall of the Exchange."[3]

On this point, too, the Report is on Thornton's lines; in this passage, apparently, his views prevailed. In his book he had observed that an unfavourable trade balance (arising, for example, from a bad harvest necessitating wheat imports) reacted on the exchanges and set up a demand for bullion for export, thus raising its price. This is an example of a movement of exchange rates that has nothing to do with an "excess" of paper. The same argument was later put forward by Malthus in an unsigned review of Ricardo's pamphlet, published in the *Edinburgh Review* of 1811; the principal defect in

[1] Thornton, *loc. cit.*, pp. 254 and 255.

[2] Thornton was fully aware of the influence exerted by the *demand* for money. He observes that paper money is hoarded when it is expected that it will rise in value, and points out that it was because they were in *demand* that the *assignats* retained their value when they were first issued.

[3] *The Paper Pound*, p. 35.

Ricardo's work, he says, is the far too narrow view he takes of the factors influencing exchange rates.

Although he was as familiar with these arguments as anyone, Ricardo deliberately ignores them and maintains that the only cause of the depreciation of paper money is an increase in its quantity. In so doing, he takes up an entirely new and wholly individual position in English currency theory. It may be this too is merely an expression of his patriotism, of his desire not to shake the confidence of the public and of other countries in the English currency. It would be diverting to believe that the "quantity theory" originated in the author's anxiety not to provide even the slightest justification for the reproach that he had shaken confidence in the country's currency in time of war. Or did Ricardo believe that by formulating this theory he would be in a better position to persuade the Bank of England to undertake the reform on which his heart was set, that is, to *reduce the note circulation* in order to raise its value and hasten the return to convertibility? It is difficult to say, although the second hypothesis seems highly probable. It is also probable that his habit of generalisation induced him simply to ignore the more complex aspects of the problem, and to regard it solely from the one standpoint which seemed to provide the key to all monetary phenomena, the aspect of *quantity*. It was a convenient position, allowing him to make the quasi-perfect analogy which he upheld so strongly, between the operation of paper money and the operation of metallic money.

He held rigidly to this standpoint against both Thornton and the *Edinburgh Review*. In his reply to the latter he again asserts that "an unfavourable balance of trade, and a consequently low exchange, may *in all cases* be traced to a relatively redundant and cheap currency."[1]

The word "relatively" introduced here is the only concession he makes to his critics; he does not even admit the truth of their contention that a favourable exchange rate can coincide with an expanding currency, and unfavourable exchanges with a diminishing currency.[2] It is true that this one word "relatively" can make a great deal of difference, as we shall see later. It may be, too, that Ricardo, who had an unrivalled knowledge of the money market, had been impressed by an incident in the history of the Bank of England

[1] Ricardo, *Economic Essays*, p. 53. [2] *Ibid.*, p. 51.

which apparently received a great deal of attention in the discussions of that time, as both Thornton and Ricardo dealt with it at considerable length.

Adam Smith noted[1] that before the recoinage of 1774, when bullion stood at a premium over the worn coinage, the Bank of England bought gold bullion (for which it paid in notes) and had it coined into standard guineas; these were immediately melted down by the public and the gold brought back to the Bank and paid for at the price of bullion. Adam Smith attributed the continuation of such transactions to an excessive note issue. Obviously, if the Bank had refused to buy gold (and assuming that the Mint would not have bought it either) the scarcity of coin would have reached a point at which, despite its bad state, its price would be on a par with bullion; but that would undoubtedly have involved an extremely awkward currency restriction. Moreover, in this case, the cause of the trouble lay in the bad state of the coinage and the remedy consisted, not in ceasing to issue notes, but in reforming the coinage.

Nevertheless Ricardo used this incident to explain the loss of gold when bank-notes are in use. In this case the only way of putting a stop to the loss of gold is to cease *granting credit*, for if the Bank issues notes when it grants credit, notes will be brought back to the Bank to be exchanged for gold, no restriction will be felt on the money market, and there is no reason why the public should cease exporting gold.

Ricardo was unquestionably right in this contention. Anybody who has had experience of such a state of affairs knows how quickly, in such circumstances, the cessation of discounting changes the direction of the movement of gold, and makes the metal reappear. That is because the growing scarcity of money *on the money market* is felt immediately. In order to conduct its operations the money market needs a minimum of media of payment and relies on the normal amount of credit, the absence of which is immediately felt. The quantity theory is confirmed on this market more quickly and more exactly than anywhere else. In this case the scarcity occurs in the currency instruments required for normal banking operations or for the current transactions of commerce and industry, not in the instruments required for the transactions of the general public.

[1] Bk. II, Chap. II, p. 285.

This scarcity has an almost instantaneous effect on the money market, but influences the other much more slowly. Without adequate justification Ricardo maintained that the same effect was produced in both cases.

What does this mean if not that a scarcity of paper money, when carried beyond a certain point, will inevitably bring back metallic money, or, to use Ricardo's expression, raise the value of gold in the exporting country and attract gold from abroad? Was this not an example of the quantity theory in its strictest formulation? Had not such cases frequently occurred since, and were they not calculated to support his contention that the quantity of money exercises a decisive influence on its relative value? It was this same conception, applied with the same strictness, which Ricardo used to explain the distribution of gold among the different countries of the world.

§ VI. *Mechanism of the World Distribution of the precious Metals*

This is one of Ricardo's most famous theories; the events of the last few years, during which the world distribution of gold has been affected in ways entirely new and unexpected, give that theory a new interest. Admittedly it explains only one aspect of the truth; it is one-sided and exclusive, like all the theories put forward by Ricardo, who was so strongly inclined to simplification and generalisation; it is not so much an original theory as a synthesis of the ideas of the eighteenth century on this question; nevertheless, it is highly instructive and touches the root of the problem.

Ricardo considered that the way in which the precious metals are distributed represents a further verification of the quantity theory. The single moving force behind the movement of money from one country to another is the "superabundance" of the precious metals.

He begins his argument with the assumption, to which reference has already been made, that at any given time there is for every country a certain state of monetary equilibrium. Given the level of commercial activity, the system of banking, and the rapidity of currency circulation, a country needs a certain quantity of the precious metals to effect its transactions; this quantity will obviously vary from country to country.[1] From the point of view of their distribution, it does not matter at all whether the *absolute* quantity of precious metals in the world is large or small. Each country will simply acquire more or less of them, but the proportion of the total which it gets will be that which corresponds to its banking system, trade, etc.

"The variation in their quantity would have produced no other effect than to make the commodities for which they were exchanged comparatively dear or cheap."[2]

He has nothing to say about the influence of an influx of precious metals on the general prosperity of the world, a matter to which eighteenth-century writers gave considerable thought; as far as the abundance or scarcity of the precious metals is concerned, his attitude approaches one of complete indifference; this was to become the gospel of his followers and was strongly criticised by Newmarch when the Californian and Australian gold discoveries were made.

In the initial state of equilibrium which Ricardo postulates, the money metals have "the same value" in each country, or, as we should say to-day, "the same purchasing power" in relation to commodities. If this were not so, if prices were higher in some countries than in others, countries where goods were "dear" would immediately begin buying goods in the "cheap" countries, and there would be a movement of bullion from the former to the latter. The result would be a diminution of money in the dear countries, and an increase in the cheap, which would re-establish the price equilibrium as between the two, for "I assume as a fact which is incontrovertible," says Ricardo, "that commodities would rise or fall in price, in proportion to the increase or diminution of money."[3]

[1] "In certain countries this proportion is much greater than in others, and varies, on some occasions, in the same country. It depends upon the rapidity of circulation, upon the degree of confidence and credit existing between traders, and, above all, on the judicious operations of banking. In England, so many means of economising the use of circulating medium have been adopted, that its value, compared with the value of the commodities which it circulates, is probably (during a period of confidence) reduced to as small a proportion as is practicable." *High Price of Bullion*, p. 34. He adds in a footnote: "In the following observations I wish it to be understood as supposing always the same degree of confidence and credit to exist."

[2] *High Price of Bullion*, § 1.

[3] *Reply to Bosanquet*, in *Economic Essays*, p. 93, note.

On this assumption, gold will never move from one country to another, and all transactions will be settled by bills of exchange "so long as their relative situation continued unaltered."[1] Ricardo leaves it to the reader to discover what he means by "an unaltered relative situation" as between, for example, two countries such as England and France, where everything is always changing.

On the other hand there will be a movement of gold in either of the following cases:

1. When one country grows wealthy more rapidly than others; there prices will fall, "it will need more money and it will obtain it from the rest of the world."

2. When gold mines are discovered in one country. In this case "the currency of that country would be lowered in value in consequence of the increased quantity of the precious metals brought into circulation, and would therefore no longer be of the same value as that of other countries. Gold and silver, whether in coin or in bullion, would immediately become articles of exportation; they would leave the country where they were cheap, for those countries where they were dear, and would continue to do so, as long as the mine should prove productive, and till the proportion existing between capital and money in each country before the discovery of the mine, were again established, and gold and silver restored everywhere to one value. In return for the gold exported, commodities would be imported; and though what is usually termed the balance of trade would be against the country exporting money or bullion, it would be evident that she was carrying on a most advantageous trade, exporting that which was no way useful to her, for commodities which might be employed in the extension of her manufactures, and the increase of her wealth."[2]

To put it briefly, and in more modern language than Ricardo used, one circumstance alone regulates gold movements from one country to another—the relative level of prices, the level itself

[1] "While the relative situation of countries continued unaltered, they might have abundant commerce with each other, but their exports and imports would on the whole be equal. England might possibly import more goods from, than she would export to, France, but she would in consequence export more to some other country, and France would import more from that country; so that the exports and imports of all countries would balance each other; bills of exchange would make the necessary payments, but no money would pass because it would have the same value in all countries." *High Price of Bullion*, p. 4.

[2] *Ibid.*

being a function of the quantity of precious metals circulating within the country and of the more or less developed organisation of payments. The price levels in different countries express the relative dearness or cheapness of the precious metals in each country. Any increase in the production of goods in one country will bring the price level down, or in other words make gold dearer and thus attract it from other countries. Any increase in the production of gold will lower its value as against goods and will lead to its export. Gold is in fact a wholly superfluous metal. When new gold mines are discovered, the only effect is to disturb the normal relations between different countries which, in the absence of gold, would be established on a barter basis, by the simple exchange of commodities.[1]

But together with this contemptuous and wholly absurd opinion about money, which puts it in a far lower category than other kinds of goods, Ricardo held that the export or import of gold is no more important than the export or import of any other commodity, and that no obstacle should be placed in the way of its loss or acquisition. If coin or bullion is a commodity like any other, that is an object of consumption or a means of production, why should its appearance in international trade be nothing but a nuisance, and why should an increase or decrease in its quantity make no difference in the economic situation? That is not true of any other commodity—the absence of coal, copper or cotton would certainly not be a matter of indifference.

But that is only one minor point, one example among many of a singularly defective terminology which ill conceals the gaps in an argument that is too anxious to reach conclusions determined beforehand. The main conclusion is that the one and only cause of

[1] "Gold and silver having been chosen for the general medium of circulation, they are, by the competition of commerce, distributed in such proportions amongst the different countries of the world, as to accommodate themselves to the natural traffic which would take place if no such metals existed, and the trade between countries were purely a trade of barter." Ricardo, *Political Economy*, § 48.

This is a curious conception! In his book on *Gold and Silver* (p. 40) Wolowski subjects it to pertinent criticism. Who can believe that trade between countries *would be the same* in the absence of gold to settle debts? It is as if it were argued that exchanges between individuals would be the same in a barter system and a money system. Classical monetary theory made the mistake of regarding money as a mechanism which is *superimposed* on a pre-existing exchange system, whereas in fact it constitutes an integral part of the economic system.

gold movements is the relative dearness or cheapness of metallic currency in different countries, or as Ricardo prefers to put it, the relative *scarcity* or *abundance* of such money.

The fact that Ricardo made no distinction between these two expressions—dearness or cheapness, and scarcity or abundance—is very important; many others have followed him in this, but the identification is incorrect and vitiates his entire theory of the distribution of the precious metals. Unless there were some confusion of this kind, it would be difficult to understand how a man as well informed as Ricardo could have deliberately ignored gold movements arising from other causes—not only those changes in the balance of trade which his contemporaries adduced in opposition to his theory, but movements of capital which, although far more extensive to-day than they were in his time, were well known then; and the movement of money resulting from loss of public confidence as to its safety which was very widespread after the World War but was also well known in the eighteenth century, during the periods of augmentation and diminution of the coinage, as Law and Cantillon had observed.

All movements of capital, of income, of services and of goods, whether occurring simultaneously or separately, may start a movement of gold. The Ricardian formula of "relative abundance" of gold as the sole cause of its export seems so completely false that one hesitates to admit that a writer as far sighted as Ricardo could have given it the meaning which tradition still attaches to it. Nevertheless he did. But when it is remembered that Ricardo was a broker on the foreign exchange market this is not so surprising. It was from this standpoint that he followed and interpreted the movement of the precious metals. What view did he get from this observation post? What follows when, as a result of *whatever* cause (credit expansion, poor harvest making additional imports necessary, foreign loans, etc.), there is a rise on the foreign exchanges, that is to say, in the price of international claims which serve as means of payment? A rise in the price, expressed in the national currency, of all foreign goods, *including gold in other countries*. The means for making payments abroad—commercial bills and cheques—having grown dearer, all foreign commodities, including gold, immediately become dearer for the country whose exchange has fallen and which has to acquire these means of payment. Let us assume that France is in this position; the price in francs of a bill of exchange on London rises, to obtain a "sovereign" in London—a coin corresponding to 25.22 fr. at Paris—a bill of exchange is bought in Paris at a price *above 25.22 fr.* In other words gold, paid for in francs, is dearer in London than in Paris. If the difference in price exceeds the cost of transporting the metal, it will be cheaper to export gold from Paris to London and to sell in Paris the bills on London obtained from the sale of gold there.

Ricardo was right in saying that all gold exports arise from the fact that gold bought in national currency is relatively dearer in the importing countries than in the exporting countries.[1] That is undoubtedly the determining factor in all gold movements, which do not take place unless the exchange rate of one country—that is to say the price of international means of payment—rises sufficiently to make it profitable to export the metal from one country to the other—a process which is true of any commodity whatever.

Ricardo adds that the profit arises from the *abundance* of gold. The origin of the mistake lies in the confusion of "relative dearness and cheapness" with "scarcity and abundance." If wheat and potatoes are dearer in London than in Paris, and are therefore exported from Paris to London, can it be taken for granted that there is a surplus of wheat or potatoes in Paris? There may be a shortage in both countries, and yet wheat and potatoes will be sent from France to England if the prices are different.

The same is true of gold. Gold is the international means of payment *par excellence* because its price, expressed in any national currency, is always stable. There is no uncertainty as to its sale. For all kinds of reasons, international means of payment other than gold may become dearer in Paris, or, in other words, there may be an insufficient supply of them to cover all the payments that have to be made. In that case gold, which always costs the same in francs, is used to make up the difference; this is reflected in a difference in the price (reckoned in francs) of gold in London and in Paris, enabling a profit to be made on its export. But that does not mean that Paris has "too much" gold, or that London is short of it. It merely means

[1] Ricardo has still another theory. He says that if gold is exported in preference to other goods from a country with an unfavourable exchange rate, it is because *gold is cheaper* than other goods. The entire discussion on this question—his contemporaries pointed out that gold rose along with other commodities—is extremely obscure and not worth further attention.

that, at a given time, Paris has a greater indebtedness in London than London has in Paris.

As a broker, Ricardo was correct in saying that gold exports always originate in a rise on the exchange, that is to say in a rise in the price (in national currency) of gold in other countries. But as an economist he was mistaken in thinking that there is an equilibrium—impossible to imagine or to define—between a country's gold "requirements" and the actual quantity of gold which that country acquires, and in assuming that the movement of gold from one country to another brings about this equilibrium, the implication being that if one country exports gold it is because it has "too much," and if another imports gold it is because it has "too little." In fact the contrary is often the case. In recent years France and the United States have acquired immense quantities of gold, far beyond their requirements, but these movements are to be attributed to the results either of the depreciation of currencies, or of the stabilisation of currencies at levels which, in regard both to capital and commodities, are a true expression of price differences which cause large scale movements of gold from one country to another.

In actual fact, gold—international money—serves the same purpose for countries as reserve funds for industrial or commercial concerns. Certain undertakings have their reserve funds lying idle; they always have liquid funds, either as cash in hand or lent on short term; when their current expenditure temporarily exceeds their current receipts, they are not at a loss to cover the difference; they call in their short-term credits. This was true of England before the war. Other undertakings have their reserves tied up; either their surplus funds are lent on too long term, or there are sudden interruptions in their sales, while expenditure continues unchanged, or they immobilise their profits. This was true of Germany before the war. When such concerns have an urgent debt to settle they have to liquidate their stocks of goods at a low price, or borrow on short or long term, or call in credits granted to other concerns.

A country has to meet its payments in the same way. These payments do not always coincide with the proceeds of sales. At times the liability side of the balance sheet exceeds the asset side. In the absence of credit, the difference cannot be made up except by the export of gold. But this is not a result of an excess of gold in the exporting country; it is the result of the totality of purchases and sales, of loans made and received, of payments and repayments which, in the aggregate, may not balance at a particular moment, so that the difference can only be covered by gold. Whenever gold is exported, it is because it is dearer in the country to which it is sent than in the exporting country. This difference in price arises because *the means of payment other than gold* available in the one country are not enough to meet all the debts that have to be settled. This shortage may arise from any of the factors which determine the balance of payments, that is to say the country's receipts and expenditure in foreign currency.

Ricardo selects only one of these factors—the shortage and plenty of gold within the country in relation to the operations to be transacted and the consequent difference in price levels. In answering the objections put forward by Malthus and Thornton, who pointed out that a deficient harvest would necessitate extra wheat imports and the export of gold to pay for them, Ricardo used a purely verbal argument, similar to that which Marx was to use later. He contended that a bad harvest, by diminishing the volume of goods while the volume of currency remained the same, makes that currency "relatively" excessive. This is obviously a feeble verbal trick. In fact, Ricardo recognises only one important and permanent cause of gold movements—the gold mines themselves; it is their output which brings about a dislocation between the price levels of different countries. Gold movements arising from a disequilibrium in the balance of payments (assuming that the quantity of money in the world does not change) are in his opinion quite unimportant. The only gold movements that are important are those produced when the countries which mine the precious metals mint the new metal; the increase in the quantity of currency raises the price level, that is to say, *lowers the purchasing power of gold in relation to goods below its purchasing power in other countries*, which is followed by variations on the exchanges. In fact, Ricardo is wholly bound by the experience of the eighteenth century.

In the nineteenth century the distribution of gold throughout the world was effected without much difficulty because the comparative freedom of international trade facilitated the rapid adjustment of variations in the balance of payments. Large scale movements of gold were rare and were managed fairly easily because bimetallism acted as a moderating influence. In this respect France was an important factor in maintaining price equilibrium, particularly after the discovery of the Californian mines. The gold exported from the Transvaal after 1895 caused a slow rise in prices everywhere. It was bought and sold everywhere at a price fixed and announced beforehand. Once it had reached the buying markets the influence of this new supply gradually made itself felt over the economic field as a whole. Gold was distributed in the way that Ricardo had described.

But the post-war movements of gold, which excited such agitation, were of an entirely different character; they may be grouped in three categories:

(*a*) Movements of capital connected with the enormous credits granted by certain countries to certain other countries (American credits to Germany, investments made by all countries either in London or at other times—for example in 1929—in New York), and with the withdrawal of capital when the panic started. These sudden withdrawals in 1931 drained Germany and Austria, and eventually London, of their gold. Ricardo had no idea of the part which these migrations of capital were to play in international life, or of the extent of the resulting movements of gold. They are one of the elements in that balance of payments which he persistently ignored.

(*b*) Other large-scale movements of gold were caused by the arbitrage operations that followed the *arbitrary fixing of a gold purchase price in national currency irrespective of the exchange rate of that currency.*

There are two outstanding examples of this; the first and more famous is the absorption of gold by the United States immediately after the war.

The buying price of gold in London was kept at the same figure as it had been before the war, although the pound had depreciated against the dollar. Since the price paid for gold in London left the depreciation of sterling out of account, newly mined gold was sold in New York for dollars, for which a larger amount of sterling could be obtained than if the gold had been sold to the Bank of England. That is why New York accumulated gold up to 1925, when the pound was stabilised. When England succeeded in restoring the pound to the old rate of 4.86 dollars, there was no longer any advantage in selling gold in New York. When the relationship between the exchange rate of the pound and the dollar coincided with the relative weight of gold in the sovereign and the dollar, gold ceased to flow exclusively to New York.

Similarly, when in 1935 President Roosevelt suddenly decided to fix the gold content of the dollar at the equivalent of 15 French francs, whereas the dollar was worth 16 francs in Paris, gold was at once sent from France to America. There was a profit to be made in buying gold in Paris at 15 francs, sending it to New York where dollars could be bought for fifteen francs, and selling those dollars in Paris in the form of bills on New York at the Paris market rate, that is, at 16 francs. Thus enormous quantities of gold were sent from London and Paris to New York to take advantage of the difference, suddenly created by devaluation in America, between the price of gold and the price of other means of international payment; the difference was eliminated by the effect of these very gold exports on exchange rates, bringing the dollar down from 16 to 15 francs. This example shews that prolonged gold movements may arise from the fact that there is a difference between the rate at which two paper currencies are exchanged, and the official price, as expressed in those currencies, quoted for gold by the banks of issue.

(*c*) After the war all countries with paper currencies had to determine anew the gold content of their monetary unit. As a rule this was fixed at the weight calculated as consistent with equilibrium in the balance of payments, that is to say at the level corresponding to stability on the foreign exchanges. In England, for example, since the pound sterling had risen to its old rate, it was decided to go back to the former gold content of the pound. In France the rise of the franc after the 1926 crisis made it possible to fix the gold content of the franc at the level at which it seemed that its exchange rate could be maintained without the loss of gold.

These attempts at stabilisation were based on the exchange rates of the respective currencies and were designed to keep them at that rate; they did not however give sufficient weight to another consideration, the relation between purchasing power on the home market and purchasing power in foreign markets. At this point Ricardo's theory can be applied. To stabilise the pound against the dollar at the rate of 4.86 means that a pound when changed into dollars can buy the same quantity of goods in America as in England. But if the English price level is so high that a pound in England commands fewer goods and services than it does in America when changed into dollars, English purchases in America will increase while American purchases in England will decline. The balance of payments moves against England and there will be a tendency for gold to be exported from England to America—not, it should be noted, because there is *too much* gold in England, but simply because, given that exchange rate, the English price level expressed in gold is higher than the American price level.[1] It is quite true, as Ricardo says, *that the difference in price levels* is the cause of the export of gold from the country where it is "relatively cheap"; but not, it should be emphasised, "relatively excessive," for its cheapness is the result of a governmental measure which, in fixing the gold content of the pound sterling, by the same act fixed the gold price of all commodities, and may have fixed it too high or too low in relation to prices in other countries.

It is clear that there are more reasons for differences in the price levels of different countries than that given by Ricardo, whose theory was based only on the experience of the eighteenth century. Similarly, there are many causes which determine the movement of gold, attracting it to those countries where it can command a higher price. The conception of a constant tendency towards equilibrium between the "monetary requirements" of every country and the amount of gold of which it is actually possessed should be definitely discarded. What is correct and useful in Ricardo's theory is the idea that there is a relationship between the rate at which two currencies exchange and the price level obtaining in the two countries, and that if this relationship is modified gold will be either exported or imported. What is lacking in Ricardo and in the *Bullion Report*, is a clear conception of the different markets and their mutual interaction, and of the equilibrium established between them. Actually there are at least four price relations to be taken into account, changes in any one of which influence the others:

(*a*) The rate at which money is exchanged for commodities, capital, and services in country A;

[1] Ricardo might perhaps still argue that there was too much gold in England in the sense that when a currency is stabilised at too low a rate, the total gold value of the existing currency is reduced, that is to say *its quantity diminished*; the reverse being true if the stabilisation rate is too high. The pound being stabilised at its old parity, total currency expressed in gold was *increased*, which led to the export of gold.

(*b*) The rate at which money is exchanged for commodities, capital, and services in country B;

(*c*) The rate of exchange of the two currencies on the international exchanges, where the respective claims of one country on the other are bought and sold;

(*d*) The fixed price at which gold is exchanged in each country for the country's currency, when such a price exists (which may not be the case either for one of the countries, or for both, if they have paper currencies)—that is to say the legal parity of the gold content of the two currencies.

Any change in the rate on any one of these four markets immediately reacts on the rates of the other three. Disequilibrium may therefore originate *now in one, now in another market and not in one only of the four*. It may be caused by a greater issue of paper money in country A, or by a bad harvest leading to a rise in prices which affects the balance of trade and therefore the exchange rate. It may have its origin in the foreign exchange market if confidence in the soundness of currency A or B is shaken. Finally, it may arise when, for one reason or another (devaluation, stabilisation, etc.), there is a change in the price of gold expressed in the national currency. Without a general theory of equilibrium it would be hopeless to try to explain the various gold movements to which international relations give rise; but nothing was further from Ricardo's mind than such a theory.

§ VII. *Ricardian Conception of Credit*

The concept of quantity completely dominates Ricardo's monetary theory: the level of prices depends on the quantity of money, whether that money is metallic or paper. The influence excercised by paper money on prices is the same whether the paper is convertible or not, its influence being strictly proportional to the quantity issued. Exchange rates are determined solely by the quantity of paper money issued in a country with a paper currency, the changes in the rate being an exact measure of the depreciation consequent upon an increase in quantity. It is by limitation of quantity that token money or copper coins retain their value in a currency system. Falls in price as well as rises are regulated by quantity. Ricardo is fully aware of the disadvantages of deflation, but he is quite convinced that a reduction in the quantity of paper, like a reduction in the quantity of coin, will raise its value, that is, lower the price of goods, almost as easily as an increase in the quantity of paper will send prices up. "A more economic use of money," on the other hand (by which he means the system of current accounts and cheques), has the same effect as an increase in its quantity and will compensate for a shortage of currency; thus there is a constant relation between the price level, the quantity of money, and the use made of other means of payment, an extension of which makes up for a decrease in currency.

Such a simplified conception of the relations between money (of whatever kind) and the price level had never been formulated before Ricardo. In it the idea of money as a mere "voucher to purchase" which was, as we have seen, held by John Law and Adam Smith, reaches its narrowest expression. The idea of money as a means of storing value has completely disappeared. That one part of the currency may be withdrawn from circulation and hoarded because it has a more stable value than goods does not seem to have occurred to him. He makes no mention of the demand for money. The importance of this omission in Ricardo's theory, as well as in the Report of the Bullion Committee, has been dealt with by Mr. Hawtrey in an extremely interesting passage.

Accepting Ricardo's argument, what, it will be asked, is the use of a monetary standard and why should such a standard be metallic? What is the point of linking the system of payments to such a standard? The answer to these questions again introduces the concept of quantity. In a most revealing sentence of his *Proposals for an Economical and Secure Currency*, Ricardo says: "The only use of a standard is to regulate the quantity, and by the quantity, the value of the currency."[1] Metallic money, according to this view, is not wealth in circulation, possession of which, as of all other commodities, is desired for its own sake, as all the great writers of the eighteenth century—Cantillon, Turgot, Galiani—had thought. The use of metal for standard money is important only because the metal is limited in quantity; consequently the quantity of money and the price level cannot rise arbitrarily and indefinitely. Ricardo's

[1] *Economic Essays*, p. 162.

train of thought is not for a moment disturbed by the idea of conserving wealth, the idea of establishing a link between the present and the future by means of an imperishable and valuable object. Or if such an idea does occur to him, it is only brushed aside; for him all the qualities of the money standard are summed up in the idea of limitation of quantity.

His conception of credit follows necessarily from this conception of money. Bank-notes are money, and the function of the banker is *to create money*. This is the first instance of those conflicting interpretations which we shall encounter later in regard to the cheque, one side contending that the issue of a credit instrument (bank-notes or current accounts available by cheques) merely puts into circulation deposits received beforehand, the other side contending that *money is created* by such issues. Cantillon's idea that bank-notes are credit instruments which make a more rapid circulation of money possible, but are not themselves money in the real sense of the word, is completely discarded. Ricardo makes no distinction between the issue of convertible notes and the creation of paper money. He sees that precautions have to be taken in regard to those who issue money, and admits that they should be compelled to provide the government with certain guarantees against over-issue. He is not shocked by the suggestion that fixed interest bearing securities can serve as sufficient guarantee. Never for a moment does it occur to him that careful selection by the banker in granting credits and responsibility for the convertibility of his notes provide adequate protection for the public. For him there is no difference between money and other circulating media of payment; the only thing that matters is limitation of the quantity.

As to *cheques*, Ricardo thinks of them not as instruments of circulation, but as a *means of economising the use of money*. He was the first to make a distinction between cheques and bank-notes (called to-day bank money[1] and notes) as currency instruments; the eighteenth century had made no such distinction, and it was a long time before the error was eradicated. He came to this conclusion because he did not regard cheques as currency instruments; they could not therefore affect prices. This is the origin of all the debates and discussions that were to lead to the passing of the Peel Act in 1844.

[1] The term used in the French original is *la monnaie scripturale* (Trs.).

These ideas, in the aggregate, constitute the *quantity theory* of money; it would be more correct to use the term *Ricardian theory of money*. It was so one-sided and exclusive that it led many later economists to regard with suspicion any theory of money or prices in which the quantity factor plays a part. The vastly exaggerated importance which Ricardo gave to this factor made them question all explanations of price movements which attached significance to the increase or decrease in the quantity of money, whether the money was made of metal or paper. When the complicated and artificial mechanism of the Peel Act of 1844 was added thereto, the Ricardian theory fell into complete disrepute.

It has however left a deep mark on all English currency theory, and even on continental theory. It is not difficult to trace that mark right down to some quite recent writers, who still think that it is possible to maintain the price level by credit operations, and see only superficial differences between convertible bank-notes and forced paper currency. The confusion between credit and money that, as we have seen, existed from the very beginning, when bank-notes were first introduced, a confusion of which John Law was the chief protagonist and which Adam Smith unconsciously popularised, is definitely formulated by Ricardo, who identifies credit instruments and standard money with a frankness that nobody before him had achieved.

This confusion is manifest in his *Proposals for an Economical and Secure Currency* published in 1816, and still more obvious in his *Plan of a National Bank* which was found among his papers after his death and published in 1823.[1] Examining the details of this plan to-day, and particularly the grounds on which Ricardo justifies them, the reader can scarcely believe that he is not dreaming; but it was this plan which was taken as the basis for the Reform of 1844 and which for a long time dominated the English conception of the bank-note. In it, Ricardo states that the sole advantage of paper money consists in this, that it enables a country to dispense with a large quantity of metallic money, which can be used in the purchase of materials, machinery, food, etc. This is a more rigorous form of Smith's idea. Since paper money is merely a convenient

[1] This has been reproduced in *Minor Papers on Currency Questions*, 1809–1823, by J. H. Hollander, Baltimore, 1932. It is of the greatest importance for an understanding of the origins of Peel's Act of 1844.

substitute for metallic money, its quantity should be fixed once and for all. To achieve this, it is only necessary to replace the notes actually issued by the Bank of England by notes issued by the State, and also to redeem the notes issued by private banks. When all the notes issued by these banks have been redeemed, the State alone will henceforth have the right to issue paper money, and it will only be able to issue new notes against a backing of new gold from abroad. The quantity of paper money in circulation in England would thus be fixed at the level at which it stood at the time Ricardo was writing, and would be increased or reduced in exact proportion to the imports or exports of bullion which might take place thereafter. A further element of elasticity would be provided by operations undertaken by the government *on the open market:* when it is desired to increase the quantity, it will buy government bills, when it is desired to decrease the quantity of money it will sell these bills. These purchases and sales will be determined by changes in the exchange rate, which will serve as a thermometer by which the government can at any moment measure the relation between the value of the paper money and the value of metallic money. It will be seen that the idea of such operations, which are sometimes regarded as the height of modernism, is really very old; as early as 1837 Gilbart sharply criticised the Bank of England for putting it into practice.

But, it will be asked, who will provide the means for discounting commercial bills? These, says Ricardo, will henceforth be provided by the deposits of the public which will constitute the resources available to the deposit banks for the purpose of discounting bills of exchange. Ricardo sees no connection between these discount operations and the issue of bank-notes. *The creation of bank-notes and the provision of credit are two entirely different functions which should not be carried out by the same body.*

Here, clearly expressed, is the idea underlying Peel's Act of 1844 and the famous division of the Bank of England into two departments. The only difference is that Ricardo wanted the Treasury to issue notes, whereas Peel's Act entrusted this function to the Bank itself.

In other words, Ricardo never for a moment imagined that bank-notes may be regarded as credit instruments, the essential function of which is to make existing money circulate. Paper money and bank-notes—they are all one to him—are money and therefore should be strictly limited in quantity, as should all money; the function which they fulfil is entirely different from that fulfilled by credit instruments.

This brief summary of Ricardo's ideas brings out clearly the incompatibility of the conception of the bank-note formulated by the leading English monetary theorist, and the conception which, at the same period, was applied by a man like Mollien to the organisation of the Bank of France. Mollien thought of the bank-note as a *credit* instrument used to replace other instruments of credit—commercial bills—and thus facilitating their circulation; conceived in this light, the bank-note is itself a sort of commercial bill. Ricardo thought of bank-notes as money; their quantity was to be determined not by the requirements of trade, but by the volume of currency existing at the time he was writing, and that quantity should thenceforth be increased or reduced only in accordance with increases or decreases in the volume of metallic money. Mollien thought the quantity of bank-notes fluctuated with fluctuations in the volume of credit; for Ricardo these fluctuations were determined by changes in the volume of metallic money. The identification of bank-notes and money, the confusion between credit operations and monetary operations, could not be more complete.

This conception of the bank-note, covered either by gold or by government bills, but in no circumstances by commercial bills, was to create a fundamental difference in the rules governing the issue of notes in Anglo-Saxon countries and on the continent. The idea was adopted by the United States in 1863 and was discarded (but with some reservations) when the Federal Reserve Banks were established in 1913.

It is difficult to exaggerate the influence exerted by Ricardo's ideas on the development of credit institutions in the nineteenth century; it is equally difficult to exaggerate their disastrous effect on the development of theories concerning credit. After Ricardo one rigid conception—the quantity of money in circulation, and the limitation of that quantity—took the place of all others in the explanation of monetary phenomena. Some writers even went so far as to disregard all legal and economic differences between metallic money, paper money, cheques and bank-notes, and attempted to explain all currency phenomena by reference to quantity alone, without making it clear whether they were dealing with the quantity of precious metals, of paper money, of bank-notes or of deposits.

Ricardo has frequently been credited with the invention of what is to-day known as the Gold Exchange Standard; this, however, was first elaborated by Walras. The error is one of interpretation. Two things impressed Ricardo: the first was the bad state of the English coinage and the heavy expenditure necessitated from time to time for its reform; the second was the ease with which, throughout the period of suspension of specie payments, Bank of England notes were used as money. He concluded that all that was required was to issue bank-notes in exchange for bullion and to discontinue the actual circulation of coin; but the notes issued against bullion should not, in principle, exceed the quantity of bullion itself. These notes as conceived by Ricardo were in effect gold deposit certificates issued by the Treasury, the notes issued by private banks being limited in quantity by certain guarantees which they should be required to provide. This system adds nothing new to credit theory. It is merely a technical contrivance designed to spare the State the cost of maintaining the coinage in a good condition. It was very useful to those who were in favour of concentrating the entire bullion reserve in the hands of the State or of the central bank, a course which is very widely advocated at the present time. Under Ricardo's system the ownership of small quantities of gold would be impossible; on the other hand wealthy persons could own as many gold bars as they liked. While everyone would have the right to the possession of as much iron, copper, or aluminium as he liked, the quantity of gold he might acquire would be limited by the quantity of bullion held by the Bank. This system, which might be justified in war time, when the State requisitions the possessions of individuals and certain goods essential to the defence of the country, cannot be justified in peace time.

Ricardo was the first to enunciate the idea that the use of metal coins in the currency is a "pure caprice."[1] To-day it has become as it were common property in England, although, of all the doubtful ideas put forward by Ricardo, this has the least in its favour.

[1] *Proposals*, § 11.

APPENDIX

It may be of interest to give here some extracts from the *Plan of a National Bank* published in 1823, which was not republished until 1932 when Hollander reproduced it in *Minor Papers on the Currency Question, 1809–1823*, by David Ricardo, published in Baltimore. This *Plan* is more lucid than the *Proposals*, and much more significant.

Ricardo begins by asserting that the sole use of bank-notes is to provide a cheap currency in the place of an expensive one. He refuses to recognise their function as credit instruments.

"The Bank of England, as well as every other bank in this country, is only of use as it substitutes a cheap currency for a dear one, a paper currency for a metallic one" (p. 164). The metallic currency thus saved can be used for the purchase of productive capital goods.

He then maintains that there is no connection between the Bank's commercial operations and its issue of notes. "The Bank of England unites in itself two operations of Banking which are quite distinct and have no necessary connection with each other; it issues a paper currency as a substitute for a metallic one; and it advances money in the way of loan to merchants and others" (p. 166). These two operations may be completely separated, the first being entrusted to the government, without any inconvenience to trade; as the quantity of paper meney in existence beforehand will remain unchanged, the banks will have the same amount at their disposal with which to conduct their operations. Ricardo, it will be seen, omits altogether the function of a bank of issue to act as a "safety valve" by granting credits to other banks. What follows is still more interesting. Proceeding from these principles, Ricardo proposes that the issue of notes should be entrusted, not to the government, but to a Committee which should have no connection with the government. The Committee would work as follows:

"It should be a part of the constitution of the board which I propose to establish that they should at no time and under no circumstances lend money to government;" (the government having the right to obtain money only by floating loans on the market or by the sale of Treasury bonds), "but that if their funds were so ample as to permit them to dispose of money they should purchase government securities in open market, and if on the contrary they had occasion to reduce their floating securities they should in like manner sell them in open market . . . (pp. 171–172). It must be recollected that these transactions would be few in amount, as the circulation would be kept at its just level by being exchanged for coin and bullion when it exceeded its proper proportion, and by the sale of gold bullion or of coin to the Commissioners when the amount of paper money was below that proportion. It would only be in the case of the stock of coin and bullion in the coffers of the Commissioners being too low that they would be under the necessity of selling some of their securities in the market in order to purchase with the paper money which they obtained by such sale the gold which they might deem necessary. On the other hand, if the gold came into their coffers too fast, and accumulated in too great a degree, by the issue of more of their paper in the purchase of these securities such a tendency would be checked" (p. 172).

Further on, Ricardo explains that the board would have to regulate the quantity of notes issued according to the price of gold, whenever that price fell below £3 17s. 10½d. an ounce, which is the price at which it should be coined.

"The 13th Regulation provides for a due issue of paper money by obliging the Commissioners to issue more money when its low value as compared with gold shews that it is not in sufficient quantity. This is the case when £3 17s. 10½d. in paper will purchase more than an ounce of gold, for by law an ounce of gold is coined into £3 17s. 10½d. and therefore it is of less value than paper money if an ounce of it will not sell for £3 17s. 10½d. in paper money. If the Commissioners regulate their issues by the comparative value of gold and paper they cannot err and they might carry on the whole business of currency with a very small quantity of paper according as its value was high or low compared with gold. As it is however desirable to be on the safe side in managing the important business of paper currency for a great country it would be expedient to make such a provision of gold as occasionally to correct the exchanges with foreign countries as much by the exportation of gold as by the reduction of the quantity of paper" (p. 178).

A little later he estimates that a circulation of 25 to 29 million pounds sterling could be adequately covered by six million in gold coin and bullion; the country would thus be freed from the necessity of keeping a reserve of 23 million which, at 3 per cent interest, yields £690,000; this figure represents the profit which would thus accrue to the public.

It will be seen that the idea of regulating the volume of currency on the London market by open market operations dates back to Ricardo, although the actual practice of such transactions by the Bank may be older.

There is scarcely one point in common between Ricardo's conception of the issue of notes and the conception which prevailed on the continent and which was later embodied in the organisation of the Federal Reserve Banks. Ricardo believed that the value of paper currency in relation to gold could be maintained by regulating its quantity on the home market. The export of gold to keep up the exchange rate is, in his view, merely a subsidiary device. It is difficult to imagine a more unrealistic conception, or one less supported by actual experience.

This is not the place for further elaboration, but some mention should be made here of the British Exchange Equalisation Account. The conception underlying that Fund, which consists in maintaining banking deposits (regarded to-day as money) at a more or less constant level, seems to be directly inspired by the ideas which moved Ricardo to formulate his plan; the most characteristic passages have been given in this Appendix, but it deserves a more detailed study than has as yet been devoted to it. There is, of course, a difference in the object aimed at. Ricardo's plan was designed to maintain the exchange rate. The Equalisation Fund appears to have as its primary object the maintenance of a stable price level.

CHAPTER FOUR

Tooke the Historian and Ricardo the Logician

§ I. PROBLEMS CREATED IN ENGLAND BY THE RESUMPTION OF CASH PAYMENTS.—§ II. TOOKE'S EXPLANATION OF THE PRICE RISE DURING FORCED CURRENCY—§ III. THE RETURN OF THE POUND TO PAR IN 1819.—§ IV. PAPER MONEY AND BANK-NOTES.

After the astonishing digression introduced by Ricardo, the tradition of the eighteenth century and of Thornton was restored in a brilliant fashion by Tooke.

"It is impossible to exaggerate the importance of this unique book," writes Jevons, referring to Tooke and Newmarch's *History of Prices*. Published in six successive volumes between 1836 and 1858,[1] it gives an invaluable collection of facts, and of the ideas expressed during the great currency controversies of the post-Napoleonic period.[2] On almost every point Tooke takes the opposite view to Ricardo. "Abstract arguments," as Tooke is pleased to call Ricardo's reasoning, find no place in his book. His conclusions are always preceded by a detailed description and analysis of facts, and are so superior to and so much more comprehensive than the Ricardian simplifications as to make the latter seem unrecognisable. History and theory go hand in hand. All six volumes are amazingly alive; Tooke deals not only with credit questions, but with all the

[1] The exact title is *A History of Prices and of the State of the Circulation during the Years 1793–1856*. The first part, in two volumes, appeared in 1838. Tooke's first book had been published in 1823; it contains a study of prices from 1793 to 1822 and provided the material for his best-known book, apart from the *History of Prices—Considerations on the State of the Currency*, published in 1826. Interest in Tooke's ideas, revived by the war, led in 1928 to the publication of a photostatic reproduction of his great book, with a long and suggestive introduction by Professor Gregory. All relevant historical and bibliographical details will be found in that introduction, as well as a learned if not wholly convincing criticism of Tooke's ideas.

[2] "One of the most valuable contributions to economical science which the present century has produced," writes Fullarton in his *On the Regulation of Currencies*, p. 5.

economic problems that arose in the course of the fifteen years during which Europe was at war with France.

Tooke was a merchant with a good knowledge of international trade and banking operations, engaged in business of the most varied kinds, familiar with the continent and in particular with Russia—the great field for all kinds of paper money experiments. When he began to write—in the very year in which Ricardo died—he was nearing the age of fifty.[1] With a great deal of practical experience behind him, supported by direct and accurate observation, and speaking with authority but without pedantry, he challenged the successors of the great metaphysician of political economy. He illuminates every aspect of every problem which he discusses—the role of banks, the nature of bank-notes and cheques, the origin of crises, the rate of interest. Even to-day there is no more instructive and helpful guide to the complicated labyrinth of present-day events. The World War and its sequel have confirmed his ideas on almost all points.

After Peel's Act was passed, Tooke's ideas became extremely popular. It is true that the very passing of the Act constituted a victory for the *Currency Principle*. But scarcely had the Act come into force than the 1847 crisis, by making it necessary to suspend the Act, justified all the criticisms which Tooke had levelled against it. In England, Germany and France the most celebrated economists adopted his standpoint. In Germany, Adolf Wagner popularised Tooke's ideas in a book which has become a classic.[2] John Stuart Mill came over wholly to the ideas of Tooke and Fullarton. In France the advocates both of monopoly and of competition in banking based their arguments on Tooke. But this victory was confined somewhat too exclusively to the principle of elasticity of issue, which Tooke had upheld. Other sound ideas were too often ignored, perhaps because the very size of these volumes made them rather inaccessible. It is a pity that nobody had the courage to undertake a French translation. This was as grievous for the development of sound credit theory in France as the absence of an English translation of Cantillon had been for England. In the

[1] He was born in St. Petersburg in 1774 and his first book appeared in 1823. He died in 1858. As Fullarton said (*loc. cit.*, p. 18), his ideas evolved gradually, attaining greater and greater precision, and reached their final form about 1840.

[2] A. Wagner, *Beiträge zur Lehre von den Banken*, Leipzig, 1857.

twentieth century, after the World War, there was even in England a revival of Ricardian ideas and a reaction away from Tooke. In the important introduction to the recent edition of Tooke, Professor Gregory finds more to criticise than to praise in his works. The present writer, on the other hand, believes that his books are full of original and sound ideas.

§ 1. *Problems Created in England by the Resumption of Cash Payments*

The events which excited the controversies in which Tooke played so great a part are well known. The twenty-five years following the Napoleonic wars were as fertile in economic and social problems as were, a century later, the years following the World War. In both cases the difficulties were of the same kind. A steady fall in prices, interrupted by periods of boom and depression, marked the years from 1815 to 1850. The political and social events which accompanied this price fall were of decisive importance in English history. The crises of 1825, 1836 and 1847, the Reform Bill of 1832, the Chartist movement, and the prosperity of the 'fifties, are the high lights of this period. The fall in prices, and the crises which accompanied it, gave rise to two main currents in credit theory.[1]

The first was brought into being by the "Birmingham School" and the advocates of the devaluation of the pound. Although on other points their opinions were far from identical, they were united in believing that the return of the pound to parity in 1819 had been a serious mistake. They believed that the fall of sterling, and the inflation which preceded it, should simply have been acknowledged and ratified by a reduction in the metallic content of the pound. It is the same point as that on which Locke joined issue with Lowndes, and Newton with Cantillon. They attributed the economic difficulties of the time to the currency "restriction" which followed the resumption of payment in specie.

[1] An extremely interesting article on this subject was published by Mr. Sayers in the Supplement to the *Economic Journal* of February 1935, under the title *The Question of the Standard, 1815–1844*.

"We all remember," writes Fullarton, "the popular hostility which for many years was directed against the measure of 1819, for the restoration of cash payments; a hostility by no means confined to the unreasoning herd, but conscientiously entertained by many well-meaning people of education, and even by men of considerable talent. Whatever went amiss, whether prices fell, or trade became stagnant, or speculations failed, the blame was invariably laid on the unhappy Peel's Bill. To this origin were traced the great commercial revulsions of 1825; and every man who chanced to impair his fortune by absurd and hazardous adventures, found a salve for his self-reproaches in attributing to the Bill the consequences of his folly and improvidence." [1]

Hostility to the resumption of payment in specie was as strong in England in 1819 as was the objection to the return to the gold standard in 1925 and particularly in 1931.

The better known of these pessimists belonged to the group known at the time as the Birmingham School, to which attention has of late again been drawn by R. G. Hawtrey[2] in England and Elie Halévy[3] in France. This school was inspired by a certain Attwood, a banker and Member of Parliament, to whose ability Tooke, though he disagreed with him, gives due recognition.[4]

From the moment when the first consequences of the slow fall in prices which followed the resumption of payments in specie began to appear, Attwood, in numerous writings, denounced the return to the old parity and the "deflation" of prices which had been the result. He was of the opinion that this deflation was the cause of England's economic difficulties and of the successive crises which shook its social and political structure. Attwood went further than anti-deflation; he advocated systematic inflation. He wanted the volume of paper in circulation increased by means of State loans to be subscribed by the bank, on a scale large enough to keep the wage level steady. His programme was greeted with derision by the adherents of both Ricardo and Tooke; John Stuart Mill, who

[1] Fullarton, *On the Regulation of the Currencies*, pp. 6 and 7. The Peel Act referred to here is that which re-established the convertibility of notes; its author was the father of the Robert Peel of the 1844 Act.

[2] One chapter in *Trade and Credit* is devoted to the Birmingham School.

[3] In his excellent *History of the English People in the 19th Century*, Vol. II.

[4] "Mr. Matthias Attwood must be considered as being not only the most eloquent but one of the most able and best informed of the expounders of the doctrine, which refers all the great fluctuations in prices to alterations in the system of our currency." *History of Prices*, Vol. II, p. 87.

refers to it briefly in his chapter on paper money, compares Attwood's ideas with those held by Hume, which have been discussed in the second chapter of the present book. Later Attwood joined the Chartist movement, and the outcry against deflation died away when English economy took an upward turn in 1851.

In so far as Attwood directs his criticism to the return to parity after an interval of paper money, he was in agreement with J.-B. Say, whose hostility to the return to pre-war parity never flagged,[1] and perhaps with Ricardo himself, who seems at times to have questioned the expediency of this step,[2] of which Say wrote: "One bankruptcy followed another, since contracts are broken when debtors are made to pay more than they owe no less than when creditors do not receive all that is due to them." [3]

In so far, however, as Attwood wanted a managed currency, in the form of paper money the issue of which would be regulated by the State on the principles outlined above, he profoundly shocked his contemporaries, for whom exchange fluctuations represented the most serious economic embarrassment.

Tooke steadily opposed these ideas. He always stood out against any suggestion of devaluation; he came out against inflationists like Attwood, and against those who advocated simple devaluation, like Baring, Lord Folkestone and Lord Ashburton.

[1] "One of the expedients suggested was to reduce the pound sterling to the quantity of gold which the bank-notes could in fact buy; if this had been done, with precautions against the Bank's increasing the number of notes in circulation, the notes could have been redeemed on demand; it is probable that commodities would not have fallen in price, industry would have enjoyed the same facilities; contracts would have been carried out on the same terms as they were made, and the State would not have had to pay its debts, pensions and salaries at a rate about one third as high again than they were formerly. Vested interests were opposed to this step and the body of the people, in addition to the ills which the labouring classes then endured, will for a long time be bowed down by the burden of a debt, three fourths of which may be attributed to a contest which national pride may call glorious, but which costs the nation dear and brings it no profit." J.-B. Say, *Traité d'Economie politique*, 2nd ed. Vol. II, pp. 76–77. What would Say have said in 1919?

[2] In his remarkable preface to the English edition of Andréadès' *History of the Bank of England, 1640–1903* (Trs. by Christabel Meredith, London, 1924), Professor Foxwell quotes the following passage from a letter which Ricardo wrote to a friend in 1821: "I never should advise a government to restore a currency which was depreciated 30 per cent to par. . . . It was without any legislation that the currency from 1813 to 1819 came . . . within 5 per cent of the value of gold, and it was in this state of things, and not with a currency depreciated 30 per cent, that I advised a recurrence to the old standard."

[3] Say, *loc. cit.*, Vol. II, p. 75.

He contended that the resumption of cash payments had not been accompanied by any restriction of the currency (which was true, but after a period of paper money the very *cessation of an increase* in the volume of paper constitutes deflation); he would not admit that the fall in prices and the accompanying economic difficulties were the result of the return to the old parity. He believed that devaluation was inimical to the interests of the working classes.[1]

Nothing is more difficult than to take sides in controversies of this kind after such a lapse of time. In all probability, the output of the gold and silver mines being what it was, the increase in the volume of goods produced would in itself have been enough, once the war was over, to bring prices down. It has frequently been asked whether the return to gold in England, by affecting the amount of gold in circulation on the continent, did not contribute to the subsequent fall in prices. Fullarton raises this question and replies that "so extensive an operation must, to some extent, have affected the value of the general stock of gold." [2]

The same question was raised in France in an excellent study of the Bank of France, unfortunately forgotten to-day, published in 1839 in the *Encyclopédie du Droit*; its author was Gauthier, a French peer and Vice-Governor of the Bank.

Even without the assumption of a relative decrease in the quantity of gold on the continent, it is obvious that the very high level to which prices in England and on the continent had been raised by the war and by paper money could not be maintained once the increase in the quantity of paper issued, which had been continuous up till then, was interrupted by the return to gold. The normal lowering of prices which would in any case have followed from a greater output of goods while the volume of currency remained the same, was intensified in England by the rise in the gold value of the pound sterling. Since this made English prices higher for foreign purchasers, it tended to impede the flow of English goods abroad and to create difficulties in the industrial world. The same course of events was observed after the World War. On both

[1] Pages 67–77 of Vol. II of the *History of Prices* should be re-read in the light of recent controversies concerning devaluation. The arguments in favour of devaluation are given at full length and discussed with that wealth of detail with which Tooke liked to embellish his expositions.

[2] Fullarton, *loc. cit.*, p. 10.

occasions the scarcity of gold was made responsible for what was in fact the obvious result of war and inflation. In any case the real burden of the public debt was increased, which was the chief reason for J.-B. Say's vehement opposition to the return to parity.

The second current of thought, contemporary with the first, was far more influential; this set out to explain the successive crises which shook English economy in that period, and which were all accompanied by the issue of notes on a large scale by the private banks, and by a severe strain on the Bank of England's gold reserves, which fell from £13.5 million in January 1824 to £1.2 million in December 1825, and from £8 million at the beginning of 1836 to £3.6 million at the end of November in the same year.

Naturally enough, each generation tends to apply to its own difficulties the remedies which served (or which are believed to have served) the preceding generation. Ricardo had shewn that the fall on the exchanges and the export of gold during the wars against Napoleon had been the result of an excessive issue of paper money. After 1819 public opinion was unanimous in support of this explanation. Could not the analogous phenomena of the post-war period be attributed to the same causes? Were not the crises, the loss of gold which followed the fall on the exchange, also due to an excess of paper money and could not the appropriate remedy once again be found in limitation of its quantity? This line of argument indicates the origin of the so-called Currency School of thought.

It was against this school of thought, and the practical conclusions which, it was claimed, followed therefrom, that Tooke's writings were, at bottom, directed. In the course of the contest itself—in which he was supported by many writers, of whom the most notable was Fullarton[1]—he formulated and elucidated a number of theories of cardinal importance, which completely discredited the Currency School and were finally adopted as part of economic doctrine.

[1] Fullarton is an excellent writer to whom recent economic dictionaries do not give even a single paragraph. He was not an economist by profession; it was on his return from India, where he had served as a doctor, that he took part in the controversy. His book *On the Regulation of Currencies* was published shortly before Peel's Act was passed.

These may be summarised as follows:

> The similarity between paper money and convertible bank-notes is only superficial. One is money, the other instruments of bank credit. It is therefore absurd to apply the same regulations to both. It is equally absurd to lay the blame on bank-notes rather than on cheques or bills of exchange, which are also credit instruments. All these instruments have the same character, none is money in the full meaning of the word. What should be fought against is the abuse of *credit* as a whole, not one form of circulating credit; for it is these abuses *in all their forms* which are the cause of crises. No mechanical or automatic device will serve as a remedy. For this purpose the discount rate must be used and the Bank of England's reserves strengthened.

That is the kernel of his argument. But to get it adopted he had to revise completely the Ricardian ideas on the subject. In the course of this revision he set down a number of truths which are of far greater importance for us to-day than his out-of-date dispute with the Currency School. Taken as a whole, they represent the most modern and the most far-sighted treatise on credit that has ever been written. They deal with the effects of paper money, the nature of bank-notes and their identity with cheques, the theory of the rate of interest, and the theory of crises. We shall examine them one by one.

§ II. *Tooke's Explanation of the Price Rise during Forced Currency*

It is primarily as an historian that Tooke takes up arms against Ricardo. In his *History of Prices*, which is really a chronicle of English economic life in the forty years covered by the work, he uses his amazingly varied knowledge to correct two legends, one referring to forced paper currency, the other to the resumption of payments in specie, both of capital importance in the economic doctrine of foreign exchanges, prices and forced currency.

It will be recalled that when Ricardo attempted to explain the rise of prices and of foreign currencies in England during the period of forced currency, he took into consideration the *supply* of paper money only. Tooke shews that the *demand* for English currency on the exchanges was at least as important.[1] Before Tooke, Thornton and Malthus had contended, as against Ricardo, that a bad harvest, by upsetting the balance of trade, lowered sterling in comparison with other currencies although the volume of sterling did not increase. Ricardo's answer was little more than a verbal evasion. Tooke expanded this criticism: the foreign exchange market responds to all fluctuations in demand, from whatever cause they arise. Exceptionally heavy imports are not the only factor affecting demand. During the war British subsidies to allied governments imposed a heavy burden on the sterling exchange, without there being any corresponding increase in the issue of paper money. Thornton had pointed that out in the *Bullion Report*,[2] but Tooke had a far wider knowledge of exchange fluctuations under a paper money system than the members of the Bullion Committee.

His Russian experiences were particularly useful. During the war, the paper rouble had fluctuated in the most unexpected fashion. When Napoleon decided on the Russian expedition the rouble, contrary to all expectations, rose on the foreign exchanges. That was because other European countries accelerated their purchases in Russia, while Russia ceased purchasing in Europe, fearing that, if the French were victorious, they would confiscate all imported goods, since such imports were made in defiance of the continental blockade. Later, with the news of the collapse of the Grand Army and the safety of Saint Petersburg, the rouble, just as perplexingly, began to fall.[3] On the other hand, observes Tooke, the exchange value of paper money can be kept stable, without any reduction in quantity, by means of a foreign loan. He

[1] The term "demand for money" will be discussed in Chapter VIII. Here it should be noted that there is an *internal* demand and an *external* demand for national currency. The external demand arises in foreign markets for the purpose of paying for goods and services *imported* from the country under consideration (or for purposes of hoarding a foreign currency). It is not directly a demand for that country's money, but for the *claims drawn in that money* (bills of exchange or cheques on banks); the amount available is determined by the volume of goods and services (including gold) exported by the country seeking the means of payment, and by the credits which it obtains abroad. Variations in this demand are reflected in the *exchange rate*. As to the *internal* demand for money, it consists in the requirements of all who have need of money either as a means of payment (for the purchase of goods or settlement of debts) or for purposes of hoarding.

[2] Tooke (Vol. I, p. 157) himself refers to the views of Thornton and Horner, the two editors-in-chief of the *Bullion Report*.

[3] *Ibid.*, Vol. IV, pp. 214–215. This is a most instructive passage.

adds that paper money does not always and necessarily depreciate in value[1] "if its quantity is strictly limited."[2]

In short, the foreign exchange market is subject to fluctuations arising from the *conditions of that market* and from all the circumstances, favourable or unfavourable, which make for the greater or lesser demand for a particular currency on that market. This elementary truth has been substantiated so often since Tooke's time that no further proof is necessary. The American Civil War[3] provides a famous illustration; the World War offers still more striking examples in the stability of the French and English exchanges thanks to American loans, the rise of Scandinavian exchanges when the policy of returning to parity was announced, the rise of sterling up to 1925, etc.

Now these fluctuations—and this is what Tooke considers of primary importance—have an immediate effect on *domestic prices* in the country with a paper currency.[4] The rise in prices is thus effected not through one channel alone, as Ricardo imagined, but through two different channels—expansion of the home demand for goods due to successive increases in the amount of paper money put into circulation, and a *rise in the price of goods imported due to the depreciation of the paper money on the foreign exchange market.*

[1] Tooke, Vol. IV, p. 177, note: "Discredit is not an essential element in variations of the value of an inconvertible paper, nor is depreciation always a necessary consequence of inconvertibility. The notes of the Bank of England, and of the private banks of this country, were for two years after the restriction of the same value as if they had been convertible, and never experienced any discredit. There were great fluctuations in the credit of the paper money of the United States of America during the War of Independence, and also in the case of the French *assignats*, arising from fluctuating opinions as to the chances of redemption; and both descriptions became ultimately valueless by excess, when all prospect of redemption had ceased. But the Russian government paper, although during the progress of its depreciation by successively increasing issues, no certain or probable prospect of redemption had been held out, seems never to have suffered any discredit; and the variations of the exchanges beyond those produced by the mere excess of the paper, were such only as are incidental to variations in the state of trade."

[2] *Ibid.*, Vol. IV, p. 215.

[3] Cf. Mitchell's famous book *Gold Prices and Wages under the Greenback Standard.*

[4] The argument is summarised in Vol. I, p. 168, in the following passage: "As the depression of the exchanges constituted an element of increased cost of all imported commodities, and thus, directly or indirectly, affected the price of a considerable proportion of native productions, the restriction may be considered to have been the condition without which so much of the rise of prices as was attributable to increased cost by adverse exchanges could not have occurred."

Tooke contends that the rise in English prices during the Napoleonic wars was to a large extent the *effect* of the depreciation of sterling on the exchange, whereas Ricardo regards that depreciation merely as a repercussion of the preceding rise in the prices of English goods.

On this point Tooke's opinion prevailed. Of course, certain economists carried his arguments too far. Starting from his propositions, they concluded that fluctuations on the exchange, and *these alone*, explain the rise of prices under a paper standard.[1] In the reaction from Ricardian doctrine they swung round to the belief that, of the two possible (and as a rule simultaneous) ways in which paper money influences prices, the second only was of importance. Tooke never went as far as that. He never denied that paper money affects domestic prices and thereby, indirectly, the exchanges. On the contrary, he was most emphatic on this point.[2] He contended that in fact *that part of the rise in English prices above the rise due to exchange depreciation* was the result of an excessive issue of paper money. Nor did he for a moment think of

[1] We cannot agree with M. Nogaro, for whom "the internal depreciation of a currency expressed in a general price rise is a *phenomenon absolutely distinct* from external depreciation, expressed in falling exchange rates. Of course," he adds, "the latter affects the general price level by raising the price of imports and even of exports. But the reverse is not true: depreciation of the currency in relation to goods has no direct effect on the exchanges because the internal currency (paper money) does not serve as a means of payment abroad" (Nogaro, *Traité d'Economie politique*, 2nd ed., 1921, p. 255). Nevertheless, the rise of internal prices affects the balance of trade and therefore the exchanges. In a remarkable article in the 1934 issue of the *Revue d'Economie politique* Mr. Robert Wolff has given an admirable account of the twofold action of the exchanges on prices, and of prices on the exchanges.

[2] Cf. the note on p. 157 of Vol. III: "Mr. Gurney very properly guards himself in his answer to the question, whether an addition of 5 millions to the circulation would not have an effect upon prices *ultimately*, by saying 'I cannot give an opinion as to the ultimate remote result.' Of course he could not; for if the addition were the consequence of an influx of gold which was to remain permanently in the country as our share of a general increase from the mines, the prices of all articles, other things remaining the same, would rise in the proportion which the 5 millions should bear to the previous circulation. There can upon this point be no difference of opinion. A permanent increase of this kind, in whatever way it were introduced, would enter into and pervade all the channels of circulation, reaching ultimately wages, and thus come into contact with every description of commodities. And a government inconvertible paper, issued in direct payments not on terminable securities, and not returnable on the issuing bank, would also, if not discredited, enter into and pervade all the channels of circulation, while the increased currency and the consequent advance of prices being beyond the bullion level, would be marked by a difference of exchange, and by an agio on gold and silver."

denying that exchange depreciation was closely bound up with an increase in the quantity of paper money, for in a country where the volume of paper money is growing, the price that can be offered for foreign currency also grows, which is another way of depreciating the exchange.[1]

Tooke was no theorist, and was not concerned to find one general formula adaptable to all concrete cases. He propounded no theory of the equilibrium of the different markets, such as we outlined when dealing with Ricardo, which alone could account for all the phenomena under consideration. He was content to emphasise, as against Ricardo, those factors which, under a paper money standard (apart from any variation in the quantity of paper), cause variations in the rate of exchange and *by means of the rate of exchange influence the price level*. It was a long time before the economists accepted his view. The opposite process described (after Thornton) by Ricardo, which is set in motion by a previous rise of domestic prices, was for a long time regarded as the only explanation, in any case as the chief explanation.

A curious illustration of the oblivion into which Tooke's ideas fell, and of the victory of the Ricardian doctrine in England, was provided, forty years after Ricardo's death, by Goschen's explanation of the premium on gold in his famous *Theory of Foreign*

[1] There is one passage in which he seems to go further, and which calls to mind certain formulas put forward quite recently: "While the amount of the Bank issues was from 1797 to 1817 undergoing, with trifling exceptions, a progressive increase, the exchanges upon every pause from the pressure of extraordinary foreign payments tended to a recovery, and when the pressure had entirely ceased, the exchanges and the price of gold were restored to par, while the Bank circulation was larger in amount than at any preceding period: thus affording the strongest presumption that the previous increase had not been the cause of the fall of the exchanges; and had not been greater than would have been required if there had been no restriction, but also no extra foreign payments, in order to supply the extended functions of money incidental to an increased population, and to a vast extension of trade and revenue, and generally of pecuniary transactions;—or, in other words, that, in the divergence between the paper and the gold, *it was the gold that, by increased demand departed from the paper, and not the paper by increased quantity from the gold*." (My italics, C. R.) It was probably arguments of this kind that Ricardo had in mind when he wrote, indignantly, in his *Principles of Political Economy*: "It will scarcely be believed fifty years hence, that Bank directors and ministers gravely contended in our times, both in parliament, and before committees of parliament, that the issue of notes by the Bank of England, unchecked by any power in the holders of such notes, to demand in exchange either specie, or bullion, had not, nor could have any effect on the prices of commodities, bullion, or foreign exchanges" (Chap. XXVII).

Exchanges published in 1863. Goschen was a banker whose daily occupation should, one would have thought, have made clear to him the incompatibility of the Ricardian doctrine with certain phenomena of the foreign exchange market. He should have realised, in particular, that the premium on gold in a country with a paper currency merely reflects the exchange rate, every variation in which necessarily results in a rise or fall within that country of the gold premium over paper. The demand for gold comes almost exclusively from exchange speculators or bankers who find it profitable to export gold whenever foreign exchanges rise; but Goschen was infected with the Ricardian doctrine, and persistently puts the cart before the horse. Gold, he reiterates, is, under a paper standard, "a commodity like any other." When there is an increase in the quantity of paper money issued, the price of gold will rise like the price of any other commodity. "Accordingly, on examining the price of bills in New York and the price of gold [during the war of secession] we shall see that they constantly rose and fell together."[1] But, after the battle of Gettysburg, which called a halt to the early successes of the Confederates, foreign exchanges and the premium on gold fell although there was no change in the volume of paper. Goschen finds this embarrassing—not because he cannot explain the fall in foreign exchanges: that, he declares with conviction, is merely the result of the lower premium—but because, as there had been no reduction in the volume of currency, he could not explain the fall in the gold premium, since "an over-issue of paper money can only be counteracted by a subsequent contraction."[2] He thereupon elaborates a number of explanations, all of which are thoroughly unsatisfactory, for the only valid explanation is precisely the opposite, that *foreign exchanges fell first* (the effect of intelligible speculation on the anticipated victory of the Northern States) and that, by an immediate counteraction, the gold premium *followed* the exchanges.

Goschen here is following Ricardo's theory word for word:

[1] Goschen, p. 102. It is possible that the internal gold premium may for a time be *greater* than the premium on the exchanges. This is what seems to have happened in France during the *assignat* period, as Hawtrey has shewn, and was due to the strong desire to hoard. But it is difficult to see how the premium can be *less* than the exchange premium for in that case the profit to be made from exporting gold and selling the foreign currency thus acquired would immediately lead to a rise in the price of gold.

[2] *Ibid.*, p. 113.

Paper money depreciates, causing prices on the home market to rise, and creating a premium on gold ("which is a commodity like any other") leading to a rise of foreign exchanges; a series of phenomena which cannot be checked except by eliminating the initial cause, the "excess of paper money." Unfortunately for Goschen, actual events took place in the reverse order. Moreover, it was not a reduction in the quantity of paper money which, some years later, brought the famous "greenbacks" up to parity with gold, but an influx of gold. In other words, as Tooke shewed, though Goschen had forgotten, it was through the foreign exchange market—and not by a policy of intense deflation—that Great Britain returned to the gold standard, as the United States was to do later.

§ III. *The Return of the Pound to Par in* 1819

This brings us to the second point on which Tooke, historian and business man, confuted the "abstract arguments" of Ricardo the logician. It concerns the method by which a depreciated currency can be brought back to parity. The problem with which Tooke deals is the problem underlying all currency stabilisations. How many mistakes would have been avoided if greater notice had been taken of him!

According to Ricardo the only way of bringing the pound back to par was to reduce the note circulation. Since the currency had been depreciated by excessive issues, was it not obvious that a reduction would be followed by appreciation? Are not inflation and deflation two logically corresponding processes?

Unfortunately for Ricardo the logic of facts worked differently from *a priori* logic. How was the pound brought back to parity in 1819? By reducing the note circulation? Not at all! Simply by an improvement on the exchanges which, once the war was over, brought gold back again from abroad to the Bank of England. And what had the Bank done to attract gold, or to raise the value of its notes? Nothing at all! It remained "purely passive;" its directors themselves admitted this, and the following excerpt from the statement made by one of their number, Mr. Pearse, in the House of Commons in 1822, was naturally seized on by Tooke: it is in fact decisive:

"Mr. Ricardo had charged the Bank with error and indiscretion, in having become too extensive purchasers of gold, in consequence of the passing of the act of 1819. The fact was, that the Bank were quite passive in taking the gold from the merchants who offered it for their purchase. The consequence, however, had been, that bullion had been paid whenever it had been demanded; that an issue of ten or eleven millions of sovereigns had taken place." [1]

Tooke's interpretation, which is confirmed by all the facts,[2] and is accepted to-day by the most authoritative historians,[3] can easily be verified by reference to the figures of note circulation, which, in 1821, when cash payments were resumed, stood at the same level as at the end of the war, although they had more than doubled since cash payments were suspended; but it did not prevail against the legend that the return of the pound to par had been brought about by a systematic reduction in the number of notes.[4]

[1] Tooke, Vol. II, p. 100.

[2] "The resumption was eventually carried into effect two years in anticipation of the term prescribed by law, by the spontaneous course of circumstances, without the slightest effort, as Mr. Tooke has incontrovertibly shown, on the part of the Bank, and in coincidence with an enlargement, instead of a contraction, of the Bank issues" (Fullarton, *loc. cit.*, p. 9).

"With regard to the effect of Mr. Peel's bill on the Bank of England, I can state, from having been in the direction during the last two years, that it has been altogether a dead letter. It has neither accelerated nor retarded the return to cash payments, except as, by ordering the repayment of ten millions of exchequer bills to the Bank, it enabled it to expend those ten millions in the purchase of bullion without in any way curtailing its other advances. The directors of the Bank of England, as plain practical men, have pursued plain practical means, without turning to the right hand or to the left, as converts to the new doctrines promulgated by the Bullion Committee, and by so doing, have already thrown into general circulation within the last twelve months, more than eight millions of sovereigns, without having diminished, except in the most trifling degree, the usual average of its notes of five pounds and upwards" (Tooke, Vol. II, p. 99).

[3] Cf. Hawtrey, *Currency and Credit*, Chap. XVIII. Cannan (who however advocated deflation) recognises that the decrease in the number of notes was insignificant—19 per cent of the highest point reached in 1817, and that it was the *increase in gold holdings which was important*. Reference to the statistical material which he published in *The Paper Pound*, p. xxxiii, provides sufficient confirmation of the first point.

[4] What had happened was that the government had repaid to the Bank the ten million that it had borrowed, thus giving proof of its desire to balance the budget. This repayment does not seem to have affected the note circulation; the number of notes was reduced by 19 per cent of the figure for 1817, when it reached its maximum, that is to say *after* the end of the war, but this reduction was apparently compensated by the issue of metallic money, as shewn in the statement of Mr. Pearse quoted by Tooke.

The passage which we have quoted from Goschen shews this, and right up to our own times, from MacCulloch, United States Secretary to the Treasury, to Adolphe Thiers and M. Poincaré, American, French and English statesmen, and with them many prominent economists, have adopted as an "orthodox" truth what is, in fact, nothing but a legend.

There are few more striking examples of the persistence of a theory that has been exploded by the facts, simply because it appears to be supported by logical reasoning. Cannot deflation undo what inflation has done? Those who reason on these lines forget one important fact, that economic phenomena are "irreversible." After inflation has raised prices to a far higher level than they were before, it is impossible to return to the starting point except by destroying the income represented by the money withdrawn from circulation. J.-B. Say saw this clearly. Events in the United States after the Civil War, in the countries of South America,[1] in France after the war of 1870–1871, in Italy after the difficulties of forced paper currency, from 1883 to 1914, and finally in all the countries which participated in the World War, were to prove this over and over again. In all these cases attempts were at first made to apply Ricardo's policy, only to be given up in face of the obstinate refusal of the facts to accommodate themselves to this policy. In all these cases there was an unwillingness to admit that it was enough to *stop inflating*, without actually *withdrawing* notes from circulation, to set going all the processes which bring gold back to a country and make it possible to re-establish the convertibility of notes.[2]

It would have been enough to consult Tooke's great work to find some of these ideas formulated with the utmost lucidity; Tooke himself summarises them in the following words:

"The restoration, therefore, of the value of the paper to its metallic standard, having taken place within six months after the appointment of the Bullion Committee, and within three months after the passing of Peel's bill, no reduction of the amount of bank-notes having taken place in the interval, and the final resumption of cash payments having taken

[1] An excellent account is given by M. Subercaseaux in *Le Papier-Monnaie*, Paris, 1920, published by Giard.

[2] I should like to refer to my *La Déflation en Pratique*, Paris, 1924, in which I have analysed the most outstanding historical examples of this process.

place in 1821 and 1822, after a substitution of sovereigns for the small notes of the Bank of England, coincident *with an increase of the issues*, paper and coin together from the Bank, Peel's bill must be pronounced to have been wholly inoperative in producing any contraction, none having occurred in the basis of the currency." [1]

§ IV. *Paper Money and Bank-notes*

Tooke was only interested in the past because of the present. Ricardian doctrines falsified the interpretation of the past; but more important for Tooke, they hindered correct interpretation of the present; attempts were being made to apply false remedies derived from false principles.

In the first place, Ricardian doctrine, without any justification, identified bank-notes with paper money; secondly, it detected an equally illusory difference between bank-notes and other credit instruments (current accounts drawn on by cheques, bills of exchange). Identification and differentiation led to the same result: bank-notes, alone among credit instruments, were given an exceptional position and were made subject to an equally exceptional procedure of issue which, far from mitigating crises, only aggravates them.

On both these points later doctrine has come over completely to Tooke's point of view.

The only difference which Ricardo saw between inconvertible paper money and bank-notes was the greater ease with which the quantity of the latter could be limited. He recognises no differences in their character; for both quantity alone determines value.

Tooke protests against this confusion. Forced paper currency is *money*. Convertible bank-notes are *credit instruments*. He insists on the distinction between money and credit, between paper money and bank-notes, which English economists from Smith to Ricardo refused to recognise. The extraordinary thing is that his view has not yet completely won the field. Colonel Torrens and Lord Overstone contended that, in this famous controversy, Tooke was

[1] Tooke, Vol. II, p. 102.

in the wrong; and their opinion is echoed in our own day by an economist as eminent as Professor Gregory.[1]

On the continent, on the other hand, nobody ever disputed the difference. In 1810 Napoleon wrote to Mollien: "The people have sense enough to understand that bank-notes are not paper money." From the time of Storch and J.-B. Say, through Sismondi and Adolf Wagner, right up to modern economic treatises, all continental writers maintain the difference between notes and paper money. In England alone was there any uncertainty, although John Stuart Mill, following in this respect Fullarton and Tooke, was in line with continental theory.

The reason for this has already been given. It was that, from 1797 to 1819, the Bank of England used paper money almost entirely for the purpose of granting private credits, whereas on the continent paper money had always been an instrument of State finance. English economists consequently were of the opinion that the real difference between convertible notes and paper money was the difference between use and abuse, but not one between the nature of the two instruments themselves.

Tooke, however, maintains that there is a fundamental difference between inconvertible paper money and bank-notes. The first is issued to meet the requirements and cover the expenditure of the State; it represents a final income (that is to say, not subject to repayment) for those individuals who come into possession of it, increasing their purchasing power, thus increasing their demand for goods and making prices rise. In brief, paper money acts on prices in the same way as metallic money does.

Convertible bank-notes, on the other hand, are *credit instruments*. They are only issued as *advances*. Far from being incorporated in the currency, they are bound to *return* to the bank which has issued them when the advances are repaid. It is true that these credits, once repaid, can be renewed or replaced by others, and the total sum advanced may remain the same or slowly increase. But the necessity of having at any moment to pay back in coin the deposits made at the bank prevents it from issuing too many notes, and if

[1] Gregory: Introduction to the new edition of the *History of Prices*, p. 88: "A more complete confusion of the issues involved can hardly be imagined," he writes of Tooke's doctrine. The present author does not share that opinion. L. von Mises, in his well-known *Theorie des Geldes und der Umlaufsmittel*, does not recognise the difference between the two instruments.

it finds that it has issued too many, it need only cease renewing its loans to get its notes back again. Bank-notes, therefore, merely *anticipate* definitive income which, once it is acquired, itself puts an end to the existence of the notes. They can therefore affect prices only *provisionally*, for in order to repay the advances a sum exactly equal to those advances has to be taken from the final income. An advance from the bank enables the borrower to spend to-day an income which he will in fact receive only later, but he will not spend that income since it will be used to repay the advance. In other words, the total of the credits granted by the banks—and consequently the total quantity of bank-notes—constitutes what we called before a "renewable aggregate," while paper money, once it has entered into circulation or income, definitely becomes part of it.

This theory of "reflux"—so elementary that it is difficult to believe that it could ever have been disputed—is the backbone of Tooke's argument. It was formulated in full detail not only by Tooke, but also by Fullarton in his notable book *On the Regulation of Currencies*, published in 1844; John Stuart Mill adopted all his conclusions.[1]

The reply made by Tooke's opponents was that there was nothing to prevent the same method being applied to paper money, its use being confined—as had in fact been done in England—to the discounting of commercial bills, and that therefore the distinction drawn by Tooke falls to the ground.

"There is no conceivable difference," wrote Colonel Torrens, "as regards the nature and character of the action upon prices, between the action produced by convertible, and that produced by inconvertible paper. There is, however, a difference between the degree and extent of the action; the effect being, in the one case, unlimited, and in the other, limited by the speedy diminution in the quantity of the convertible paper money as soon as its value in relation to gold begins to decline. Mr. Tooke's argument, when fairly analysed, amounts to this—An increase in the quantity of convertible paper cannot reduce its value, because, when the increase of quantity has reduced its value, a diminution in its quantity will raise its value; therefore the quantity of convertible paper has no influence upon its value."—Q.E.D.[2]

[1] The essential passages in Tooke are to be found in Vol. IV, pp. 176 *et seq.* He reproduces the passage from Fullarton as a footnote. It occurs on p. 65 of *On the Regulation of Currencies.*

[2] Quoted by Tooke, Vol. IV, p. 182. The passage is taken from Torrens' *An Inquiry into the Practical Working of the Proposed Arrangement for the Renewal of the Charter of the Bank of England*, 1844, pp. 46–48.

Torrens' argument is specious, for inconvertibility changes the *legal character* of bank-notes, and therefore the value which their holders place on them. Bank-notes are *claims* on a defined quantity of gold. Paper money is a *means of payment* whose purchasing power over goods (or gold) is fixed on the market according to variations in supply and demand. It is a legal claim, and it is only the law which gives it the power to settle debts. But it is not a claim in the strict sense of the word. In saying that "purchasing power [in the sense of claims] commands a value like any other right over wealth,"[1] Mr. Hawtrey forgets that there is a great difference between a right over a volume of wealth fixed and determined beforehand, and a right over "wealth" in the abstract without specifying how much. The quantity of goods which paper money commands varies with market fluctuations and, more important, depends in part on the quantity of paper issued, without the present holders of the paper being able to exert any control over that amount. It may of course be said that the same is true of metallic money, but that raises the question of the difference between paper money and coin, which is quite different from the question of the difference between paper money and bank-notes.

The question of quantity to which Ricardo and his disciples would reduce all these problems, is only one of the factors that have to be taken into account. One is always brought back to the wider problem of determining what is the monetary standard—the international standard, gold, by means of which all the national price systems are brought into relation with each other, or paper, the purely national standard, which isolates the price systems of the different countries. Convertible notes (or, what comes to the same thing, current accounts drawn on by cheques) may, if their quantity is increased, affect the purchasing power even of national gold coin; in such cases gold will be exported, and the *international level of gold prices* will be affected (although only very slowly); but the national price level will not be dissociated from the international level. It will continue to follow the fluctuations of the latter. Thus, to the extent that cheques and bank-notes become more widely used, they have a certain influence on the price level, but so long as the connexion with gold is maintained, and gold is a product for which both as coin and as bullion there is an international

[1] *Currency and Credit*, London, 1928, p. 444.

demand, that influence can only be very limited and very slow in its action. But from the moment that convertibility is suspended everything is changed; the rope which binds the national monetary system to the international system is severed. The "reflux" method is designed to keep that rope intact.

It is, of course, true that Tooke's argument remains valid only so long as the banks really put the "law of reflux" into operation and confine themselves to making short-term loans and not advances which immobilise their funds for indefinite periods. Tooke makes this assumption throughout his argument. If the notes issued by the banks cease to be convertible, they become irrecoverable, or only partly recoverable claims, and their value fluctuates like that of any other credit claims, the payment of which is not absolutely certain.

In short, convertibility is not a mere device for limiting quantity; convertibility gives notes *legal and economic qualities* which paper money does not possess, and which are *independent of quantity.*

Tooke and Fullarton freely admit that, if inconvertibility did not have the same disastrous consequences in England as it did elsewhere, it was because neither the State nor the Bank abused the opportunity.[1] Tooke notes that, throughout the entire period, market rate was lower than bank rate, for which a legal maximum of 5 per cent was fixed, and borrowers preferred to seek the funds which they required on the market. Had the market rate risen above 5 per cent, the number of notes issued by the Bank would have increased (since it would have been to the advantage of the banks to rediscount their bills at the Bank of England) and their depreciation would have been much greater.

One last point. If Tooke refuses to identify bank-notes with forced paper currency, he is equally opposed to an identification of bank-notes with metallic money. For Ricardo and for Smith the term "money" is applicable to all currency instruments. Tooke refuses to give the name money to credit instruments. Money is more than a simple medium of exchange or a common denominator of values; it is the "subject of contracts for future payment," and "it is in this latter capacity that the fixity of a standard is most

[1] Tooke comes to the conclusion that the quantity of notes issued never exceeded the requirements of a growing population and more extensive production. He adduces as proof the ease with which the pound sterling, once peace was made, returned to parity. But this is not convincing. Then, as in 1925, speculation helped to raise the pound above its normal level.

essential." "Both the seller and the buyer of the goods, and the lender and borrower on mortgage, are willing to take their chance of what the value of gold may be at the expiration of the term. It is true that gold may vary in value; but there is no other commodity, silver perhaps alone excepted, so little liable to vary. And there is, accordingly, no other commodity than gold, or silver, which it would suit both parties to look to for eventual payment."[1]

Now the value of the convertible bank-note is derived precisely from its connexion with the metallic standard. As to the paper standard, it is, of course, a standard, but a bad one, because there is nothing to guarantee its stability.

Many of the misconceptions in English theory, and its divergence from continental theory, arise from this application of the term money to all currency instruments; Tooke correctly restricts its use to standard money. Ricardo's refusal to stop short at the legal characteristics of media of payment—which in their turn entail economic characteristics—only to stop short at "quantity" as the distinctive feature of media of payment, is the origin of these misunderstandings.[2]

[1] The passage quoted above continues: "As a mere instrument or medium of exchange, at the same time and in the same place, invariableness of value, though desirable, is not of so much importance; the immediate purpose of money in this capacity being to serve as a point, or rather a scale, of comparison more convenient than actual barter between any two commodities or sets of commodities. It is in the latter capacity, that is to say, as the subject of engagements or obligations for future payment, that in every view of justice and policy, the specific thing promised, in quantity and quality, should be paid at the expiration of the term." Tooke, Vol. IV, pp. 145–146.

[2] In Robertson's *Money*, published in 1921, the author applies the term "money" to all means of payment, which he divides into different species (common money, deposits, etc.) of which one is *Standard money*. It is this standard money, he says, which determines the quantity of all the others. Thus Robertson re-introduces (he cannot do otherwise) a terminology in which money in Tooke's sense has a special place. Would it not be easier and more convenient to confine the term only to this standard money, and to call other means of payment circulating credits?

To identify money with currency instruments is tantamount to thinking of money merely as a "voucher to purchase," as Law, Adam Smith, and Ricardo did. In *The Value of Money*, published first in 1916 and re-published in 1936 (Smith. New York), Benjamin Anderson subjects this idea to the liveliest criticism. His book is full of interesting ideas, and frequently represents the standpoint put forward in this book. Chapter VII, entitled *Dodo-Bones*, which demonstrates the impossibility of thinking of money without a value of its own, either in virtue of the substance of which it is made or in virtue of the rights (measurable in economic terms) which it confers. is particularly significant.

CHAPTER FIVE

Tooke, Creator of the Credit Theory The Currency and Banking Principles Controversy

§ I. FUNDAMENTAL IDENTITY OF BANK-NOTES AND BANK DEPOSITS.—§ II. TOOKE'S THEORY OF CRISES: INCOME CREATED BY CREDIT AND FINAL INCOME.—§ III. DIFFERENT EFFECT OF AN INFLUX OF GOLD ON PRICES ACCORDING TO WHETHER IT COINCIDES WITH A BOOM OR SLUMP.—§ IV. INFLUENCE OF THE RATE OF INTEREST ON PRICES.—§ V. PEEL'S ACT OF 1844 AND THE CURRENCY AND BANKING PRINCIPLES CONTROVERSY.—§ VI. ECHOES IN FRANCE OF THE CURRENCY AND BANKING CONTROVERSY.

In the previous chapter we examined Tooke's criticism of the interpretation given by Ricardo and his disciples to the events which occurred during the war and the period of forced paper currency. That criticism in itself is charged with positive lessons; and in the course of his argument, Tooke was led to formulate many other theories of considerable importance in regard to credit theory as a whole, echoes of which were heard again in the controversies which followed the World War:

1. Tooke upheld the idea, which had been maintained throughout the eighteenth century, that there is a fundamental identity between the different credit instruments, in particular between bank-notes and cheques;

2. In opposition to the theory which explains crises as the result of abuses in the issue of bank-notes, Tooke put forward an explanation based on the abuse of credit in general; he is thus led to formulate a theory concerning the relation between long-term price movements and cyclical price variations which, although little attention has been paid to it by the majority of economists, is of the greatest importance;

3. Similarly, in regard to the effects on prices of an increase in

the precious metals, and to the relation between these effects and cyclical variations, he makes observations of a wholly original character which are also extremely valuable;

4. Finally, he puts forward an entirely new theory of the influence exerted on the price of commodities and stock exchange prices by a fall in the rate of interest; the application of this theory to present-day problems is particularly interesting.

All these theories were formulated as by-products of the discussions which preceded the passing of the Peel Act in 1844 and the reorganisation of the Bank of England effected thereby. We shall attempt to shew why Tooke's theories were not accepted in England, and what were the consequences, in regard to credit organisation, of the monopoly in fact conferred on the Bank of England; we shall deal also with the repercussions in France, where credit was organised quite differently, of the famous controversy between the partisans of the Currency principle and the partisans of the Banking principle. The actual subject of the controversy has no more than a retrospective interest, but the truths which Tooke and his followers enunciated in the course of their argument remain of prime importance.

§ 1. *Fundamental Identity of Bank-Notes and Bank Deposits*

Bank-notes are not money. They are credit instruments, circulating credits. As such they belong to the category not of paper money, but of commercial paper, bills of exchange and current accounts drawn on by cheque, of what is called to-day "bank money." This is one of the elementary truths which Ricardo failed to grasp and on which Tooke always insisted.

In this he was in complete agreement with the best traditions of political economy; with Cantillon, from whom quotations on this point have been given in an earlier chapter, with Thornton, who treats the Bank of England's deposits and its notes in the same way, with Fullarton, who devotes some eloquent chapters to this subject, with Gilbart, one of the most able bankers of his time, and, somewhat later, with MacLeod. Bank-notes are merely commercial bills payable on sight, and not bearing interest, drawn on and accepted by a banker. A current account entry is similarly a banker's undertaking to pay on sight. When a bank's client discounts a bill, the bank substitutes its promise to pay for the promise of the acceptor; whether this promise is registered by a note which circulates from hand to hand, or by an entry in the bank's books, the sum mentioned in which can be transferred by means of cheques detached from the cheque book issued by the bank to its depositors, makes absolutely no difference to the economic effects.

"There is not," writes Fullarton, "a single object at present attained through the agency of the Bank of England notes, which might not be as effectually accomplished by each individual keeping an account with the Bank, and transacting all his payments of five pounds and upwards by cheque. I do not say, that such a plan would be necessarily free from inconveniences or difficulties in practice. I only affirm, that there would be no obstacle to it in principle, and that in this manner, a book-credit circulation might be universally substituted for our circulation of bank-notes, and would perform all the offices of exchange quite as certainly and efficiently." [1]

And he adds: "Bank-notes are the small change of credit, the humblest of the mechanical organisations through which credit develops itself." [2]

It was necessary to elaborate this simple idea because the entire Ricardian school and the Currency school insisted on the difference between bank-notes and other credit instruments, and regarded bank-notes as money. Their most authoritative spokesman, Sir Robert Peel, said when introducing the Bill:

"I must state at the outset, that in using the word 'money,' I mean to designate by that word the coin of the realm and promissory notes, payable to bearer on demand. In using the word 'paper currency,' I mean only such promissory notes. I do not include in that term bills of exchange, or drafts on bankers, or other forms of credit. There is a material distinction in my opinion between the character of a promissory note payable to bearer on demand, and other forms of paper credit, and *between the effects which they respectively produce upon the prices of commodities, and upon the exchanges*. The one answers all the purposes of money, passes from hand to hand without endorsement, without examination, if there be no suspicion of forgery; and it is what its designations imply it to be, currency or circulating medium." [3]

[1] Fullarton, p. 41. [2] *Ibid.*, p. 51.

[3] Quoted by Tooke, Vol. IV, pp. 154–155.

Tooke marshalled all his polemical ardour to combat this idea, reproducing for this purpose the arguments used by Fullarton and by one of his friends, Pennington, who took an active part in the controversy. "When a London banker discounts a bill of exchange, he gives credit for the amount of the bill, less the interest, for the period which the bill has to run, in an account opened in his ledger: when a country banker discounts a bill of exchange, he pays the amount of the bill, less the interest, in promissory notes. In both cases payment from the banker of the amount of the bill, less the discount, may be immediately demanded in gold, or in Bank of England notes." [1]

He concludes that there is only a formal difference between the two procedures.

The beliefs of Peel and the Currency School were not weakened by Tooke's arguments; this provides a further striking example of the weight carried by great names and by over-simplified thought in the tradition of political economy. It was for this reason that in France, for example, Napoleon's contention that the issuing of notes is in fact the equivalent of "minting money" carried conviction. Tooke said on this point: "The confusion between paper credit and paper money seems to have given rise to the dogma of the currency theory, that the issue of promissory notes payable on demand, in coin, is a prerogative or function of the sovereign!" [2]

From time to time economists have found it necessary to repeat the proof of Tooke's contention;[3] that did not prevent the banks of issue (in France as in Germany) from advocating the use of cheques rather than bank-notes during the World War, on the ground that cheques, unlike notes, would not involve a rise in prices.

It is interesting to observe that, a hundred years after these disputes concerning the nature of bank-notes, the very same ideas are put forward in regard to cheques, which are called money since their use is so widespread. What, it is asked, are bank credits that can be drawn on by cheques if not new money? In his famous *The Meaning of Money*, published in 1908, Hartley Withers calls deposit banks "banks of cheque issue," and, before him, MacLeod, in his *History of the Bank of England*, had elaborated a long argument

[1] The passage is given in full in Vol. II, p. 372. [2] Vol. IV, p. 171, footnote.

[3] Cf. for recent examples, Ansiaux's article in the *Revue d'Economie politique*, 1912, p. 553, Bendixen's pamphlets in Germany, and Hartley Withers' *Meaning of Money*.

to prove that credit creates "capital." For what does a banker do when he grants credit against, let us say, a bill of exchange? He allows his client to enter into his credit account the amount of the loan, and to draw cheques on that account; these cheques may be paid to a third person, who will then enter the amount of the cheques in his account at another bank (or at the same bank). On the asset side, the banks' holdings, taken as a whole, have been increased by the bill of exchange; on the liability side, deposits are increased by the amount of the loan made against the bill. Thus bank credits *create deposits* and deposits available by means of cheques are "purchasing power" and therefore "money." In other words, deposit banks are just as much creators of money as banks of issue, for in their case, as in the latter, advances which the bank agrees to make end in the issue of a note and notes are money. "Loans create deposits"—that is the new formula which has misled so many writers and which was to lead a man like Wicksell to make the amazing statement that the supply of credit always and inevitably adapts itself to the demand. To dispel this illusion it is only necessary to point out that, as deposits are "created," the cash in hand by which these deposits are covered represents a diminishing percentage of those same deposits. The banks are thus made aware that their credit *margin* is narrowing and that the time has come to limit their advances. This concept of the credit margin, fundamental in banking (whether as regards banks of issue or deposit banks), occupies a very insignificant place in the majority of works devoted to this subject. The credit margin is the *stock of credit that is still available* and, assuming that cash in hand remains the same, diminishes to the extent that bank advances expand.

Of course this margin varies; its extent is determined by the banker's estimate of what he considers a "liquid" position, that is to say by the proportion of his deposits which he has always to keep ready in the form of notes or of a current account at the central bank. Each banker, naturally, will make a different estimate, and his calculations will be influenced by the degree of liquidity of his investments, which in its turn varies according to the banking and stock exchange system of the country in question.[1]

[1] In Anglo-Saxon countries, for example, it is considered quite correct to use short-term deposits for the purchase of stock exchange securities, because the securities market in New York and London is far better organised and much larger than the Paris securities market.

The formula "loans create deposits" demonstrates once again the identity of the two credit instruments in question (the difference, as between the two periods, arises from the fact that commercial banks have everywhere taken the place of private banks of issue and that, in England and America, the public as a whole use cheques rather than bank-notes); it also indicates the tendency, in Anglo-Saxon countries, to apply the term "money" to what is only a credit instrument.

In the last few years numerous articles have been written about this so-called creation of money. Actually, what was said in the first chapter about bank-notes may be repeated in regard to cheques. The commercial bank, operating by means of "credit entries," fulfils the same function as the bank of issue granting credit by means of bank-notes: *by their advances deposit banks put into circulation the surplus cash entrusted to them by the public.* Bank-notes and bank money are issued in the same way. What the public deposit at the bank is the funds for which at the moment they have no use, whether these funds are deposited as cheques, notes or coin.

It is clear that these deposits, in whatever form they are made, are necessarily reflected in an increase in the bank's cash holdings (including in that term coin, notes and current accounts with the central bank). Similarly withdrawals by the public, in whatever form they are made, are reflected in a decrease in those holdings. The public pay in to the bank their gold, notes or cheques. Each of these payments is represented at the bank by a deposit to the account of the client who makes it, and each puts the bank in possession of gold (which it immediately deposits at the central bank), notes, or payments to its account at the central bank made by the banks on which the cheques which its clients hand in are drawn. These are the funds which the bank uses to make loans. Every day the bank receives cheques drawn on other banks, and is presented with cheques drawn on itself. In the end the difference between these two sums is paid to the bank, or is paid by it out of its cash (or its account at the central bank). In the same way the bank every day receives repayments of loans which it has made, either in the form of cheques drawn on itself and in its favour, which diminishes the balance of creditor accounts, or in the form of notes and coin, which increases its cash in hand; in both cases the proportion of cash to deposits rises. The reverse is true when the bank makes advances. The terms "deposits" and "creditor accounts" are here regarded as identical.

Thus in all cases what the bank lends is the cash surpluses of the public, deposited at the bank by the public; but instead of giving it to the borrower in the form of notes or of gold, it enters the amount of the loan in the client's credit account. This is a deposit represented in the bank's assets not by cash (gold, notes, current accounts at the central bank) but by advances (discounts or loans against securities). These deposits circulate like other deposits, from bank to bank, by means of cheques. They can no longer be distinguished from deposits made originally by the public, just as it is impossible to distinguish among the notes in circulation those originating in a discount by the central bank or in a deposit made in gold, or again to distinguish in a country with a metallic currency the coins held as the result of a loan from those held as the result of a sale of property. As these deposits, originating in the bank's credit operations, increase, the proportion of the bank's total deposits represented by cash in hand, that is to say the sum held in notes and coin or at the central bank, grows smaller. It is the decrease in this proportion which warns the bank that its credits must be restricted—which is exactly what happens in a bank of issue. The creation of a deposit by the grant of an advance or by a discount is the exact equivalent of the creation of a bank-note by the same transactions. The difference arises from the fact that in countries where there is a central bank of issue, which has the exclusive right of issuing bank-notes and of providing for their cover, the deposit banks have come to regard bank-notes, and not coin, as the currency which they must use for payments. In these countries, indeed, notes have become the chief currency instrument; banks settle their accounts with each other by means of notes or by transfer through the central bank, and their chief concern is to be able at any moment to repay in these notes the deposits entrusted to them. In other words, for deposit banks, "money," what constitutes their "cash in hand" (corresponding to the gold holdings of the bank of issue), means the notes which they hold or their current accounts at the central bank, which can at any moment be changed into notes. It is left to the central bank to provide for the exchange of these notes into gold.

There is a second difference: we have said that deposit banks limit their responsibility to payment in notes. Now, in modern currency systems, the number of notes that a central bank can issue is *elastic*. Provided that its bills can be rediscounted at the issuing bank, the deposit bank can as a rule be sure of getting a credit from the bank of issue, granted in the form of notes. On the other hand the quantity of gold available for the redemption of notes is at any moment limited; it is not elastic; consequently the bank of issue has need of greater caution than the deposit bank.

It follows that deposit banks are in a position to exercise *greater freedom in granting credits* than the bank of issue, and, in fact, their cash reserves (notes and deposits at the central bank) are maintained, in relation to the sums which they have received, at a much lower level than the normal proportion of the bank of issue's gold holdings to the total number of notes issued. The credits granted by the deposit banks are not as a rule paid out in notes to the borrowers, but are left on current account at the bank and are transferred by cheque to other accounts. Thus, in countries where the use of cheques is widespread, the figure of deposits (or current accounts) grows; as against these deposits the asset side of the balance sheet shews the bank's cash in hand (notes held at the bank and current account at the central bank) and the credits which it has granted.

It is clear that the system of "bank money" has replaced the "bank-note" system. The effect of both is to *put into circulation* the hard cash originally deposited at the banks. In fact however, this circulation is only nominal, since the gold, like the notes, is not actually moved, or only to a small extent. Deposit accounts represent, very largely, the amount of money constantly being put into circulation by credit, and constantly being brought back to the banks.

It is often asked how such a mighty credit structure can be erected on such a narrow cash foundation.

Let us take a country with a hundred million in coin. The coin is brought in to the bank of issue, which gives in exchange notes to the same amount, and also grants credits up to fifty millions. There are now notes to the value of 150 millions in circulation, of which 50 represent the putting into circulation of coin. The public prudently place their notes in the deposit banks, which transfer them to the central bank. The 150 millions of notes in circulation are now replaced by 150 millions on deposit; the deposit banks hold, instead of the notes, current accounts at the central bank to the value of 150 million. But the deposit banks grant credits; let us say that their credits amount to 140 million; these too are immediately re-deposited, and are now represented by current credit accounts. Total deposits now amount to 290 million, to meet which the banks hold 150 million at the central bank. They realise that they can lend still more, and lend again part of their 290 million deposits, let us say 125 million, and then a further 125 million; this makes a total deposits figure of 540 million, still with a total cash reserve of 150 million.

These transactions continue until the deposit banks consider that further credits would involve the risk of their cash reserve being insufficient to meet possible demands for withdrawal, even taking into account the re-discounting of their bills at the central bank. The bankers now keep their eyes on their cash holdings, and the relation of those holdings to the total of their deposits which they may be called on to repay. This is what English writers mean when they say that "bankers construct a credit edifice on a given gold basis." But what in fact happens is that the bankers have received 150 millions, 140 millions, 125 millions and a further 125 millions, making a total of 540 millions, all of which have been deposited with them exactly as the first 150 million were. Thus cash in hand always remains the same, while the deposit total increases; but that total, it should be noted, cannot go on increasing *indefinitely*. For every new credit granted by the bank *narrows the credit margin*. To use the terms adopted earlier in this book, the velocity of the currency circulation cannot increase to infinity.

In short, everything that is true of bank-notes is true also of deposits. This has been clear to many writers, and Cannan, for example, never ceased to protest against the idea that banks *create* money.

"But whatever some bank chairmen and some monetary theorists may think, every bank-manager knows that the customers who provide the funds which the bank lends and invests are substantial people who have property of their own which they find convenient to entrust to the bank. They could, if they had time and inclination, lend direct to the same people to whom the bank lends, but they find it better to entrust the business to an intermediary, the bank, which is expert at it and, by clubbing a number of them together as its customers, is able to let each of them have the money at any time when they happen to want it."[1]

This is more than a mere verbal point; for we have often seen how dangerous words themselves can be in these matters. This is but another instance. Certain writers to-day, for example Irving Fisher, would have the same action taken in regard to current accounts available by cheque as Ricardo and the Currency School advocated for notes: that these deposits on sight should be covered by "state money" of an equal amount, and that the banks should not be allowed to use this money for granting credits (cf. Fisher's *100 per cent Money*, New York, 1935). It is the principle underlying Peel's Act of 1844, and repeats *word for word* the proposal made by Ricardo in 1823, although here it is applied to cheques. It is significant that this proposal should be made after a large-scale war during which the State carried to excess the creation of money, *disguised as credit instruments*. What a dazzling light that throws on the suggestion!

In England and the United States, the war was financed not directly by the bank of issue, but indirectly by the deposit banks, which themselves had recourse to the Treasury (in England) and the Federal Reserve Bank (in America) for the means of payment required in ever increasing quantity by the public. In France and Germany, on the other hand, the governments issued treasury bonds to the central banks in exchange for direct advances, in notes, with which to make their payments.

Between these two methods there is a difference only in *form*.

[1] E. Cannan, *Money, its Connection with Rising and Falling Prices*, London, 1923, p. 82. Elsewhere Cannan says: "Within, I think, the last forty years a practice has grown up among the people who talk and write on such subjects, of regarding the amount which bankers are bound to pay to their customers on demand or at short notice as a mass of 'bank-money' or of 'credit' which must be added to the total of the currency (of notes and coin) whenever variations in the quantity of money are being thought of as influencing prices. This is one of the most obstructive of all modern monetary delusions." Further on he says that, if this definition of money is accepted, there is no reason why, for example, deposits in saving banks should not be included in the term as well as bank deposits; only, he adds, their "inclusion would have made the doctrine taught about banks too ridiculous for acceptance." Cannan, *Modern Currency and the Regulation of its Value*, London, 1931, pp. 88 and 97.

They had the same effect: as government expenditure put into circulation the sums thus created, the public brought them to the banks, and *private* deposits were thus increased. They also brought about a rise in prices, since they originated in expenditure not covered by revenue, and a growing demand on the part of the public for currency. In France the government paid these sums *directly* to its contractors, whose expenditure distributed it throughout the country; the public thus came into possession of larger monetary resources, part of which was deposited in the banks, whereas in England and the United States this creation of money occurred *indirectly*. The British government provided the *banks* with notes called currency notes whenever the public wished to draw on their increased deposits for currency. In America the government empowered the Federal Reserve Bank, established in 1913, to make in notes the advances required by the banks.

These currency notes (since become bank-notes and incorporated as part of the normal note circulation of the Bank of England) and Federal Reserve bank-notes were, like the notes issued by the Bank of France and the Reichsbank, "fiat money" or "necessity money," a paper money created to meet State needs.

After the peace the banks, misled by the abundance of money, granted private credits in excess (particularly in the United States); at the same time production, which had been arrested during the war, again expanded, and prices fell; the inevitable result was the failure of a large number of banks and the destruction of many milliards of deposits. When these disasters occurred blame was laid, not on the financial policy of the governments during the war, but on the banks; they were charged with having created too many deposits, and it was proposed that these deposits should be replaced by money guaranteed by the government, which the banks would not be allowed to use for making loans.

The fact that the very same proposals should be made in regard to cheques as, one hundred years earlier, writing after the Napoleonic wars, Ricardo had made in regard to bank-notes, is so curious and so significant that it should be emphasised. No more convincing proof could be asked of Tooke's contention that bank-notes and cheques are identical. The superficial difference—that one loan is made in the form of an entry in a current account, and the other in the form of bank-notes—does not affect the issue.

Having established this identity, Tooke draws two important conclusions:

1. Since all credit instruments are essentially the same, it is absurd to put bank-notes in a class apart. If credit has been granted in excessive quantities, the situation cannot be remedied merely by limiting the number of bank-notes issued, as the Currency School argued; it is necessary to deal with credit as a whole.

2. The banks' creation of credit, in all its forms, and particularly in the form of bank-notes, takes place only because the *public demand credit*. Banks cannot create notes *at will*, any more than they can create deposits. They are only created if the public demand them. That is why it is impossible to get out of a crisis by creating paper. Whereas paper money is created by the government at will in order to meet expenditure which cannot be covered by its ordinary revenue, credit instruments are created only in response to public demand. The State creates paper money at will but cannot withdraw it from circulation; the banks do not create credit instruments at will, but can withdraw them by ceasing to renew credits.

"There is," says Fullarton, "this broad and clear distinction between all currencies of value and currencies of credit, that the quantity of the former is in no degree regulated by the public demand, whereas the quantity of the latter is regulated by nothing else. . . . New gold coin and new conventional notes are introduced into the market by being made the medium of *payments*. Bank-notes, on the contrary, are never issued but on *loan*, and an equal amount of notes must be returned into the bank whenever the loan becomes due."[1]

[1] Fullarton, pp. 63–64. Tooke uses the same argument, as shewn in the following characteristic passage: "It will hence appear that the difference between paper money so issued, and bank-notes such as those of this country consists, not only in the limit prescribed by their convertibility to the amount of them, but in the mode of issue. The latter are issued to those only who, being entitled to demand gold, desire to have notes in preference; and it depends upon the particular purposes for which the notes are employed, whether a greater or less quantity is required. *The quantity*, therefore, *is an effect and not a cause of demand.* A compulsory government paper, on the other hand, while it is in the course of augmentation, acts directly as an originating cause on prices and incomes, constituting a fresh source of demand in money, depreciated in value, as compared with gold, but of the same nominal value as before." Vol. IV, p. 177.

§ II. *Tooke's Theory of Crises. Income Created by Credit and Final Income*

The foregoing clears up preliminary questions of definition. The essential problem is: What is the explanation of crises? How can they be overcome? It was this problem which lay at the heart of the controversy between the adherents of the Currency Principle and the adherents of the Banking Principle. Tooke's theory of crises, almost completely ignored by the historians, is one of the most penetrating that has ever been formulated.

The partisans of the Currency School believed that crises resulted from an excessive issue of bank-notes, and would disappear if such an excess were made impossible.

Tooke does not agree. Notes are merely one of the forms assumed by credit. They are not the only form, nor even the most important—a crisis is accompanied by an excess of credit in *all its forms*—too many bills of exchange, too great a volume of purchases on credit, an excessive creation of current accounts; it is mere chance, a pure accident, which determines whether the credit granted will be used in the form of notes or the form of cheques. An increase in the circulation is the result or the symptom of a certain credit position. It is therefore the abuse of credit in general that must be prevented, or, if it cannot be prevented, then checked in time.

According to Tooke, this abuse of credit is the result of the "spirit of speculation"—of what he elsewhere calls "overbanking,"[1] which is itself brought into play by a *given price situation*. Credit does not give rise to speculation, but follows it; credit is always the response to a *demand*, and this *demand* is itself the result of a given economic situation.

[1] Cf. Vol. III, p. 262. "The phenomena of the great occasional derangement of the country circulation have been referable in a much greater degree to over-banking than to mere over-issues of paper money. By over-banking (which is a phrase of modern introduction) I mean advances, either on insufficient or inconvertible securities, or in too large a proportion to the liabilities. The disproportion of the securities to the liabilities might, perhaps, be set wholly against the deposits; and but for the excess of inconvertibility of the securities, on occasion of unexpected demands by depositors, there might, in the instance of many of the country bankers who failed, have been no unusual demands for payment of their notes."

This brings us to the heart of the theory of crises, which Tooke attacks boldly from its most difficult angle. How does a period of boom begin? Once it has begun, how can it be checked? What is the connexion between *temporary price fluctuations* and the *general price movement* of the time, the long-term tendency in prices? In short, how are cyclical price movements superimposed on the long-term price tendency, and how do the two act in combination? This question clearly defines the terms of one of the most difficult of all economic problems, on which a great deal of ink has been spilt. Here we shall deal only with those aspects of the problem which interested Tooke, and with the guidance which his theory can give in a consideration of the problems of credit and currency regulation.

Tooke distinguishes between: (*a*) speculative price movements, and (*b*) price movements which can be called (though he himself does not use the words) permanent or fundamental. Tooke uses the phrase "general prices" as opposed to speculation prices.

Speculative movements are inevitable in a national economy as complex as the English. These movements—or as we would say these cyclical boom periods—originate not in an expansion of credit, but in a *favourable price situation in certain commodity markets*. This situation is exploited by speculators with the aid of credit which, it must be repeated, is granted in response to previous *demand;* an increase in the volume of such credit cannot be directly provoked at will. A low rate of interest, as we shall see, cannot in itself give rise to credit expansion, but it facilitates such an expansion when demands for credit are made.

The points which Tooke considers essential are: 1, that speculation originates in the situation of the commercial or industrial market, and not in an increase in the note circulation; 2, that the steady expansion of credit is an effect, and not a cause of this speculation, for there is no expansion of credit without the demand for it; 3, that the contraction in the currency which follows a crisis is the consequence and not the cause of the slump.

"As book credits and bills of exchange are the medium through which a considerable portion of the purchase of commodities are effected, constituting prices computed in money, as completely as those which are made by the intervention of bank-notes or coin, the greater or less degree of credit that enters at different periods into the markets for commodities will naturally operate as a temporary or disturbing cause in those markets. But credit in this sense is not confined to banking advances or discounts. . . . If the facility of credit as from producers, whether manufacturers or farmers, or from importers and merchants, to dealers, and from them to shopkeepers, be, as in periods of confidence it is apt to be, carried to an undue extent, prices may be inflated, and a cessation of the excess of confidence, terminating in distrust, will cause a collapse. An extension of the issues of bank-notes, and a subsequent contraction, have been commonly the consequences, and not the causes, of occasional undue expansion alternating with collapse of credit."[1]

When there is a favourable market situation there will be what Tooke calls a speculative price rise. This rise precedes expansion of the circulation.[2] But how does it end?

This is where the fundamental or general price level enters. How is this fundamental level determined? *It depends, in the last analysis, on the permanent incomes of consumers, which can be divided into wages, interest, the profits of entrepreneurs, and the rents of landowners.* If these permanent incomes are not enough to absorb commodities at the prices to which they have been raised by the speculative movement, prices will fall; this constitutes the crisis, which will have the effect of bringing the "speculative" level into line with the normal or "general" level, which is determined by the incomes of consumers.

This is Tooke's theory, which is given, in his own words, in the following quotation:

"And here we come to the ultimate regulating principle of money prices.

"It is the quantity of money constituting the revenues of the different orders of the state, under the head of rents, profits, salaries, and wages,

[1] Tooke, Vol. III, p. 277. On p. 245 of the same volume he writes: "[I conclude] that the prices of commodities are not liable to be influenced in any perceptible degree by variations in the issues of the Bank, in a convertible state of the paper, according to the system by which, since 1825, those issues have been regulated; that variations in the state of credit may and often do arise from circumstances extrinsic to the state of the circulation, and that no regulation of the issues of paper money can operate as an infallible preservative against occasional great fluctuations in the state of credit, and in the rate of interest."

[2] "In point of fact, and historically, as far as my researches have gone, in every signal instance of a rise or fall of prices, the rise or fall has preceded, and therefore could not be the effect of, an enlargement or contraction of the bank circulation." (Fullarton, p. 100.)

destined for current expenditure, according to the wants and habits of the several classes, that alone forms the limiting principle of the *aggregate of money prices*,—the only prices that can properly come under the designation of *general prices*. As the cost of production is the limiting principle of supply, so the aggregate of money incomes devoted to expenditure for consumption is the limiting principle of demand for commodities."[1]

Thus, according to Tooke, the origin of crises lies in a contradiction between the level to which speculation has carried prices, and the level at which the money incomes of the public devoted to expenditure can absorb production. Mr. Hawtrey, writing in our own times, has put forward such a striking objection to this theory that it must be mentioned here. It represents one more instance of formal economic logic in conflict with the observed facts.

The objection, which seems at first unanswerable, is as follows: *credit itself creates income*. What is done with the sums borrowed from the banks? They are used to pay wages and to purchase raw materials, the price of which includes the profits of the entrepreneur and interest on the capital invested. Thus *credit itself creates the incomes with which, later on, the manufactured products are bought;* these credits are part of the cost of production which, as Tooke himself says, is made up of wages, profits, interest and rent. Will not these incomes be equal to the cost of production, and why should they not be sufficient to absorb commodities at prices which they cost to produce?

This is the apparently irrefutable argument advanced by the logician. But a national economy is not a closed world, in which every sum put into circulation necessarily reappears somewhere as consumers' purchasing power. Every economy is dependent on others. If the harvest is bad, and large imports of wheat lead to capital export, the income diverted abroad will decrease home demand. If a crisis occurs in countries indebted to England, accompanied by the suspension of payments, the income figures for England will shew a fall. If external markets are closed the same result will follow. Even within the country itself, a large-scale re-orientation of demand (the result, for example, of a bad harvest), and a diminishing demand for the products of those industries which had recourse to credit in the preceding period, are enough for the prices of such products to fall and for the industrialists to

[1] Vol. III, p. 276.

be unable to repay the banks, thus bringing about bankruptcies in the course of which a part of the income previously created by credit is destroyed. The same result will follow if the credits are granted on long instead of short term, and the bank whose funds are thus immobilised is met with a sudden demand for the withdrawal of deposits. Tooke mentions some of these circumstances.[1] Many others could be given which (in an economy which is not closed and where, even internally, credits are repaid to the banks not without some frictions and delays) prevent the income of consumers from reaching a level exactly equal to the cost of production of commodities as a whole. Frequently a small gap between the two is enough to bring about a fall in the market price of one single commodity, and for that fall to involve all other prices.

Tooke saw this quite clearly. The present writer would add to his arguments a theoretical argument which remains valid even on the assumption that the credit-income-demand circuit is working without any friction and without any interference from outside.

Let us start with the hypothesis that a part of wages and costs has been paid, up to a certain stage of production, by means of bank credits. By this means new purchasing power has been created which should reappear in the incomes of the public and permit of an increased demand for goods and services at higher prices. After a time, if all goes well, the sale of the products at

[1] "The most striking, the most extensive, and the most distressing, is that which has been noticed in the first chapter of this work, namely, the reduced earnings of the manufacturing population, and the large proportion of those reduced money earnings which must go to the purchase of food at comparatively high prices. This cause, in its ramifications, will apply also to the power of expenditure of some of the classes immediately above the poorest. The disturbed state of our trade with America, and with China, will of course account, among other causes, for the reduced demand for some of our manufactures, and the consequent diminished employment of the workmen. There is also a cause, of minor importance, however, which affects the power of expenditure of persons in the middling walks of life. I mean the very large amount of capital which is absorbed, and wholly unproductive of immediate income (whether permanently so is another question), in railway and other joint stock concerns, but chiefly the former, in which the sums invested, and for the present yielding no net returns, are computed to amount to many millions. The absence of all income from such an outlay might not, in ordinary times, have a sensible influence on the general scale of expenditure in consumable commodities, and it might be, in a prosperous period, more than compensated by the savings of those same and other classes; but in the present instance it may be mentioned as being possibly among the minor aggravating causes of the present depression." Vol. III, p. 278.

these higher prices which have been established, will enable the borrower to repay the loans he has received, and still make a profit. If, at this stage, he wishes to continue production he has (1) to get his credits renewed; (2) *to get a somewhat larger credit*, corresponding to the higher general price level which has been established in the preceding period. This process continues from stage to stage; in other words, the continuation of production *at the same level* is only possible if the credits are *increased* from stage to stage. The time will come when—*in the absence of a wider foundation for credits*, that is to say of the bank's cash resources—the banks fear that their credit margin may be exhausted and will either refuse to grant further credits or will grant them only at prohibitive rates. This point having been reached, producers will curtail production, thereby reducing the incomes of those who depend on them, workers, providers of raw materials, etc. This reduction in purchasing power starts a slump which involves the destruction of a large part of the incomes created by means of bank credits.

Tooke does not bring forward this theoretical argument. As usual, he merely enumerates facts, though these in themselves are enough to shew that the objection of the logician cannot be maintained. The distinction which he makes between the "general level" of prices and the temporary level established during a "period of confidence," as he calls it, seems to the present writer of fundamental importance. Its truth is permanent; it does provide an explanation of the cyclical fluctuations about an *average price curve* which may have an upward or a downward tendency; these fluctuations present the economist with one of his most difficult problems.[1]

§ III. *Different Effect of an Influx of Gold on Prices according to Whether it Coincides with a Boom or Slump*

Unlike certain of his successors, Tooke, although so strongly opposed to Ricardo, does not deny the influence exerted on prices by an influx of gold or by the creation of paper money. On the

[1] It appears that Tooke's opponents were inclined to accept this theory, judging from a statement by Lord Overstone quoted by Tooke, with obvious satisfaction, on p. 269 of Vol. III.

contrary, he makes the point in several places.[1] But he is less inclined than others to arbitrary simplifications of fact, or to attribute price variations to one single cause.

In particular, he was deeply impressed by the effects of the coincidence of a period of economic boom or depression with an influx of gold, or with supplementary issues of paper money. He describes these effects in a number of passages which, even to-day, provide a satisfactory explanation of facts which, at the first glance, seem to contradict earlier experience.

Tooke notes, first of all, that even in the absence of paper money, and *when the currency consists entirely of coin*, "there are expansions and contractions of the circulation, without any corresponding movements of the metallic basis," and continues: "But if from accidental circumstances there should coincidently with the tendency to speculation, through the means of credit, happen to be an enlargement of the metallic basis, an increased facility would arise, to the extension of the circulation, and to the spirit of speculation; and the converse would be the consequence of a contraction of the basis coinciding with a reaction from speculation and its attendant discredit."[2]

Thus variations in the rapidity of circulation of money may occur under the influence of speculation, apart from *any change in the quantity of metallic money*. Conversely the normal effects of changes in the quantity of money may be strengthened or weakened by speculative movements, by what we should now call cyclical price variations. "For short periods, therefore, considerable variations of prices might take place consistently with a uniform amount of money, as, on the other hand, an undisturbed state of prices might prevail consistently with marked variations of the quantity of money."[3]

Here Tooke provides the explanation of many facts which have frequently astonished economists: the impossibility, for example, of reviving an economy weakened by crisis by supplementary note issues or by the creation of additional credits (cf. the United States before 1933); the slowness of the price rise usually brought about by an influx of gold when that influx coincides with a period of depression (as was the case between 1890–1895);

[1] See in particular the footnote on p. 157 of Vol. III.

[2] Vol. I, pp. 151–152.

[3] Vol. I, p. 156.

the aggravation of cyclical crises in periods when there is a slowing down in the output of the precious metals, and their mitigation in periods when there is a large influx of bullion (phenomena characteristic of the periods 1873–1895 and 1895–1914).

Fullarton has given a detailed and striking description of what takes place when there is an influx of gold at a time when markets are depressed:

> "If there has been no pre-existing demand for an addition to the circulating medium, if there be no new capital to be distributed, no new channel of commerce to be opened, nor any great discovery in mechanics to be worked out into active and profitable existence, the arrival of a million of new gold from abroad will assuredly create none of these things. The gold will be sold to the Bank for a million in notes, and those notes will fare just as all the issues of the Bank invariably fare, which are sent into a market having no employment for them. The holders will immediately become competitors for a share of the productive securities floating in the market, for a share of the Exchequer bills, the Consols, and the discounts. In the discount-market they will come into immediate competition with the Bank of England; and by offering the money at a rate of interest below the Bank rate, they will be enabled to intercept a portion of the bills on their way for discount to the Bank. The sellers of the Exchequer bills and of the Consols, into whose hands another portion of the notes may be supposed to have come, will in their turns have to find new investments for their money, and many of them may be expected also to resort to the discount market; and thus the process will go on from hand to hand till the discount-market shall have absorbed the whole million. The Bank meanwhile will have its notes flowing in fast, in payment of the bills of exchange previously in its hands, as they successively become due, while there will be no vent for its notes in fresh discounts; and the result of the whole will be, that, at the end perhaps of a week, the Bank will find itself with a million more of coin in its coffers, and a million less of securities. So long as the Bank has a sovereign out on credit, the channel of reflux must remain open, and the Bank is utterly impotent to add a superfluous note to the currency." [1]

Thus new gold, coming on to a depressed market, takes refuge at the central bank and does not leave it.

This reciprocal action of cyclical variations and of the rate of bullion inflow on the price level—of the utmost importance for an understanding of price movements—has been explained by

[1] Fullarton, pp. 78–79.

nobody so well as by Tooke and Fullarton. Once again they seem to us the most up to date of the writers about credit. The same is true when they deal with gold movements from one country to another. Tooke agrees with Ricardo that differences in price levels have a permanent and profound influence on such movements.[1] But that influence may be modified by a number of circumstances. He mentions in particular (apart from temporary disturbances in the balance of trade) the situation in the capital market and the state of credit in other financial centres, where a local crisis may be enough to cause a drain of gold from London. These are all factors to which recent writers, such as Mr. Hawtrey, have quite rightly given prominence; but Tooke was the first to indicate their importance, a hundred years ago. One of the chief causes of the movement of gold from one place to another is the fact that periods of boom and depression do not occur simultaneously in different countries.

§ IV. *Influence of the Rate of Interest on Prices*

In recent years there has been a great deal of discussion about the question of the influence of the rate of interest on economic recovery. A systematic policy of lowering the discount rate has been advocated as the best means of overcoming the crisis. As far as I know nobody has called attention to Tooke's ideas on this subject, although on this, as on so many other questions, he might be read with great advantage. Here only his two most important observations will be noted:

1. A low discount rate cannot by itself stimulate the price level;
2. A low discount rate can affect prices on the stock exchange without having any effect on commodity markets.

A fall in the rate of discount,[2] by bringing about a rise in the price of capital and a reduction in its yield, impels capitalists to seek higher profits in more risky investments, and induces borrowers to take advantage of the low rate to extend their undertakings. But

[1] Cf. Vol. III. pp. 70 *et seq.*

[2] In the passage on pp. 360–361 of Vol. II Tooke speaks of the "rate of interest," but it is obvious that he is referring to the discount rate, as will be seen by a comparison with p. 153 of Vol. III, in which he does refer to the rate of discount.

that will be done only on one condition, which is that it "should coincide with a tendency from other causes, to a speculative rise of prices, and with the opening of new fields for enterprise."[1]

"There are, doubtless, persons who, upon imperfect information, and upon insufficient grounds, or with too sanguine a view of contingencies in their favour, speculate improvidently; but their *motive* or *inducement* so to speculate is the opinion which, whether well or ill-founded, or whether upon their own view or upon the authority or example of other persons, they entertain of the probability of an advance of price. It is not the mere facility of borrowing, or the difference between being able to discount at 3 or at 6 per cent, that supplies the *motive* for purchasing, or even for selling. Few persons of the description here mentioned ever speculate but upon the confident expectation of an advance of price of at least 10 per cent; the instances are rare in which an advance to that extent would hold out any inducement to speculate, in the sense of the word here assumed."[2]

If these additional motives are not present "any forced operation of the Bank, with a view to extend its circulation, could have had no effect whatever upon prices."[3] At this point Tooke appeals to the authority of a famous banker, Samuel Gurney, one of the founders of the banking house of that name which collapsed in 1866, "whose experience and knowledge of the money market are certainly not inferior to those of anybody else"; Gurney was of the opinion that an artificial addition to the Bank's circulation would have only this effect, "that the bankers would have more bank-notes than they could use, and would lock them up in their tills; such addition would not come into actual circulation, at least no more than the transactions of London cause a demand for."[4]

Thus a low rate of interest may foster and support a rise which *began from other causes*. "If there exist grounds for speculation in goods, a coincident facility of credit *may*, but will not *necessarily*, extend the range of it."[5] And Tooke adds that a low rate of interest is at the bottom of all cases of "overtrading" and "overbanking."[6]

The events of the last few years and the experiences of open market operations in both England and the United States in the course of the crisis have fully confirmed Tooke's ideas. The sums

[1] Tooke, Vol. II, Appendix A, p. 361.
[2] *Ibid.*, Vol. III, p. 153.
[3] *Ibid.*, p. 156.
[4] *Ibid.*, p. 156.
[5] *Ibid.*, p. 166.
[6] *Ibid.*, Vol. IV, p. 271.

"artificially" put into circulation (that is to say, against the purchase of State bonds) always came back to the banks, until an upward movement brought about by devaluation began to affect prices. Tooke's observation (made not casually or incidentally; it is one to which he frequently returns) was once again verified by experience.

His second observation is no less important: it is that the lowering of the discount rate, although it cannot by itself cause a rise in the price of commodities, can certainly affect *stock exchange prices.* This distinction between the two markets—the market for goods and the market for securities—is of the utmost importance, and was first pointed out by Tooke.

"When the market rate of interest happens to have fallen, if there has not previously been an equivalent rise in the price of government securities, there may be such a rise of the public funds as may have the character of speculation; on such occasions, the anticipation of the prices to which they ought to attain, may be an exaggerated one, but the foundation for the rise would substantially exist in a tendency to an adjustment of the relative value of different securities for investment. On the other hand, a rise in the market rate of interest, more especially if combined with political apprehensions, has a necessary tendency to reduce the prices of all securities, quite independently of any forced contraction of the circulation of the Bank. In truth, 'the putting on of the screw' by the Bank, which is the modern phrase for raising the rate of discount, is nothing more than the Bank's following the rise of the market rate; the main well-founded charge against that establishment having been, not that it raised the rate unnecessarily or too soon, but that it did not follow that rise sufficiently soon, nor with sufficient effect. . . . *But the effects of variations in the circulation and in the rate of interest, on the prices of securities, have no analogy in the markets for commodities.*"[1]

A number of recent illustrations can be given of the difference between the effects of an increase of money on the capital market and on commodity markets respectively. One of the most notable is provided by France in 1926, when the rise of the franc caused a large-scale reflux of capital, followed by the *de facto* stabilisation of the franc. The reflux of French capital and the investment of foreign capital in France assumed enormous proportions. It coincided with a commercial and industrial crisis bound up with the rise of the

[1] Tooke, Vol. III, p. 165.

franc, a crisis which quickly subsided when the franc was stabilised. The vast sums which entered France in 1927 were employed entirely *on the capital market*; there was at that time no rise in the prices of goods. The funds which flowed into France were sent there with the sole object of profiting from the anticipated rise in stock exchange values, which did take place, and from a still more marked rise in the franc which speculators hoped for but which in fact did not take place. The rise in stock exchange values went on for a long time, while commodity prices remained stable.

Tooke's experience enabled him to arrive at conclusions of outstanding value in the interpretation of money market phenomena; unfortunately they were too easily forgotten by those who came after him.

§ v. *Peel's Act of* 1844 *and the Currency and Banking Principles Controversy*

Since Tooke's ideas were undoubtedly correct, and the majority of continental economists supported his views, as well as, in England, such men as John Stuart Mill, how can we explain the success of the Currency School, and the embodiment of their ideas in the Peel Act of 1844? To do so we must take into account the dominating influence of facts and sentiments which count for more in the decisions of statesmen than reasoned arguments.

Peel was up against a problem which disturbed public opinion deeply. One crisis followed another, usually accompanied by an increase in the number of notes in circulation; then, suddenly, certain banks would fail and the bearers of their notes, who quite often had never had any business with the banks, would find their holdings repudiated. Similar events occurred in America, where crises were followed by the failure of innumerable banks. No doubt it might be argued theoretically that current account deposits are the equivalent of bank-notes, that notes always come back to the bank if they are in excess, that the quantity in circulation is therefore subject to automatic regulation, and that notes cannot be thrust on the public. But was it in fact possible to dispute that credit was excessive? Tooke himself had been compelled to admit it. If the conduct of many bankers was beyond reproach, there were nevertheless many others who took advantage of periods of boom to grant credits in too great abundance, to offer their services at very low rates of interest. Competition among banks increased their natural tendency to persuade the public to take up loans. Moreover, the multiplicity of different kinds of bank-notes was a source of embarrassment. To accept a cheque as payment is to display confidence in the payer, whom the payee knows; to accept a note is an act of trust in an unknown bank, whose standing is known only by hearsay. Therefore it was *essential to have only one kind of bank-note*; this idea prevailed against all opposition and ended in the recognition of only one bank of issue.

These, no doubt, were the wholly practical reasons which induced Robert Peel to accept the principles of the Currency School. On this point—when it was merely a question of limiting the private banks' right to issue notes, and of granting the Bank of England a monopoly—there was in fact no divergence between the two schools. Tooke was in favour of note regulation and of Bank of England monopoly. He agreed with those who cried: freedom of banking is freedom of swindling.

Although the idea was never given precise formulation, bank-notes henceforth were regarded as privileged currency instruments; they were there to satisfy *abnormal credit requirements*, to meet exceptional circumstances and to act as a safety-valve in moments of monetary tension. The theoretical identity of credit instruments is one thing; their identity, as a matter of practical functioning, is another. By giving one bank only the right to issue notes, it was given a means of action which other banks did not possess, and also a means of control. The role of "national central bank" which history had gradually conferred on the Bank of England was ratified, and, most important, the currency of the country was unified.

Looking back to-day, it is this aspect of the Peel Act which strikes us as the most important. Later developments in all other advanced countries were to confirm the usefulness of one central bank charged with the privilege of issuing notes. But the dispute between the two schools was concerned not so much with this point (on which, at bottom, they were both agreed) as with the organisation of the Bank of England itself. In regard to organisation, Peel accepted principles which history has shewn to be false, and which Tooke and Fullarton contested with arguments whose validity is no longer disputed.

The Currency School, blindly following the suggestions put forward by Ricardo in 1823, advocated two measures:

1. The division of the Bank of England into two departments, an issue department and a banking department;
2. All note issues to be covered by coin or bullion, with the exception of a small quantity, for which the Bank should hold State bonds.

It was on these two points that the two schools differed. It is precisely these two points that have lost all interest for us to-day. In the first place, eighty years after the Act was passed, both these measures were abandoned in fact if not in law. In addition to its legal balance sheet, the Bank of England has for some years past published a statement similar to those published by all issuing banks, in which the two departments are treated as one. Moreover, new laws put into force since the war give the Bank the right to issue notes without metallic cover in excess of the amount legally laid down whenever the need should arise. The unissued note reserve which the Bank of England uses for granting credits, that is to say its "margin of issue," formerly wholly inelastic, has now become as elastic as that of any other bank.[1]

The Bank of England has thus regained that elasticity of issue which Tooke advocated so warmly. The controversy is ended. Peel's Act is nothing but a memory. To-day it is clear (and many writers said so at the time) that the organisation laid down in the Act was one of the most irrational that has ever been devised: it required all the sound common sense of the English to make it work, all the ability of its governors, and sometimes the co-operation of continental banks. It is unnecessary to discuss the question further; but—for the sake of completeness—it is as well to summarise the ideas which guided the promoters of the Act, in particular Lord Overstone.

Starting out from the erroneous idea that bank-notes are money,

[1] The reader is referred to the series of Acts which have, since the war, changed the legal position of the Bank of England. Here I would refer only to the fact that the Bank is no longer obliged in emergencies to consult the Chancellor of the Exchequer before increasing its note issue, and that the consent of the Treasury is assured in all circumstances.

whereas other credit instruments are not money, and that rises in prices (even when notes are convertible) are the result of an excessive issue of bank-notes (which are mistakenly regarded as paper money), and that, finally, crises are the consequence of excessive issues—all of them ideas which Tooke and Fullarton shewed to be false—Lord Overstone concluded that the way to avoid crises was to *limit the paper in circulation to the amount that a purely metallic currency would have been* (as though crises were avoided in countries with a purely metallic currency). If there is an excessive amount of coin in circulation, gold will leave the country and the exchange rate of the currency will fall. The same symptoms will be manifest with "mixed" currencies, consisting of both coins and bank-notes. (This conception of a "mixed" currency is also absurd since, even in the absence of bank-notes, coin is never the sole circulating medium.) Once these symptoms appear, the number of bank-notes must be reduced. This will be achieved if the quantity of notes is strictly limited and if gold can only be obtained in exchange for bank-notes. To get gold, the public will have to use the notes in circulation, and thus their quantity will be automatically reduced.

This was Lord Overstone's theory. It met with every kind of objection, of which the most important may be summarised as follows: In a country such as England, with a highly developed credit system, the notes which the banks use to obtain gold are *not drawn from the notes in circulation*, but from the re-discounting of their bills at the central bank. The process envisaged by the Currency School, based on the idea of notes coming in from those already in circulation, does not in fact operate. As we shall see in Chapter Nine, Lord Overstone misunderstood the function of a central bank, assumed henceforth by the Bank of England. The only way to reduce the circulation, or rather to *rectify an excess of credit*, is to make credit dearer, that is to say to raise the discount rate.

Tooke maintained that the raising of the discount rate, coupled with a strong cash position, would enable the Bank of England to mitigate the effects of a crisis and to prevent it from developing. Mere limitation of notes will only make the crisis *more acute*, for it is the function of notes to provide additional temporary currency in times of crisis, which will make it possible to avoid bankruptcies and collapses. This concept of the necessity of elasticity in a credit system is one to which Tooke attached great importance. It was to be fully confirmed by the crisis of 1847, when the bank was compelled to ask the Treasury to authorise the issue of notes in excess of the legal maximum. Three years after it was passed, events proved the worthlessness of the Peel Act.

§ VI. *Echoes in France of the Currency and Banking Controversy*

It might seem that the disputes aroused by the Peel Act could find no echo in France, since there were enormous differences between the credit systems of the two countries at the time when the controversy was in full swing.

In England, in addition to the central bank whose notes had been made legal tender in 1833, there were a large number of country banks of issue which had made notes a means of payment in general use, and also commercial banks, gradually becoming more powerful, which were accustoming the public to the use of the cheque;[1] the first of these was the London and Westminster Bank founded by Gilbart in 1833. The country as a whole was "thoroughly banked," as Robert Giffen was to say later. Unity was achieved by all the banks having an office in London, where deposits were kept, while the London banks, thanks to the Clearing House, had reduced cash payments in London to a minimum. Finally, outside the banking world, there was the market represented by the great acceptance houses, which discounted international bills of exchange and made London the recognised centre for international payments and foreign loans.

No such institutions existed in France. Under Louis Phillipe, as under the *ancien régime*, cash payments continued to play the most important part. The amount of coin in circulation was very great, far in excess of that in England. It was composed for the greater part of silver, held by a large number of country landowners with small and middling estates, of artisans, and of small-scale manufacturers, who were accustomed to keep large sums of coin in their own coffers. Balzac, a close observer of his times, describes in one of his novels the notary Crottat, who kept 400,000 francs in his own house, and who was murdered for his money. In the country,

[1] A full description will be found in Fullarton's book.

and in many towns, the notaries were the real purveyors of credit, and their operations were transacted wholly in coin.

The Bank of France and the few country banks alone were empowered to issue notes. At first the Bank had difficulty in discounting in notes. The public demanded coin. Writing to Mollien about the Havre branch, Napoleon insists that bills be discounted in notes. On the other hand, the Bank would only discount bills on Paris, and the country banks would only issue notes against bills drawn on the town where they were established. There were a certain number of bankers in Paris—those who formed the *Haute Banque*—undertaking financial operations, discounting foreign bills, acting as correspondents for provincial discount bodies; but none of them issued notes, and the cheque was still unknown. It was used only by a few very great personages in the financial world. Here, again, we can learn from Balzac. In his *Splendeurs et Misères des Courtisanes*, he describes how the Baron de Nucingen, when threatened by some ruffians, drew from his pocket a booklet from which he withdrew "one of those little slips of stamped paper which the Bank issues to bankers, and on which they have only to write out, in words and figures, the desired sum, to make it an order payable to bearer." He is describing a cheque. The little slip of paper is rejected by the mistrustful villains, who demand notes. In the country, in market towns, discounters would accept bills drawn on different places, giving in exchange either bills drawn on Paris, or notes. But a great part of their operations was transacted in coin.

Far from being plentiful, bank-notes were still very scarce. In 1840 the total number of notes issued by the Bank of France and the country banks did not exceed 250 million, of which 50 million were not covered. Notes were a convenient means of transporting large sums of money, rather than credit instruments.[1] Up to 1840, the lowest denomination of a note was 500 francs; it was then brought down to 200.

The Bank of France was partly responsible for this restricted use of notes. Notes could not be exchanged for coin elsewhere than in Paris. With the exception of some districts, the notes were almost unknown in the provinces. "In France," writes Rossi, "the

[1] In 1846 the Bank printed some 5,000-franc notes for no other purpose but convenience of carriage.

bank-note is unknown in the majority of departments." It was regarded as a bill on Paris and was subject to a discount which at times exceeded the discount on bills because the risk of loss or theft was greater, notes being payable to bearer whereas bills have to be endorsed. To guard against such misfortunes notes were sent in halves.[1] Consequently, in 1839, the Bank decided to issue promissory notes, endorsable and payable within fifteen days.

Bank of France notes were often refused in the provinces, and Courcelle-Seneuil suggested that they should be made legal tender, as had been done for Bank of England notes in 1833.[2]

Besides the Bank, there were some "caisses" (the Bank of France forbade them to use the name of bank) which attempted to put paper into circulation. The best known was the Caisse Lafitte, founded by the famous banker of that name. It issued *interest bearing* short term bills (and also non-interest bearing three months' bills). But the circulation of bills of this kind, despite the advantage in the way of interest, was necessarily restricted, the more so as, like Bank of France notes, they could only be cashed in Paris.[3]

Despite the disjointed character of credit organisation in France, there was an element of unity in the circulation and of centralisation in the money market. That element was provided not by the notes of the Bank of France, but by the *bill on Paris*. As in the eighteenth century, but on a far wider scale, Paris acted as the clearing house for many of the payments that had to be made from one part of France to another, and the bill on Paris was used as the medium. "In our political and financial organisation," wrote Clapier in 1844, "there is a secret force which tends to concentrate the entire currency of France at Paris: almost half of the budget is spent in Paris, the largest fortunes are made and unmade at Paris; the greater part of

[1] Cf. Ramon, *Histoire de la Banque de France*, p. 179.

[2] Cf. Courcelle-Seneuil, *Le Crédit et la Banque*, a pamphlet published in 1840, p. 86. In an anonymous pamphlet published in the same year by Guillaumin entitled *Des Banques en France, Nécessité d'une Enquête avant de renouveler le Privilège de la Banque de France*, we read on p. 55: "With notes which can be cashed only in Paris, which do not bear interest however long they are kept, the difficulties of redemption and the fear of their loss if sent to Paris are so great, that in many places the paper money of the Bank of France is persistently refused and in other places it is accepted only as a sort of commodity for which a purchaser must be found at a reduced price; the loss to the bearer in many departments is as great as 1 per cent."

[3] For the Caisse Lafitte, see Vergeot, *Le Crédit comme Stimulant et régulateur de l'Industrie*, pp. 214 *et seq.*

the commercial transactions of the country are drawn up and settled in bills drawn on Paris."[1]

Gustave d'Eichthal said in the Chamber in 1848:

"It seems that there are in France two distinct and separate beings: Paris, which carries on its special business, and the departments, which carry on theirs. We are always told that if the Bank of France had branches everywhere, it would sacrifice the departments to Paris. Nothing is further from the truth: there is only one body, one body with its limbs: Paris and other towns. Let us see how large-scale banking operations are carried on. How is the cotton bought in the United States for Le Havre paid for? By bills on Paris. How is payment made for the finished cloth sent from Lyon to America? By paper on Paris. What I say of foreign trade is true also of trade between one town and another in France. Paris is a great centre for settling the business of the country; we should organise and extend this great instrument for the greater benefit of all; there is no question of monopoly or despotism; it is a question of having a unified paper circulation, of the greatest possible equality in rates of interest and exchange rates, of cutting down to the minimum the costs of transporting capital from one place to another." [2]

Bills on Paris thus constituted the element of unity in French monetary organisation, and as such bills could be discounted at the Bank of France, it automatically became the central monetary reservoir which could be drawn on in difficult times.[3]

If its function were extended, if the number of its branches were increased, and the public everywhere made familiar with its notes, those notes would supersede the bills of exchange on Paris and become the chief currency instrument and the chief credit instrument in France. Leon Faucher put forward this view with notable lucidity in the same debate:

"Although we have a system which seems to involve the joint existence of a central bank, stretching out towards the different parts of the country, and of country banks, as unconnected as they are uncontrolled, the

[1] Clapier, *Des Banques aux Etats-Unis, en Angleterre et en France*, pamphlet, 1844, p. 49.

[2] Speech in the Chamber of Deputies, February 22, 1848, quoted by Wolowski, p. 496.

[3] An excellent account of the concentration of money at the Bank of France is given in a remarkable article, to which reference has already been made, by M. Gauthier, a vice-governor of the Bank, in the *Encyclopédie du Droit*, 1839, Vol. I, pp. 584 and 601.

existence of monopoly side by side with freedom, in fact things are gradually developing towards the establishment of a single bank. These country banks, which it was hoped to isolate from each other, are coming to find a point of contact in the Bank of France. Instead of confining themselves to discounting bills on the place where they are established, and for which they have the right to issue notes, they have taken to negotiating bills on Paris and have therefore, either directly or indirectly, very close connections with the Bank of France. In 1847 the country banks discounted bills on Paris to the value of 206 millions, that is to say, something like a quarter of their total transactions. When the country banks require coin, they negotiate this paper at the nearest branch of the Bank, or through Paris bankers who themselves get the cash from the great reservoir, the Bank of France, which becomes, especially in moments of stress, the *point d'appui* of the local banks. Thus the country banks become in fact branches of the Bank of France; with this difference, that they give no guarantee either to the Bank or to the public. The Bank of France has no control over their operations; it is compelled for national reasons, and for reasons of public security, so to speak, to come to their assistance when they are in danger, because it knows, as everybody knows, that all credit institutions are intimately connected, and that the failure of one is a danger to all the others. Thus the single bank, *or rather the central bank*, is very nearly a *fait accompli* in France. That should not astonish you, for it is in the nature of things."[1]

In France the question was one not of restricting but ofextending the use of notes, not of curbing credit but of developing it, and the most effective way was to give a wider currency to the notes of the Bank of France, which already enjoyed public confidence.

It was because the Peel Act gave the Bank of England a practical monopoly that the controversy between the Currency and Banking Schools interested France, and not because the same Act imposed limitations on the Bank. Books on banking written in France at that time should be read with this in mind.

The Saint-Simonian group was of course the first to put forward the ideas which, developed during the course of the century, were to have such a strong influence on the economic organisation of the country. Such of their ideas as related to the provision of long-term capital are so well known that they need no elaboration here. They were put into effect in the building of the railways and later

[1] Speech in the Chamber of Deputies, February 21, 1848, quoted by Wolowski, p. 482.

in the *Crédit Mobilier* established by the Péreires, and became universally known. But the Saint-Simonians were also interested in short-term credit and put forward an original idea about ank-notes. It was worked out by Enfantin, but it did not meet with success in practice, and it must be confessed that on this question the Saint-Simonians shewed less insight than on a number of others. Enfantin starts from the idea (held by Mollien) that notes payable on sight are analogous to bills of exchange. But for the bearer, as for the bank which issues it, the note holds a danger, since it is never fully covered in the cash reserves of the bank. This explains rises in the rate of discount, by which the bank tries to protect its cash reserves, and which are, he considers, the origin of commercial and industrial crises. This mechanism should be changed. "When the Bank discounts bills it should give in exchange, not notes payable at sight, but notes payable *on the same date as the bills* and bearing interest at a lower rate than the discount rate. Thus the dates of repayment will always coincide with the dates when it collects money, and it will be freed from worry about the relation between the number of its notes in circulation and its metal reserves, a relation which at present is constantly fluctuating. It might be feared that giving the notes a fixed date for maturity would injuriously affect their ease of circulation, but that would be countered by making them interest bearing. The adoption of this device would put an end to those sudden rises in the rate of interest, and those sudden restrictions in discounting, and consequently to the economic disorders which arise from the faulty constitution of present day banks."[1]

This is in fact the idea underlying the notes issued by the Caisse Lafitte, which can scarcely be said to have been successful. The same type of note was issued later by the *Crédit Mobilier*, but only in small quantities.[2]

There is not a great deal of difference between these notes and current accounts drawn on by cheque; but the difference is great enough to make their extension difficult. The first bearer of the note, who is also the person seeking credit, proves his adherence to the system by the very fact that he accepts the note; on the other

[1] Quoted by J.-B. Vergeot, *Le Crédit comme Stimulant et Régulateur de l'Industrie*, Paris, 1918, p. 104. This excellent book is a history of Saint-Simonian ideas concerning credit.

[2] Vergeot, p. 158.

hand, those to whom it is subsequently offered in payment usually prefer a currency that is *immediately available, and immediately convertible* into coin, such as notes payable on demand or cheques. The circulation of maturities is therefore limited (despite the attraction of interest) to a much narrower circle than notes payable at sight.

The Saint-Simonians did not realise that to issue notes is merely to put into circulation *existing funds*, and that it provides the means of substituting ready money for money due at a future date. Notes are undoubtedly bills, but bills *at sight*, and it is this that gives them their ease of circulation.

Enfantin's conception of the bank-note is derived from his conception of long-term credit. Just as railway bonds, redeemable at the termination of the concession, are issued to raise the capital required for their construction, so interest-bearing bank-notes are issued against commercial bills and mature at the same time as the bills. Bank-notes are a kind of short-term bond issued by the bank to the public with the object of raising the funds required to finance the bills. In both cases the public bring out their savings. The truth of the matter, however, as we see it, is that notes represent the money which the banks put into circulation, and which is constantly re-deposited at the bank. Enfantin also applied his argument to current accounts which he thought should bear interest "on condition that the sums deposited are withdrawn not less than three, or perhaps six months after the date of deposit."[1] The same suggestion was made, in practically identical terms, by Walras in 1885.[2]

After the decline of the Saint-Simonian school no important ideas in regard to banking were put forward in France until the question of the renewal of the Bank of France's charter came up for discussion in 1840. Then articles and pamphlets were numerous and shew a striking similarity to the speeches in the House of Commons and the House of Lords.[3]

[1] Article on *Discount Banks* in the *Producteur* of 1828.

[2] "Deeds of ownership of circulating capital should not be used for money; they should be kept by the capitalists who create savings, like deeds of ownership of fixed capital. Discounts should be made by means of three months' interest-bearing deposits placed in the bank." Walras, *Etudes d'Economie appliquée*, 1936 edition, p. 4.

[3] It is unfortunate that M. Ramon's book on the Bank of France, in general well documented, does not deal with these extremely interesting writings, which are as a rule strongly critical of Bank of France policy. In addition to the writers

All are agreed on one point, the inadequacy of credit in France and the necessity of developing the credit system. This inadequacy was attributed to circumstances but also to the policy of the Bank, which came in for fairly severe criticism. "It is difficult," writes in 1844 Courcelle-Seneuil, who to the end of his life retained a bad opinion of the Bank, "to imagine the terror which it inspires in the commercial world. This terror stifles requests and even complaints, as those who wished to obtain information about the Bank have reason to know." He objects to the stipulation of a third signatory, because it necessitates "the assistance of a highly paid intermediary." But his chief complaint is that, except in the chief towns and the large commercial houses, credit is practically unknown; other producers can get it only at an exorbitant price.[1] In his speech in the Upper Chamber Rossi expressed the same opinion:

> "Instead of regarding credit paper with the utmost confidence, France displays a somewhat excessive distrust. . . . We should reassure and encourage, rather than frighten and restrain. For that we must have a system of guarantees that will set at rest the minds of even the most cautious; the reassuring example of what happens now should help us to catch a glimpse of the progress which may perhaps one day be made."[2]

There was complete agreement that credit had to be extended and not restricted; differences arose only as to the methods to be employed. Across the Channel the debates between the Currency and Banking Schools bear a wholly different aspect. There was one point on which Tooke and Overstone were in complete agreement, the necessity of regulating banks of issue. Neither of the two parties (in this they were following Adam Smith) advocated complete liberty of action. The advisability of a Bank of England monopoly was challenged by nobody.

mentioned in the text and in footnotes, and to the well-known speakers who took part in the notable parliamentary debates from 1840 to 1848 (their speeches are reproduced in Wolowski's book), there were less well-known writers such as d'Esterno (*Des Banques Départementales*), Courtet de l'Isle (*Du Crédit en France*), Louis de Noiron (*Des Banques en France*) and others whose pamphlets give an extremely interesting picture of the credit system functioning in France at that time. Above all, there was Gauthier, whose article on the Bank of France in the *Encyclopédie du Droit*, 1839, gives the most comprehensive and most intelligent account of the Bank at that time.

[1] Courcelle-Seneuil, *op. cit.*, p. 68.

[2] Quoted by Wolowski, p. 190.

In France the liberal school, with the dogmatism by which it has always been characterised, and whose chief representatives were Chevalier and Courcelle-Seneuil, transferred the argument to a new field: freedom for the banks, or monopoly for the Bank of France? The dispute had no real practical interest, for in fact the provincial banks of issue played a very minor part and could not have carried on without the support of the Bank of France. The parliamentary debates of 1848 shew that they were really branches of the Bank of France, which supplied them with gold when they required it. In the course of the dispute, Tooke's position was completely distorted, for he had advocated *elasticity of issue*, not *competition among banks of issue.*[1]

Those who advocated a monopoly for the Bank of France eagerly seized the opportunity. They demanded that monopoly in the name of the Currency Principle. They accepted the erroneous idea (with some slight modifications, as shewn in Rossi) that the right to issue notes was the same as the right to mint money, and proposed that that right should be conferred on one institution under state control. They expected that the grant of this privilege would lead to a wider use of notes. In France there was still a deep-rooted distrust of *assignats*, and if bank-notes were to be accepted freely, they must be hedged around with such guarantees of security and inspire such confidence that even the most timid would not refuse to accept them in payment. There had to be *one kind of note only*, and therefore a monopoly was essential. They could be issued only by one bank, and that bank must enjoy such unquestioned prestige, and such a standing, that it would seem ridiculous to reject its notes.

In this controversy, which was ended by the 1848 revolution but was resumed in 1863 in regard to the Bank of Savoy, Michel Chevalier took on himself the defence of liberty and was supported by Courcelle-Seneuil and Courtois. On the other side were Rossi, Wolowski and d'Eichthal, vigorous advocates of monopoly. One side used the argument that the Scotch banks were successful; the other side pointed to the failure of the American banks.

[1] Wolowski says on p. 324: "Failing to distinguish between the principle of the free expansion of the note issue in accordance with trade requirements, and the principle of free competition in the issuing of notes, those who invoked the authority of Tooke in favour of the latter course were singularly mistaken."

From the Currency School the advocates of monopoly borrowed the idea of a clear-cut distinction between the function of issuing notes fulfilled by "currency banks" and the function of discounting, or commercial function which they thought should remain free, because it does not concern the general public as a whole.[1] This controversy was the origin of the hard and fast distinction drawn by the majority of French economists, and by almost all business men, between bank-notes and cheques, notwithstanding all the decisive arguments brought forward by Tooke and Fullarton.

It should be noted that curiously enough they never demanded limitation of the Bank of France's *issues*. The Bank was organised on the purest "banking principle," since there was no minimum fixed for its cash reserves, no minimum laid down for the proportion between cash holdings and note issue, no maximum set to the number of notes that might be issued. It was to enjoy complete liberty of action, and had only to concern itself with the needs of commerce and the monetary situation at any given time.[2]

Thus, in the midst of these purely theoretical controversies, France organised a banking system very different from the English—or rather similar to the English as it was in the eighteenth century when it first came into existence: a central bank quite free to issue notes and provided with strong cash reserves, with local banks closely bound to the capital by their holdings of bills on Paris, obtaining gold by means of these bills from the branches of the central bank. As to a market for international bills, it existed in Paris, but was quite small. A small number of private houses of the highest standing dealt in these bills—they were known as *hors banque*, because the discount rate was lower than the Bank of France rate—which represented a reserve of foreign gold that was readily available, since most were drawn on London, and facilitated payment for French imports.

[1] "To separate issuing from discounting, and to subject it to strict regulations... while leaving discounting entirely free—this was the starting point of the proposed reforms, which differentiated between what is, for a currency ban , essentially the exercise of a kind of public function, and those functions which concern private affairs. This was the fundamental idea underlying the Peel Act of 1844." Wolowski *Banques*, p. 232. The reader will remember that this was the basic idea in the plan which Ricardo drew up in 1823.

[2] It was only after 1871 that a maximum limit was fixed for the Bank's note issue, but this limit was always changed by Parliament at the request of the Bank, whenever the need arose.

CHAPTER SIX

Gold Output and Price Movements 1850—1936

§ I. INFLUX OF GOLD FROM CALIFORNIA AND AUSTRALIA AND THE WORLD RISE IN PRICES AFTER 1851.—§ II. QUANTITATIVE AND ANTI-QUANTITATIVE EXPLANATIONS OF THE 1873–1895 DEPRESSION.—§ III. ECONOMIC PROSPERITY FROM 1895–1914 AND THE TRANSVAAL GOLD MINES.—§ IV. THE QUANTITY THEORY AFTER THE WAR.

For some time after the passing of the Peel Act there were no major controversies about credit. All the arguments on both sides had been exhausted, and the whole subject was dropped in weariness. Twenty-five years later Bagehot was to open his book on *Lombard Street* with an assurance to his readers that he did not intend to converse on a subject of which he knew they were tired. But a different problem was to arise which had, as it were, lain dormant since the beginning of the nineteenth century, the problem of the action of the precious metals on prices. Unanimity on the question had been reached in the eighteenth century, but the discovery of gold in California, the demonetisation of silver, and the exploitation of the Transvaal gold mines, gave it a new urgency; the unanimity of eighteenth-century writers was replaced by differences of opinion which are still in evidence to-day. This problem will be dealt with in the present and the following chapters.

In the second half of the nineteenth century, and the first third of the twentieth, large-scale price movements were of frequent occurrence: the rise in prices from 1851 to 1871, the steep fall from 1873 to 1895, the equally pronounced rise from 1895 to 1914; then, once the gold standard was re-established in a large number of countries after the war, the slow fall, beginning in 1925, accelerated in 1929 and ending in the catastrophic crisis of 1929 to 1935. Each of these periods coincided with important changes in the output of the precious metals or of money tokens. The question of the extent to which these changes were bound up with the price movements gave rise to the most heated arguments. There was almost complete agreement as to the reason for the rise that took place between 1851 and 1871. On the other hand the fall between 1873 and 1895 gave rise to a number of new theories which completely contradicted previous explanations, and have had a remarkable influence on the controversies concerning the present world crisis.

An enumeration and brief examination of these theories is therefore of direct interest in any diagnosis of the present crisis and the most recent controversies. We shall not again discuss, in its broad outlines, the so-called quantity theory; in its most extreme form, it is quite different from theories about the action of the precious metals on prices;[1] we intend merely to review the explanations offered, firstly of the rise or fall of prices at these different periods, secondly of the relation between these movements and changes in the output or the utilisation of the precious metals.

§ 1. *Influx of Gold from California and Australia and the World Rise in Prices after* 1851

In 1848, when the discovery of gold in California opened a new period in monetary history, the quantity theory as formulated by Ricardo had suffered a setback.

Ricardo's theory is so narrow and exclusive that it has little in common with the far more flexible and discriminating theories of the eighteenth century, of Henry Thornton at the beginning of the nineteenth, and of Tooke and his school between 1820 and 1847. It can be summarised as follows: Forced paper currency and metallic money have exactly the same economic effects; their quantity determines the price level, and changes in that level have little or no bearing on economic prosperity or depression; forced paper currency and convertible bank-notes are subject to the same laws; they are both supplementary currency added to metallic money, and can replace the latter; the value of bank-notes is

[1] Even such writers as Benjamin Anderson, who are strongly opposed to the "quantity theory" as enunciated by Ricardo or Irving Fisher, admit as self-evident that an increase in the production of the money metal must result in a fall in its purchasing power.

maintained not by convertibility, but by the limitation of their number; a deficiency in the quantity of money can be compensated by an increase in its rapidity of circulation; when the quantity of money declines, its velocity of circulation grows, and conversely.

These simple formulas, nearly all of which were in the course of the century to be disproved by facts, were never accepted by all economists. From the very beginning they found powerful opponents in England, and on the Continent they were adopted only with reserve. In 1847 they sustained a great setback. The Peel Act of 1844, based on the principles of the Currency School, which were inspired by Ricardian theories, broke down in the 1847 crisis and had to be suspended. All the warnings uttered by Tooke and his followers were borne out by events, and the authority of the Ricardian formulas in regard to bank credit suffered a serious blow.

The discovery of new goldfields was to provide a further opportunity of verifying their validity, this time in regard not to bank money, but to metallic money.

The Ricardian theory was not completely discredited until the price fall of 1873–1895. Then the reaction from it was so violent that many writers went so far as to deny that the price level can be influenced in any way by an abundance or scarcity of gold, although this was a fact which Tooke and other opponents of Ricardo had never dreamed of disputing. But, before that happened, the discovery of gold in California and Australia was to provide an opportunity for questioning another part of his doctrine, the denial that an influx of gold and the consequent rise in prices can have any bearing on economic activity and *prosperity*. Ricardo considered that such a rise was a purely transitory phenomenon that would pass and leave the national economy in the same state as before. His opinion was warmly disputed by Newmarch, Levasseur and Chevalier in the period which opened with the discovery of the new goldfields in 1848 and 1850.

For, from 1850 onwards, under the influence of a large influx of gold, the poverty and distress of deflation suddenly gave place to a general feeling of security and well-being, and to an upward movement in English and European economic affairs. These events elicited various responses from the economists. Some, such as Austin (quoted by Levasseur), merely repeated the old Ricardian doctrine that "the country which buys gold gains nothing and loses all." Others, mentioned by Newmarch (there is no point in enumerating their names; in themselves they are completely forgotten, and survive only in the criticisms of their opponents), maintained that "it is a gross error to suppose that the New Supplies of Gold have made any addition to the Real Wealth of the world; or have been productive of any clear and important benefit to this country."[1]

They were behind the times. The effects of the influx of new gold were too striking, and the resulting prosperity too universal to admit of an instant's doubt, except among those whose minds were already irrevocably made up. Nobody could remain blind to the progress of international trade, which reached an hitherto unknown magnitude, to the general increase in wealth that accompanied the rise in prices not only in the countries producing gold, but in all countries engaged in trade, to the improved position of state finances, and the stronger position of banks. It was not long before unanimity reigned as to the part played in this advance by the discovery of Californian and Australian gold; the gold rush excited the interest and curiosity of the whole world.

In France Levasseur in his *Question de l'Or* (1858), and Michel Chevalier, in his *La Monnaie*, noted the facts of increasing prosperity and a simultaneous price rise. Levasseur used the facts as a basis for once more formulating the quantity theory; his version might be termed moderate, for while recognising the action of gold on prices, he points out that in fact the rise in prices is not proportionate to the increase in gold, for this effect is partly offset by an increased production of goods. Chevalier points out the "fall in the value of gold" and in 1859 devoted an entire book to the question. He gives a clear account of its consequences for California; "for mankind as a whole the significance of this event is incalculable."[2]

But the writer who most deserves attention is Newmarch, for his opinion came to be accepted as giving the correct interpretation of the facts. Although he is faithful to the tradition of Tooke (to

[1] Newmarch, *History of Prices*, Vol. VI, pp. 213 and 198.

[2] *La Monnaie*, p. 476. This book, published at Brussels by Méline, Cans et Cie, reproduces the lectures given by Chevalier in the 'fifties; he proposes that if the use of gold for payments is to be continued, "its value, which is now falling, should be fixed each year, by the legislative body, according to the comparative rates of the two precious metals on the principal markets of the world" (p. 474). This is a plea for a return to silver monometallism.

whose position he succeeded when he edited the *History of Prices*), continuing to deny the direct action of gold on prices[1] and to reject what he calls "the abstract argument" (that is, the argument that prices will rise in *proportion* to the increase in gold output),[2] he is constantly referring to the beneficial effects ef the new gold discoveries and the increase in *income* of which they were the cause.[3]

There is, it is true, a certain vacillation in Newmarch's ideas. Must not an increase in income send prices up? On the other hand, was it possible to maintain that the price level had hardly risen between 1851 and 1857, when a study of the index numbers of the period, as well as the facts ascertained by Levasseur and later by

[1] "That as far as can be ascertained by a careful examination of the course of Prices in this country as regards a considerable number of leading commodities, it does not appear that the Prices prevailing in the early part of 1857, when compared with the Prices prevailing in 1851, justify the inference that, in any manifest or appreciable degree, the increase in the quantity of Metallic Money, by means of the New Gold, has raised the Price of Commodities;—in other words, in every instance of a variation in Price, a full explanation of the charge is apparently afforded by circumstances affecting the Supply or the Demand." Tooke and Newmarch, *op. cit.*, Vol. VI, p. 232.

[2] "The abstract argument assumes that the quantity of money being doubled, prices will be doubled; alluding in the faintest manner, if at all, to the length of the interval which will elapse, and to the magnitude of the changes which will take place in connection with the process.

"But it is precisely these omitted elements which constitute the essence of the question.

"The theory supposes, in effect, that the doubling of the quantity of money leads hastily to the doubling of the prices of all commodities; and that hence the only consequences which flow from the augmentation of the money, are the inconvenience of having to count two coins instead of one; and the disappearance as regards the recipients of fixed incomes of one half of their means of subsistence.

"But it is not true that the effect of even a largely increased quantity of metallic money in raising prices is a hasty process; nor is it true, that, according to the facts of the last three hundred and sixty years, a doubling of the quantity of metallic money has led either hastily or ultimately to a doubling of prices; nor, further, is it true, that the circumstances connected with the diffusion of the larger quantity of metallic money are so purely collateral that they may be left out of view. On the contrary, we have already found, and we shall find still more, that by the process of the Diffusion there are brought into operation causes which go very far to invalidate the *a priori* inferences adopted on abstract grounds." *Ibid.*, Vol. VI, pp. 194–195.

[3] "That the whole process of the Distribution of the New Gold, in the first instance among the Labourers and Capitalists of the Gold Countries,—and in the second instance, among the Capitalists and Labourers of this and other countries,—resolves itself into a Demand for more Labour; and through the Demand for more Labour into a gradual rise of all classes of Incomes." *Ibid.*, Vol. VI, p. 234.

Jevons,[1] proved the contrary, and Newmarch himself admitted that the price of raw materials and metals had risen, and wages and profits still more?

With this reservation,[2] Newmarch's account of the discovery of gold in California and Australia, and of the effects of its greater output, remains a model of economic observation and analysis. Even after this lapse of time it has lost none of its freshness.

Newmarch is concerned first of all to emphasise the powerful and beneficial effect of an influx of gold on the wealth and prosperity of nations:

> "The Influence of the New Supplies of Gold, year by year, has been probably that particular Cause, or train of Causes, which has modified, in the most powerful degree, the Economical and Commercial History of the last Nine Years." [3]

He considers that an increase of gold plays the same part as the construction of better and wider roads:

> "An inadequate Stock of Money produces evils very similar in their nature to the impediments, the accidents, the disappointments, and the suffering, material and moral, occasioned by the pressure of a large and swelling traffic within the limits of a narrow, irregular, and unsound Road. And still greater are the evils, when the Road is not only inadequate in width, but insufficient in length; when it is not only incapable of bearing all the traffic, but also incapable of carrying it more than half way to its destination." [4]

[1] "I was so much struck with the enormous and almost general rise of prices about 1853, that I was led to suspect an alteration of the standard of value." W. S. Jevons, *A Serious Fall in the Value of Gold Ascertained*, in *Investigations in Currency and Finances*, London, 1863, Preface, p. 1.

[2] It is easier to understand Newmarch's insistence on this point if it is remembered that, according to Ricardo and his followers, the effect of an excessive quantity of gold on prices is realised in two stages: firstly, by the depreciation of the gold, secondly, by the rise in prices. Nobody has ever been able to understand how gold depreciation can *precede* the price rise. The depreciation in the value of gold and the rise in prices are one and the same phenomenon. Newmarch apparently was bent on discrediting this idea of a direct and previous depreciation of the metallic currency. Ricardo's standpoint can perhaps be explained by reference to the similarity which he always maintains exists between paper and metal. Paper money depreciates in relation to metal, and this direct depreciation is due wholly to its excessive quantity. Gold undergoes a similar process, for more of it has to be offered to obtain the same quantity of goods.

[3] This refers to the period 1848–1857. (Tooke and Newmarch, *op. cit.*, Vol. VI, p. 135.)

[4] *Ibid.*, Vol. VI, p. 216

Once more Tooke's followers contest the view, so deeply rooted in English economic theory, that the welfare and economic activity of a country are not affected by the quantity of money; they are referring, it should be noted, to countries with *metallic currency*:

"Within the Gold Countries the effects of the Discoveries have been to create rapidly and largely accumulations of Real Wealth and real resources. The adult population of those countries has been increased three- or four-fold within as many years. The erection of houses; the cultivation of the soil; the reclamation of waste lands; the construction of railways; the embellishment of towns; the provision of harbours and docks; the foundation of schools and universities; and, more conspicuous than all, the establishment, almost at a single stride, of an enormous Foreign Trade;—in a few words, the vigorous prosecution of every enterprise, and the swift advancement of every art which can render a country opulent and powerful, are results which have been nearly all accomplished in the Gold Countries, by the exportation to other countries, year by year, of their supplies of New Gold.

Within those other countries to which the Gold has been sent in exchange for commodities the continuous effective demand for commodities has produced the same effects, but in a limited degree, which have taken place in Australia and California. In the United Kingdom, for example, the continuance, year by year, of an effective demand for commodities has led to improvements and extensions in the means of production,—has led to accumulations of capital, as savings out of the large incomes of capitalists and labourers,—and has diminished within the country the pressure of unemployed and destitute persons."[1]

Newmarch is careful to point out, and it is of the utmost importance, that these beneficial effects flow *only from an increase in gold.* Similar results cannot be expected, for example, from an increase in paper money:

"It also seems to be forgotten that between brisk and constant markets, arising out of the Influx of New Gold; and enlarged demand, in any particular country, arising out of any devices of compulsory Paper Money; there is scarcely a quality in common. The compulsory Paper Money has no intrinsic value; and the point is presently reached when the contracted area within which alone it can circulate, renders every emission at once operative on prices to the full extent of its amount in

[1] Tooke and Newmarch, *op. cit.*, Vol. VI, pp. 192–193.

mere quantity. . . . Gold and Silver, on the other hand, are objects of universal desire; and constitute the circulating medium of all nations. The enlarged demand, therefore, which they occasion, is diffused over a circle which becomes wider every day; and is sustained by causes which are continually extending into new regions the advantages at first confined to a single spot."[1]

The friend and successor of Tooke, who had, in opposition to Ricardo, insisted with so much energy and good sense on the fundamental difference between inconvertible paper money and convertible paper credit, continues the battle by insisting with equally well-founded energy on the difference between the effects of an increase in gold and the effects of an increase in the quantity of paper money; Ricardo and his school had maintained that they were identical.[2]

"In a few words, therefore," writes Newmarch, "it is the prodigious impulse imparted to production during the considerable interval which must elapse before additions to the quantity of Money can be neutralised by corresponding additions to the range of Prices; which have rendered, and will continue to render, the New Supplies of Gold a powerful means by which the real and solid wealth of the world will be increased."[3] David Hume had said the same thing, though considerably better, about gold from America.

This was written on the eve of the crisis of 1857 which was for a time to interrupt (and very harshly) the extraordinary prosperity that followed on the discovery of new gold; it has lost nothing of its validity. The events of the period from 1895 to 1914 provided a striking confirmation of its truth.

The coincidence of a gold influx with economic prosperity and with the price rise which began after 1850 has not been denied, and it greatly impressed the economists, who interpreted the phenomena as cause and effect. Marshall—and his opinion cannot be neglected—saw in it nothing but coincidence. In his evidence before the Gold and Silver Commission of 1887 he recalled the

[1] Tooke and Newmarch, *op. cit.*, Vol. VI, p. 218.

[2] It is true that Ricardo realised the *different extent* of the market for gold and the market for paper money, and grasped the international character of the first and the purely national character of the second; but that—though it is in truth big enough—was the only difference he recognised in the two currency instruments.

[3] Tooke and Newmarch, *op. cit.*, Vol. VI, p. 217.

events of that time and, while admitting the simultaneity of the phenomena, made a curious distinction between the two chief effects of the influx of gold from Australia—the rise in prices and economic prosperity. The first he attributed to the new gold that had come into world circulation, but he maintained that the second was due to the introduction of free trade in England after 1851. His interpretation does no doubt appeal with particular force to Englishmen, but "continentals" may be forgiven their stubborn scepticism. For the prosperity of the years 1850 to 1873 was very widespread; it was enjoyed by the Continent as well as by England, and the decade 1851 to 1860 was, for all countries, a period of vigorous activity in all branches of production. Free trade, on the other hand, was until 1860 an almost exclusively English practice, that did not spread to the Continent until the following decade. It would seem to follow that the progress made in that period was due chiefly to gold, although the effect of a steadily widening British market on European economy is not thereby denied.[1]

Marshall's opinion is given not merely as a curiosity, but as one more illustration of the difficulty of *isolating* causes and effects in economic affairs. That opinion was not shared by others. If it diverges from Newmarch in regard to the effect of an influx of gold on economic prosperity, it does shew how general was the agreement as to the effect of such an influx on price movements. The quantity theory, not in its Ricardian, but in its broadest and most classical form, seemed to have been decisively confirmed by fact. It was only in the subsequent period of depression—between 1873 and 1895—that serious differences of opinion were expressed by economists; some of them went so far as to deny (not as a matter of theory, but in practice and in the interpretation of the concrete facts which they observed) any causal relation between the two phenomena.

[1] Sir David Barbour put the following question to Marshall: "But do you think that the rise of prices which took place from 1848 or 1850 up to 1873 was due to free trade?" to which Marshall replied: "I think that was due chiefly to the influx of gold and to the development of the banking system. It was the increase of prosperity that I ascribed to free trade." Barbour: "And if that increase in gold had not taken place prices would have fallen very much probably?" Marshall: "That is my opinion." Alfred Marshall, *Official Papers*, p. 58.

§ II. *Quantitative and Anti-quantitative Explanations of the Depression of* 1873–1895

The period of general prosperity inaugurated in 1851 was followed after the Franco-Prussian War and the crisis of 1873, by a long period of depression in Europe and over a great part of the world; with a few brief respites, it lasted until 1895.

The period opens with the adoption of the gold standard by the new German Reich, a step which was soon followed by the Scandinavian countries. A few years later the countries in the Latin Union closed down the Mints which had undertaken the free coinage of silver, and in 1893 the silver mints of India were closed. In 1873 the United States, which was still using the forced currency of the Civil War, adopted the gold standard as the basis of its prospective currency when payment in specie was to be resumed in 1878. After an unsuccessful attempt in 1871, Japan adopted the gold standard in 1897. Thus, in the space of 25 years, the Continent of Europe moved towards the general adoption of the gold standard, the United States returned to it after an interval of paper money, and Asia began to take the same road. As a money metal, silver was steadily losing ground.

In the course of this period the yearly output of gold fell below its former level, the annual increase representing a steadily decreasing proportion of the total stock. It was therefore natural to ask whether the general abandonment of the free coinage of silver, and the almost exclusive use of gold as the money metal were not—since agricultural and industrial production was increasing steadily, fostered by a long period of peace—in large measure responsible for the prolonged fall in prices and the economic depression.

The old controversy was once more resumed. Unfortunately, it cropped up in circumstances that were *peculiarly unfavourable to a scientific consideration of facts*, for it was dominated by a practical problem of currency organisation: was it desirable, or not, to retain bimetallism where it was still in existence? Was it desirable, or not, to adopt the gold standard everywhere?

The dispute was particularly sharp in countries such as France, which—if bimetallism were maintained—was in danger of losing the stock of gold that it had accumulated as the result of a legal price favourable to its import; if the rate were to become unfavourable, that stock—following Gresham's law—would be lost. What was at stake in this controversy was the retention or loss of a metal which *had become the money standard of the chief commercial countries* (England, the United States, Germany), countries which accounted for the most important part of the foreign trade and capital transactions of France and the Latin Union. All business men, all those who considered that the maintenance at Paris of a financial and money market capable of competing with the chief financial centres of the world, was a matter of primary economic necessity, were in favour of the gold standard, or rather of the limping double standard, under which there would be a limited minting of silver coin. Those, on the other hand, who regarded the steady fall in prices as the chief evil, and who were concerned chiefly with the bad state of agriculture and industry, were in favour of bi-metallism.

The dispute broke out before 1873: it began in the preceding decade, when the change in the relative prices of gold and silver favoured the import of the latter metal. Here we shall deal only with the arguments relating to the influence of the production of the precious metals on prices, leaving aside the arguments for or against the retention of the *loi de Germinal*, and the more abstract arguments concerning the nature of the money standard, although they occupied an important place in the controversy. Nor shall we attempt to enumerate the names of all who took part in it, for such a list would include not only French, Belgian, German, American, Swiss and Dutch economists, all of whom voiced their opinion on the question (de Laveleye in Belgium, Soetbeer and Bamberger in Germany, Walras in France, Marshall in England), but also the official representatives of the countries in the Latin Union at the conferences of that body, the witnesses who gave evidence before the English Gold and Silver Commission of 1887,[1] and the speakers who, in Parliament and at the meetings of Parliamentary Commissions, debated this question. The amount written about

[1] The Report of this Commission has recently been republished by the Columbia University Press (New York, 1936) under the title: *The Monetary Problem: Gold and Silver Commission*. The 1887 Commission had been preceded in 1886 by a Royal Commission on the Depression of Trade and Industry, which had also gone thoroughly into currency questions.

currency questions during the last thirty years of the nineteenth century is scarcely less vast than the post-war literature on monetary problems. It is to be hoped that one day a writer with the requisite learning and industry will extract what is useful in it.[1]

As to the problem with which alone we are here concerned—the relation between the output of the metals and the price level—we shall give the views of the most important writers, and not burden the argument with the manifold variations of these views as given by economists of lesser stature.

The bimetallists were in no doubt as to the effect on prices of a scarcity or plenty of the precious metals; they remained undeviatingly faithful to traditional doctrines. The abandonment of silver, and the limitation of free coinage to gold alone, were bound to bring about a fall in world prices. Wolowski made the point again and again between 1865 and 1870, particularly in his book *L'Or et l'Argent* which gives, alongside its brilliant argumentation, a comprehensive summary of all the major ideas of the bimetallist group.[2] He was in fact its real leader. He had translated Nicolas

[1] A lively summary of these controversies is to be found in M. Gonnard's *Histoire des Doctrines monétaires*, the second volume of which has just appeared.

[2] The group included Courcelle-Seneuil, Cernuschi, de Lavergne, A. Allard, and E. Théry in France; Rau, Prince-Smith, and Max Wirth in Germany; de Laveleye, the Belgian, was converted from the gold standard to the "double standard." In England Stanley Jevons admitted that in theory Wolowski was right, but in practice he was inclined to favour gold alone: "Although I am far from being certain on this point, I admit that *in theory*, you and the other advocates of what might be called the *alternative money standard*, are right. But from a *practical* point of view the problem takes on a different aspect, and I am inclined to hope for the extension of the gold standard." These words are addressed to Wolowski (cf. *L'Or et l'Argent*, p. 64); Jevons believed—and events justified the belief—that the output of gold would increase. Chevalier, who had advocated silver monometallism from 1850, went over to the advocacy of gold monometallism in 1867; he was constant only in his support of monometallism and in the dogmatism of the arguments which he applied to each variety in turn. Among the partisans of bi-metallism in France mention should be made of M. Rouland, Governor of the Bank of France, who was supported by many of his colleagues, including Alphonse de Rothschild, and by a number of bankers including Adolphe d'Eichthal. In this, as in all currency crises, the Bank of France was concerned to defend the *status quo*. Having defended bimetallism, it became the defender of the limping double standard when that was made the legal standard; after the war, and up to 1926, it advocated the revalorisation of the franc at the pre-war parity, just as, in 1935, it favoured the retention of the Poincaré franc. Its attitude in this respect is similar to that always adopted by banks of issue in similar circumstances. They have always left to the government the initiative in and responsibility for changes in the currency system.

Oresme's and Copernicus' treatises on money, and considered himself the heir to the doctrine of the seventeenth and eighteenth centuries;[1] drawing the logical conclusions from that doctrine, he constructed a clear picture of the probable course of events if silver were abandoned.

"The role of money in trade," he writes,[2] "dominates everything; what we must avoid is *price* changes. . . . The total stock of gold and silver held by civilised countries to-day is estimated at fifty odd milliards, each metal accounting for roughly one half. Assume that one of these two is *demonetised*, involving the light-hearted renunciation of half the hard cash used in effecting transactions; the inevitable result would be an alarming rise in the value of the favoured metal, which would henceforth alone be accepted in settlement of debts; I use the word *alarming* for, at whatever rate it was valued, that rate would represent a new burden on debtors. All long-term contracts—rents, mortgages, loans, leases, etc.—would be affected. The law, whose duty it is in case of doubt to ease the position of the *debtor*, would aggravate it.

"All states have large public debts; the burden of that debt would become heavier, to the detriment of all tax-payers and the exclusive benefit of rentiers. At a time when Italy, the United States, Austria, are hoping to emerge from a paper-money regime and to return to the *terra firma* of a metallic currency,[3] the abandonment of silver as a money metal is being advocated. *Have those who favour such a course calculated the outcome of a greater demand for metal currency coinciding with the arbitrary disappearance of the raw material of which that currency is made?*[4]

"The re-establishment of a metal currency in these vast countries with a population of more than one hundred and sixty millions will absorb a great deal of gold and silver. A worse moment for advocating the demonetisation of silver could not have been chosen." [5]

Nobody will deny that the depression of 1873–1895 fully justified these forebodings (and economic prophecies are so seldom

[1] Cf. his evidence before the 1870 Inquiry, published as an Appendix to *L'Or et L'Argent*, where his argument runs on the purest classical lines. He foretold the fall in land values which did occur in the following years; it is true that one of his opponents, M. de Parieu, was equally correct in prophesying that if Germany adopted the gold standard before France, France would be flooded with German silver. This did in fact happen, and it was this which led to the abandonment of the free coinage of silver in France.

[2] Wolowski, p. 386.

[3] "We all belong to the metallic school," says Wolowski on many occasions in answer to the advocates of paper money. Many present-day advocates of bimetallism would not agree.

[4] My italics.—C.R.

[5] *L'or et L'Argent*, pp. xxxiv and xxxv.

verified by the facts that the point is well worth making); the reply given by the advocates of gold monometallism must be dealt with in two sections, for here we must distinguish between a *first* and a *second* generation of economists.

The first—represented by Victor Bonnet, de Parieu and Michel Chevalier—did not wait for the depression to express their opinion. They too believed in the quantity theory and would not for a moment have denied the influence on prices of changes in the quantity of bullion. But they maintained that if the free coinage of silver continued, the resultant rise in prices would be as disastrous as the fall foretold by the pessimists. Looking at things from a purely French and wholly practical point of view, they thought that the really important question was whether bi-metallist France was to submit passively to becoming the reservoir into which other, countries could pour their demonetised silver, while she herself gradually lost her gold.

The *second* generation—writing in the midst of the economic depression—followed a wholly different line of reasoning. They did not deny that *in theory* the price level depends on the quantity of goods offered for sale and on the output of the precious metals. The writings of, for example, Leroy-Beaulieu in France and Lexis in Germany, follow on this point the purest eighteenth-century lines.[1] As far as I know de Foville was the only one who seems to have questioned this principle by attributing the rise in prices in the areas where gold was mined to difficulties of transport, the inaccessibility of the new workings, the influx of population, etc.—an argument on which we need waste little time.[2]

What these writers question (in this they were supported by Nasse, an excellent German economist) was whether *in fact* the world fall in prices which followed the demonetisation of silver was due to inadequate gold output. This was a question of inter-

[1] See, in particular, Leroy-Beaulieu's *Traité théorique et pratique d'Economté Politique*, Vol. III, pp. 147–148.

[2] Unfortunately I have been unable to find a precise passage in any of de Foville's articles (a complete bibliography was published after his death by Fernand Faure), but I have a very clear recollection of conversations in which de Foville put this argument forward with great conviction, unmoved by the objection that high prices could not have been paid in the gold-producing countries if the metal itself had not been plentiful. M. Arnauné, his successor at the Mint, shared his opinion, although he did not absolutely reject any idea of gold appreciation. (Cf. *La Monnaie, le Crédit, et le Change*, 5th ed., p. 59.)

pretation, not of principle; a diagnosis, not a theory;[1] and their diagnosis was strongly influenced by the desire to defend, in France, the suspension of free silver coinage, in Germany, the recent introduction of the gold standard, and by the fear that the fall in prices would be attributed to these measures.

In countries where no such anxieties were felt (such as England, which had long been on the gold standard, or Italy, which had a paper currency), the majority of writers were in favour of gold monometallism, but freely admitted that the suspension of silver coinage and the increased demand for gold due to the wider

[1] Cf. Leroy-Beaulieu, *op. cit.*, pp. 311 *et seq.* Lexis put forward the same views; they are of interest because he expressed his opinion both on the fall and on the rise of prices. Speaking before the English Commission of 1887, he denied that gold was scarce at the time but added: "It is certainly possible and indeed probable that in the future, if the circle of gold countries is enlarged and the production of gold further decreased, scarcity of gold and consequent appreciation of gold as compared with commodities might be occasioned." His ideas about the later rise in prices are to be found in an article *Gold und Preis*, published in 1913 in a symposium in honour of Professor Riesser. In this Lexis makes the decisive observation that gold constitutes *new* purchasing power, whereas commodities "only provide purchasing power after they have been sold" (p. 97), and he adopts the quantity theory in its traditional form in the following passage: "When the mass of commodities put into circulation increases in the same proportion as gold used for money, there is no reason to assume that a given price rise is the result of greater gold production, still less when the rate of increase in the production of goods exceeds the rate of increase in gold production. On the other hand it is *possible* (Lexis' italics) that if gold increases more rapidly than production prices will rise. . . . But that does not happen necessarily nor in all cases" (p. 98). Like Leroy-Beaulieu, Lexis accepts the *principle* of the quantity theory, but insists that in each case the actual facts must be considered and interpreted. What interpretation did he offer for the rise of prices in the first twelve years of the twentieth century? According to him, this was due primarily to the rise in wages (p. 102), although he admits, after studying Fisher's figures, that, at least between 1898 and 1902, gold accounted for some part of that rise. "It is possible that the increase in currency instruments during those years did contribute, though not to any great extent, to the rise in prices" (p. 113). Similarly, the mitigation in the violence of crises during that period "may" have been the result of an influx of gold (p. 102). Lexis thus takes up the same position as other "anti-quantitative" writers; he does not deny the theoretical validity of the action of gold on prices, but refuses to admit it *in concrete cases*. But he still has to explain the striking change in the long-term price tendency after 1895, and this he does by reference to the market situation of different commodities; he finds a *special* reason for the rise in the price of each of the principal commodities, just as he had found a special cause for its fall before 1895 (p. 91). But that is precisely the point. It is difficult to understand how somebody as scientific as Lexis failed to realise that it is precisely this *simultaneous* reversal of movement on all markets which constitutes the problem to be solved. It cannot be explained except by the intervention of a new factor—gold production.

adoption of the gold standard had contributed to the fall in prices; this opinion was held by Marshall, Jevons, Sir Robert Giffen, and Pantaleoni.

Marshall tries to find a half-way solution in what he calls "symmetallism;"[1] Jevons thinks that the temporary scarcity of gold, the effects of which he does not dispute, will soon be succeeded by a period of abundance. In France, Walras and Charles Gide shared his opinion, and Walras advocates a "subsidiary silver coinage for purposes of adjustment" to meet the difficulties of the moment.[2] The constantly repeated assertion of the "anti-quantitatives" that the cause of the fall in prices was to be sought in the tremendous increase in the production of goods, in the improvements in means of transport, in the introduction of steamships instead of sailing vessels, in the great reduction in costs generally resulting from the innumerable scientific discoveries and inventions, was met with the reply: "All this is true, but the fall in prices which has resulted shews that at the moment that output of the precious metals is not great enough to offset the indisputable and undisputed effect of all these factors on the price level." All the more, they added, as the same factors were in operation before 1873, perhaps even in greater degree, without any fall in prices taking place; on the contrary, prices rose. How could the fact that the same causes produced different results be explained except by the intervention of a new factor, the monetary factor?

In short, the controversy between those who attributed the fall to the increase in production, and those who insisted on the "appreciation of gold" ended by becoming a merely verbal dispute:[3] once it is recognised that both the supply of goods and the flowof gold must be taken into account in an explanation on price move-

[1] In his *Official Papers*, p. 14, Marshall describes his proposal to the 1886 Commission on the Depression of Trade as follows: "My alternative scheme is got from his [Ricardo's] simply by wedding a bar of silver of, say, 2,000 gram es to a bar of gold of, say, 100 grammes; the Government undertaking to be always ready to buy or sell a wedded pair of bars for a fixed amount currency. (It would be somewhere about £29.) This would be true bi-metallism. The value of the currency would be fixed absolutely by the means of the value of a gramme of gold and, say, 20 grammes of silver. It would have no chance of deteriorating into a silver monometallism."

[2] Cf. Walras, *Etudes d'Economie politique appliquée*, 1936 edition. The original article appeared in 1884 in the *Revue de Droit International*.

[3] Cf. Sir David Barbour's Memorandum to the 1887 Commission on Gold and Silver.

ments, the question whether the supply of the precious metals is inadequate or the supply of goods excessive seems somewhat idle. Scientifically, the only precise formulation of the question is to discover what level of output of the precious metals *would be enough to keep prices stable*, and whether it does in fact correspond to that ideal. This was a question which Cassel was later to investigate.

But the "second generation" invokes another argument, which was to have far greater bearing on the development of theory and still to-day continues to influence the attitude of those who deny that the output of the precious metals has an appreciable effect on the price level: *this concerns the more extensive use of credit instruments, cheques and bank-notes, as means of payment, and the secondary place henceforth taken by metallic money as a factor influencing prices.*

As early as the currency inquiry of 1870, Victor Bonnet said, in an attempt to dispel the fear of an inadequate supply of currency: "As we go on, we shall do more and more business with less coin,"[1] to which Wolowski immediately replied: "Experience shews that the greater the extension of credit, the greater the need of a large metallic reserve; England's gold reserve has grown parallel with her credit institutions."[2] The dispute begun then has continued to our own times, but it was most acute at the depth of the 1873–1895 depression. The economists of that time brought forward as proof *the steady fall in the rate of interest* since prices had begun to fall, arguing that if the supply of money were inadequate, the rate of interest would rise, and not fall.

The ideas underlying this argument had such a serious effect on the subsequent development of currency doctrine that they deserve close examination.

To deduce from a fall in the rate of interest during a period of falling prices that there is therefore no shortage in the supply of precious metals represents a marked divergence from eighteenth-century doctrine. This theory was put forward by Nasse in a famous article entitled *The Fall in the Prices of Commodities during the last Fifteen Years.*[3] Economists from Cantillon to Turgot had tried to

[1] Cf. Wolowski, *op. cit.*, p. 42.

[2] The same argument was taken up by Benjamin Anderson in 1916, in the book to which reference has been made above.

[3] In the *Jahrbuch für National Oekonomie* of 1888.

destroy the false association of ideas between "an influx of specie" and a "fall in the rate of interest," between the "purchasing power of money" and the "price of money" on the capital market. And now, a century after them, the fall in "the price of money" is once more adduced as evidence of monetary plenty. Indeed Adam Smith had, in a significant passage, envisaged the very state of affairs that existed in Europe from 1873 to 1895—a fall in the price of commodities resulting from their increased production while the quantity of coin remained unchanged. He shewed that this would be followed by a steady fall in industrial profits and consequently by a fall in the rate of interest, since entrepreneurs would naturally offer lower and lower rates for savings as their hopes of profits fell, and the amount of credit required for the same operations diminished with the fall in the price of commodities.[1]

The apparent paradox of a fall in the rate of interest in a period of steadily falling prices—accompanied by an inadequate output of the precious metals—and of a rise in interest rates when prices are rising owing to an influx of the precious metals, was witnessed in its two aspects successively between 1873 and 1895, and 1895 and 1914. But it is wholly consistent with the facts of economic experience and reason; there is in fact nothing paradoxical about it. The explanation (on which Wicksell's researches were based), which shocks the prejudiced for whom "monetary abundance" means both an abundance of money available on the market and an abundance of the precious metals, is really quite simple. It is to be found in the marked changes in the *demand* for capital in periods of falling and rising prices. It is obvious that, as a whole the demand for capital declines when prices are falling, and rises when prices are rising, from the point of view both of the quantity demanded and the rate which is offered. Nasse entirely failed to see this point, which the events of the following years were, by reversing cause and effect, clearly to confirm.[2]

At the same time two writers, Sir Robert Giffen, an Englishman,

[1] *Wealth of Nations*, Vol. I, p. 338: "The interest of money, keeping pace always with the profits of stock, might, in this manner, be greatly diminished, though the value of money, or the quantity of good which any particular sum could purchase, was greatly augmented."

[2] May I be permitted to refer to my article on the *Rate of Interest* published in 1912 and reproduced in my *Essais sur Quelques Problèmes Monétaires*, 1932.

who was already famous, and Irving Fisher, an American, who was soon to win great fame, worked out the theory explaining these facts. Sir Robert Giffen's article on *Gold, the Discount Rate, and Prices*, published in 1886, is an admirable attempt to analyse the mechanism by which a greater or lesser influx of gold affects prices and the discount rate. At that time "the City" was pleased to maintain that it was only through changes in the discount rate that an abundance or scarcity of gold could affect prices: "In our present complicated banking system, it is urged, [as it was after the World War] there is no direct connection between gold coinage and commodities; it is only through the discount market that prices can be affected at all."[1]

Giffen did not share this view. He argued that prices are influenced both *directly* by the quantity of gold put into circulation, and *indirectly* by the raising or lowering of the discount rate, and the interaction of these two influences is extremely complex. The originality of Giffen's article consists in his account of this process; it was the first attempt of its kind in economic literature. He reaches the following conclusion: when there is a fall in prices as a result of the greater output of goods and of an inadequate supply of gold, this fall "is equivalent to a diminution of nominal capital, and so tends for the moment to relieve the disproportion between borrowing operations and the cash available to move them. . . . The fall eases the money market and prevents a rise in rates of discount, or produces a fall in them, such as would not otherwise have occurred."[2] In other words, the fall in prices means that a smaller sum of credit will be enough to make the same quantity of goods circulate; or, to put it in another way, the *nominal* demand on the money market declines and the discount rate will not change as much as if (bank reserves remaining the same) the price level were higher. Giffen produces statistical evidence shewing that between 1874 and 1884 the figures of Clearing House transactions and the volume of bank-notes in circulation declined, while the Bank of England's reserves remained stationary and gold in circulation diminished. The fall in the discount rate, far from proving that gold was abundant, was only a result of the fall in prices.

Giffen's article is the more remarkable as it was written before the

[1] Giffen, *Essays in Finance*, Second Series, p. 54, 1886. This article was not republished in the third series. The first series appeared in 1880.

[2] *Ibid.*, p. 55.

influx of gold from South Africa provided, as it were in reverse, a re-endorsement of his argument. It also throws light on the attitude of "banking circles" which, oblivious to any but short-term phenomena, refuse to recognise the effect on the money market of the general movement of prices and the relation between gold production and the production of goods. The theory advanced by Nasse and Lexis[1] reflects this attitude, which was maintained by the highest banking circles in America in 1924 and 1925.

Two other points in his article should be mentioned. The first is the clear distinction he draws between movements in the long term rate of interest, and the far more frequent and rapid fluctuations in the discount rate and the rate for short-term loans; it is a distinction which the majority of economists at that time ignored, but its great importance was to be brought out by post-war events, the second is his prophecy (verified by events, as Wolowski's had been fifteen years earlier) that unless new sources of gold were discovered the average level of prices and of nominal values would be lower in the ten years to come than it had been in the past ten years.[2] Once again the "quantity" theory enabled a *correct* forecast to be made.

In an article called *Appreciation and Interest*, published in 1886 and later reproduced in his book on the rate of interest, Irving Fisher shews that the parallelism between long-term movements in the rate of interest and in prices had been recognised since the eighteenth century, and that the fall or rise of the rate of interest over long periods is simply the adaptation of the rate to the increased or decreased purchasing power of money.

But this simple explanation takes for granted the assumption on which it is based—the initial fall in prices caused by an increase in the production of goods while the output of gold remains stationary. It is this fall in prices which alone can explain the fall in profits and, by direct reaction, the fall in the rate of interest. Until 1898 nobody dreamed of questioning this assumption. In that year however, a book was published which at first passed almost unnoticed, but later won wide fame. In his examination of monetary

[1] In his *Rate of Interest*, published in 1907, Fisher devotes the whole of Chapter XVI to refuting this theory which "in spite of having been refuted by economists for over a hundred years, is still dominant among many if not most business men" (p. 318).

[2] Giffen, pp. 47 and 97

problems, the author, Knut Wicksell, a Swede, gave proof of unusual insight and of a marked taste for paradox. He coolly maintains that "increased productivity cannot by itself be responsible for any general fall in prices."[1] It was the first time in the entire history of economic thought that such an assertion had been made. Indeed, the author himself does not seem wholly convinced; he appears rather to be irritated by the repeated contention of the monometallists that the fall of prices after 1873 was the result of a lowering in *costs of production*, when they should have said that it was due to a greater abundance of goods.[2] Denying that an increase in the volume of goods can cause a price fall, he asserts that this fall is due to the fact that the discount rate has not fallen enough. The lowering of the discount rate is not the result of a fall in prices; it is the cause of that fall; for, says Wicksell, it is not lowered as much as it should be, taking into account the simultaneous fall in what he calls the "natural" rate of interest.[3] In other words, having to explain why the fall in prices is accompanied by a fall in the discount rate, Wicksell argues that the fall in the bank rate of interest is deceptive; in fact that rate is *too high*, in comparison with a certain natural rate which has fallen, and the continued fall in prices is the result of the disparity between the two rates. The rate of interest, and in particular the short term bank rate of interest, which all economists before Wicksell had regarded as a *resultant* of general market conditions, is here put forward as the factor which *gives rise* to the price fall. The astonishing conclusion follows that when a long period of falling prices is accompanied by an equally steady fall in the bank rate of interest, the latter rate must be regarded as *too high*, and when a long term price rise is accompanied by an equally steady rise in the bank rate of interest, this rate must be regarded as *too low*. The terminology Wicksell

[1] Wicksell, *Interest and Prices*, transl. by R. F. Kahn, with an Introduction by M. Ohlin, 1936, p. 172.

[2] Theoretically, a fall in the cost of production of one commodity might not lead to any increase in the quantity of that commodity sold; thus a certain amount of income would go to swell the demand for other commodities and send up their price. The general price level would remain unchanged. This is a purely theoretical hypothesis which Wicksell elaborated in his *Lectures*.

[3] We shall deal with Wicksell's theory of the natural rate of interest in the next chapter. At the moment we are concerned only with his fundamental idea that the abundance of goods resulting from technical progress cannot be considered as an independent and direct cause of a fall in prices.

uses is not calculated to facilitate the description of economic phenomena.

By seizing on a fundamental proposition upheld till then both by the "quantity theorists" and their adversaries, Wicksell gave evidence of great polemical skill. The "quantity theorists" of that time can be criticised for failing to draw from that proposition all the conclusions to which it led. By insisting on the inadequate supply of gold they placed themselves in a difficult position. All economic arguments which proceed from the absence or insufficiency of something (as when Senior spoke of the *abstention* of the capitalist) inevitably give rise to the question: insufficient in comparison with what? Absence in comparison with what "presence"? Their position would have been much stronger if they had said: "normally—and assuming that all other things, including the quantity of money, remain equal—an increase in the production of goods exercises a steady pressure on prices as a whole (little matter whether those prices are in fact paid in cheques, notes, or coin). That is the permanent and essential fact which must provide the starting point in all arguments on this subject. This pressure will be greater or less according to whether credit methods and ways of economising the use of money develop more or less quickly; but it represents the normal tendency of prices in a progressive economy, where savings are constantly creating new capital. *Such falls have at times been interrupted, and these breaks, disregarding cyclical variations, have always coincided with periods during which the output of the precious metals used for money has been rapidly increased.* There is nothing astonishing in this, since the new bullion creates an additional demand for products which *has not been preceded by any supply of commodities*. This demand becomes a factor making for a rise, which in its turn increases the volume of credits and the rapidity of currency circulation. Thus, in prolonged periods of falling prices the greater supply of goods is not offset by a large enough output of the precious metals to counterbalance the pressure of the goods on prices. In these periods the active factor is not the insufficiency of the precious metals, but the plenitude of commodities. On the other hand, when new mines are opened, the active factor is the abundance of the precious metals. Thus the increase in the volume of goods is a permanent factor with a direct bearing on prices, which should never be left out of account."

By refusing to admit this fundamental proposition, Wicksell deprived his opponents of the very foundation of their argument.

We have insisted on this curious paradox because, in the first place, Wicksell's book, which was completely overlooked when it was published, has since the war (although in the meantime, as we shall see, the author modified his original conception) been regarded as giving the best explanation of the phenomena we are witnessing to-day; and in the second place he shews what rash and unreal conclusions were reached, what revolutions in the most firmly and widely held ideas were caused, in the period which we are now studying, by the desire to escape at any cost from what is contemptuously referred to as the quantity theory of money—a theory with which Wicksell, as a final paradox, declares he is, in principle, in agreement.[1]

Let us now turn to the second argument brought forward by the "anti-quantity theorists," that the increased use of credit and bank money has practically eliminated metallic money as a factor influencing the price level: here again we shall come across Wicksell's name.

The development of credit institutions, and particularly of large deposit banks, is one of the most important facts in nineteenth-century economic history. Roughly contemporaneous with the Peel Act in England, it assumed significant proportions in France and Germany after the war of 1870–1871. It is true that it was accompanied by the gradual disappearance of a number of local banks, so that in many instances it was a case of one bank taking the place of another rather than an increase in the actual number of deposit banks. In England the spread of banking encouraged the use of cheques as means of payment. The writings of Jevons and Bagehot, coming after MacLeod's great book, had made economists familiar with the workings of the London Clearing House and the mechanism of bank money. In France and Germany the establishment of more and more branches of the Bank of France and the Reichsbank respectively, and the clearing system organised by

[1] The reader will find in the chapter of his book called "The Quantity Theory and its Opponents" an extremely ingenious and original analysis of the mechanism by which an inadequate supply of money causes a fall in prices. In the same chapter he criticises all those writers who have tried to replace the quantity theory by another; he presents his theory as an attempt to rid the quantity theory of the inadequacies which disfigure it.

these two great institutions, enabling a vast volume of transactions to be settled without the transfer of coin, made a great impression; and it is not surprising that among many people the idea should grow up that coin had had its day and could very well be replaced by a general book-keeping system, somewhat on the lines proposed by Ernest Solvay for Belgium. Until that could be attained, they contented themselves with the statement (expressed in the vaguest of terms) that though coin was still used for the settlement of debts, it no longer exerted any influence on the price level, except in a quite roundabout and remote way.

These ideas are imaginative rather than sound.

In the first place, they ignore the fact that in countries like France and Germany—and even in England—gold and silver were still very widely used in day to day transactions. They ignore the fact that bank-notes—in so far as they are not merely gold certificates (in which case they are equivalent to actual gold currency), that is, in so far as they represent credit operations—have very largely merely *taken the place of* a vast number of bills of exchange, the circulation of which has practically ceased. They ignore the fact that the circulation of cheques was, outside England, limited to a very small part of the population. Finally they ignore the fact that the clearing houses were used very largely for the settlement of stock exchange operations which do not affect the prices of goods.[1]

Moreover, the overwhelming majority of wage payments and retail purchases were still made in hard cash. But even if the proportion of "circulating credits" to coin had been much higher than in fact it was, it would not have changed the situation. Would the increasing quantity of goods offered on the market have exerted less pressure on prices? To counteract such pressure, in the absence of an increase in gold, the quantity of circulating credits would have had to increase as the volume of goods increased; in other words

[1] In an essay on the rise in prices written in 1872 (published in the first series of his *Essays in Finance*) Giffen writes: "The common notion is that . . . the gradual perfection of the Clearing House arrangements [have] economised currency since 1850. . . . So far as the use of sovereigns is concerned, the necessities and habits of the people are unchanged. Deposit banking was quite as much developed in 1850 in proportion to the population, as it is now. . . . We may assume then that every increase of population and business since 1850 must have involved a proportionate expansion of the sovereign circulation" (pp. 93–94).

the fall of prices not being offset by an access of gold, it would have had to be offset by an extension of credits. *But it was precisely the opposite that occurred during those years.*[1] The volume of circulating credits (cheques and notes), and in particular that part of credit arising from advances and discounts, far from growing, decreased or remained stationary. This was true of France, of Germany, and of England.[2] Indeed *it could not have been otherwise*, for the reasons already given. When the increase in the volume of goods offered on the market begins to depress prices—and is not offset by a commensurate increase in bullion—this fall, by reducing profits, reduces economic activity and consequently the *demand* for credit. "When prices fall, business contracts, and production is checked—capital in the form of gold accumulates in the banks, and the rate of interest and discount falls," said Sir Louis Mallet to the 1887 Commission on Gold and Silver.[3] Speaking of the part credit plays in determining prices, he said: "The question is one of such complexity, and has hitherto been so imperfectly investigated by economists, that it cannot be adequately discussed in connection with our present inquiry; but I believe the operation of credit to be rather that of adding incalculably to the number of transactions, as well as to the circulating medium required to effect them, than of

[1] Referring to this period (*The International Gold Problem*, p. 75) Mr. Hawtrey says that the abnormal demand for gold was offset by an "equally abnormal development of credit substitutes." Quoted in *The Future of Monetary Policy*, p. 198. But in fact the reverse was true; such a statement by so eminent an economist indicates how little known are the facts relating to this subject.

[2] The statistical evidence is readily available. As far as France is concerned, the reader need only refer to the bank reports between 1890 and 1895 to find constantly reiterated complaints about the scarcity of "discountable paper." Between 1880 and 1895 the figure of commercial bills in circulation fell from 30 to 26 milliards (cf. Roulleau, *Le Règlement des Effets de Commerce*, Paris, 1914); the average of Bank of France bill holdings and advances fell from 901 to 856 million. These figures give a more telling picture when compared with the rapid increase in the corresponding figures after 1895. The same observations apply to Germany, where the same contrast between the two periods is evident. As to England, Sir Robert Giffen shews (*Essays in Finance*, second series, pp. 79 and 82) that with the fall in prices there was a decline in Clearing House transactions, in the note circulation and in taxable income. It is difficult to exaggerate the contrast presented by the money markets of all the great States before and after 1895, that is to say before and after the influx of gold from the Transvaal.

[3] The Report of the Royal Commission was republished in 1936 by Columbia University under the title: *The Monetary Problem, Gold and Silver Commission*, cf. p. 267.

diminishing the quantity of metallic money necessary to supply the requisite currency."[1]

The economists of the time had in fact very little to say about the effect of credit on long term price tendencies. Mill had given an entire chapter to the question, on which he throws a fair amount of light. Cairnes, with a more clearly defined attitude, had pointed out that in countries with a highly developed credit system the influence of an influx of bullion on prices was *reinforçed* by credit facilities, a theory which accords *greater* and not *less* influence to the precious metals on prices in highly developed credit systems, and which is in complete contradiction to Nasse's views. Other economists had expressed the opinion that the volume of credits circulating in any country remained in more or less constant relation to the stock of money, and that, as credits adjusted themselves to this stock, they could not serve to offset an inadequate stock (as Ricardo thought). This relation is not fixed, but elastic, and varies with cyclical fluctuations of boom and depression. Somewhat later, Irving Fisher demonstrated, more clearly and completely than any writer before him, that the relation of the volume of circulating credits to the volume of metallic money changes very slowly.[2] He shewed also that in prolonged periods of rising prices the velocity of currency circulation and the volume of credit do not diminish, but increase, and that they diminish in periods of falling prices. Consequently, when these rises and falls are due to an influx or to an inadequacy of the precious metals, credit and the velocity of circulation, far from mitigating the effects of such an influx or insufficiency, *reinforce* them. The argument based on the extension of credit is not only unsound theoretically, but is directly contradicted by actual historical facts.

Wicksell alone had the courage to maintain the opposite opinion; on this point too he carried the vague and confused ideas of the anti-quantity theorists to one simple and logical principle; unfortunately, that principle is contradicted by fact. Starting from the fact admitted by all writers about the money market, that the provision of credit by a bank results in the creation of a deposit at another (or at the same) bank, he concludes that *in a system in*

[1] *The Monetary Problem, Gold and Silver Commission*, cf. pp. 262–263.

[2] I. Fisher, *Purchasing Power*, p. 50.

which the banks are not subject to demands for repayment, credit can be indefinitely extended.

"We have seen that in our ideal state every payment, and consequently every loan, is accomplished by means of cheques or *giro* facilities. It is then no longer possible to refer to the supply of money as an independent magnitude, differing from the demand for money. No matter what amount of money may be demanded from the banks, that is the amount that they are in a position to lend (so long as the security of the borrower is adequate). The banks have merely to enter a figure in the borrower's account to represent a credit granted or a deposit created. When a cheque is then drawn and subsequently presented to the banks, they credit the account of the owner of the cheque with a deposit of the appropriate amount (or reduce his debit by that amount). The 'supply of money' is thus furnished by the demand itself."[1]

Here the price level is completely liberated from the stock of metallic money; if it were in fact independent there would be no point in keeping any bank reserves at all. The old eighteenth-century and Ricardian formula is revised. It had been maintained that whatever the supply of money it will find a corresponding demand; here it is argued that supply adapts itself indefinitely to demand. Money, like air, becomes a free good. What a marvellous discovery! And to put the discovery into practice it is only necessary that the public should never withdraw their deposits . . . and that "the security provided by the borrower should be adequate."

This one little condition to which Wicksell (as it were in passing) makes his conception subject, illustrates the fantastic nature of the whole idea, for bank guarantees are not unlimited. Wicksell simply forgets that with every new advance the bank's *credit margin is narrowed*. But there is really little point in going on. Is there a banker in the world who, attempting to grapple with the difficulties of keeping his position liquid, would not laugh outright at such a dazzling prospect?

If anything could shew up the contradictions in the various theories which claim that the volume of metallic currency is not a factor in explaining price movements, it is the two arguments which Wicksell, impenitently logical, was led to uphold: firstly that an increase in the volume of commodities does not lower the

[1] Wicksell, *Interest and Prices*, p. 110.

price level; secondly, that the demand for credit creates the necessary supply of credit. When these two propositions shall have been, not merely stated, but proven and accepted by economists and business men, the corollaries therefrom may be seriously examined. Meanwhile we shall regard them as theorems in non-euclidian economic geometry.

Wicksell's book marks the extreme theoretical limit of the refusal to admit a diminished output of the precious metals as one of the elements in a prolonged price fall, when one of those metals has been deprived of its currency function and the other has to meet the monetary demands of countries formerly on the double standard or on the silver standard. Having shattered the foundations of the theory of long term price tendencies held until that time, he has to find a new reason for such movements: to this end he brings forward the theory of the divergence between the discount rate and the "natural" rate of interest which we shall deal with in the next chapter, and in which Wicksell himself ended by not believing, though some of his slower followers have not yet given it up.

§ III. *Economic Prosperity from* 1895 *to* 1914 *and the Transvaal Gold Mines*

In the same year (1898) in which Wicksell made a last attempt to explain the fall in world prices without reference either to the volume of commodities or to the quantity of currency, events were already occurring to disprove his contention.

Gold, which had been absent too long from the world scene, made a brilliant reappearance. The discovery of gold in the Transvaal, where mines were opened in 1890, enormously accelerated the rate of its production. Ample reserves, which only waited the end of the depression to be put into circulation, were accumulated by the central banks of issue between 1890 and 1895. In a few years the curve of world economic activity began to move upwards; after 1895, having fallen for twenty-two years, prices began to rise.

Those who lived through that period of change, and who had been brought up in the idea of an irreversible economic decline, will never forget the astonishment with which they witnessed this wholly unexpected renewal of economic activity and prosperity; this was particularly true of France, where there was a widespread public belief that it was due to the *Exposition Universelle* of 1900!

Walras, who remained steadily faithful to the quantity theory (although he was opposed to bimetallism) indicated what was going to happen as early as 1895, that is, *before any effect on prices was visible*:

"Deducting the 14 or 15 milliards of gold which should come from the Witwatersrand alone as the value of the gold which will be used for industrial and luxury purposes, the price rise which will take place within the next ten years or so as a result of the increase in the output of gold may, without exaggeration, be put at 12 or 15 per cent. All those whose profits are derived from the difference between cost price and selling price, entrepreneurs in agriculture, industry, and trade, and holders of ordinary shares, who will raise the selling price of their products long before they raise the price for productive services, will bathe in a sea of prosperity. On the other hand all those whose incomes are fixed in advance, landowners, labourers, bondholders, will find their position grow worse. Landowners who also farm their land are entrepreneurs, the others will try to raise their rents as quickly as possible; but the workers will have to resort to strikes, so costly and so painful to them, to get their wages raised; clerical workers and employees of the central and local authorities will find it still more difficult to get their salaries increased; as to the small capitalists, the bondholders, they have no way of getting their income raised, for the interest on their bonds is fixed, and from now onward their capital can be redeemed only in depreciated currency."[1]

His prophecy was to be verified as precisely as were Wolowski's in 1869 and Giffen's in 1886, which foretold the opposite order of events.

The change in regard to credit is striking; the bill holdings of the deposit banks and banks of issue increased rapidly; money circulated more rapidly, the discount rate and long term interest rate rose steadily. The events of the preceding period were reversed as in a mirror. The importance of the *demand* for credit now stands out with unmistakable clarity. It increases in volume and is granted at a rate which rises steadily just as, previously, it had diminished

[1] Léon Walras, *Etudes d'Economie Politique Appliquée*: *Le Péril bimétalliste*, p. 676. The article quoted from above first appeared in the *Revue Socialiste* in 1895.

in volume and been granted at lower and lower rates. Far from acting as a sort of counter-balance to an abundance of currency, compensating for an inadequate supply of coin or diminishing when the quantity of money increases (as Ricardo would have us believe), credit and the velocity of currency circulation act in an exactly opposite way. Wolowski, who had from the beginning of the controversy insisted that the quantity of money and the volume of credit move along parallel lines, was shewn to have been right. At the same time there was less of the hoarding that had been so characteristic of the previous period. That was because *the demand for metallic currency with the object of keeping it* (as opposed to the demand for credit) diminished. Having to choose between keeping their wealth in the form of money or in the form of commodities, the public chose the way which offered a chance of increasing the value of their property. The purchasing power of money was falling, whereas the price of commodities was rising. The function of acting as a store of value tended to pass from gold to commodities, as it does whenever there is a rapid increase in the quantity of currency.

The years from 1896–1914 will always be remembered as one of the most prosperous and brilliant periods in world economic history. In almost every sphere the phenomena of the previous period were reversed, and those of the years 1851–1870 reproduced. Everywhere the gold standard was strengthened as a result of the vastly extended production of the metal. Even South America, notorious until then for its monetary crises, stabilised its currencies. As a result of the rise in the price of agricultural products Argentine and Brazil at last managed to cease issuing forced currency and to stabilise their exchanges. Italy, that had for so long been compelled to use paper currency, gradually brought the lira to par, which was reached in 1912. Spanish currency steadily climbed to equilibrium on the exchanges. For a short space of time Russia abandoned paper money, which was its usual currency, and established the gold standard in 1899, in the same year as Austria-Hungary. The Indian rupee was stabilised without difficulty, and the gold exchange standard introduced in an increasing number of countries. All the beneficial effects of an influx of gold enumerated by Newmarch in reference to the years 1851–1857 made their appearance once more. No longer did anybody speak of a scarcity of the precious metals. The attempts of international conferences to get bimetallism widely re-established broke down in face of British opposition. The only complaint came from consumers, particularly the working classes, whose cost of living was rising. Towards the end of this period it was being suggested that an international conference should be convened to discover ways and means of checking the rise in the cost of living, and President Taft had declared himself ready to do so. Economists, including Irving Fisher, worked out plans for stabilising the value of money. They were concerned not, as at the present day, with schemes for checking a rise in the value of gold, but with schemes for preventing the steady decline in the purchasing power of gold. Irving Fisher advocated an increase in the weight of the monetary unit. Just as, after the 1930 crisis, certain prophets foretold an uninterrupted fall in prices, so at that time a great number of writers envisaged an uninterrupted rise, and drew the darkest conclusions as to the future of the working classes and the general welfare.

However, the difficulties of a high cost of living were forgotten in the general industrial prosperity, the ease with which states and individuals settled their debts, and the mounting reserves of the banks of issue. What was the attitude of economists during this new period in monetary history?

A few writers clung to the ideas of the previous period and continued, either to deny any relation between the rise in prices and the new influx of gold, or to make the latter a factor of secondary importance.[1] Others, who had formerly denied any relation between the fall in prices and the slowing down of gold output, no longer hesitated to acknowledge the influence of the new gold discoveries. From 1906, as we shall see in the next chapter, Wicksell openly dropped the theory that prices moved independently of gold. In the Preface to his *Lectures* he admits that the change in the price tendency after 1895 is associated with the rapid increase in the quantity of gold.

The economists who had always maintained this thesis saw

[1] M. Lescure, and M. Nogaro, whose writings have shed such useful light on certain aspects of crises, and of the relation between prices and the exchanges, represent these two tendencies, although, on various occasions, M. Nogaro does admit, regretfully as it were, that gold output has a certain influence. For Lexis, see *supra*, pp. 249–250.

their contentions confirmed by facts. Of these, Irving Fisher was the one whose works, quite rightly, attracted most attention.[1]

At the same time—there being no longer any fear of a return to bimetallism—it was possible to make a more objective statistical investigation of the actual relations between price movements and world gold output. Those who undertook this research became more and more firmly convinced that the price fall from 1873 to 1895 originated in the demonetisation of silver and in the relatively stationary output of the gold mines until 1890. Their explanation did not imply either the desire to return to an out-of-date currency system, or criticism of the decisions taken after 1875 by countries formerly bimetallist. It merely emphasised the dependence of the world price level on gold. In this connexion special mention should be made of the work of a young statistician, Marcel Lenoir, too early lost to science;[2] the work of Aupetit, Fisher and Cassel is already well known to all.

Cassel's investigations made a particularly great impression. Taking as basis the Sauerbeck and Jevons price index, he notes that the index figure reached in 1910 was the same, or very nearly the same, as the figure for 1850, and that the average for the years 1848–1851 (following the 1847 crisis) was the same as the average for the years 1908–1911 (following the 1907 crisis). He then takes the level of 1850 and 1910 as *normal* and uses this as his base, or index number of 100, on which to calculate the levels for the period 1800–1910. Making allowance for loss by wear and tear, he calculates the amount of gold in the world at the dates 1800, 1850 and 1910, and gets the figures (in milliards of pre-war marks) 5·735, 10 and 52. Thus, between 1850 and 1910, the stock of gold increased 5·2 times, corresponding to an average annual increase of 2·8 per cent of the existing stock; and as the price level is the same at both the beginning and end of the period, he concludes that precisely such a rate of increase was required, given the economic development that took place over that period, to keep prices stable. A steady increase of 2·8 per cent may therefore be regarded as the *normal* rate for the period under review. He plots the curve of the *normal* gold stock back to the year 1800, using the same base.

[1] In particular *The Purchasing Power of Money*, 1911, and *The Rate of Interest*, 1907.

[2] Lenoir, *Etude sur la Formation et le Mouvement des Prix*, Paris, 1913.

On this assumption, the price variations which occurred during that period can be attributed to divergencies between the actual and the normal stock of gold. These divergencies he calculates by dividing the actual stock for each year by the normal stock, thus obtaining figures varying above and below the figure 1 (representing the two years 1850 and 1910, when the actual stock and the normal stock are taken as equal). The curve obtained represents the *relative* stock of gold. A comparison of this curve with the price curve obtained in the manner described above shews a clear correspondence between its movements and the rises and falls of prices.[1]

The method Cassel used has been criticised because of its arbitrary choice of the years designed to serve as a basis for calculating the "normal" increase in gold;[2] but the striking contrast between the movement of prices before and after the discovery of the Transvaal mines would not be weakened whatever years were chosen. It is this contrast, this complete reversal of the price tendency, with all the phenomena of greater economic activity by which it was accompanied, which has to be explained.

§ IV. *The Quantity Theory after the War*

The last episode in price history which aroused controversy began with the war and the extraordinary gold and price movements which occurred after the war.

During the war, the movement of prices was determined almost exclusively not by the production of gold (which practically ceased to play any part in monetary affairs) but by the issue of paper money in the great majority of belligerent countries and even in some countries which remained neutral. Convertibility was suspended almost everywhere and the requirements of the state led to the issue of paper money in enormous quantities, either by the central banks or by the governments themselves; the result of this

[1] G. Cassel, *Theoretische Sozialökonomie*, Leipzig, 1918, § 54.

[2] This criticism is made by M. Nogaro in a recent edition of his book *La Monnaie et les Phénomènes monétaires contemporains*, Paris, 1935. In a pamphlet published by Sirey in 1936 called *Interprétation de la Baisse des Prix depuis la Crise*, the present writer has attempted a statistical analysis of the question which, though differing from Cassel's, reaches the same conclusion.

policy was a violent rise in prices, or, if it is preferred, an enormous decline in the purchasing power of the national monetary unit which, with the introduction of forced currency, became a simple paper claim completely detached from gold. Nobody to-day denies that the origin of that steep price rise lay in the creation of paper money by the state and the creation of inconvertible bank credits to cover state expenditure. Disputes as to the effects of an abundance or scarcity of gold on the price level did not arise until a certain number of the great powers returned to the gold standard.

Between 1920–1930 most of the important currencies were stabilised and again made convertible. In all these stabilisations the United States dollar, the only currency which had remained almost uninterruptedly convertible, was taken as the basis. It had been possible to maintain the convertibility of the dollar because of two facts:

1. The United States had created bank money in enormous quantities to provide the government with means far in excess of their normal revenue; this would have led to the introduction of forced currency but for the fact that during the war the belligerent countries sent their gold to the United States to pay for part of their purchases there; consequently it was possible to maintain convertibility almost the whole time;

2. After the war the convertibility of the dollar was strengthened because all the gold newly extracted from the mines was sent to the United States; this happened because the *large European banks refused to change their pre-war gold purchase price* and to buy gold at the new price established on the market as a result of the depreciation of paper. The sterling price of gold in London, and its price in francs in Paris, remained at the legal rate fixed before the war, but the pound and the franc had depreciated against the dollar, so that by selling a certain amount of gold in New York for dollars *a much larger number of pounds sterling or of francs would be obtained by purchase with these dollars* than if the gold had been sold direct to the banks in England and France. That was the sole and effective reason why gold was sent to the United States. The charge that America was anxious to accumulate gold is absurd, particularly when it is made by those countries which caused that accumulation by their own currency policy.

The gold which strengthened the reserves of the United States banks was, however, being accumulated in a country where the price level, even after the fall that occurred in the 1920–1921 crisis, was still nearly 50 per cent higher than it had been in 1913. There had been no change in the rate of increase of world gold production that could explain a rise of nearly 50 per cent in gold prices in the short space of eight years. In the twenty years from 1895 to 1914 world gold output had doubled, but prices had only risen from 25 to 30 per cent. The American gold price level was therefore wholly abnormal, the result of exceptional circumstances, of the artificial situation temporarily created by the war.

In 1924 and 1925 two great European powers, Germany and Great Britain (the latter soon followed by its dominions and colonies), returned to the gold standard. The level of gold prices in these countries was then linked up with the American level. The paradox of such a high price level, which now became a world price level, was immediately obvious: from that moment it began to fall. A similar fall had occurred on the general adoption of the gold standard after 1873; silver had been demonetised, leaving gold alone as the standard; in 1925 it was paper that was abandoned in favour of gold, and prices dropped.

The countries which returned to the gold standard immediately ceased issuing paper money. *The mere cessation of the issue of paper money, even without any reduction in its quantity, is enough to begin a price fall.* After the war the output of goods had resumed its normal dimensions (which means that it was steadily increasing); the effort to absorb these goods with nominal incomes that were henceforth stationary exerted pressure on all markets.

The fall in prices which followed was particularly steep and prolonged; there were two reasons for this: the price level had itself been pushed up to excessive heights by the abundance of currency. The competition of producers on the market operates by means of a reduction in cost prices, enabling them to supply a larger quantity of goods at a lower price per unit. Now, when prices have once been raised by 50 per cent (working population and technical equipment remaining roughly stationary) an *equal quantity* of labour or capital economised in the manufacture of a commodity is *reckoned at a price* 50 *per cent higher than it would have been before that price rise.* An economy in the use of labour or material which, at the earlier price level, would have represented 100 francs, represents an economy of 150 francs at the higher price level. Consequently, at this higher level, technical improvements which would formerly have meant a reduction of 100 francs in selling price now permit a reduction of 150 francs. The first effect of competition, when it was resumed after the war, and of the reduction in costs which was meant to stimulate a demand no longer swollen by inflation, was a *very rapid fall* in the prices of goods offered on the market. But as the general price level falls, the rate of its fall slows down. It is as if it were a spring, which is easy to compress at first but offers greater resistance as the pressure is increased.

The fact that in England paper money had rashly and prematurely been declared convertible against gold, and that in America the influx of gold had concealed the normal effects of paper inflation, did not affect the process itself. It merely meant that the fall was a fall in *gold prices* and not in *paper prices*; but the rise of prices in relation to what they were before the war was not less exaggerated, and the fall occurred in the same way as if gold prices had been paper prices.

The second reason was this: a prolonged fall in prices normally goes on until the mining of new gold begins to act in the opposite direction and creates a new demand for goods. If cyclical variations are disregarded, the history of prices can in fact be shewn to consist of a steady tendency to fall, offset from time to time by the effect of new discoveries of the precious metals.

Now, the abundance of a paper currency *artificially restored to pre-war gold parity* (in the United States by the influx of gold from Europe, in England by stabilisation at the old rate) meant that the *influence of new gold was reduced to practically nil.*

To make this clear, let us suppose that in 1913 the quantity of metallic currency serving as basis for trade was equal to 10 milliard francs, each franc representing 0·3225 gr. of gold, or 322·5 kg. per milliard, and that, because of war inflation, this quantity is replaced by 40 milliards of paper money. When the currency is restored, by various measures, to par, these 40 milliards are regarded as equivalent to gold. Total currency, now all convertible, is 50 milliards, and the bank continues to give one franc for every 0·32 gr. of gold brought to it. If the annual output of gold in 1913 was 322·5 kg., one milliard francs would have been added to a total monetary stock of 10 milliards, thus increasing it by 10 per cent. But in post-war conditions (when the 40 milliards of paper money have been brought back to par) the same output will still add one milliard to the monetary stock, but this will represent only an increase of 2 per cent, instead of 10 per cent. In other words, the influence of new gold on incomes, and consequently on prices, will be attenuated to one-fifth of what it was before.

This is precisely what happened in the United States and in England. These two countries had created a large volume of paper money, but decided to maintain that paper at pre-war parities. In other words, after having trebled or quadrupled their currency they tried to give each unit of currency the same gold value as before the war, while at the same time maintaining its purchasing power at the lower level caused by the war. It followed that an annual output of gold equal to the pre-war output represented, *in comparison with existing purchasing power*, a much smaller increase in purchasing power. In other words, the action on prices of newly-mined gold was reduced to insignificant proportions.

This was counteracted by the effects of devaluation in England and America.

Starting again from our earlier hypothesis, let us suppose that the weight of gold contained in one franc is reduced by a re-definition of its standard content to one-fifth, and let us suppose again that annual output is still 322·5 kg. This amount of metal can now be coined into 5 milliard francs instead of one milliard, or (what amounts to the same thing) the central bank can now issue five milliard in notes. The addition to purchasing power will again reach the figure of 10 per cent a year. After the first year, unless the annual output of gold is increased, the rate of increase in purchasing power will slow down. That is what will happen in any case. *The point to be emphasised is that the factor which, before the war and inflation, countered the fall in prices, was re-established at its former level.*

Like all widespread falls in gold prices, devaluation greatly stimulated gold production. The cost in pounds of working the mines remained practically unchanged, whereas the yield of gold sales in devaluated sterling rose by the full extent of the devaluation. For the last five years the figures for gold production in all the old mining areas have risen steadily, and new mines, like those in Russia, have been opened. Thus devaluation in England and America restored the influence on prices of new gold, and provided a powerful stimulus to gold production.

On the other hand it sent the English and American gold price level down at one stroke, leaving the volume of nominal income reckoned in sterling and dollars unchanged. It had the same effect as slow deflation, with this difference: that deflation involves a progressive reduction in all nominal incomes, which is not without grave consequences for all debtors.[1]

The facts and arguments given above strongly support those doctrines which attribute preponderating influence in the determination of the price level to an increase in the supply of goods, creating a downward price tendency, and to an increase in the output of gold, creating an upward tendency. They contradict the theories at first put forward by Wicksell, who denied the first, and by the disciples of Lexis, Nasse and de Foville, who denied the second. It is therefore not surprising that the great majority of economists have ascribed to gold paramount importance in the sensational fluctuations of the world price level during the present crisis.

A brief review of the theories put forward reveals that there is a twofold tendency underlying the explanations given of the world economic crisis.

Certain writers have concentrated particularly on the "reversal" of prices and the "outbreak" of the crisis in 1929–1930. The mechanism of this "outbreak" does not differ in any obvious respect from that which came into action in former crises. The catastrophe which transforms a rise into a fall of prices has always presented economists with a peculiarly difficult subject for analysis. But in this respect the crisis of 1929–1930 does not differ in essentials (except for circumstances of fact) from former crises. It is perhaps more dramatic than others, and more complex because it was so

[1] What would in fact happen in the case of deflation? Let us again take the hypothesis made above; let the total currency be 50 milliards, and the price index 500, corresponding to a commodity output of 1,000 milliard tons at an average price of one franc per ton. If prices fall so far that one franc will purchase not one ton, but five tons of commodities, the purchasing power of the franc will be increased fivefold, and the purchasing power of 0·32 gr. of gold, which had been reduced by the rise in prices from 5 to 1, will again stand at its earlier level. But to get to this point prices must have fallen very steeply, with all the ill effects of such a fall for debtors. From then on, the new gold produced will represent per gramme the same increase in purchasing power.

long delayed; but it is nevertheless a particular example of a familiar species.[1]

The problem presented by the present crisis is less that of its beginning, than that of its *persistence* and its *depth*. It is the period of depression following the crisis—similar to the long depression which followed the crisis of 1873—that makes it necessary to examine the problem of the influence of gold and of paper money on prices. It is from this point of view and in the light of the theories just enunciated above that the explanations put forward in the last ten years will be examined.

In the first place, the deliberations of the League of Nations Gold Delegation—whatever one may think of some of their conclusions—shewed that all the experts consulted were agreed in ascribing fundamental importance in the determination of prices to the production of gold. The *leit-motif* of their discussions was the insufficiency of gold. It would be unfair to criticise the Delegation for failing to foresee the subsequent course of gold output, in the first place because the predictions of economists and geologists as to the future of gold output have always been belied by events (from those of Chevalier and de Launay to Mr. Kitchin), and in the second place, because it would have been unreasonable to expect the Committee to have foreseen devaluation in England and the intensive exploitation of the Russian mines.

The Report of the Macmillan Committee (1931) also deals with currency problems. There too the quantity theory is accepted without reservation: "Obviously the general price level must be governed by the volume of purchasing power directed to the buying of current output relative to the volume of this output."[2] It is true that the authors of the Report attribute great influence in the creation of purchasing power to banks of issue as well as to gold; but it is precisely to compensate for an inadequate gold output (on this point they accept the conclusions of the League of Nations Gold Delegation)[3] that they propose a more extensive use of credit. In neither report is any doubt expressed as to the influence of gold on prices.

[1] The literature on this subject is so vast that it is impossible to select a few books without doing an injustice to those omitted. But we would mention Professor Robbins' *The Great Depression* for England, the works of Messrs. Warren and Pearson for America, and of M. Nogaro for France.

[2] *Macmillan Report*, p. 93.

[3] *Ibid.*, p. 65.

As to the economists, as distinct from the official Committees, their belief in the action of gold on prices was strengthened. Edwin Cannan and Maynard Keynes—two English economists whose theories were wholly opposed in tendency—are in complete agreement on this point. After the war Cannan steadily proclaimed his adherence to classical doctrine,[1] while Keynes, having diligently sought an explanation of price fluctuations in a theory of saving and investment, ends up in a notable article, with an assertion of the importance he attaches to the recent increase in the production of gold.[2]

In France classical doctrine was greatly strengthened.

François Simiand cannot be accused of arriving at his conclusions on a superficial examination of the facts. Nobody has studied the history and statistics of the subject with more scrupulous care, with a more painstaking conscientiousness, with a more passionate determination not to ignore a single fact or argument that might appear to contradict his views. Nor can he be charged with a prejudice in favour of classical doctrine, for nobody is more free of dogma or tradition. Having made a really exhaustive study of price and wage movements, he says:

> "The origin of the rise of wages, and more broadly of the generally favourable tendency in economic development as a whole during the nineteenth and twentieth centuries, does not lie in the organisation of the economic system, nor in economic liberty; it does not lie in technical progress, nor in capitalism, nor in socialism; it is to be found in the discovery and exploitation of the gold mines of California, and later of the Transvaal and the Klondyke. A subsidiary cause, in the early years of the nineteenth century and again in the second and third decades of the twentieth, lies in what is generally known as 'fiduciary inflation.' "[3]

Like the members of the Macmillan Committee, Simiand attaches importance not to the absolute volume of gold production at any given moment, but to its annual rate of increase. It is the magnitude of this rate which determines a rise or fall in the price level through the action of rising or falling profits. It is true that he applies his theory not merely to gold, but to currency instruments as a whole, including paper money. On this point his theory may be contested;

[1] See *Money*, 1923, and *Modern Currency*, 1931.

[2] See *The Economic Journal* for 1936.

[3] *Le Salaire, l'Evolution sociale, et la Monnaie*, Paris, 1932, Vol. I, p. xiv.

here we are concerned only to note how strikingly his researches confirm the importance at all times attributed to gold in the establishment of the general price level.[1]

At the same time as Simiand's book there appeared the work of two Swiss economists, MM. Guillaume, who demonstrated mathematically the importance of gold in general price movements. They start from the idea that "rationalisation," that is to say technical progress, by reducing costs, must lead to a fall in prices accompanied by a real "enrichment" of the community. To compensate for this fall (which Wicksell maintained, paradoxically, was not inevitable) an increase in gold is normally required, since gold, as MM. Guillaume very rightly said, has the peculiar characteristic, that an increase in its quantity increases the demand for commodities directly, without any preceding sale of existing commodities, that is to say without any simultaneous and contrary pressure on the prices of commodities.

Gold, however, does not necessarily increase as rapidly as prices, owing to rationalisation, fall. The same result as would follow from an increase in gold can be brought about by indebtedness, that is to say by the banks or the State creating credit.[2] Indebtedness, however, places on the future the burden of repayment and of

[1] "If our analysis of production pressures in phase A is correct, the central factor therein, rising profits, increased for all economic activities, was obtained by a simultaneous increase in the quantities produced and in prices per unit, and therefore in the total values of the products, which *in the end* was met by the realisation of final exchanges; we say in the end because, from the beginning of the complex and graduated processes which characterise the working of an advanced exchange economy until their end in the purchases for final consumption, the diverse economic activities successively implied would remain in temporary suspension, if the means of realising in advance the parts which should correspond to them in future values were not available to store them up until that time, thus permitting operations to be regulated and transacted in virtue of this anticipated cover. Now these anticipated realisations, without which, as we have seen, the economic system could not function, much less develop, consist directly of money, or indirectly of the credits which provide the basis for money resources" (François Simiand, *Les Fluctuations économiques à Longue Periode et la Crise Mondiale*, p. 45). This is a characteristic example of Simiand's somewhat rugged style, in which he tries to make the reader share his own effort to overcome one by one the series of barriers obstructing the solution of an economic problem, of which he is determined to leave not one standing.

[2] This is a simplification of MM. Guillaume's ideas; their conception of indebtedness is more extensive than I have made it here, but this is not the place to give a detailed account of their theory, which has been very carefully elaborated and deserves a special study. Cf. *Sur les Fondements de l'Economique rationnel*, Gauthier-Villars, 1932.

interest and consequently, if the rise in prices is to be maintained, annual income must always be increased by new indebtedness. In their eyes the origin of the present crisis is to be found in the enormous "indebtedness" of the war period and in its subsequent cessation. This conception is similar to that put forward by the present author; it restores gold to its rightful place as a factor influencing the price level. The originality and value of the work of MM. Guillaume consist in the exactness with which their ideas are presented and in the remarkable precision with which they describe the reactions of the different factors affecting the price level. Their book is an extremely original and suggestive contribution to the explanation of the post-war crisis.

Another writer in this group is M. Aftalion, who insists that long term price rises are caused, not by the mechanical action of gold, but by the increase in *income* which follows from new gold production, and conversely that falls are due primarily to the pressure of commodities. His chapter on *Gold and Long Term Movements in World Prices*[1] gives an excellent account of the alternating action of the increased demand for products and of the growing pressure of the supply of commodities, as a result of which the movement of world prices is from time to time reversed.

But the most significant of all the ideas provoked by the war and the post-war period are those of Mr. Hawtrey, which he has so ably defended in a number of books. Mr. Hawtrey has never denied the abnormal character of the post-war level of gold prices, but he is convinced that this level can be maintained by *appropriate credit manipulation*, as a result of which "the value of gold will conform to the value of the currency units instead of the value of the currency units conforming to the value of gold."[2] The formula is as significant as it is paradoxical. It is in the purest Ricardian tradition, and seems completely to have forgotten the teachings of Tooke. The problem which Mr. Hawtrey set himself to solve after the World War consisted in no less than this: *how, instead of creating new gold currency units with purchasing power equal to the reduced purchasing power of the paper units of the same denomination, to adjust the purchasing power of the old gold units (without changing their old content) to the diminished purchasing power of the paper units.*

[1] In *L'Or et sa Distribution Mondiale*, Paris, 1932.

[2] *The Gold Standard*, p. 94.

To solve this problem, which far exceeds in magnitude the problem that England had to face after the Napoleonic wars, or France after the war of 1870, it is necessary, says Mr. Hawtrey, *in the absence of new and large supplies of gold* (which there are no grounds for believing will be available), *to reduce the demand for gold*, so that the quantity of gold available for payments may correspond with the new price level. He envisages three ways of bringing about such a reduction in the demand for gold: The extension of the Gold Exchange Standard (as was proposed at the 1922 Genoa Conference), a reduction in the legal reserves of the banks of issue and the pursuance of an open market policy to counteract the effect of a drain of gold, and finally, co-operation between the central banks of issue to bring credit movements in the different countries into line.

This is not the place to discuss in detail these methods, which were recommended by the Macmillan Committee in the face of strong and well-reasoned opposition from Lord Bradbury. For events themselves provided a solution of the problem, though in another sense. It was the purchasing power of paper money which was brought into line with the purchasing power of gold, and not the other way round. The reasons for this have already been given. No human purpose could prevail against the ineluctable and violent fall of world prices after the war. Indebtedness, as the Guillaumes said, had reached such exaggerated proportions that it could not be counteracted by credit, which is itself only a system of indebtedness. The forced devaluation of the pound followed a bare few weeks after the publication of the Macmillan Report, in which this remedy had been strongly repudiated. But the only point which concerns us here is that Mr. Hawtrey's proposal was based on his conviction of the profound influence exercised by an abundance or scarcity of gold on prices.

The ideas of the period 1880–1895, which represented the departure of political economy from an age-old tradition constantly confirmed by events, did not survive the test of facts.

If, in this sphere, the economists can be criticised, it is on the grounds that they did not realise clearly enough, after the war, that the American gold price level was wholly disproportionate to the pre-war level, and were not firm enough in their belief that such an anomaly must inevitably right itself, unless that level were maintained by an enormous and most improbable increase in gold output. The American price curve after the War of Secession should have served as an example. It would have shewn how paper inflation prices fell rapidly to reach the level of world gold prices. But if, in 1922 or 1925, anyone had declared that it was impossible for American prices to stay at the level they had then reached, his argument would have been called fantastic—and by Americans first of all. Clear insight on this point would have been of the greatest possible service in demonstrating the futility of an individual or concerted effort to combat the inevitable.

The gradual return to a price level in harmony with the real state of affairs was achieved through a period of great difficulty and hardship. To future eyes this period of economic history will appear as the result of a great illusion. Belief in the economic omnipotence of governments suffered a severe setback. It is to be hoped that no further experiment will be made to control the world price level. Events can only be controlled if the effort to do so is based on experience. When this particular attempt to order events was made, the experience of an entire century had been overlooked.

Postscript.—In returning to a more correct idea of the action of the precious metals on prices, we should not at the same time return to the more regrettable exaggerations of Ricardian doctrine. Belief in the action of the precious metals is far from being the same as belief in Ricardo's version of the quantity theory. There are certain economists who view the rapid increase in gold output in 1935, 1936 and 1937 with the same apprehension as Ricardo's disciples in 1850. The panic that seized Holland at that time led, it will be remembered, to the adoption of the silver standard, as suggested by Michel Chevalier. The Dutch regretted the step later. In March and April 1937, it was being suggested in London and New York that "the price of gold should be lowered," that is, that the dollar and the pound should be revalorised for fear of a too steep rise in prices. On the contrary, this is the moment to remember the teachings of Tooke and Newmarch, to realise that there is "as it were no point in common" between currency expansion due to gold and currency expansion due to paper. It is the moment to remember that the countries which have no gold (Germany, Italy, the Balkans, China, etc.) are anxious to increase the demand for gold, and that the stability of exchanges and the strength that would be given by an influx of new gold to the entire banking and financial structure, which has been so profoundly shaken in the last twenty years, as well as the expansion of international trade which would follow, would more than offset the inconveniences of a rise in prices which, being international, could only be moderate in extent.

CHAPTER SEVEN

The Action of Gold and of the Discount Rate on Prices

§ I. FROM CANTILLON TO NEWMARCH.—§ II. MARSHALL'S EVIDENCE BEFORE THE CURRENCY COMMISSION.—§ III. KNUT WICKSELL AND HIS CONVERSION.—§ IV. CASSEL'S THEORY.—§ V. KEYNES, HAWTREY, AND THE RETURN TO CANTILLON.

In principle nobody has ever disputed the existence of a connexion between the output of the money metal and the price level. But we have seen that when it is a question of interpreting actual long term price movements, many economists hesitate to apply this general principle to the facts of a given case, and to recognise the influence either of a larger output of goods or of a larger output of gold.

The way in which gold exercises its influence on prices still appears a mystery to many people. In the preceding chapter we dealt with the way in which it brings about a fall, with special reference to the marked price movements of the periods 1873–1895, and 1925–1935. We also indicated the way in which a price rise is caused by referring to the argument of many writers (among others Lexis) that the production of gold and its transformation into money (either directly by coinage at the mint, or indirectly by the banks of issue purchasing bullion in exchange for notes) is equivalent to the creation of new purchasing power, which, when added to existing purchasing power, increases the nominal total of incomes; in the aggregate, these incomes constitute the demand for goods, and the greater demand naturally tends to make prices rise. Whereas, in the normal process of exchange, the acquisition of a money income necessitates the *preliminary sale of a commodity on the market*, which is equivalent to a *downward pressure on market prices*, gold mines yield a product which is *immediately* transformed into purchasing power in the form of money, and which therefore can influence prices only in an upward direction.

Other writers confine their arguments to the point that the money metals, when their quantity is increased, fall in value, like all other economic goods; this fall is expressed automatically by a diminution in the quantity of other goods for which they can be exchanged.[1]

Despite the simplicity of these arguments, the mechanism by which the production of gold affects prices continues to present difficulties to many, who have attempted to find other explanations of long term price movements. In the present chapter we shall survey the theories which have been put forward in regard to this mechanism.

§ 1. *From Cantillon to Newmarch*

The question was first asked (and answered) by Cantillon, the great eighteenth-century master of everything relating to the working of currency and credit:

> "M. Locke lays it down as a fundamental maxim that the quantity of produce and merchandise in proportion to the quantity of money serves as the regulator of market price . . . he has clearly seen that the abundance of money makes every thing dear, but he has not considered how it does so. The great difficulty of this question consists in knowing in what way and in what proportion the increase of money raises prices."[2]

To the answer to this question he devotes three lengthy chapters, full of interesting historical observations. The essential point in his explanation is that the new gold extracted from the mines exerts its influence in two ways, firstly, as new capital on the money and finance market; secondly, and chiefly, as the additional expenditure which those who mine the gold are enabled to make, thus directly affecting prices. He considers this second channel the more important of the two, and concentrates his attention on it.

> "I consider in general that an increase of actual money causes in a State a corresponding increase of consumption which gradually brings about increased prices."[3]

[1] A striking demonstration of the action of the precious metals on prices was given recently in a most interesting study by M. Marjolin, published in *Activité Economique*, October 1935 and January 1937.

[2] Cantillon, p. 161.

[3] *Ibid.*, p. 163.

But he does not under-estimate the first point; indeed, he has a better understanding than some of his successors of the different effects that the two processes will have on the rate of interest:

> "If the abundance of money in the State comes from the hands of money-lenders, it will doubtless bring down the current rate of interest by increasing the number of money-lenders: but if it comes from the intervention of spenders it will have just the opposite effect and will raise the rate of interest by increasing the number of Undertakers who will have employment from this increased expense, and will need to borrow to equip their business in all classes of interest."[1]

This concise passage contains all that is required for a complete solution of the problems of the relation between the discount rate and an influx of the money metals. As to making the fall in the rate of interest the *cause* of the rise in prices which follows an influx of gold—as did some of the writers we shall presently examine—the idea never occurred to Cantillon.

He shews in detail how the greater expenditure of those who own the gold mines gradually increases the incomes, and consequently the expenditure, of other classes; how those with fixed incomes are hurt by rising prices, how such a rise encourages the import of foreign products, leading to the export of gold from one country to another, until the trade balance of the first becomes unfavourable and it again sinks back into its earlier poverty (Spain as an example),[2] how the new countries which have acquired the gold in their turn lose their foreign customers because all their products have risen in price (France between 1648 and 1684 as an example), and how only those countries can win lasting benefit from an influx of gold and silver where "the facility and cheapness of its shipping for the transport of its work and manufactures . . . may compensate the high price of labour caused by the too great abundance of money"[3] (England and Holland as examples).

All that has now become classical, and later writers did not even touch on the problem. Adam Smith saw no difficulty; the mechanism

[1] Cantillon, p. 215.

[2] *Ibid.*, p. 185: "The too great abundance of money, which so long as it lasts forms the power of States, throws them back imperceptibly but naturally into poverty."

[3] *Ibid.*, p. 169.

was obvious. Hume, Thornton,[1] Ricardo, entertained no doubts at all as to the direct action of the precious metals on prices.

They are concerned with another problem: the *distribution of the precious metals among the different countries of the world* and the proportion of them which each manages to retain. Later Senior[2] and Mill were preoccupied with the same question. In the first half of the nineteenth century England was the great reservoir for gold, the country where it circulated most abundantly, and where the price level was highest. In all the analyses of how and why this came about, Cantillon's description is taken as the basis, but it is made more precise, and gradually elaborated into a general theory.

Nothing really new on this subject was brought forward until 1850 and 1851, when gold was discovered and mined in California and Australia. The impression created by these events was enormous; intense commercial activity was apparent almost everywhere, but most notably in England and France; prices rose, prosperity grew, and, once again, the attention of economists was directed to the mechanism by which the precious metals influence the price level and wealth in general.

In France Levasseur and Chevalier, the one in his *Question de l'Or*, the other in his book *La Monnaie*, follow the beaten path, the former more methodically and accurately, the latter with more talent and less lucidity, carefully avoiding any analysis of the mechanism and losing himself in vivid historical digressions or in prophecies which, like all Chevalier's prophecies, were subsequently contradicted by events.[3] But for both of them the mechanism by which gold affects prices remained that of direct exchange between the countries producing gold and the countries exporting com-

[1] His *Enquiry into the Nature and Effects of the Paper Credit of Great Britain*, 1802, contains all the ideas about credit that were to be discussed in England in the first half of the nineteenth century.

[2] Cf. Senior's writings, which have recently been republished by the *Economic Journal*.

[3] Cf. Levasseur, *Le Question de l'or*, 1856, p. 157, and Chevalier, *La Monnaie*, Brussels, 1850, p. 151, and p. 458, where he writes: "The precious metals fall gradually when thrown on to the market in large quantities: for, to sell their bullion in their own countries, the holders of gold and silver, whoever they are, have to have it minted, and when the quantity of money has been doubled, for example, each coin, other things being equal, will only exchange for half the quantity of commodities in comparison with what it was worth before." Chevalier thought that gold would probably be abandoned as the money metal because of the excessive quantities in which it was being produced.

modities. The initial profits increase general demand, new profits are made which in their turn increase demand, and so on. The series of reverberations by means of which the rise is spread from one country to another, in the end embracing the entire economic world, is described by Levasseur with as much care as by Cantillon himself, and in almost identical terms.

In England, on the other hand, the work of Newmarch (who, after Tooke's death, continued alone their great *History of Prices*) brings to light a more complex view of the problem. His description of the consequences of the new gold discoveries is, with Levasseur's, the most lively and exciting of all, while his view of events is even more direct and more vivid than the Frenchman's. He is principally concerned to shew, as against the disciples of Ricardo, firstly, that an influx of gold is a *real addition to the wealth* of the countries where it takes place, and does not merely give rise to a price movement without economic consequences; secondly, that the rise in prices is not the result of a *direct depreciation of gold*, as the Ricardians would have it, but is brought about by the rise in all *incomes* (profits, wages, etc.) drawn from industries that are stimulated by a growing demand.

Newmarch is correct on both points. As far at any rate as the second is concerned, it is really a question of terminology.[1] Like Cantillon, he asserts that it is by means of international trade, by the increased expenditure either at home or abroad of those who get the gold from the mines, that the new wealth is spread over the world.[2]

But Newmarch indicated a second mechanism in addition to this "direct" mechanism, and it is in this that his originality lies. His description of the way in which gold affects prices *through the money market* deserves to be given in his own words.

"Those New Supplies [of gold] were sent to this country either in payment for Goods bought of this country; or as remittances of capital seeking profitable investment, or profitable employment in some kind of trade; and they gradually accumulated in the Bank of England as the

[1] The propriety of the terms used by Newmarch may be questioned. The rise of prices originating in increased demand is the effect not only of the expenditure of *net income* (wages, profits, etc.), but also of *expenditure on the maintenance of capital equipment*, as, for example, when the mining companies buy machines with their gold to replace the old machines.

[2] Cf. Tooke and Newmarch, Vol. VI, pp. 234 and 235.

safest and most convenient place of deposit pending their ultimate application.

"The natural and inevitable effect of so sudden and large an addition to the Reserve of the Bank was (under its present constitution and system of management) to reduce the minimum Rate of Discount from 3 per cent in January, 1851, to 2 per cent in April, 1852; and in the general market to reduce the rate still lower, namely, to about 1½ per cent during the greater part of the year 1852.

"It is true, therefore, that the first effect of the Gold Discoveries was to reduce the Rate of Discount, and through the Rate of Discount, to reduce the Rate of Interest on advances made for long periods on Mortgages and other similar securities. But this effect was in its nature but temporary, and was accompanied by circumstances which tended day by day to counteract its continuance. The most immediate consequence of the extreme reduction of the Rate of Interest was to lessen the cost of producing commodities, and to increase the profits of all persons requiring the accommodation of advances for short or long periods. *In other words, the low rates of* 1852 *set in motion in some important degree the extended trade and exterprise of* 1853; and that extended trade and enterprise rapidly raised the requirements for capital beyond the supply; and led, therefore, to those successive elevations of the rate of interest which were the most striking feature in the early commercial history of 1853."[1]

Thus, in contrast to the predictions of many of his contemporaries, Newmarch sets forth the twofold phenomenon of an initial fall in the discount rate followed by a steady rise in that rate with the continuation of the gold influx, and argues that this initial fall acts as a stimulant to business. (The same double effect was produced in 1895 and the following years when Transvaal gold spread over the world.)

This is what is new in Newmarch, and subsequent theories were all based on the sentence that we have italicised. It was, however, not wholly original, for Cantillon—who had been completely forgotten by Newmarch's time—had in the eighteenth century set forth the same facts and explained in clear and concise terms both the initial fall and the subsequent rise in the discount rate. For both Cantillon and Newmarch the rise in the discount rate after its initial fall is a normal phenomenon; for both of them the two ways in which gold affects prices—the "direct" way by means of greater expenditure, and the "indirect" way by means of the money market,

[1] Vol. VI, pp. 200–201.

are in operation simultaneously and reinforce each other, the first preceding the second. The stimulus directly given to production by the new gold leads to a greater demand for short-term credits, and this demand is made at a higher and higher rate. On the other hand the gold accumulated by the banks enables them to meet this new demand, at first at a very low rate, and then at a rate which steadily rises. The demand for long-term savings and the rates at which they are obtained present the same picture. Thus the phenomenon of an influx of gold followed after a short interval by a rise in the discount rate, which appears at first glance paradoxical, is in fact wholly natural. Later, after 1873, the converse and apparently no less paradoxical phenomenon was observed of a steady and more and more marked fall in the discount rate as the fall in prices and the "appreciation" of gold continued. The fall in the discount rate indicates that there is a cheap *supply* of credit; for it to be followed by a rise there must be an increased and sustained *demand* for credit. Now, unless it is argued (as some of the writers we shall mention did argue, although the facts do not confirm their contention) that the fall in the discount rate is *in itself* and without any other external cause enough to stimulate the production of commodities and to give rise to a steady demand for credit, it must necessarily follow that the precious metals, in order to have the effects which in fact they are observed to have, must act in a twofold manner, both directly on the demand for commodities, and also on the money market.[1]

[1] Between 1858 and 1860 Cairnes devoted four essays to the action of the precious metals on prices, which he republished in 1873 under the title *Essays in Political Economy*. He is concerned primarily to explain the reaction of an influx of gold on different countries and on the prices of different categories of commodities. He describes in detail the re-distribution of industries and of wealth which follows. It is diverting to note that he supports Chevalier as to the probable depreciation of gold at the very time (1872) that the long period of price depression was about to begin—a further proof of the difficulty of prophecy in the economic field. But what I would emphasise here is that not once in his four lengthy essays does Cairnes make the *slightest allusion to the influence which the discount rate may have on the price level*, He is thoroughly familiar with the work of Newmarch, whom he quotes on several occasions, but the sentence on which later Marshall was to construct his theory does not seem to have struck him at all. He limits himself to the assertion that gold acts in two ways:

1. Directly by raising demand prices;
2. Still more markedly in countries such as England and the United States where the use of credit instruments is highly developed, for these instruments reinforce the action of gold and make it possible for a small quantity of gold to produce as

§ II. *Marshall's Evidence before the Currency Commission*

In 1887, in his famous deposition submitted to the English Commission of Enquiry into the Circulation of Gold and Silver,[1] Marshall repudiated the idea of this twofold action, and made the discount rate exclusively instrumental in bringing about a price rise. His evidence had a decisive influence on the subsequent development of currency theory. Mr. Keynes called it "the most important contribution to monetary theory in England since Ricardo."[2] An almost identical theory was put forward by Walras at the same time, but its formulation was so abstract that it did not arouse much response.[3]

At the time that Marshall was giving his evidence the economic and monetary situation was the exact reverse of what it had been in 1856. Prices had been falling for fifteen years. The depression in trade and agriculture was a source of great anxiety to governments, the fall in silver disturbed economic relations between Asia

great an effect as a much larger quantity would in other countries (cf. in particular, pp. 57 *et seq.*).

In a characteristic passage he rejects the idea that gold can act apart from demand, *merely in virtue of its quantity*;

"According to Mr. Newmarch, the depreciation of money may occur by a process which is neither of these, when money operates upon prices neither through demand nor yet through supply, but 'by reason of augmented quantity.' I must confess myself wholly unable to conceive the process here indicated" (p. 57, note).

Finally, he contends that the increase in the currency rendered necessary by the increase in the precious metals and their consequent depreciation *constitutes an evil* (p. 93) compelling the countries affected by it to devote part of their labour to the acquisition of currency instruments which, apart from this function, do not represent wealth at all. This argument is largely directed against Newmarch, who was of the opposite opinion, and recalls the similar contention of Ricardo on this same point.

Taken in the aggregate, Cairnes' ideas shed no new light on the problem discussed here, although his analysis of the successive price changes in Australia, England and India after the new gold discoveries is extremely interesting.

[1] Marshall's evidence is taken from the *Official Papers of Alfred Marshall*, edited by J. M. Keynes in 1926. It will also be found as an Appendix to the *Final Report of the Royal Commission on Gold and Silver*, published officially in 1888, which contains the evidence of a large number of experts of the time that provides valuable material for an understanding of the currency situation of that period.

[2] Cf. *Economic Journal*, 1911, p. 395, footnote.

[3] Cf. Walras, *Eléments d'Economie pure*, p. 318, 1900 edition. Cf. also the excellent articles by Marget in the *Journal of Political Economy*, 1933–1934, for an appreciation of Walras' contribution to this subject.

and Europe. Gold was rising in relation both to silver and to commodities. Hoarding was becoming more widespread. The discount rate and the rate for savings were falling on the principal markets to levels long unknown. The controversy between the bimetallists and the monometallists—so prejudicial to an impartial examination of currency theories—was in full swing. In 1856 the economists were being asked to explain the rise in prices; in 1887 they had to account for the fall.

The natural and traditional explanation was to attribute the fall in prices to the enormous increase in the volume of goods produced, which had not been adequately offset by a corresponding supply of new money since silver had been abandoned as standard. The fall in the long and short term interest rates then appeared as the necessary *consequence* of the fall in prices which, by reducing nominal profits, reduced the rate which entrepreneurs could pay for the capital they borrowed on long or short term. This reduction in the demand price for credits coincided with an increasing supply of available capital on the money market, due to the rapid expansion of the deposit and cheque system and to a reduction in the amount of cash which the public thought it necessary to hold. The inevitable result was a fall in the discount rate.

Marshall approaches the question from an entirely different angle. Nowadays, he says, the precious metals operate principally through the banks. Foreign gold rarely enters into national circulation except through some intermediate process.[1] It is by means of the banks and the credits which they grant that it exerts its influence, and, obviously, when it is being produced in large quantities, the rate of discount falls as the banks' reserves grow.

This fall, in its turn, encourages borrowing on the part both of speculators and of industrialists; it therefore acts as a stimulus to the production of goods, to the demand for raw materials, the services of labour, etc. This is followed by a general rise in prices which, by a well-known reaction, necessitates a larger monetary

[1] In Marshall's time people seemed bemused by a kind of ill-defined mysticism about *gold in circulation* and its influence on prices. Otherwise it is difficult to understand how anyone with as open a mind as Marshall could have attached any importance whatever to the fact that gold is put directly into circulation by the Mint, and indirectly by the banks of issue in the form of notes or current accounts. It is to a vague idea of this kind that Cairnes is alluding in the passage quoted on p. 291, footnote.

circulation. The public's need for coin, the amount of cash which they wish to hold, increases, and their demands are satisfied without difficulty.

If the production of gold is slowed down, or if countries newly adopting the gold standard attract large quantities of the metal, the converse series of events occurs. The gold reserves of the countries which have long been on the gold standard cease to grow; they may even diminish. In these circumstances a fall in the discount rate might well stimulate production, but the subsequent price rise will soon be checked because the banks will find it impossible, with their stationary or falling reserves, to meet the public's growing demand for cash. To protect their reserves they will have to raise the discount rate; prices will sink back again and the fall will be resumed.

The Commission were obviously surprised by this explanation, in spite of their respect for so eminent a witness as Alfred Marshall. They were taken aback by the distinction he drew between earlier times, when gold entered directly into circulation, and the present, when it is put into circulation via the banks. And in fact what difference does it make if the producers of gold themselves have the bullion which represents their gross output coined at the Mint, or whether they hand it in to the bank in exchange for notes or entries in their current accounts which they can use instead of gold as means of payment? The only question which arises is whether the gross output of the mines is *spent directly* (it matters little where) on sinking funds, replacement of machinery, new investments, wages, and, in so far as it is paid out as dividends to shareholders, for personal consumption. On this point there can be no doubt. The gross output of the mines is *spent*, and spent *directly*; now, as formerly, this expenditure represents an exactly equivalent increase in the demand for the goods and products existing in the world, and consequently tends to make their prices rise. It is precisely this tendency which provides the initial stimulus, that is later reinforced by the greater elasticity of bank credits.

A second and equally pertinent question was put to Marshall; it directed the discussion into the instructive sphere of the interpretation of facts:

From 1873 until to-day (1888), observed in substance many members of the Commission, we have had a steady fall in prices and a parallel fall in the rate of discount. On your theory, how do you explain the fact that these lowerings of the discount rate did not check the price fall and give rise to an upward movement? What difference is there between the falls in the discount rate that have occurred in the last fifteen years and the predicted fall which, when there is an influx of gold, would according to you provoke a rise in prices?

Marshall answered this clear question by advancing a subtle theory which, in varied terms, has been taken up by his successors, and may be summarised as follows:

The normal rate of discount is directly dependent on the long term rate of interest. When the latter falls as a result of the rapid accumulation of savings, the discount rate follows suit. At such times lowerings of the discount rate can only *follow* falls in the long term interest rate, and these successive falls, being merely the *effect* of the general situation on the market for savings, cannot act as a *cause*. For a fall in the discount rate to affect the movement of prices, the rate must fall *below the normal rate* corresponding to the rate for savings, thus creating, between the two rates, a gap which will bring entrepreneurs profits large enough to set going a movement towards higher prices. This is precisely what is done by an influx of gold. On the other hand, the falls in the discount rate between 1873 and 1888 were not of this peculiar kind. The rate was always lowered to adjust it to the fall in the rate of interest on capital, which had *already occurred*. Conversely, when the long term interest rate rises as a result of greater profits on capital there will be a gradual rise in the discount rate, brought about by the rise in the rate for savings. The peculiar kind of fall in the discount rate following an influx of the precious metals, which marks the change in the direction of interest rates, is, to use Marshall's term, only a temporary "ripple" on the surface of the discount level, which soon gives way to a rise; but this "ripple" is enough to provoke a reversal of the price movement, which will last as long as the influx of precious metals, and their direct or indirect entry into circulation, is great enough to maintain the new price level.[1]

[1] The essential passage from Marshall's evidence is as follows, p. 130 (see also pp. 51, 52 and 157 of *Official Papers*): "In my view the rate of discount is determined by the average profitableness of different businesses; that is, determined partly by the amount of capital that is seeking investment as compared with the openings for new

In these explanations bullion continued to play its part as an essential factor determining the rise or fall of prices; the mistake lies in Marshall's failure to trace the fall in interest rates to its source, that is, to the *preceding* fall in prices. The members of the Commission remained sceptical. They returned to the point two or three times, and asked Marshall for further elucidation.

They asked why—if the origin of a price rise lies in the gap between short and long term interest rates—this gap, and the reversal of the price tendency which results, cannot exist *apart from any exceptional influx of gold.* Marshall had explained the fall in the long term rate of interest between 1883 and 1888 as due to the rapid accumulation of savings in that period. Assuming that to be correct, why had the discount rate during the same period never

docks, new machinery, and so on; and the extent of these openings is itself practically determined to a great extent by the belief that people have that prices will rise or fall, other things being equal, for people are unwilling to borrow if they think that prices will fall. The supply of loans on the one hand and the desire of people to obtain loans on the other, having fixed the rates of discount at anything, 8, 6, 5, or 2 per cent, then the influx of a little extra gold, going as it does into the hands of those who deal in credit, causes the supply to rise relatively to the demand; the rate of discount falls below its equilibrium level, however low that was, and therefore stimulates speculation. . . . A fall which had been produced by the thinning out of the field for the investment of capital relatively to the supply of capital could not increase speculation, because it had itself been caused by the difficulty of finding a profitable opening for speculation. But when discount has already fallen sufficiently low to absorb the capital even in spite of the thinning out of the field for profitable employment of speculative capital, so that a new equilibrium at the lower rate of discount has been arrived at, then an even lower rate is required to again establish equilibrium between the demand for loans and the supply of them; this new rate effects the equilibrium by causing capital to go into the hands of speculators who would not take capital at the old rate, but do take it at the new; and whatever form their speculation may take, it is almost sure, directly or indirectly, to raise prices. This is the main issue. There is, however, a side issue which should not be overlooked and may be in some cases more important than the main issue. It is this: when the gold comes to the country it is known and people expect that prices will rise. Now if a person doubting whether to borrow for speculative purposes has reason to believe that prices will rise, he is willing to take a loan at 3 per cent, which before he would not have taken at 2½ per cent, and consequently the influx of gold into the country by making people believe that prices will rise increases the demand for capital and raises, therefore, in my opinion, the rate of discount." We fully agree with this part of Marshall's analysis, made with that admirable care characteristic of all the work of this great economist, which states that an influx of new gold into a market where the discount rate has long been falling, gives an extra turn of the screw which for a time sends the discount rate still lower and encourages business men to borrow in order to take advantage of the difference between the discount rate and the long term interest rate.

fallen *below* what he called the equilibrium rate? Why had it always *followed* and adjusted itself to the long-term rate? Why, in the absence of a *spontaneous* fall (which is quite possible since the long and short term markets are comparatively independent) to the level required to bring about a reversal in prices, had not the banks tried *deliberately* to bring it down? All the more as, throughout the entire period—this was pointed out by Sir David Barbour and Marshall agreed—the Bank of England's cash holdings had increased considerably, which would have facilitated a reduction in the rate.

The mistake made by Marshall, misled by his purely banking interpretation of the rise in prices, was to attempt to explain not only *long-term rises* exclusively by variations in the discount rate—which would have been rash enough—but also long-term falls, which was impossible. For it is obvious that in these cases the discount rate plays no part at all; unlike gold, goods do not pass through the hands of the banks. The pressure which the normal increase in the volume of commodities exerts on markets—if it is not offset by the creation of enough new purchasing power—necessarily brings prices down and leads to a fall in the rate of interest and in the discount rate. Marshall loses himself in futile efforts to find the cause of price falls in the *money market* and admits ingenuously: "It puzzles me down to this moment."[1] Mr. Leonard Courtney, a member of the Commission, tried to extricate him from his difficulty. But between them they only succeeded in explaining what happens when *gold is sent from one country to another*—a purely temporary phenomenon which has no connexion with a fall in world prices and which moreover is accompanied, as we have seen (this would have struck Marshall as paradoxical), by a slight increase in the gold holdings of the Bank of England, that is to say by an increase, and not a decrease, in the means for granting credit.[2]

All this can be explained very simply if the doctrine embodied in the best economic tradition is accepted, that the supply of commodities directly influences the price level; but it becomes incomprehensible if the discount rate is regarded as the essential

[1] *Official Papers*, p. 126.

[2] This increase is explained by the depression itself, during which the loans formerly made by the banks are repaid and only partially renewed. The banks therefore have larger supplies of loanable capital, but the depression prevents the public from making use of them.

intermediary in all upward or downward variations of the general price level. Quite recently the same misunderstanding has led certain English economists to believe that it is enough to lower the discount rate a little more to reverse the downward price tendency which has been in operation for the last ten years; the initial cause of that fall was the absurdly high price level which, after the war, it was thought possible to maintain.

However that may be, the idea that variations in the discount rate are not only one factor, but the chief and almost the sole factor in the reversal of price tendencies, has become, since Marshall gave his evidence, an important part of English doctrine.

What has been said here refers of course to long term price movements, and not to so-called cyclical movements. These may be attributed to different causes from those which determine what the English call secular price movements, on which cyclical movements are as it were grafted. Writers after Marshall did not always draw this distinction, sometimes applying and sometimes refusing to apply his ideas to cyclical price variations. In what follows we are concerned, unless otherwise stated, with the interpretation of long term movements.

§ III. *Knut Wicksell and His Conversion*

Dubious as Marshall's theory was, it provided valuable support to some of the most unfortunate tendencies that have been apparent in the broad stream of ideas relating to currency and credit. It strengthened all those who rejected the theory that an influx of precious metals directly influences prices—and they had become plentiful since the bimetallist controversy, some out of a spirit of good fellowship, others in the stubbornness of their monometallism. It strengthened the idea, natural to bankers, that with the increase in the number of notes and cheques credit instruments, and credit instruments alone, independently of the output of the precious metals, influence prices—as though the total of these instruments were not itself directly and obviously bound up with movements in the gold reserve.[1] Finally, it lent powerful support to those who

[1] Cf. the illuminating graphs published by M. Marjolin in No. 3 of *Activité Economique*.

were still, after so many centuries, seeking the philosopher's stone of political economy, the way to stabilise the constantly moving level of prices. They profited most from Marshall's theory. It is they who are so anxious to-day to convert governments to their belief in the practicability of a managed currency. They all ascribe the vital role to the discount rate.

An extremely erudite Swedish economist with a vigorous mind, M. Knut Wicksell, took up Marshall's theory and developed it to its final consequences in a book which was published in German in 1898.[1] He has since reiterated his ideas in his *Lectures*, which appeared in Swedish in 1906 and in German translation in 1922.[2] A rise in prices may be initiated, he says, by a wide enough gap between the bank's discount rate and what he calls the "normal" or "natural" or "real" long term rate of interest. He does not consider that this rate is identical with Marshall's "equilibrium" rate, but the two conceptions are very close to one another.[3] In both cases it is a question, not of a rate that is actually in operation, but of a *theoretical* rate, an intellectual construction, and that in itself is enough to indicate how embarrassed the banks would be if they had to direct their policy by this abstraction. For Wicksell, the "normal" rate is the rate at which "there is exact equilibrium between the demand for and the supply of savings." [4]

When the rate for bank loans is lower than this theoretical rate, entrepreneurs can hope for a margin of profit which is wide enough to encourage the initiation of new production; this involves the purchase of raw materials and the services of labour and tends to raise prices and wages generally. *This rise may continue indefinitely*,

[1] *Geldzins und Güterpreis*: this is very difficult to find in the original, and the present author has used the English translation which appeared in 1935.

[2] The English edition appeared in 1935 as *Lectures on Political Economy*, translated by E. Classen and edited by Professor L. Robbins. M. Wicksell gave a summary of his theory in the *Economic Journal* for 1907, p. 213. In this article he suggests international co-operation of the banks to maintain prices, and indicates the opposition between the maintenance of the price level and the maintenance of exchange stability on which Mr. Keynes in particular has since insisted so strongly.

[3] In his Introduction to the reprint of Tooke's works, Professor Gregory identifies this idea with I. Fisher's conception of "real" interest, but this is an error of interpretation; see the Appendix to this chapter.

[4] P. 220. It is, he adds, "more or less equal to the anticipated yield of new capital effectively employed in production." This is what he calls the "Grenz-produktivitaet des Wartens," a complex concept which is explained in the first volume of his *Lectures.*

the rate of interest adjusting itself to the new price level, *provided that the banks keep their discount rate below the normal rate as defined above*. The rise in prices is thus the means by which the two rates are adjusted to each other.

It should be observed that Wicksell apparently believes that short term credit from the banks can take the place of long term credit for the industrialist, or, as he says, can "compete" with it; obviously, then, it can *make up for* a temporary absence of long term credit.[1] It is the volume of long term savings which, in the end, is the most important for production. It is a low rate for long-term savings which favours the development of production, and this rate is of far greater import than any gap which may exist (and which in fact nearly always does exist) between the long-term rate and the discount rate.

Here, however, we are most interested in the sequel to this argument. For the rise in prices provoked by the divergence between the two rates to be continued, one condition, says Wicksell, is necessary. The monetary system, and this is the crux of the argument, must be "of unlimited elasticity."[2]

It is precisely this elasticity, he continues, not unlimited but relative, which is given to a monetary system when an inflow of gold, as a result of the new output of the mines, increases the reserves of the banks. But it can also be given in another way—for example, *if the banks extend their credit indefinitely*. "There can scarcely be any difference if for gold we substitute bank-notes, fictitious deposits, or other bank credit. The *causa efficiens*, the direct and active cause, is in both cases the same, namely a rate of loan interest below the normal, and in both cases the consequences must be the same."[3]

Let us ask the question in our turn: what is the difference? It is merely the difference between gold and paper money!

[1] At a time when short-term banking deposits are increasing steadily as a result of an increase in currency (as happened from 1900 to 1912) the banks can indeed without any great obvious danger place part of the short-term funds deposited with them in long-term investments. The German banks did this at the beginning of the twentieth century. In this case short-term savings (what we have elsewhere called reserve savings) do really provide long-term funds. But this is a dangerous practice if the rise is followed by a prolonged fall, or if a slight crisis precipitates large withdrawals.

[2] *Lectures on Political Economy*, Vol. II, p. 197.

[3] *Ibid.*, Vol. II, p. 198.

Here, according to Wicksell, we have a way of stabilising prices. Let us first of all give the banks "unlimited elasticity" of credit. Then let us induce them to fix their discount rate below or above the famous "normal" rate of interest, according to whether we want prices to rise or to fall. And the goal is achieved. Only we may ask whether there will still be a "normal" rate of interest or any saving at all, if the banks enjoy "unlimited" elasticity of credit, and short-term credit can compete "indefinitely" with long-term savings. There will no longer be any need for a gap between the discount rate and the normal rate. The price rise will take place by itself.

In brief, what Wicksell says may be summarised as follows: Give the banks the monetary means, in gold or paper, which will enable them to extend credit indefinitely, and compel them to lower their discount rate. You will get an equally indefinite rise in prices. But take care; avoid the error of the vulgar who attribute the rise in prices to the unlimited abundance of gold or paper. No! The origin of the rise, its *causa efficiens*, lies in the fact that the banks have kept a correct distance between their discount rate and what I call the "natural" or "real" rate of interest; this, I confess, I cannot define in thoroughly precise terms; my colleagues, Cassel and Keynes, for example, and many others, dispute its theoretical validity, and the banks which would eventually be charged with the control of prices, have, I admit, no means whatever of establishing or verifying that normal rate.

Voltaire said that a sorcerer could always destroy a herd of cattle by his incantations, on condition that the incantations were accompanied by a large enough dose of arsenic. In Wicksell's case the incantation is the gap between the discount rate and the "natural" rate of interest. The arsenic takes the form of an influx of gold or unlimited credit creation. He regards the incantation as the principal, the arsenic as a subsidiary cause.

This is what Marshall's theory, stripped of all the reservations and conditions with which the great English economist naturally qualified it, led to. In this form it is carried further. The discount rate is no longer the intermediary through which an abundance or scarcity of gold exerts its influence on prices. It has become the "efficient cause," and gold is now the intermediary—an intermediary which, it is true, is admitted to be indispensable. Marshall is not merely surpassed; he is contradicted, for Wicksell goes on to dispute at least one of the ideas which Marshall held most firmly. The latter regards the discount rate as normally a function of the long term interest rate. In Wicksell the short term discount rate ends up by imposing its level on the rate for savings. Neither contention is correct. Sometimes the two rates are largely independent of each other, sometimes they are closely connected. The two markets are in constant contact, but they are supplied from different sources and are approached by different demands. We have analysed elsewhere the differences between the two.[1] But, as between Marshall and Wicksell, the former's point of view is far more often in accordance with the facts than the latter's, although it is Wicksell's theory which has been dominant in Anglo-Saxon financial policy in the last few years.

This was Wicksell's position in 1898. He was to make a notable change in it eight years later, and the change marks a curious and significant incident in the history of economic thought.

After 1895 the world monetary situation changed once again. The exploitation of the Transvaal mines, and the enormous influx of gold which followed, dominated all subsequent events. The prolonged price fall was succeeded by a marked rise; in all important centres the rate for savings and the discount rate rose too; in the field of production and finance all the phenomena which astonished the world in 1851 and 1856 were reproduced.

It would appear extremely difficult to attribute this reversal to any other cause than the sudden abundance of the precious metals after their relative scarcity. Only those did so who were still influenced by the bimetallist controversy and the opportunist arguments of the gold monometallists. Others saw the lesson of events clearly. The same zeal which formerly went into the search for antidotes to the fall in prices was now applied to finding means to check the rise. By the same token the traditional doctrine of the *direct* influence of an influx of the precious metals on prices regained its former prestige.

This is what Wicksell said in the preface to his *Lectures* of 1906:

"I was earlier of the opinion, which was in complete accordance with the ideas of the classical school, that the action of an influx of gold on

[1] Cf. the present author's study of *Saving*, published in 1922 and reproduced in his *Essais sur quelques Problèmes Monétaires*, 1934.

prices operates principally through the medium of the discount rate, in the sense that when the output of gold exceeds requirements, the gold reserves of the banks are increased; this induces them to lower their discount rate, which in its turn causes a rise in prices great enough to bring the new gold stocks in circulation.

"On a more thorough consideration of the question, I have come to the conclusion that in this process chief emphasis should be laid on the increased demand for goods in the gold-producing countries. If this demand is not accompanied by an equally great additional supply of goods, or in other words by greater gold requirements in other countries, it must have as a direct result a rise in prices, whether or not the discount rate is thereby affected, or even moves in the opposite direction."[1]

Here he has returned to the idea of the direct action of gold on prices, and, in the course of his book, he explains in detail how, in his opinion, this mechanism works.[2] In his conclusion he summarises his point of view in these words:

"There are two essential causes of change in the commodity price level. *Firstly*, the demand for goods from the countries producing the precious metals, especially gold, followed by shipments of gold in payment thereof. . . . *Secondly*, the fact that interest on borrowed money is for one reason or another either below or above the level which would normally be governed by the real rate ruling at the time, a circumstance which, so long as it lasts, must cause a progressive rise or fall in prices and during which the *medium of turnover* is adapted to the changed demand, not by an increase or decrease in the quantity of money (gold) but by an increase or decrease in the (physical or virtual) velocity of circulation of money through the agency of credit."[3]

It is therefore only so-called *cyclical* movements, and not secular movements, which originate in the gap between the natural and the actual rate. Long term movements are linked up with gold produc-

[1] *Lectures on Political Economy* (French edition, Introduction, p. xii). The same statement is made in the article he published in 1907 in the *Economic Journal*. He goes on: "This modification of my former views does not affect the practical conclusions to be drawn concerning the rational regulation of the value of money, for in my opinion such regulation presupposes a complete separation between the value of money and gold fluctuations." Thus he admits that his system is conditional on a paper currency.

[2] Cf. pp. 194 *et seq.* of his *Lectures*. His explanation is on the lines of those given by Cantillon, Levasseur, etc., but rather more technical.

[3] *Ibid.*, p. 215.

tion. Cyclical movements are effected by means of greater rapidity in the circulation of money, that is to say by means of an increase in bank credits; the long-term movements are due to the direct increase in the volume of purchasing power represented by the new gold.

Wicksell, however, fails to draw all the consequences of his change in attitude. Taking the case in which the output of gold is clearly insufficient, bringing about a prolonged price fall, that is, a long-term movement, he suggests that this can be met by a decisive and steady lowering of the discount rate.

> "An adequate lowering of interest rates should successfully counteract the otherwise inevitable pressure on prices; the only obstacle to its realisation would be the fact that the banks' supplies of gold would no longer suffice to fill the vacuum in the circulation of gold among the public which would be caused by the diminished production of gold."[1]

To avoid this obstacle he recommends the holding of foreign securities to make up the gold reserve of every bank, and finally, if no other means is effective, the substitution of paper money for gold.

Here are the essentials of the programme proposed, and to some extent applied, in the Anglo-Saxon countries in the last ten years. It will be seen that the idea is older than the present crisis, and is not exclusively English. But Wicksell ignores one important measure, precisely the one measure which could be effective in the situation he has supposed, but which would have occurred to nobody before the war: that measure is devaluation which, by changing the content of the monetary unit, ratifies the fall in the general price level without subjecting the national economy to the sufferings involved in the alternative method of lowering prices, that is, in deflation. Wicksell overlooked this measure because, among the causes of a change in the long term price tendency, he forgot to mention one, and not the least important one, which acts in a contrary direction to an abundance of gold: *the abundance of goods*, which *also acts directly* on prices, making them fall when the output of gold is not great enough to counteract the pressure. Against this pressure, as we said in the previous chapter, so long as prices are expressed in the only recognised international

[1] *Lectures on Political Economy*, p. 216.

currency, that is to say in gold, a lowering of the *discount rate* will have no more effect than a wisp of straw in a storm. But it is precisely pressure of this kind which has been exerted in the last ten years on a price level artificially created by the war. As to substituting paper money for gold, that is a national currency for an international currency, its effect is to unleash all the powerful forces which determine the prices of national currencies in relation to each other and, by means of the rate of exchange, burden the price level of each country with a weight which manipulations of the discount rate are totally incapable of lightening.

Wicksell's conversion was not complete. In spite of everything he remains faithful to the idea of controlling the price level by means of the discount rate, although he admits that the discount rate is ineffective when there is an influx of gold (since the rise of prices then, he agrees, is produced independently of the discount rate), and powerless when there is a scarcity of gold, since any rise which it might bring about would immediately be checked by inadequate bank reserves and consequent limitation of credit. That is why Keynes and Hawtrey advocate another method: the purchase of securities by the banks.

§ IV. *Cassel's Theory*

Wicksell was not alone in returning after 1900 to the correct idea of the direct action of gold on prices. Others also came back to it, and many never abandoned it. Irving Fisher, for example, considered it so self-evident that he did not even attempt to describe the mechanism in detail—for which he has been criticised. Others, like Keynes, before the war, while supporting Marshall's theory, were cautious enough to add that the mechanism is not always the same.[1] Edwin Cannan never hesitated a moment. For him it was scarcely a problem, the mechanism was so clear.[2] He found it almost impossible to believe that anyone could ever doubt this explanation, but adds "fifty years after Cairnes"; Cairnes himself

[1] Cf. his review of Fisher's *Purchasing Power of Money* in the *Economic Journal* for 1911, p. 393: "There is of course no single explanation suited to all times and places."

[2] Cf. his *Money*, p. 66, and *Modern Currency*, p. 52.

remarked with some bitterness that in fact misconceptions on this point were very widespread.

But at the end of the war, and after the beginning of the 1931 crisis, the problem of a stable price level assumed a new urgency. Since 1925 there had again been a prolonged fall in prices, and the idea of utilising the discount rate as an instrument of stabilisation regained popularity. Those who advocate this policy, Cassel, Keynes, Hawtrey, all rely in varying degrees on Wicksell's ideas and proposals. All ascribe preponderant influence to the discount rate: some see in it a means of counteracting the fall in prices; others (Hawtrey) find the actual cause of the crisis in the inopportune raising of the discount rate by the banks of issue. But if we look for the scientific basis of their ideas, the precise mechanism by which they believe the discount rate affects prices, we are somewhat surprised to find that the account of this mechanism, which was faulty enough when Marshall described it, has not made the slightest advance, and that not one of the writers who aim at price stabilisation agrees with the others on the methods by which this can be achieved. This absence of agreement between the inventors of systems of general price stabilisation recurs, it will have been remarked, throughout the history of economic doctrine.

Walras considers the "symmetallism" proposed by Marshall ineffective, and Marshall finds Walras' monometallism, with subsidiary silver issues, impracticable. When, later, Irving Fisher put forward his plan for the compensated dollar (one of whose minor defects was that it applied only to the United States, and left the rest of the world in darkness) he encountered criticism from Cassel and Wicksell, Keynes and Hawtrey. We shall soon see that both Cassel and Keynes had a different idea of the "natural" rate of interest from Wicksell, although this conception underlies their theories, and that Keynes and Cassel define the term differently. As to Keynes' currency theory, which may be said to have convinced nobody, it was Hawtrey who subjected it to the most decisive criticism. In themselves these disagreements are wholly natural and arise in perfect good faith. Nevertheless it must be confessed that when such highly qualified specialists all differ on the most difficult point in monetary theory, on the principles and methods of price stabilisation and on the chances of such plans succeeding, the eagerness they display to get governments (either individually or collectively) to adopt one or other of these methods, has in it something to arouse anxiety.

On what arguments, for example, does Cassel rely, to demonstrate the possibility of stabilising prices by the banks' discount policy? On new observations that have been scientifically verified? Not at all; but on a series of purely logical deductions, innocent of any experimental authority, which are peculiarly reminiscent of the dialectical method of Marx.[1]

How does gold get into circulation? Through the banks, answers Cassel, following Marshall. "It is therefore the banks which, in the final analysis, control the currency." The rashness of this generalisation is immediately obvious—for the banks remain passive in the face of a gold influx, which as a rule they merely submit to. But how do they control currency, and thereby the price level? Through the discount rate (as though a large volume of currency instruments did not enter circulation without the mediation of credit, merely by an increase in cash holdings, in the notes and deposits by which they are represented)!

> "Consequently," says Cassel, "the movements of the general price-level, in so far as they are controlled by factors on the monetary side, are at all times mainly determined by the bank rate."[2]

This series of general propositions, each of which, taken alone, is incorrect, but which appear to follow logically the one from the other, diverts the reader's attention from the influx of gold as a factor in the price level and directs it to the discount rate. It is Marshall's theory, minus his *nuances*. But Cassel goes far beyond Marshall. What, he asks, has been the object of the banks' discount policy up to the present? To allow gold to exercise its influence on prices by maintaining the convertibility of credit. The discount rate has thus been used to achieve a price level *in conformity with a certain goal:* the subordination of the price level to the supply of gold.

But—and this is the crux of the argument—are there no other objectives which could be reached by using the same m thod? For example, the maintenance of a stable average price for a given

[1] Cf. *The Theory of Social Economy*. Transl. by J. McCabe, London, 1932, section 58, entitled: *The Regulation of the Price Level by the Discount Rate.*

[2] *Ibid.*, p. 475.

group of commodities? "A rate-policy that aims at the gold-parity of the standard, or, in other words, at a constant price for gold, will bring about a price-level with secular variations in inverse ratio to the value of gold and with certain independent annual variations. It would hardly be too bold to infer from this that a rate-policy that aimed at the fixing of any other price could bring about the same result. As such aim of a rate-policy the main thing to be taken into consideration would be the fixing of a definite average of a certain group of commodities or, which comes to the same thing, the fixing of the total price of a definite quantity of commodities. It must, therefore, be possible by means of a suitable rate-policy to obtain a price-level with secular variations in inverse proportion to the fluctuations in value of this quantity of commodities relatively to the sum total of commodities.

"By choosing a sufficiently representative quantity of commodities such changes of value could not take place to any great extent, and it would therefore be possible to stabilise the general price-level by means of a prudent rate-policy to such an extent that there would be no secular variations."[1] Here we are where we wanted to be!

It might be pointed out to M. Cassel that it is not the discount rate, but the *convertibility of credits into gold*, which makes the price level vary in relation with the supply of gold. It might be pointed out that all that the banks have so far done is to assist in *maintaining that convertibility*, leaving prices to find their own level in relation to gold. He might be asked how, in the system which he proposes, the banks will act to maintain convertibility against "a group of commodities," which seems rather more complicated than the maintenance of convertibility against gold. He would reply—and the similarity to Ricardo is curious[2]—that convertibility is of secondary importance, that in fact the discount rate is all (as if convertibility had not been maintained almost throughout the entire eighteenth century in England and a great part of the nineteenth century in France *without any appreciable variations in the discount rate*, and with prices fluctuating freely). And if you were

[1] *The Theory of Social Economy*, p. 477.

[2] Ricardo considered the convertibility of notes a matter of secondary importance, useful only because it ensured limitation of the quantity of paper. Limitation of quantity alone maintained the value of the paper.

to ask for more precise instructions for bankers who (poor things!) will find it rather difficult to determine whether any given price movement indicates a "secular" or an "annual" variation,[1] he will reply that they must maintain the discount rate *in accordance with* (*in Uebereinstimmung*) the "real" rate of interest on capital; this conception of a real rate, M. Cassel himself declares, is "conventional," and the only certain thing we know about it is that it is different from M. Wicksell's conception.[2]

From this phantasmagoria—for indeed it is nothing else—we can extract one thing: that, like Wicksell, but with fewer reservations, M. Cassel thinks that the ideal currency system is a paper money system (he uses the term *freie Währung*) under which variations in the discount rate would at all times determine the price level. His theory is applicable to such a system, but not to a gold system. But we know that in a paper money régime the discount rate scarcely counts at all (as we saw earlier on) as against the far more powerful reactions set up by "confidence" in the paper and by variations in the exchange rate.

Marshall would certainly have been astonished by this currency utopia, but its origin can be traced back to his theory, and to the role which he incorrectly assigns to the discount rate.

But better follows. After this great verbal dialectical effort (in the best traditions of Marx and Ricardo), M. Cassel is suddenly seized by a doubt. After all, he asks, is this price stabilisation so desirable? And in a truly odd passage he shews—this time by arguments whose validity no one will dispute—that, except where the national economy is stationary, it would have thoroughly inequitable consequences. The passage should be quoted in full. It demonstrates that M. Cassel's doctrine of price stabilisation is as doubtful from the point of view of social utility as we have found it to be inadequate from the point of view of practical operation.

"The moment we consider a progressive national economy, we see that the question has other aspects. Progress consists in raising the productivity of human labour as well as in multiplying the labour. If the productivity increases in a certain annual percentage, we may suppose, on the one hand, that the prices of commodities remain unchanged and the incomes of the producers are increased by the aforesaid percentage

[1] Cassel is of the opinion that only secular variations can be controlled by the discount rate.

[2] *Theory of Social Economy*, p 437.

or, on the other hand, that the incomes of the producers remain constant and the prices of commodities are reduced to the amount of the percentage."

He continues with a description of the effects which this change would have on the relations between borrowers and lenders:

"If productivity rises and the prices of commodities are unchanged, a lender of money will receive back a sum that represents the same amount of commodities as the original loan. He will therefore derive no advantage from the increased productivity; relatively, he will be worse off. The whole advantage falls to the borrower of money, who, if he is a producer, as he generally is, has made a direct profit by the increase of productivity without alteration of prices; if he is a State, borrowing for purposes of consumption, he sees his financial position strengthened by the rise of the general income. If, on the other hand, the prices of commodities fall in the same measure as productivity increases, the loaner gets his share of the increased productivity, while the borrower gets no profit from it in connexion with the loan.

Which alternative is to be preferred, or whether a middle course should be adopted, is essentially an economic-political question in which great interests are opposed to each other."[1]

Price stabilisation is thus an objective which it is far from easy to define. It is like the problem of "just distribution" which nobody has succeeded in defining; if it were put into effect it would immediately give rise to new problems; up to the present his followers have been as little able to give precise answers to these problems as M. Cassel himself.

§ v. *Keynes, Hawtrey and the Return to Cantillon*

Cassel remains true to Marshall's theory in the sense that for him the rate of discount is the chief instrument for controlling prices; this is not enough for Messrs. Keynes and Hawtrey; the discount rate has to be reinforced by a new method: the purchase of securities on the market.

Referring constantly to Wicksell in the two large volumes of *A Treatise on Money* published in 1930, Mr. Keynes sets forth a

[1] *Theory of Social Economy*, pp. 484–485.

theory which differs noticeably from that of the Swedish economist, as well as from M. Cassel's.[1]

Mr. Keynes' book aims at formulating a policy which will enable the banks to influence the price level, but it is rather surprising, after the writer's great effort, to note the extreme caution of the conclusions he reaches. In the first place (and this is remarkable in a disciple of Marshall) he regards the discount rate as a defective instrument for the control of prices. A lasting effect on the price level can only be exercised by means of the rate for savings, that is the long term interest rate. By lowering the discount rate all that the banks can do is to inaugurate a tendency, on the part of depositors, to invest their funds in government securities, which will naturally cause a rise in their price, that is to say a fall in the long term rate of interest.[2]

But something more must be done if this latter rate is to be directly affected. In fact the only thing that can send prices up is that the actual long term rate of interest shou d differ from its "natural" rate. What is this "natural" rate? It is not the rate as defined by Marshall, nor by Cassel, nor even Wicksell. "The natural rate of interest," says Mr. Keynes, "is the rate at which saving and the value of investment are exactly balanced";[3] for—and this is his entire theory—once this equilibrium is not in force (because the actual interest rate is either below or above the natural rate, and therefore savings are either in excess of or less than the investment demand) the prices of goods are immediately affected. Prices rise when the actual rate is lower than the natural rate, and fall when it is higher.

We shall not stop to criticise this theory, advanced by Keynes with a wealth of algebraic formulas. That has been done fully in an article by Mr. Hawtrey. We shall simply point out that Mr. Keynes' "natural" rate is only an intellectual construction, that it can neither be established in theory nor affirmed in reality, which means that as a theory it is incapable of scientific verification and

[1] An account of his ideas on this point is to be found in the excellent Swedish review, *Index*, for 1930.

[2] *A Treatise on Money*, Vol. II, pp. 363 *et seq*. He admits that up to the present the discount rate has not exerted much influence, and that only the future can shew whether the methods which he proposes, "confidently employed in the right degree and at the right time," will have the desired effect.

[3] *Ibid.*, Vol. I, p. 155.

in practice it is utterly useless for bankers who would wish to use it as a guide.

Let us however examine the conclusions to which these premises lead Mr. Keynes. If his initial theory is correct, a reversal in the price tendency can be brought about by having a rate of interest that is lower than the natural rate. But this result cannot be obtained by mere manipulation of the discount rate. Something more effective must be done; he suggests the direct purchase of fixed interest-bearing securities on the open market. This policy must be pursued by the banks "to the bitter end," that is, until the fall in the rate of interest has reached a point at which the rise in prices can begin.[1]

Thus Keynes, like Wicksell, requires unlimited creation of credit by the banks, or, more exactly, unlimited issue of banking credit, not in the form of normal bank advances but for the purpose of buying securities on the market. Keynes, too, goes far beyond Marshall: Wicksell's theory of unlimited credit elasticity has got the upper hand. It is more than doubtful whether an issue of this kind can achieve anything but a rise in stock exchange values by encouraging speculation, the effects of which might be very different from those anticipated by Keynes. The advantage that such a policy would have for state finances is obvious; what is not so clear is how this artificial rate of interest can affect the position of a national economy in which progress or depression obviously depends on a large variety of factors.

Mr. Hawtrey's theory, though in principle very different from Mr. Keynes', in practice arrives at the same conclusions.[2] He would meet a prolonged price fall by having the central banks purchase fixed interest-bearing securities on the market. These operations, combined with a very low short term rate of interest, would, in his opinion, bring about that slight rise in prices which is enough to set the entire economic machine going in the right direction.

Mr. Hawtrey is one of those who believe in the possibility of maintaining the price level by credit, and his theory really needs separate treatment; here we shall deal only with the two essential

[1] *Treatise*, Vol. II, pp. 369 *et seq*.

[2] Mr. Hawtrey has a large number of works to his credit which deserve separate study. The most important, for the section which follows, are *The Art of Central Banking*, 1932, and *The Gold Standard*, 1933.

points in it that affect the question we are discussing, that is, the method of regulating the price level. Firstly, he believes that if the gold standard has been "a disastrous failure" since 1926 (although he wishes it to be the system of the future), the main reason is that the central banks have raised their discount rate at inopportune moments. These rises in the rate have, according to Hawtrey, precipitated a "deflation" of prices which has made the crisis more severe and more violent. After all that has already been said on this point in earlier sections of this book, it seems unnecessary to repeat once more that in the price fall after 1925, and especially after 1930, when gold prices were readjusted to a world level corresponding to the real relation between the output of gold and the production of goods, the pressure exerted by the rising output of commodities was far too great to be either lightened or increased by the action of the discount rate.[1]

As to the effect which the unlimited purchase of securities on the market can have on the commodity price level, it should be noted that recourse to this method implies that Marshall's initial theory is abandoned; according to him the gap between the discount rate and the interest rate is enough to raise prices. Mr. Hawtrey returns to the old method of an unlimited issue of bank credits. He says:

> "When a bank buys long-dated securities . . . there may be a delay in bringing out the new issues and therefore in starting the capital outlay. In that case the securities in the hands of dealers will be diminished by the amount purchased by the banks, and if, as is likely, the indebtedness of the dealers is reduced to the same extent, the banks will have failed to expand their assets at all. But if the banks persist in buying more and more securities they will pass beyond the point at which the credit created can be offset by the repayment of advances, and they can thus *ensure* an expansion taking place. When they buy, they create money, and place it in the hands of the sellers. There must ultimately be a limit to the amount of money that the sellers will hold idle, and it follows that by this process the vicious circle of deflation can always be broken, however great the stagnation of business and the reluctance of borrowers may be."

The hopes founded on this method seem to me illusory. The issue of banking credit by the purchase of securities, aimed at

[1] On all these points see *The Art of Central Banking*, pp. 213 *et seq.*

[2] *The Art of Central Banking*, p. 173.

raising their value, must necessarily induce the public to come on to the market in their turn and to buy back the same securities, in other words to bring the money created by the banks back to its place of origin. The attempt to raise commodity prices by means of stock exchange operations has so far never succeeded. It might perhaps have an initial success on a completely closed financial market cut off from any contact with foreign markets (as is the case in England to-day); but in a normal market that has not lost its international connexions the attempt is doomed to failure.

However that may be, it is clear that Mr. Hawtrey, like Mr. Keynes, brings us back to Wicksell's "unlimited elasticity" of credit. In fact, he ends up by admitting that the only way we can influence prices is to increase the means of payment not for advances, but for direct purchases. After all the subtleties to which Marshall's theories gave rise, this return to a long-known truth is rather significant.

Critics of Mr. Hawtrey's and Mr. Keynes' theories were not lacking. To mention only two English writers: Cannan devotes one section of his last book to the theory of prices based on the discount rate,[1] and Mr. Lionel Robbins, in *The Great Depression*, has some excellent pages on the effects of credit expansion.

On the other hand, I do not think it has yet been pointed out that the method advocated by Mr. Hawtrey and Mr. Keynes, and regarded by some of their readers as representing the latest advances in economic science, is in fact a *very old method pursued by the Bank of England in the eighteenth century*. The purchase of securities on the market was a device used by the bank in agreement with the government when they wished to create a more favourable market for the issue of state bonds. This "dodge" was described and its effects analysed in the most comprehensive fashion by the writer from whom we have so often quoted, and who seems to be as forgotten in England to-day as he was in the nineteenth century, despite Mr. Higgs' excellent edition of his book. It is the fate of anonymous works, even of the first rank, to have their ideas pilfered by contemporaries (Cantillon had this honour done him, and was scarcely ever quoted except by Adam Smith) and to be forgotten by later generations.

In the last two pages of his book Cantillon describes the open

[1] Cf. *Modern Currency*, pp. 81 *et seq.*

market policy of his time. These pages, written between 1730 and 1735, have a particularly attractive flavour in the light of events in the year of grace 1935:

"If a Minister of State in England, seeking to lower the rate of interest or for other reasons, forces up the price of public stock in London and if he has enough credit with the Directors of the Bank (under the obligation of indemnifying them in case of loss) to get them to issue a quantity of bank-notes without backing, begging them to use these notes themselves to buy several blocks and capitals of the public stock, this stock will not fail to rise in price through these operations. And those who have sold stock, seeing the high price continue, will perhaps decide (so as not to leave their bank-notes idle and thinking from the rumours spread about that the rate of interest will fall and the stock go up further in price) to buy it back at a higher price than they sold it for. If several people seeing the agents of the Banks buy this stock step in and do likewise, thinking to profit like them, the public funds will increase in price to the point which the Minister wishes. And it may happen that the Bank will cleverly resell at a higher price all the stock it has purchased at the Minister's request, and will not only make a large profit on it but will retire and cancel all the extraordinary bank-notes which it had issued.

"If the Bank alone raises the price of public stock by buying it, it will by so much depress it when it resells to cancel its excess issue of notes. But it always happens that many people wishing to follow the Agents of the Banks in their operations help to keep up the price. Some of them get caught for want of understanding these operations, in which there enter infinite refinements or rather trickery which lie outside my subject.

"It is then undoubted that a Bank with the complicity of a Minister is able to raise and support the price of public stock and to lower the rate of interest in the State at the pleasure of this Minister when the steps are taken discreetly, and thus pay off the State debt. But these refinements which open the door to making large fortunes are rarely carried out for the sole advantage of the State, and those who take part in them are generally corrupted. The excess bank-notes, made and issued on these occasions, do not upset the circulation, because being used for the buying and selling of stock they do not serve for household expenses and are not changed into silver. But if some panic or unforeseen crisis drove the holders to demand silver from the Bank the bomb would burst and it would be seen that these are dangerous operations."[1]

Undoubtedly there is little new under the sun. The difficulties encountered to-day by the London market as a result of the vast

[1] Cantillon, pp. 321–323.

purchases of fixed interest-bearing securities by the banks were foreseen by Cantillon. And is it not curious that he should have stated so clearly the absence of any effect on commodity prices of operations confined to the money market alone?

APPENDIX

Since there is even to-day so much confusion in economic terminology concerning the question of the rate of interest, it may perhaps be of service to remind the reader of the sense in which the terms used in this book are employed, and the vital distinctions between the markets on which the different rates are fixed. English terminology has long confused "profit" and "interest." The one word "capital" is still used for what continental theory has long distinguished as "saving" and "capital." (This is done in Marshall's evidence quoted above.) The distinction between "savings" and "investments," on which Mr. Keynes rightly insists, is an old one in French and Italian theory. Identification of the discount rate with the interest rate, which is frequent among English writers, is another unfortunate source of confusion.

The theories examined in this chapter can only be properly evaluated if the following distinctions are borne in mind.

1. The yield on the material capital existing at any given time (houses, lands, factories, etc.) in relation to the savings originally employed in their purchase or creation. This is the yield of a company *in relation to its joint stock*, the figure which appears as profit on the balance sheet.

This yield is as diverse as business undertakings themselves; at any moment in any country (and in the world as a whole) there are *as many different yields as there are undertakings*, from the most prosperous to those which are working at a loss. It is therefore absurd to speak of a *rate of profit* on "real," that is to say material capital.

What happens when the general price level is rising or falling is that the *aggregate* of profits increases or decreases *on the average*; a period of rising prices increases the profits of prosperous concerns and puts the losing concerns level again; a period of falling prices produces the opposite effect.

But there is no *rate of profit* which can be referred to as *typical*; the *average* rate of profit, which can be calculated by dividing the total of the items "joint stock" in company balance sheets by the total of the dividends paid by those companies, is a *statistical* concept; it is not a price.

2. The *rate for savings*, or the long term interest rate, is the *price* paid for the *new savings* required at any given moment on the market where savers seeking an *investment* meet the business men, states, municipalities, etc., which need these savings either for consumption purposes or for investment (both uses imply the *expenditure* of the money savings of the savers).

When commodity prices are rising, and it appears that the yield of the material capital in existence or to be created with a given volume of savings will go up (or that the yield of the taxes imposed by the central and local authorities will increase), those seeking capital can *offer more interest* for a given volume of savings, and the price which is finally fixed for loans actually made naturally tends to rise. The converse happens when the price of goods and services is falling.

Thus the rate for savings has a tendency to follow the upward and downward movements in the prices of commodities and services; this tendency may of course be offset by other circumstances, but it is nevertheless there in all cases.

Of course, there is not a *single* rate for savings, but many rates according to the risks involved in the different investments, etc. For investments offering the same security these rates are usually very close to each other, and generally vary in the same direction over long periods. They oscillate around a *typical* rate which is, for example, the interest paid on the government loans of a country whose financial position is unquestioned.

3. The *discount rate*, the typical rate for *bank* advances, is fixed on the market where *short-term* capital is available. This mark is very different from the market for savings proper, because the supply consists not of savings, which are made wholly out of net income, but of the *cash which the public have free temporarily* and put at the disposal of the banks or other institutions. This cash is part of the *gross money incomes* received by individuals or business concerns.

I have discussed the essential differences between this market and the savings market elsewhere, distinguishing between reserve savings and creative savings.

The discount rate is, of course, strongly influenced by the long term interest rate since in a large number of cases reserve savings (loanable bank cash) are in demand *until* savings proper become available. The contacts between the two markets are numerous. But the *two are essentially different* in the nature both of the supplies which they handle and the demands which come to the markets to be met.[1]

At bottom, all the controversies which we have reviewed in the preceding pages revolve round one problem: is it movements in the general price level which affect the rate for savings and the discount rate, or is it rather these two rates, and the gaps which may exist between them, which influence general price movements? To me there can be no doubt as to the answer. Clear explanations on all these points are to be found in the extremely lucid and intelligent work of the Swiss economist Somary entitled *Bankpolitik*.

As to the *natural* rate of interest, it is an intellectual construction, naturally varying with all the different theories, since each gives a different meaning to the word "natural" or "normal." [2] The same cannot be said of the concept of a "real" rate of interest as defined, for example, by Irving Fisher. This is a very simple idea, corresponding to the recognised distinction between *nominal* wages and *real* wages. *Real interest* is interest evaluated in commodities, the amount of commodities which can be bought at a given moment by, for example, five francs interest. It can therefore be said that when prices are rising rapidly *nominal* interest of 5 per cent, when evaluated in terms of commodities, is the same as 4 per cent interest at an earlier time when prices were lower. In such cases it is legitimate and intelligible to say that nominal interest has changed, but real interest remained the same.

[1] I cannot agree with the views expressed in *Volkswirtschaftliche Theorie des Bankkredits* (1920), by Albert Hahn, who denies any distinction between the two (pp. 10 and 11).

[2] Mr. Keynes, who seems to attach so much importance to the idea in his *Treatise on Money*, abandons it in his later book: "I am now no longer of the opinion that the concept of a 'natural' rate of interest, which previously seemed to me a most promising idea, has anything very useful or significant to contribute to our analysis. It is merely the rate of interest which will preserve the *status quo*; and, in general, we have no predominant interest in the *status quo* as such." *The General Theory of Employment Interest and Money*, 1936, p. 243.

CHAPTER EIGHT

The General Theory of Money at the Beginning of the Twentieth Century

§ I. DEFINITION AND FUNCTIONS OF MONEY.—§ II. THEORIES OF THE VALUE OF MONEY.—§ III. KNAPP'S NOMINALIST THEORY.—§ IV. CAN THE PRICE LEVEL BE STABILISED?

After the events and the controversies which I have attempted to survey in the last two chapters, anticipating somewhat the most recent theories, it is of interest to consider how economists regarded the general theory of money at the end of the nineteenth and the beginning of the twentieth century. How are its functions defined? What role is assigned to metallic currency, to circulating credits, to paper money? How is the different action of these different means of payment on the price level explained? What is meant by the "value" of money and what is the mechanism by which at any given moment that value is fixed?

It may seem strange that final answers to these questions should not have been found long ago, since money has been in existence for thousands of years. But it is no more strange than the arguments which still go on as to the functions of the state and the best system of popular representation. Money is an historical institution whose principal function has undoubtedly always been the same, although in the course of the centuries it appears in constantly changing forms.

In the nineteenth century many currency systems disappeared, and others were established unknown to earlier generations. The concentration of metallic reserves by the banks of issue and the increase in the number of such banks are in themselves a new phenomenon. Side by side with the gold standard in its purest form, of which England presents the first example, some countries established bimetallism, others the limping double standard. A new system grew up—the Gold Exchange Standard, under which the domestic currency, composed of silver or paper, is attached to the gold standard by means of a system of conversion at a fixed rate against the (gold) currency of another country. Forced paper currency produced different effects in Spain, Italy, the United States, Austria and South America. The purchasing power of silver money and of gold money fluctuated from time to time.

In short, our monetary experience was vastly enriched. The proper task of economics is to analyse and evaluate the wealth of new material and new phenomena, and to find out to what extent it compels a revision of or an addition to traditional theories and interpretations. The currency doctrine of the eighteenth century was limited to a few very simple and very general theorems. Have they been replaced by more accurate and more certain theorems? Were economists at the end of the nineteenth century better informed than their predecessors a hundred years earlier as to the different effects of different currency systems, the essential services which a currency has to render, the influence that each exerts on the others as between different countries?

This is our immediate field of investigation, and here, more than before, we shall have to limit our enquiries to the main currents of ideas only (ignoring many writers who well deserve consideration and study) since we wish the reader's attention to be concentrated on essential doctrines and fundamental problems.[1]

Reading the principal works on this subject, one's first impression is that their authors disagree very widely, but a closer study soon reveals some theories which are common to them all, and indicates the interesting development that the presentation of currency doctrine has undergone.

In the first place there is substantial agreement as to the definition of money and its functions, if not in the words used (for the vocabulary varies according to the country and the writer) at least in the things which the words signify. As to the value of money, there is greater clarity in regard to the part played by demand, in

[1] If I had to make a choice among the books on money that have appeared in all languages, whose numbers are so vast that nobody can claim to know them all, I should suggest, as the writings which are most important to know and to study, two which in their conciseness and depth give the fullest summaries of what is most essential on this subject: Carl Menger's admirable article on *Geld* in the *Handwörterbuch der Staatswissenschaften*, and the chapter in K. Wicksell's *Lectures* which serves as an introduction to the second volume.

contrast to Ricardian theories which are concerned exclusively with its supply. There is growing realisation that the concept of the demand for money is merely the converse of the concept of the velocity of circulation, a term which, in Ricardian doctrine, comprehends all other factors than quantity. With this realisation the theory of the value of money is brought into closer harmony with the general theory of value from which, in classical doctrine, it was always more or less distinct. Finally, in regard to paper money, it is realised that in certain circumstances its value can be kept fairly steady; this encouraged the utopians who for a hundred years have dreamt of substituting paper for metallic money.

In the period we are now to study, as at all other times, currency theory has both its heretics and its cranks. At the beginning of the twentieth century the arch heretic is Knapp, with his *Staatliche Theorie des Geldes*. He again raises the entire problem of the monetary system, which the nineteenth century believed it had solved in the best interests of the economic community. At the same time other writers, with their minds turned to different goals, raise the problem of the stabilisation of the value of money. Ironically enough, this question was debated most hotly on the very eve of a war in which the governments were to destroy without misgivings, and for a long time, that modicum of stability which, thanks to gold, the nineteenth century had with so much difficulty succeeded in establishing.

§ 1. *Definition and Functions of Money*

In the first place, which, among the many instruments of circulation, deserve the name of money? In the seventeenth and eighteenth centuries it is always metallic currency that is meant when money is spoken of, and the theories of the time are concerned with metallic currency alone. The theory of paper money stands in the same relation to the theory of metallic currency as, in medicine, the study of the pathology of an organ stands to that of its normal anatomy and physiology. But in the nineteenth century a number of new means of payment came into use, bank-notes and cheques. Are they too to be considered as money? Yes, if by money we mean all instruments of circulation. No, if we agree that in order to bear the name of money an instrument of circulation must also be a standard of value, and this cannot be claimed for bank-notes and current accounts available by cheque. Mere *circulating credits*, mere claims payable in standard money, they are rather "fiduciary money."

This answer would have been accepted all round if the obsolete disputes of the Currency School and the old Ricardian distinctions had not left their mark on men's minds; and if, on the other hand, the English government in 1833, the French government in 1876, and the German government somewhat later had not made bank-notes legal tender, in order to facilitate their circulation in times of peace and to prepare the way for the change over to forced paper currency in times of war. When bank-notes are made legal tender, the false idea held by the public generally that notes are money in the same sense as metallic currency is money, is strengthened; whether or not legal tender, the value of convertible bank-notes is determined by the value of the metal into which they are convertible.

This misunderstanding gave rise to a dispute as heated as it was futile, in which bank-notes were contrasted with cheques, the former being called money, the latter not. This was the opinion of Helfferich,[1] in the book in which he summarises German monetary theory. It was also held by Irving Fisher, but not by Conant,[2] for example, in America, nor by the great banker Paul Warburg, in the series of addresses and articles in which he advocated, in a most eloquent and learned fashion, the establishment of a Federal Reserve Bank for the United States.[3] Nor was this opinion shared by the majority of French writers, who continued to confine the word money to metallic currency, and to call notes fiduciary money. The controversy was without much interest, and there is no point in elaborating it further, since it fades away once agreement is reached as to the meaning of the words used. The same writers who call bank-notes money confine the word, when they are working out their theory of money, to the money which serves as

[1] Helfferich, *Das Geld*, 1906.

[2] Conant, *Principles of Money and Banking*, New York, 1905.

[3] P. Warburg, *The Federal Reserve System. Its Origin and Growth*, New York, 1930.

standard, whether metallic currency or paper money.[1] As to those—mainly English writers—who apply the term money to all means of payment whatever (for example Robertson), in conformity with common usage, they put standard money in a separate category; this is the money which serves not only as a means of payment, but also as standard of value, in which prices are expressed. Thus all distinguish standard money from the instruments of circulation which derive their value from their convertibility into standard money. Now there are only two standard moneys: metallic money and forced paper currency, and these are the two which are referred to in any attempt to define the nature and functions of money.

Here it should be remarked that the majority of writers are dealing with *metallic currency* and with that *alone* when they discuss monetary theory. Others, however, include paper money. It is an important difference. We shall deal first with the former writers, that is, with theories concerning metallic currency.

Before going on, however, there is a preliminary question which all theorists have discussed with great relish: is metallic currency a "commodity like any other commodity," or is it not? The question goes back to the eighteenth century, and was warmly taken up by Ricardo. At a time when mercantilists ascribed overwhelming importance to a country's possession of money, economists strove to convince governments that gold and silver were no more and no less important than other commodities, that the precious metals came into or left a country from the same causes as other commodities, that is, according to their price in the different countries, and that in any case their quantity was a matter of indifference, since the price level adapted itself to that quantity, which therefore could never be either too great or too small. These were the essential arguments of Hume and Ricardo.

But the formula used to summarise this series of propositions was particularly unfortunate. For there is no commodity "like all other commodities." Every commodity has its particular characteristics, meets different needs, and answers a specific demand on the market. There is a certain amount of each and every commodity which may

[1] Two writers, one Swedish, the other Austrian, maintain the distinction between metallic currency serving as the standard, and means of circulation: Knut Wicksell, in his *Lectures*, published in Sweden in 1906, and Ludwig von Mises in his *Das Geld und die Umlaufsmittel*, which first appeared before the war; the title alone is significant.

or may not correspond with the requirements of a country at a given moment. Thus the formula "money is a commodity *like all other commodities*" has no precise meaning (apart from the practical conclusions which, it is alleged, follow from it). For what have to be defined are the *particular characteristics* of this special commodity, money (assuming, of course, that the money is made of precious metal).

The chief argument used by those who refuse to regard money as a commodity is that money is acquired not in order to be kept or consumed, but in order *to be got rid of*. This argument, used by a large number of writers (for example Gide), is similar to the idea worked out by John Law and Adam Smith, according to which money is essentially a "voucher to purchase," the "great wheel of circulation." Turgot had pointed out the error in this when he said that money is not a "token" but a part of wealth. Moreover, the majority of goods are, at a certain stage in their production, acquired "to be sold"—this is true of all articles manufactured for the market. Others, like houses and pictures, are acquired to be enjoyed, it is true, but frequently with the subsidiary purpose of being "got rid of" at one time or another. Money is like these goods, for it too is frequently acquired not to be got rid of but to be kept. Menger observes on this point, very correctly:

"The theory held by certain recent writers, according to which the distinctive peculiarity of money in comparison with other goods is that, whereas an ordinary commodity, if its purpose is to be fulfilled, that is, if it is to be consumed, must disappear from the market, money fulfils its purpose by being spent and remaining on the market—this theory is valid only in so far as the one function of money which distinguishes it from other commodities is taken into account, the function of acting as an intermediary. It is obvious that money, that is to say the commodity which serves to circulate goods, ordinarily remains on the market, whereas other commodities disappear from the market. But it is a mistake to conclude therefrom that money is not a commodity; it is more correct to say that money always has the character of a commodity, whereas other goods have this character only for a time, and that money fulfils an important economic function on the market, whereas other commodities only yield their utility when they are consumed, that is to say when they cease to be commodities."[1]

[1] Menger, *Grundsätze*, second edition, p. 261.

Thus metallic money is an economic good that is an object of desire like all economic goods; and the problem is to discover precisely what qualities it has that make it an object of desire. When we put it like this we leave sterile discussions as to the definition of money to tackle the problem from the standpoint of the functions of money, which is both far more interesting and more difficult.

The qualities of metallic money reside in its *form* and in its *substance* and it is, in my opinion, unprofitable to attempt to separate substance and form. Metallic currency is: 1, a medium of exchange; 2, a means of comparing values (so much for the form and the name); 3, a store of value.

This list of the functions of money, or of the services which it renders, is extremely old; in fact it goes back to Aristotle. It has never been abandoned. In the eighteenth century Galiani (in a passage quoted above), Hutcheson and Adam Smith repeat it; but in the course of the nineteenth century, particularly after Ricardo, many writers fail to mention the third function, and define money simply in the terms of the first two. Money, it is said, from Michel Chevalier to Colson, is the medium of exchange and the means of comparing values (valorimeter, Leroy-Beaulieu was to call it). The same formula is to be found in the most modern writers—Cassel, Hawtrey, Robertson and others.

This reduction of the functions of money to two has many drawbacks, for these two functions could be fulfilled by any "unit of account" whatever. Ricardo had pointed that out,[1] and, a century later, Cassel makes the same point. Reduced to these two functions money becomes merely a means for settling debts and the indispensable medium for judging between the prices of commodities taken two by two (the proof of this extremely important point was worked out by Walras).[2] It might even be possible to dispense with any material embodiment of money whatever if all accounts

[1] Cf. *Principles*, § 125.

[2] This is one of the most interesting elements in Walras' theory of money, which was taken up by Wicksell. It should be included in all economic textbooks, from which, unfortunately, it is nearly always absent. It finally discredits the idea that money adds nothing new to the system of exchange, and that the system would work in the same way in the absence of money, if all exchanges were made by barter. Such a system would it is true make it possible to judge the price of one commodity in terms of one other, but judgments as to two commodities of different price and a third commodity could not be made in the absence of a *tertium comparationis*, and no general equilibrium could be established.

were settled by clearing arrangements on a given day . . . and if there were no balance. *But there always are such balances, and these have to be covered; the way in which these balances are settled is of primary importance in trade.*

Metallic money has a third function, the most important of all, which is probably the origin of its other functions—that of serving as a store of value, as an insurance against the uncertainties of the *future.* It is a bridge between the present and the future.[1] It is a means of settling balances, without waiting until such balances are offset by further operations.

It should be said at once that the great majority of nineteenth-century writers *imply* this function even if they do not state it explicitly. It does not even occur to most of them that any money other than metallic money can serve as a standard; or, if it does, they reject the thought in horror. Paper money, in their opinion, is a pathological case that requires special treatment; the idea of standard money connotes to them, without any need of explicit statement, a commodity with a value of its own, and therefore a "store of value." Perhaps, too, they imagined that the dictates of formal logic compelled them to make a distinction (between the metal as a commodity and the monetary character given to the metal) where social reality has made none, and where therefore the theorist should make none if he wishes to understand the real function of money.

A characteristic example of this method of approaching the theory of money is given by Pantaleoni in his *Economia Pura* of 1889.[2] He regards money exclusively as a "medium of exchange" and consequently as a "common denominator of value." All its other functions derive from its "merceologic" character, that is to say, from its character as a commodity, and are therefore "contingent." However, even its function as a medium of exchange, says Pantaleoni, presupposes "a condition of fact," which is "that all desire and accept money, being confident that they can dispose of it whenever they want to." What creates this confidence matters

[1] I was pleased to find this formula in Mr. Keynes' last book, p. 293: "The importance of money essentially flows from its being a link between the present and the future."

[2] Translated into English by T. Boston Bruce: *Pure Economics*, by Professor Maffeo Pantaleoni, London, 1898.

little. One thing will function as money as well as any other provided it enjoys the same degree of confidence (p.223). *Here Pantaleoni is actually introducing into the concept of money the idea of an object desired for its own sake and having a value of its own*, for people will always have more confidence (in Pantaleoni's meaning of the word) in something which, *besides* its use as a medium of exchange, *is in demand for other reasons*, than in something which is in demand solely because it serves as a medium of exchange. Starting from this point, he proceeds to a demonstration of the quantity theory, taking as his basis the following theorem, taken from Ricardo, which facts have over and over again shewn to be false: "But if we suppose a commodity which is exclusively a medium of exchange, we are confronted by the fact that the utility of the entire mass of the commodity set apart for such use, be it little or great, never varies. . . . The total value of the mass of money, that is the integral value of the mass, or yet again the value of the aggreagate amount of money, will therefore be constant." "The value of the monetary unit will therefore be expressed by the formula $v = \frac{m}{qr}$, in which the volume of business transactions, *i.e.* the demand for money, is denoted by *m*, and the supply of money by the product of its quantity *q* multiplied by the rapidity of its circulation *r*."[1]

There appears to be no hint of a "store of value" in this conception of money, which seems to have been dominant in Italian and English teaching at the time when Pantaleoni's book appeared. Nevertheless it is there implicitly, for the entire argument falls to the ground if *confidence* is lacking.

In any case, the importance of the reserve function of metallic

[1] *Ibid.*, p. 231. It is extremely interesting to read the criticism made of this version of the quantity theory by Philip H. Wicksteed, an English author of the greatest ability and subtlety, a pupil of Jevons and partisan of the theory of marginal utility, who is too little known and too rarely quoted. Cf. his *Common Sense of Political Economy*, London, 1910.

In a weighty book, *Ricerche sopra la Teoria generale della Moneta* (Milan, 1932), a great part of which was written before 1914, Gustave del Vecchio criticises the attempts to apply the theory of marginal utility to the value of money. He himself makes a new application, the extremely complex mechanism of which would take too long to set forth here. I would only remark that I do not agree with the position taken up at the outset by this author, who regards money merely as a medium of exchange, and consequently the demand for money as a demand for means of exchange. It is the position taken by Pantaleoni, which is dealt with above.

currency is fundamental, and if it is ignored a number of misunderstandings are created. For man does not live merely in the present. Economic man, in particular, lives essentially in *the future*,[1] and this preoccupation with the future is quite rightly expressed in the creation of *reserves*. If men were all Robinson Crusoes, these reserves would be composed entirely of the less perishable objects of consumption and of instruments of labour. But as man is a *social being* and economic life is based on the division of social labour, he builds up his reserves for the future not merely out of objects of personal utility, but out of objects *which he knows are desired by the other members of the community*, just as he produces objects which he does not need himself, but is sure of selling. The precious metals—objects both rare and beautiful like precious stones[2]—have from the first lent themselves to the *formation of reserves*, both because they do not deteriorate and because they are the object of universal desire. Metallic money is therefore particularly

[1] This is the source of perpetual misunderstanding between economists and sociologists or historians, who are mainly preoccupied with explaining the past.

[2] I cannot resist the temptation of again quoting from Galiani's *Della Moneta*, Vol. I, pp. 61 *et seq.* (Custodi edition of 1802): "Everything is useful which produces real gratification, or allays the intensity of desire. Now our desires do not consist only in the wish to eat, or drink, or sleep: these are only our primary desires which, once satisfied, give place to others equally strong. For man is so constituted that scarcely is one desire satisfied than another is roused, which moves him with the same force as the first. . . . Thus it is that the things which make us respected have the greatest value. Such are honours and titles, rank and position, which are the chief among the non-material things. These are followed by a certain number of objects which have at all times been valued and sought for by men for their beauty, and those who have possessed them and bedecked themselves with them have for that reason been held in respect and envied. Such are gems, rare stones, certain furs, the most beautiful metals, gold and silver, and certain works of art which embody much labour and beauty. . . . But most men argue thus, with Bernard Davanzati: A real calf is more useful than a golden calf, but how much less value men place on it. I reply: if a real calf were as rare as a golden calf, its price would be as much greater than the price of a golden calf as its usefulness is greater. . . . There are those who say, a pound of bread is more useful than a pound of gold. I reply: that is a shameful sophism arising from ignorance that the words 'more useful' and 'less useful' are relative terms, varying according to the different position of men. If we speak of a man who has neither bread nor gold, then indeed bread is more useful to him, for you will find nobody who will reject the bread and, taking gold, die of hunger. . . . Leaving aside all considerations which arise from superficial and imperfect reflection, I conclude that objects which bring respect to men, give women grace and children beauty, are useful and rightly so. From which the most important conclusion must be drawn that gold and silver have a value as metals precedent to their value as money."

well suited to the formation of reserves, originally *because of its substance*, and later in virtue of that very increase in "acceptability" which the precious metals acquire when they are chosen as the means of payment. It is probable that the creation of reserves of the precious metals preceded the making of coins. At first these metals were accessible only to the wealthiest classes and to those engaged in trade. In ancient societies business transactions were few and far between, and the object chosen as means of payment had to be one whose value remained the same over long periods. Once the precious metals became more plentiful, and their coinage made them accessible not merely to a few, but to all those who engaged in business, the creation of metallic reserves became possible for all, and as coin was the form in which the precious metals were held by the public, it was (with a metallic currency) in coin that all classes of society, from the richest to the poorest, built up their reserves. (Later people kept claims or securities *convertible at will into bullion.*)

Of course, reserves can be built up under other forms. All creation of capital, all acquisitions of precious goods, objects of art, jewels, stones, rare metals, all holdings of securities, all house building, represent a reserve; but the reserve of precious metals (and for the majority of people such a reserve is possible almost solely by the accumulation of money) is by far the most convenient, the most universal, the safest, and, in case of need, the most easily negotiable. The day that a money, for any reason whatever, loses this capacity for serving as a store of value, the day, for example, that a paper money begins to depreciate, even if it does not immediately lose its capacity to subserve other functions, *it becomes less suitable.* During the French Revolution people preferred barter to using the *assignats*, whose value was "dissolving," even as a simple means of payment.[1] What did this mean if not that money,

[1] Three years ago a former President of the Council in France advocated (to the stupefaction of his hearers, it must be said) as a remedy for the crisis a "dissolving currency," that is to say, a money without that very quality which makes a currency an object of demand: fixity of value. The idea was borrowed from a German, by name Silvio Gesell, who achieved a certain notoriety (and gathered a small group of followers) by announcing the necessity of bringing the rate of interest down to nil by means of a money which people would be anxious to get rid of since a tax would be levied on all who held on to it. This resurrected Proudhonist idea has had the peculiar good fortune of winning an adherent in the person of Mr. Keynes (cf. p. 353 of his latest book).

being no longer a store of value, thereupon ceased to be a good medium of exchange?

In fact, and this point is fundamental, the function of acting as a medium of exchange, *since time is necessarily involved* (there is always a certain interval between the receipt of money and its expenditure), *presupposes* the function of a store of value. A sum of money received in payment, whether as salary, wages, the proceeds of the sale of a harvest, always serves a *double* purpose: *firstly*, *to cover expenses* as they arise during the week, the month, or the year, and secondly, to *store up the value* of the service provided or the goods sold *during the time, frequently indeterminate, which will elapse before it is entirely spent*. When we speak of the circulatory function of money, we should never forget that it *presupposes and implies* the function of a store of value, the two being as inseparable as the obverse and reverse of a medal. Any modification in the suitability of money to perform the latter function immediately affects its suitability to fulfil its other functions.

Furthermore, the desire of the different classes in the community for metallic money is in direct relation to the time which elapses between its receipt and its expenditure. The farmer, who realises the price of his harvest once a year, attaches the greatest importance to having the money paid to him in metallic currency or in paper immediately convertible into hard cash.

It has been said since John Law that the value of the precious metals arises partly from the fact that they are used for money. That is obvious, and in this respect the value of the precious metals does not differ from the value of any other object. Whenever a new use is discovered for any commodity, the demand for it, and consequently its value, tends to increase; conversely it diminishes when another good is substituted for it in some of its uses. Ambiguity begins when this observation is taken to warrant the assertion that has frequently been made, that any other object could serve just as well for money, and that its use for this purpose would give it the same value as it gives to the precious metals. This misunderstanding is cleared up if we distinguish between the function of money as an instrument of circulation and its function as a reserve of value. Any object at all might it is true serve as an instrument of circulation. But it is not true that any object whatever can serve as a store of value. It is a great mistake to believe that if, for example, gold were demonetised, it would immediately cease to serve as a store of value; it would not lose this function unless *another object* were found that would serve this purpose, and serve it better. If the demonetisation of silver made it decline in value, it was because gold took its place in its capacity as a store of value. But if gold were demonetised to-day, *without an equivalent substitute being found*, the demand for gold would not grow less; on the contrary, it would be in demand everywhere. People still look on gold as a precious object. To rid them of what certain people would like to persuade them is an illusion, it would have to be shewn that gold is neither beautiful, nor durable, nor imperishable; that nobody wants it any more, and that in accumulating it they are accumulating nothing but ashes. Up to the present nobody has succeeded in proving this. The widespread idea that by demonetising gold in certain countries you reduce the demand for gold in the world as a whole seems to me, in present world circumstances, to be erroneous. If England or the United States were to demonetise gold, the price of the gold sold by these countries would perhaps for a time fall in sterling or dollars, but the price would soon rise again because the lower price would increase the demand for gold in other countries, and because of the uncertainty aroused by doubts as to the stability of sterling or dollars.

Not all writers in the nineteenth century forgot to mention this most essential function. Tooke, as we have seen, included it. But it did not really come into its own again until the time of Jevons, Walras and Menger, who regenerated economic theory in all its branches; they were followed in this by the best of the modern theorists. "Historically speaking," wrote Jevons in his *Money and the Mechanism of Exchange* (1875), "such a generally esteemed substance as gold seems to have served, firstly, as a commodity valuable for ornamental purposes; secondly, as stored wealth; thirdly, as a medium of exchange; and, lastly, as a measure of value" (p.16). Walras insists on the role of money as a means of providing for the future and brings forward the idea of the "encaisse désirée," the amount of cash that people like to hold. Finally, in his admirable article on *Geld* in the *Handwörterbuch der Staatswissenschaften*, Menger analyses with remarkable insight the origin and functions of money, and shews how the precious metals, being in universal demand, became the medium of exchange and the means of accumulating wealth.[1] Marshall took up and elaborated Walras' idea of the "encaisse désirée," on which he constructed his entire theory of the value of money. Wicksell also made it the pivot of his theory.[2]

In the last few years, and under the influence of the World War, which emphasised the essential function of metallic currency to act as a reserve, a group of young American, Austrian, English and Swedish economists have tried to make clear the importance of this function. Money cannot be understood unless it is considered not in a society that has achieved static equilibrium, but in a dynamic society; that is to say, the changes which time brings to the life of societies and of individuals must be taken into account. Money, as we have so often said, plays the part of bridge between present and future. Its function is to guard against the uncertainties of the future.

The ideas of this group are lucidly summarised by a young Austrian economist from whom we quote the following:

> "In an economy without 'frictions' where everybody foresaw with perfect certainty his tastes, income, future prices and therefore the dates as well as the size of his purchases, nobody would keep a cash-balance. Everybody would invest all his money for exactly the periods of time allowed for by the foreseen future payments, since an omission to do so would involve loss of the interest which could be earned on it. Everybody would have an account in one central clearing bank, and all payments would be effected by the appropriate entries in the books of the bank. Short run assets as well as long run ones would be equally good means of payment, since there would be no risk and therefore no difference between the short and long run rates of interest in this state of universal certain foresight. There would be no limit to the creation of credit by the central bank in this state; the economic process would develop as if the velocity of circulation of money tended towards infinity, i.e. money

[1] In Menger's article money's function as a store of value is regarded as a consequence of its function as a medium of exchange, but this latter is itself the result of the universal demand for the precious metals because of their intrinsic value.

[2] Quite recently an eminent Austrian economist, Gottfried Kunwald, wrote in his really remarkable book *Das Leben der Erwartungs- und Kredit Wirtschaft* (1934): "Whoever acquires money wants it in order to preserve that complete liberty of future choice among the possible means of satisfaction, that anonymous and abstract power over men which is desired as instinctively as the satisfaction of any other need. . . . Whoever acquires money knows that he will spend it sooner or later, but he does not acquire it in order to spend it."

prices would become indeterminate, although relative prices would remain perfectly determined. This *reductio ad absurdum* shows that it is inconsistent to assume at the same time a state of general certain foresight and the existence of money: they are mutually incompatible. Money (as cash balance) exists only and in so far as general foresight is not certain; it is a function of the individual's feeling of uncertainty, a means of meeting it: a good satisfying the want for certainty. Since certain foresight is assumed in static equilibrium money and static equilibrium are incompatible."

This passage is taken from an article[1] in which the author, having condensed into a few pages the development of ideas on the functions of money in the course of the century, and having analysed its functions in an original fashion, summarises the most recent works of the Austrian and English schools. It took the war and the characteristic phenomena of the hoarding and migration of money to remind economists of certain very old truths, which all those, from John Law to Ernest Solvay,[2] who refuse to regard money as anything except a means for settling accounts, would have us forget. They forget that in the real world settlement is never complete, and that a means must be found for settling *balances*. Events after the collapse of currencies in 1931 have made abundantly clear the essential part played by balances in trade between individuals as well as between countries, and the necessity of paying these balances in a good universally recognised as stable.

[1] P. N. Rosenstein-Rodan, *The Co-ordination of the General Theories of Money and Price* (*Economica*, August 1936, pp. 271–272). In this remarkable article Mr. Rosenstein-Rodan mentions the chief authors and works concerned with the development of this conception of money. Of particular interest among these are F. A. Hayek's *Beiträge zur Geldtheorie* (containing articles by J. G. Koopmans, G. Myrdal and E. Lindhal), articles by Knight and Hicks, and articles by M. Marget in the *Journal of Political Economy*, in which he shews the position of Walras as forerunner. A bibliography of the writings of this school and an account of some of their theories are also to be found in an article by Pierre Raynaud, *Essais sur la Monnaie neutre* in the *Revue d'Economie politique* for July–August, 1937.

[2] We shall not deal with the ideas of Ernest Solvay's school, which derive from their failure to understand the difference between credit instruments and money, and from a primitive philosophy of history, according to which the ease with which payments can be made by credit instruments will gradually make metallic currency unnecessary and ensure its disappearance, even as a standard of value. An account of these ideas is to be found in *Le Crédit Commercial et la Banque nationale de Belgique* (Brussels, 1899), by Guillaume de Greef, an able representative of this school, written on the occasion of the renewal of the charter of the Belgian National Bank.

Once the functions of money are defined, we must consider a further factor on which Jevons particularly insisted, and which is never brought into great enough prominence—for its neglect is at the source of many errors—and that is *the distribution of these functions among different instruments.*

At the present time—and particularly since the World War—the instruments of circulation (wherever the bank of issue carries out the obligation of conversion) are bank-notes or cheques; but the standard of value is the gold into which they are both convertible, and which is kept in the form of bullion in the vaults of the bank, so that in reality it is the gold which is circulating, but through the medium of paper. During the period of inflation and of paper money (particularly between 1920 and 1926) contracts for constructional and other long-term works were more and more often drawn up not in paper francs (whose value fluctuated rapidly) but in commodities, for example wheat. The medium of payment was still the paper franc, but the function of acting as a standard of value (since contracts drawn up in terms of gold were, inexcusably but traditionally, forbidden) had passed from paper money to commodities. Jevons had noted such significant phenomena:

"In Queen Elizabeth's reign silver was the common measure of value; gold was employed in large payments in quantities depending upon its current value in silver, while corn was required by the Act 18th Elizabeth, c. VI (1576), to be the standard of value in drawing the leases of certain college lands."

And he draws the following conclusion:

"It is in the highest degree important that the reader should discriminate carefully and constantly between the four functions which money fulfils, at least in modern societies. We are so accustomed to use that one same substance in all the four different ways, that they tend to become confused together in thought. We come to regard as almost necessary that union of functions which is, at the most, a matter of convenience, and may not always be desirable. We might certainly employ one substance as a medium of exchange, a second as a measure of value, a third as a standard of value, and a fourth as a store of value. . . . One of our chief tasks in this book will be to consider the various materials which have been employed as money, or have been, or may be, suggested for the purpose. It must be our endeavour, if possible, to discover some substance which will in the highest degree combine the characters requisite for all the different functions of money, but we must bear in mind that a partition of these functions amongst different substances is practicable."[1]

This distribution of the different functions of money among the different instruments is of great sociological interest. Menger discusses it in detail in his *Geld* article. It has always existed in all monetary systems, and could serve as the basis for classifying these systems if there were any real purpose to be served thereby. It is also a perpetual source of incorrect interpretation for superficial persons who are tempted to give the name money to anything that fulfils only *one* of the functions of money, and to draw hasty conclusions as to the nature of money itself. The separate existence of means of circulation on the one hand, and standard money on the other, is liable to cause anxiety only when the denomination of the unit employed in drawing up contracts is no longer the same as the denomination of the unit which serves as instrument of circulation.

Up to the present we have only dealt with writers who have never questioned that money should be made of a substance desired for its own sake and deriving a value of its own from this demand. But towards the end of the nineteenth century the idea arose that a good "definition" of money should cover not merely metallic currency, but forced paper currency as well. This opinion was held, in particular, by Knapp.

Before him the majority of economists had refused to put paper money and metallic currency in the same boat. Pareto (more concerned with morals than he would care to admit) distinguishes the two by the terms of "true" and "false" money. Others, like Cassel, distinguish "free" (paper) money and money "tied" to a commodity (*freie und gebundene Währung*). Knapp denies the validity of these distinctions. A good definition of money, he observes, should comprehend all moneys, including paper money.

The importance given to the definition of money indicates the juridical bent of Knapp's mind, but does less credit to his scientific spirit, for a definition is never interesting in itself, but solely in virtue of the help it can render to enquiry. Jevons, himself a logician, remarks with his customary good sense and directness:

"Much ingenuity has been spent upon attempts to define the term *money*. and puzzling questions have arisen as to the precise kinds of

[1] S. Jevons, *Money and the Mechanism of Exchange*, London, 1875, pp. 16–18.

credit documents which are to be included under the term. . . . All such attempts at definition seem to me to involve the logical blunder of supposing that we may by settling the meaning of a single word avoid all the complex differences and various conditions of many things, each requiring its own definition. Bullion, standard coin, token coin, convertible and inconvertible notes, legal tender and not legal tender, cheques of several kinds, mercantile bills, exchequer bills, stock certificates, etc., are all things capable of being received in payment of a debt, if the debtor is willing to pay and the creditor to receive them; but they are, nevertheless, different kinds of things. By calling some money and some not, we do not save ourselves from the consideration of their complex legal and economical differences." [1]

What matters to the economist is not so much a good definition of money, as a knowledge and an understanding of "monetary phenomena"; [2] that is to say, of the way in which the very varied and numerous instruments that are in fact in existence and that we call money behave in different circumstances. A knowledge of these phenomena is far more important for the organisation of a currency system than a definition, however comprehensive, of money. Moreover, given the great variety of existing currencies, a definition of this sort would necessarily be so general and would have necessarily to ignore so many of the characteristics of real moneys, that it would have but little interest. A general definition of "living beings" would have to abstract, from the great multiplicity of their characteristics, the few fundamental features common alike to protozoa, the elephant and man. In the same way a definition that could be applied to all kinds of money—the English sovereign, the inconvertible pound sterling of to-day, the equally inconvertible mark, the silver five franc piece in the old bimetallist system, etc., would inevitably consist of characteristics so general that they would cease to have any interest. The definition of *money in general* is in the same class as a definition of the State that would cover the British Empire, Abyssinia, Albania and Honduras.

Furthermore, such a general definition would inevitably lead to paper money being regarded as the *monetary type par excellence*. And in fact this is the conclusion at which Knapp arrives. As soon as one gives the name money to all paper that circulates, the

[1] S. Jevons, *Money and the Mechanism of Exchange*, London, 1875, p. 248.

[2] These are the words used in the title of M. Rueff's remarkable book, *Théories des Phénomènes monétaires*, Paris, 1927.

definition of money, in order to cover everything, must include only those moneys *with the fewest characteristics and qualities*, and, in particular, it must exclude the characteristics peculiar to metallic money which are absent in the case of paper money. A definition of the State that could be applied both to the Hottentots and to the United States would have to be confined to those characteristics common to both, that is to say, in effect, to the characteristics of the Hottentot State. All others would appear as "anomalies" or "excrescences" added to "the essence" of the State, which is determined solely by the nature of the Hottentot State. In the same way metallic currency (which historically has covered almost the entire field of monetary phenomena, and which even to-day is the recognised standard in all important States) strikes Herr Knapp merely as one variety of a much larger species, of which paper money is the prototype.

In this respect Mr. Hawtrey's method differs little from Mr. Knapp's. Having defined money as "the means for the payment of debts" he shews that a paper currency or bank transfers fulfil this function admirably. The same is true of Cassel. On the other hand, when the function of acting as a store of value is in question, these writers are compelled to admit that bank money cannot fulfil this function on its own, but must have backing elsewhere.

This controversy conceals a more serious and most instructive difference of opinion.

By asserting that paper money should be considered as money, and protesting against its systematic exclusion from monetary theory, Knapp and his followers are anxious to emphasise that in fact certain paper moneys do circulate, fulfil the functions of money, and that countries such as Russia and Austria in the last third of the nineteenth century could not be regarded as having no money because they had a forced paper currency. Knapp gives the name of "metallists" to those theorists for whom money, by definition, requires a metallic basis, and who therefore cannot give a satisfactory explanation of such monetary phenomena as were witnessed in Austria-Hungary after 1875, when the paper florin, originally based on silver, was worth more in terms of gold currencies than the weight of silver in the metal florin.

In fact, "anti-metallists" like Knapp and "metallists" make the same mistake: *they deny that paper money can be used to create a store of value*. The anti-metallists (particularly Knapp) regard money merely as a means of circulation and completely ignore its function of acting as a store of value. They find it easy enough to shew that paper is as good a means of circulation as metallic currency, which nobody would dispute. The metallists, who consider the store of value function essential, refuse to recognise paper money as a "real" money, for they think it is unable to fulfil this function.

The truth is that paper *may* fulfil this function and does in fact often do so. Whether it does it well or badly is another question. I am convinced that it does it very badly. But it does fulfil this function. What is paper money? It is a legal claim, since it derives all its properties from the law. It is, if you like, a claim, but a claim of a special kind. The economic value of a claim is determined by that of the object which it commands. The characteristic of paper money is that neither the object on which it is a claim, nor the date on which this object will be obtained, are fixed. Paper money is simply a "voucher" which may be transformed into goods or services to an amount dependent on its variable purchasing power, or (if there is a chance of its becoming convertible at any rate whatever) into an undefined quantity of metallic currency, or finally into bills of exchange, the rate of which varies, on foreign countries. The only fixed right it possesses is that of settling debts. It follows that, the purchasing power of paper money being very variable, its value varies with the judgment of those who receive it as to the nature and quantity of the objects into which it will be transformed. Its capacity of serving as a store of value is dominated by this uncertainty. This capacity exists, but it is precarious. Thus the anti-metallists are wrong in denying that one of the functions of money is to act as a store of value, and in asserting that paper money is the money *par excellence*. Whereas the metallists are wrong in believing that paper money cannot fulfil this function. But it is true that it fulfils it very badly, and it is in this respect that its difference from metallic money is so striking.

§ II. *Theories of the Value of Money*

When attempting to formulate a general theory of the value of money, that is to say of variations in its purchasing power (and whatever may be the interpretations given by different writers to *real* price movements), the majority of economists at the end of the nineteenth century are inevitably drawn to formulas which make the value of money depend primarily on its supply. By general consent this has been given the name of the "quantity" theory. Knut Wicksell, one of the most vigorous intellects that have tackled this problem, goes so far as to say:

> "The only specific theory of the value of money which has been propounded, and perhaps the only one which can make any claim to real scientific importance, is the Quantity Theory, according to which the value or purchasing power of money varies in inverse proportion to its quantity, so that an increase or decrease in the quantity of money, other things being equal, will cause a proportionate decrease or increase in its purchasing power in terms of other goods, and thus a corresponding increase or decrease in all commodity prices. All other theories—and there are not many—are in reality no more than generalisations of the general theory of value applied to money, to that extent, therefore, even if they were otherwise tenable, they cannot be called *specific*."[1]

But it did not end there. In the early years of the twentieth century there are signs of a tendency to insist more and more on the part played by the demand for money in determining its value. It was realised that the idea of velocity of circulation is but the converse of the idea of the demand for money, and that the latter is infinitely more significant. For the historian this development of ideas—or of formulas—represents the most interesting aspect of the writings of that time.

A. *The Supply of Money:* According to Ricardo and Thornton, the supply of money consists of the quantity of effective money offered in a given time on all markets together. It consists of all coins multiplied by their rapidity of circulation. A coin which is used ten times in the course of the year on different markets corresponds to a supply of ten coins.

As against the supply of money, the demand is composed of the mass of transactions to be effected in the given time, that is to say, of the aggregate sales of goods or services for which the seller wishes to receive cash.

The price level, or more exactly the average of the prices actually

[1] *Lectures*, Vol. II, p. 141.

paid, will thus be the product of the quantity of metallic currency, multiplied by its rapidity of circulation and divided by the number of transactions, or: $P = \frac{M\,V}{Q}$ where P represents the average of all effective prices in the period under consideration.

This theorem is the expression of an elementary truism,[1] since, whatever theory may be held, the average price of transactions multiplied by the number of transactions cannot fail to be equal to the quantity of money which was used to settle them, that is to say to the stock of money multiplied by its velocity of circulation. But it remained practically unchanged up to the time when Irving Fisher replaced it by a more elaborate formula (which he says he took from Newcomb, but which is in fact to be found as early as Walras[2]) in which he attempts to define the concept of velocity of circulation more precisely, and then to enumerate the factors which make it vary. It is no exaggeration to say that Fisher was the first economist to attempt a complete study of this question since Thornton made his acute analysis of the different velocities of different media of payment.

Fisher first of all extends the above formula by introducing a new factor—the velocity of circulation not merely of coins and of bank-notes (which he regards as money) but also of current accounts available by cheque. According to the conception of banking credit worked out in the beginning of this book, cheques and notes—in so far as they are not covered by coin—merely represent, in the form of circulating credits, the metallic currency put into circulation by the operations of the banks; their own velocity of circulation must therefore be added to that of the original money to measure the effect of the latter on prices. Fisher's formula $P = \frac{MV + M'V'}{Q}$ is thus in complete harmony with the conception of banking credit as a means of making money circulate.

But Fisher goes further. First of all, he gives a precise definition of velocity of circulation: it is the number of times a coin or a note changes hands in a given time, or, in regard to current accounts, the number of entries in and withdrawals from this account.

He then proceeds (and this is more important) to an examination

[1] As M. Rueff so clearly points out in his *Théorie des Phénomènes monétaires.*

[2] Cf. Marget's articles in the *Journal of Political Economy*, 1933–1934.

of the factors which modify the various elements in the formula. The conclusions at which he arrives may be summarised as follows:

1. There is a fairly constant relation between M and M′. In other words, the total credit granted by the banks on a given cash position, and consequently the growth of deposits resulting from credit operations, change slowly. Any increase in metallic money automatically increases the figure of deposits and of cheque circulation by a sum corresponding to the comparatively fixed relation established by custom between M and M′. This at least can be inferred from a comparison of the statistics relating to two periods separated by a certain interval of time.

2. On the other hand, if we assume a transitional period, for example, a period when prices are rising owing to an increase in the metallic currency, there will be an increase not only in the total of credits made by the banks but also in the velocity of circulation of both money M and bank deposits M′. In other words (and this, as we have seen, has been on a number of occasions verified by experience) an increase in money leading to a rise in prices, *far from being offset by a contraction of credit or of the velocity of circulation, is in fact reinforced by these two factors.*

The converse phenomena occur when, for whatever reason, prices fall.

The chapter in which Fisher sets forth the mutual interactions of the factors at work in a transitional period is applicable to events during cyclical periods of boom and depression and to events when the output of the precious metals is rising or falling.

Once the transitional period is over and a new period of equilibrium has been entered upon, the final result of an influx of money (assuming that the number of transactions remains the same) will be a higher price level due to the increase in money, since the relation between money and credit will have changed only slightly.

3. If credit and the use of cheques become highly developed—that is, if M′ increases in relation to M—the result will also be a certain rise in prices in the country where this has occurred. Here the rise will be due not to an influx of money but to changes in banking methods. As a result of this rise a certain part of the metallic reserves of this country will be exported, which will cause a slight rise in the international price level. "In any case the effect on prices

is extremely small, being spread over the whole commercial world."[1] This reduces to their proper magnitude the exaggerated effects that earlier economists attributed to credit as a means of changing the price level. It provides, I think, the only formula for indicating the permanent effect of credit on the international price level. It is clear that the action of credit is both slow and of small extent.

4. Changes in the rapidity with which money circulates will have exactly the same effects as an increase in credit. They too occur extremely slowly and, above all, they too are a function in the transitional period of the increase in money.

5. Finally, an increase in the "volume of exchanges" tends to *attract* money to a country. Such an increase tends to lower prices and consequently to draw in money from abroad. But at the same time it tends to increase the velocity of circulation and the two tendencies may in fact cancel each other out.

These observations by Irving Fisher represent the clearest attempt so far made by an economist to elucidate the relation between prices, the quantity of money, and its velocity of circulation. One may doubt the validity of the distinction he makes between transitional and other periods, for what period is not a transitional period, and when can we say that we have entered upon a period of equilibrium? But they do summarise the facts as verified by experience on a number of occasions, which assign preponderant influence to the output of the precious metals. Thus Irving Fisher's formulation of the quantity theory is in direct line with eighteenth-century doctrine.

A slightly different formulation has been worked out by those writers—such as Hawtrey and Aftalion—who take consumable income as the starting point for their investigation of prices. Their formulas are on the same lines as Tooke's, to which far too little attention has been paid; and with which we dealt in Chapter Five. They differ more in appearance than in substance from Irving Fisher's formula.

According to Mr. Hawtrey, the factor which at any time influences the price level, or the purchasing power of money, is the net income expended, or, as he puts it, "consumers' outlay"; this constitutes the "demand" for products at any given moment. The total of this consumers' outlay is determined by the wages,

[1] Fisher, *Purchasing Power*, p. 163.

interest, rent and profits received at any given time by the population concerned, and put into circulation by them. This of course includes the sums saved, since saving is only a special channel of expenditure. At any given time the total sums thus spent form "the proximate cause in the determination of prices." The formula for expressing the quantity theory then becomes the following: "The price level is proportional to the consumers' outlay and inversely proportional to the quantity of goods (including capital goods) bought by consumers per unit of time."

This formula is very closely allied to Fisher's quantitative formula, for, says Hawtrey, "Consumers' outlay is proportional jointly to the unspent margin[1] and the circuit velocity of money. Consequently the price level varies *directly* as the unspent margin and the circuit velocity, and *inversely* as the quantity of goods bought by consumers."[2]

Mr. Hawtrey adds the following passage, which provides a clue to many of the most interesting observations in his book:

> "Here we have a form of the quantity theory which employs a quite definite index number, weighted according to quantities consumed. Our formula is based on wealth *consumed*, not on wealth *produced*. An increase in the consumers' outlay may be met for a time by drawing on stocks of goods instead of by a rise of prices. And a decrease in the consumers' outlay may involve in the first instance an accumulation of stocks instead of a fall of prices. When a tendency to a rise or fall of prices is thus masked by consumption exceeding or falling short of output, there may be said to be a 'virtual rise' or a 'virtual fall' of prices, a 'virtual depreciation' or a 'virtual appreciation' of the currency unit."[3]

If the quantity theory in one or another of these formulations is accepted, it should be pointed out that the application of formulas obtained in this way for the purpose of predicting the price level, or even of explaining its movements in the past, is particularly difficult. Everything that can be said on this point has been said, during the course of the heated controversies as to the "measura-

[1] The "unspent margin" is the aggregate of money units (metallic currency in circulation, notes, bank deposits) which is at any moment available for spending. It is really $M + M'$, although at first glance the formula used by Mr. Hawtrey on p. 62 of his *Currency and Credit* appears rather different.

[2] Hawtrey, *Currency and Credit*, London, 1928, pp. 59–60.

[3] *Ibid.*, p. 60.

bility" of the factors involved in Fisher's formula.[1] Here we shall confine ourselves to indicating a few of the difficulties, which we cannot expect to overcome in the near future unless energetic steps are taken to organise, on an international scale, the collection of accurate statistics concerning each of the factors involved.[2]

Even the quantity of money is difficult to assess accurately. When it is a question of paper money the quantity is, of course, generally known, but paper money is always a national money, and although nobody would dream of denying its effect on prices, the extent of its influence always remains singularly uncertain since it is affected by changes in the international field. On the other hand, in the case of metallic currency, the actual quantity is a matter of doubt, for any estimate must take into account the money hoarded and the respective quantities of the metal used for money and used for industrial purposes; the quantity used in industry is unknown, although it undoubtedly is a diminishing proportion of the whole. A hundred years ago Fullarton pointed out that hoarding gives elasticity to the circulation of coin; the war and the post-war period shewed that hoarding had lost none of its attraction. We are therefore compelled to simplify the problem by confining ourselves to measuring the increase in the world output of gold; this has been the method adopted by the majority of writers—for example by Cassel—who have dealt with this question.

Admitting the legitimacy of this simplification (which we for our part do) we have still to calculate the three other factors in Fisher's formula: the velocity of circulation of metallic currency; the quantity and velocity of circulation of circulating credits; and the volume of transactions. Uncertain as any calculations concerning the other three factors must be, the uncertainties attending any calculation of this last factor—the volume of transactions—are far greater, and so long as they are not dispelled (Mr. Snyder's very fine work cannot be said to be wholly successful), verification of Fisher's formula and its use in predicting future price movements must remain extremely problematical.

[1] For a discussion of these methods and an account of the controversies the reader is referred to Valentin Wagner's excellent work, published at Basel, and quoted earlier.

[2] An interesting attempt on these lines has recently been made by Mr. James Angell, the results of which were published in New York in 1936 under the title *The Behavior of Money*.

In these circumstances Fisher's formula really amounts to little more than a convenient recapitulation of the chief factors concerned in the establishment of the price level.

Mr. Hawtrey's formula, by taking the expenditure of net income as its starting point (and omitting all intermediate transactions, and all capital transactions), has certain advantages from the standpoint of elucidating price phenomena, but its statistical verification is scarcely one degree less difficult than that of Fisher's.

Up to the present only a few very general—but nevertheless very important—conclusions emerge from these discussions:

1. The action of an influx of the precious metals on prices is indisputable. There is a concurrence between an acceleration or slowing down in the output of the precious metals, and the long-term movements of prices, which cannot be accidental. We have shewn this in the chapter in which we discussed the theories of Cassel and Wicksell;[1]

2. This action is infinitely more powerful than that of credit instruments for a number of reasons: firstly, because there appears to be a certain constancy in the relation between the total of circulating credits and the total of metallic currency; secondly, and principally, because the velocity of circulation of money and the volume of credit appear, from all the statistical material on this question so far assembled, *to vary in the same direction as the quantity of money* and not inversely. When money is being turned out on a large scale, the velocity of circulation increases, and conversely. Thus, in general, the money factor may be regarded as predominant.[2] The alleged compensatory action of an increase or decrease in the quantity of money and variations in the velocity of its circulation, devised by Ricardo and still believed by certain economists to-day, is pure illusion;

3. Finally, if we wish to predict or explain price movements, the factor of variations in net income seems, from the statistical point of view, more readily intelligible than the velocity of circula-

[1] Referring to Cassel's calculations, Mr. Hawtrey says: "All you know is that there is a relative correspondence of the price-level with the gold output. All it shows is that all these forces other than the gold output did more or less cancel out." Quoted in *The Future of Monetary Policy*, A Report published by the Royal Institute of International Affairs, London, 1935, p. 198.

[2] Mr. Benjamin Anderson reaches the same conclusion in his recently republished *The Value of Money* (1936).

tion factor. Monetary factors exert their influence largely through increases or decreases in income. Income statistics, at least in some countries, are comparatively easy to calculate; in any case they can be calculated more easily than the velocity of circulation of money.[1]

B. *The demand for money:* The theories we have just reviewed, ingenious as they are, have one feature in common. Although they recognise as a matter of principle that the value of money is determined by the laws of demand and supply, in practice they omit the factor of demand, which appears merely as the aggregate sum of transactions to be effected; having mentioned this factor they deal almost exclusively with the factor of "supply," represented both by the "quantity" of money and by its velocity of circulation. So much so, indeed, that the theory of the value of money, instead of fitting into the general theory of the value of commodities—in which the element of demand is so important—seems to constitute a thing apart, as it were outside the general framework of economic theory.

This has often been noted; probably the most interesting attempt to give demand its due place has been made by those writers who, although not the first to introduce the concept of demand into monetary theory (for the term "demand for money" is very old), did at least insist on its importance.

There are two reasons why a product or a service is exchanged for money, in other words why money is "demanded" on the market:[2] Firstly, to obtain a "generalised power" of acquisition—money—instead of the special and limited power of acquisition represented by a given product or a particular service. Money is thus demanded with a view to its being spent, or to settle debts contracted beforehand; Secondly, to keep in the form of money for

[1] These conclusions appear to be confirmed by the results of the researches undertaken by M. Rueff in his *Théorie des Phénomènes monétaires.*

[2] Certain writers fail to distinguish between the "demand" for money which takes the form of a loan, and the demand for money with a view to keeping it. This is one of the many confusions arising from the terms used by those on the money market. It would not occur to anybody to include in the study of the demand for goods the demand for goods to be hired out. Why should it be otherwise with the demand for money? We have already referred to the great difference between the supply of money available for loan, and that which is to be exchanged for goods and services; this was recognised by economists of the eighteenth century but ignored in the nineteenth century.

a definite or an indefinite time, the *value* of the goods or services sold, that is, to provide against known or unknown future requirements.

In other words, it is the special qualities of the "good" money, as described earlier on—its functions as a medium of exchange and a store of value—which explain why commodities or services are exchanged for money. In the majority of cases, as we have seen, those who demand money have both qualities in mind.

The effect of this twofold demand is to raise the value of money, since the supply of goods or services tends to lower their price on the market where they are offered. But this effect is not of equal duration in all cases. When the money is immediately brought to market again (that is to say on offer once more[1]), its offer tends to send prices up, thus offsetting the previous downward tendency. On the other hand, when it is retained for expenditure later (or not at all) the tendency towards rising prices which would otherwise have offset the tendency downwards initiated by the original sale of goods and services is checked for a shorter or longer time.

It follows from this that what is known as the velocity of the circulation of money depends in fact on the length of time which sellers of goods and services, or creditors whose advances are repaid, *themselves keep* the money thus obtained. The number of transactions which a man will effect with a given income is not fixed *ne varietur*. It is a variable factor, which depends on the amount of money he decides to keep as a means of storing up value. The velocity of circulation will increase or diminish inversely to the *demand for money*, if by that we understand the demand for money in order to keep it. The concept of velocity of circulation is therefore, as we think Wicksell was the first to point out, the converse of the concept of monetary demand.

So long as the value of money in relation to goods remains fairly stable, there is no marked preference for one or the other. The demand for money to be kept, and consequently the velocity of

[1] When goods have been sold in order to obtain money to settle a debt, it no longer depends on the seller of the goods whether that money is put into circulation, but on the creditor to whom he has to repay the proceeds of the sale. In periods of depression the slowing down in the circulation of money arises largely from the fact that creditors do not again put into circulation the money they have been repaid. This is particularly true of banks.

circulation, is determined by custom and the level of trading activity. But once the value of money begins to change, the choice between keeping money or keeping goods becomes an important factor, and price movements are reinforced by changes in the demand for money. The vitally important economic operation by which an individual or a concern distributes the expenditure of income *in time*, becomes infinitely more difficult when the stability of the purchasing power of money can no longer be taken for granted. When there is a general rise in prices there is a tendency not to keep money but to purchase goods, since goods are rising in value. The velocity of monetary circulation increases because the demand for money to be kept is not so great. Conversely, when prices are falling, hoarding becomes general, since keeping money appears to be a better way of storing up value than buying goods. The two extremes of this process are the flight from money which occurs at certain periods of rapid inflation, and at the other end general hoarding, which takes place during prolonged depressions. Between these two extremes every kind of intermediate position is possible. What is true of the market in general is true of the particular markets. If a commodity—for example wheat—rises in price, those who have wheat will keep it. If it falls, they will be anxious to sell it at the best price they can get if money seems to them to be more stable in value than their wheat.

Considered from the standpoint of the demand for money, a number of phenomena which are extremely difficult to explain by the concept of velocity of circulation, become perfectly clear. This is particularly true of the characteristic differences between paper money and metallic money.

What is characteristic of paper money (except in wholly exceptional cases) is the uncertainty as to its *future* value; this gives rise to fluctuations in its *present* value; for the present demand for such money arising from the desire to keep it will increase or decline according to whether it is believed that its future value will be greater or less. The successive hoarding and unhoarding of paper money was a factor of immense importance during and after the war. When certain Scandinavian countries announced their intention of returning to pre-war parity, their currencies were immediately hoarded in great quantities, which led to a rapid rise on the exchanges and a fall in prices. During the inflation period in Germany marks were hoarded when it was believed that Reich finances would be stabilised, and put into circulation when the opposite conviction held sway. Some striking examples of this behaviour are given in M. Bresciani-Turoni's magnificent study of the vicissitudes of German currency.[1]

The same explanation can be applied to fluctuations in the exchange rates of paper currencies when there has been no expansion or restriction of the notes issued; such sudden variations greatly intrigued Ricardo's contemporaries during the Napoleonic wars, and Mr. Goschen during the American Civil War; they were simply the result of purchases of the currency by speculators whenever they believed that the war would soon be over and that therefore the currency would soon be stabilised.

A similar process occurs during periods of crisis or lack of confidence, as a result of which one kind of money stands at a premium over another kind within one and the same country. In the United States in 1907 metallic currency stood at a premium over cheques because there was widespread fear that the banks would fail, and the public therefore preferred to keep their reserves in hard cash rather than in bank deposits. In France in 1849, on the other hand, notes stood at a premium over money because they were more convenient as a means of keeping large sums, and their number was temporarily limited by the law establishing forced currency. Again, quite recently, foreign gold currencies were at a premium in France, notwithstanding the *theoretical convertibility* of Bank of France notes, because convertibility into bullion was limited to large sums, and thus only wealthy persons were in a position to hold gold. This illustration gives a further proof of the importance of the legal characteristics of a currency in determining its economic value, which Ricardo persistently ignored.

The typical example of the demand for money as a "store of value" and the abandonment of a currency which is unable to fulfil this function is provided by the phenomenon of a flight from the national currency and the purchase of foreign currencies.

These are all cases of a *direct demand* for one kind of money in preference to another, either for the purpose of keeping it, or for using it to acquire goods whose value is not affected by variations in the monetary standard.

[1] Cf. his *Vicende del Marco tedesco*, published in 1932.

To explain all these phenomena by the single formula of "rapidity of circulation" elucidates nothing, although it is true that an increase or decrease in velocity is a direct and immediate result of the greater or lesser demand for money.[1]

The importance of the demand for money was again brought into prominence by the economic disorders following the World War; but even before then it had been explicitly set forth by some of the greatest economists of the late nineteenth century, in particular by Walras, Menger, Marshall, Wicksell and Fisher.

The idea of the "encaisse désirée," the amount of cash which the public like to keep in their pockets, was first formulated by Walras. He defines it as "the sum of all or part of the consumable goods and of the permanent net income that those who come on to the market wish to buy, and of which they desire to hold the equivalent in ready cash and cash savings." [2] This is an extremely accurate definition, since it includes money destined both for consumption and for saving; its only defect is that Walras assumes that the expenditure of the money is known in advance; it thus leaves out of account uncertainty as to the future, although it is precisely as an insurance against such uncertainty that money reserves are built up. Nevertheless this definition marks a great advance in the elucidation of monetary phenomena. In his article on *Geld* in the *Handwoerterbuch der Staatswissenschaften*,[3] Menger, at the end of the century, gave an equally precise definition of "the need for money," a concept corresponding to Walras' "encaisse désirée." He elaborates the idea in the second edition of his *Grundsätze* and shews how important this factor is in providing against future uncertainties.

But, as far as I am aware, Wicksell was the first to grasp the full import of the concept of the demand for money and to demonstrate

[1] When the number of notes in a country is diminished by the export of gold the shortage is felt by merchants and manufacturers who ask the banks to grant more credit (that is to say, to increase the velocity of circulation of the money that remains). If the banks yield to this pressure there is no reason why the exported money should be brought back, since it is only by refusing to increase credits that the banks will induce concerns to repatriate their gold.

[2] *Eléments*, fourth edition, p. 305.

[3] Cf. also the last pages of his *Grundsätze* (second edition, Vienna, 1923) in which he protests against the exaggerated importance attributed by the so-called classical economists to velocity of circulation, as against the "encaisse désirée" which, varying according to circumstances, gives elasticity to the supply of money.

that it is merely the converse of the concept of velocity of circulation. The following passage summarises his argument:

"An attempt could be made to ascertain the *intervals of rest* of all the pieces of money during the given period, the actual processes of exchange being regarded as confined to single points of time. The arithmetic mean of these intervals of rest could then be obtained (intervals at the beginning and end of the given period would not be counted separately but would be combined). This would give *the mean interval of rest* of money, and, expressed as a fraction of the unit of time (the year), its value would be equal to the reciprocal of the velocity of circulation of money, as worked out above. This is as it should be. For the arithmetic mean of the intervals of rest of all the units of money is equal to their sum divided by their number, and consequently the reciprocal is equal to the number of intervals of rest divided by their sum. But the *number* of intervals of rest (as defined above) is clearly equal to the number of circulations of all the units of money, or, what is the same thing, the total value, P, of the goods exchanged. And the *sum* of the intervals of rest clearly comprises all the intervals of rest of each individual piece of money, which, expressed as fractions of the unit of time, add up in each case to exactly a year (to the unit of time itself). The total sum is therefore equal to the number of units of money, *i.e.* to the quantity, M, of money in circulation. The ratio of P to M is thus once more obtained."[1]

Wicksell used this concept as the foundation of his extremely original representation of the way prices fall when the output of the precious metals declines. Fisher elaborates the same idea, which he calls "average time of turnover" and which is the reciprocal of the velocity of circulation;[2] but, having given its mathematical definition, Fisher does not use the concept in his currency theory.

Marshall on several occasions emphasised the importance of the demand factor and after 1886 he draws attention to the effect of rising and falling prices on hoarding.[3]

But it was only after the war that the concept of the demand for money really came into its own in monetary theory. In this respect Edwin Cannan's article on *The Application of the Theoretical Apparatus of Supply and Demand to Units of Currency* which appeared in the *Economic Journal* in 1921, is particularly characteristic. Here, as in the two small but solid books on the question which he

[1] K. Wicksell, *Interest and Prices*, pp. 52, 53.

[2] Cf. *Purchasing Power of Money*, p. 351.

[3] Cf. *Official Papers*, p. 6.

published later, he compares money to other things "such as land and railways; the annual production is so small compared with the stock, that we think of the stock as furnishing the supply, and the ability and willingness of people to use the thing as furnishing the demand."

Money belongs to this category of goods, for it is a durable instrumental good the stock of which is at any time very large in comparison with the additions to or subtractions from it that are made each year.

"We may consequently think of the supply, as we think of the supply of houses, as being the stock rather than the annual produce; and we may think of this supply, as we think of the supply of houses, as being increased by net additions to the stock, and decreased by net subtractions from it.

"Following the same line with demand, we must think of the demand for currency as being furnished, not by the number or amount of *transactions*, but by the ability and willingness of persons to *hold* currency, in the same way as we think of the demand for houses as coming not from the persons who buy and re-sell or lease and sub-lease houses, but from the persons who *occupy* houses. Mere activity in the house market—mere buying and selling of houses—may in a sense be said to involve 'increase of demand' for houses, but in the corresponding sense it may be said to involve an equal 'increase of supply'; the two things cancel. The demand which is important for our purposes is the demand for occupation. In the same way, more transactions for money—more purchases and sales of commodities and services—may in a sense be said to involve increase of demand for money, but in the corresponding sense it may be said to involve an equal increase of supply of money; the two things cancel. The demand which is important for our purpose is the demand for currency, not to pay away again immediately, but to *hold*."

Cannan returned to this argument more than once, and came to the conclusion that the demand for money in this sense increases when prices are falling, and decreases when prices are rising.

The same position was later taken up by the American economist Carver in an interesting article (*Economic Journal*, 1934) in which he enumerates the different circumstances that create a general demand for money to be kept as money. A number of the younger English and Austrian writers, the most important of whom have been mentioned above, take up the same position, which may be summarised in the following terms: Everyone who has or who receives an income has always to decide what part of his income he will keep in the form of money; the demand for money is the result of this decision.

Economic decisions as to expenditure are the result of selections made, firstly as between different goods, secondly as between the *different dates* at which the selected goods will be obtained. The demand for money is the result of a supplementary choice. Everybody has to choose between keeping his income in the form of money and spending it on the purchase of goods and services, or investing it with a view to drawing interest. The choice is determined by the characteristics of money as defined above—its ability to act as a general medium of exchange and as a store of value.

Obviously this conception is incompatible with the theory which, by extending the concept of marginal utility to money, makes the value of money equal to the marginal utility of the final good that the money can buy. This theory, formulated by Wieser, represents money as a good whose value depends, not on the services which it itself performs, but on the services to be performed by the objects which that money enables its holder to buy. In deciding on his "encaisse désirée," economic man chooses between the marginal utility of the services of money as defined above, and the marginal utility of goods. I am not aware that any scientific attempt has yet been made to apply from this standpoint the theory of marginal utility to money.[1]

One last remark on this subject: It has frequently been pointed out here that the rapidity of the circulation of money increases when prices are rising and decreases when prices are falling. The reader will have noticed that all writers who regard the demand for money as the factor determining changes in the velocity of circulation reach the same conclusion. The demand for money increases when prices are falling (that is to say the velocity of circulation decreases) and conversely. Thus variations in demand accompany and reinforce upward or downward movements in the price level, *but cannot be considered as the initial factor determining such movements*. This must be sought elsewhere: either, when it is

[1] Fritsch's mathematical treatise *New Methods of Measuring Marginal Utility* (Tübingen, 1932) gives a definition of the marginal utility of money that we cannot discuss here.

a case of a prolonged fall in prices, in a rapid increase in the production and sale of goods, or when prices are rising, in an increase in the currency, or, for cyclical variations, in an increase in credit.

§ III. *Knapp's Nominalist Theory*

The great majority of eighteenth- and nineteenth-century writers on money start from the idea that the chief use of a monetary system—that is to say the object which the State should pursue in establishing such a system—is to provide the economic community with a good medium of exchange and a stable reserve of value. In drawing up the rules which govern its currency, the State should have in mind the interest of individuals, the solidity of the foundations on which their economic relations rest, and it should take no action except such as is directed to this end. It should allow the metallic money chosen as the standard to enter and leave the country freely; it should guarantee that the coins it mints really contain the weight of metal by which the monetary unit is defined, and finally it should take care that any fiduciary currency is kept up to the value of the metal standard. At that point its functions cease. Of course, the metallic standard is not completely stable, and the price level varies with the greater or lesser output of the precious metals. But these variations are unavoidable, and are smaller in magnitude than those that would accompany any other monetary system, which would necessarily be artificial. As to the international aspect of money, its utility is not disputed, since the precious metals constitute the basis of almost all important monetary systems. The twofold object to be achieved is thus stability of the value of money in relation to commodities and to foreign currencies.

In 1905 a German professor, Georg Friedrich Knapp, who had made his name as an economic historian, published his *Staatliche Theorie des Geldes*;[1] it is a vigorous and ingenious work. The title gives some indication of the author's attitude, and the book immediately excited lively controversies. Knapp asserts that money is essentially a State affair, to be regulated by the State in its own interest. "Money is a creation of law; it appears in the course of

[1] Unfortunately the translation by Lucas and Bonar, published in London in 1924, is abridged. Where possible the English edition has been used.—Trs.

history under the most diverse forms. A theory of money must therefore at the same time be a theory of the history of law."[1]

Having thus decided that monetary questions originate neither in political economy nor in law, but in the history of law (which is truly paradoxical, since history has never provided the theoretical explanation of any phenomenon) he continues: The question of the value of money is secondary; what is important is its validity (*geltung*) (as opposed to its value), that is to say the power to discharge debt given to it by the State, that to which, in virtue of the law, money gives a right. On what in fact does the State confer this power of money? On a given weight of metal stamped with the insignia of the State? Not at all! This power is conferred on a unit of value which has a different name in different countries—it may be called a franc or a florin or a dollar—and has the power of finally discharging debts. The particular material embodiment of this unit is not important; it may be paper or gold, and the State has its own reasons for choosing now one material, now another. It is this unit (irrespective of the substance in which it is embodied) which possesses the power of discharging indebtedness, and the only quality which counts is its validity.

The monetary unit, represented by the instrument of circulation called money, is therefore purely "nominal." The franc, the dollar, and the florin do not connote a fixed weight of metal. They are *abstract units.*

It is easy, says Knapp, to prove this contention, for it is apparent in all currency history. Does not the State from time to time change the content of the monetary standard? For example it announces that from such and such a date the franc will be represented by a certain weight of gold, whereas until then it was represented by a certain weight of silver; at the same time it fixes the amount of gold that must be paid to settle debts incurred in silver francs. Such a decision can be explained in one way only: the debt was not incurred in a certain weight of silver, but in *francs, abstract units*, and these debts can be settled in silver money at one time, in gold money at another, as the State decides. If it were otherwise the decision of the State would be incomprehensible. In the interval of time during which the definition of the monetary unit changes—that is, between

[1] Knapp, p. 1. Walras also upheld the rights of the State in regard to money, but in quite different fashion from Knapp.

the moment when a debt in francs represents a certain weight of silver, and the moment when it represents a certain weight of gold[1]—it is obvious, Knapp contends, that the debt can represent only francs pure and simple, francs which are neither gold nor silver. "Each alteration of the means of payment implies that the unit of value, at least at the moment of transition, should be regarded as nominal. Once a money has been established, it can only be changed by an admission of the nominal character of the monetary unit; this character consists in the possibility of the State changing the means of payment, while the relative magnitude of different debts remains unchanged." [2] In these conditions a money is defined by the number of units of debts in old money that the new money can discharge. Thus the definition of a money is exclusively an "historical" definition.

"This definition has absolutely nothing to do with the material in which the old means of payment consisted, nor yet the new. It only contains the proportion of the new to the old unit of value, *i.e.* it relates the new unit back to the old one." [3]

This is the kernel of Knapp's thesis. The rest of his book is merely the logical and systematic development of this basic conception. He works out an extremely elaborate and complicated vocabulary to describe different monetary systems,[4] and makes an ingenious attempt at their classification. But a classification and a nomenclature, however instructive they may be, do not explain monetary phenomena. Of greater interest and importance is his attempt to shew that the essential object of the principal monetary systems is to establish a fixed rate of exchange with the chief commercial countries and in particular with England, which is the

[1] Why should there be such an interval of time? As a rule a change in legal status is effected instantaneously, immediately on promulgation of the law or decree introducing the change.

[2] *Staatliche Theorie*, p. 16 (*The State Theory of Money*, p. 19).

[3] *Ibid.*, p. 18, English edition, pp. 21–22.

[4] Here is an example of Knapp's language: "The order in which lytric phenomena are dealt with here is not arbitrary but necessary. (1) We presupposed the hylogenesis of the means of payment, for only hylic means of payment allow of pensatory use. (2) Then morphism appears; only morphic means of payment can be proclamatory and therefore Chartal. (3) Finally, it is only in the case of Chartal means of payment that the hylic basis can disappear; they alone, therefore, can be autogenic" (English edition, pp. 31–32). The idea expressed here is quite simple; Knapp is describing the transition from metallic to paper currency.

largest buyer and seller of goods.[1] The gold standard (of which, he says, he is in favour) is in his opinion merely a convenient way of maintaining exchange stability. But it is not the only way. The system in force in British India, or in Austria-Hungary, shews that it is possible to have a currency administration which assures exchange stability without any internal circulation of gold. Moreover, gold is being used less and less for domestic purposes, and reserved for international payments (there is nothing new in this observation, for Thornton noted this development in 1802, and it has been pointed out by practically all writers on money since). The most interesting part of Knapp's book is his account of the different systems of exchange stabilisation; this has been done many times since, but at the time Knapp wrote his book such systems were still a novelty. What is original in his work is the thesis outlined above, which caused a great stir and excited long-drawn controversies.

As a juridical thesis, there is nothing new in it. It is merely a philosophic version of an old principle that was formulated in article 1895 of the French Civil Code, according to which existing contracts (unless containing a specific clause to the contrary, although such clauses are forbidden in most countries) can, or rather must be paid in the new currency whenever the State alters the definition of the monetary unit. Changes in the unit of currency in the last twenty years have been the cause of endless dispute and

[1] Cf. the characteristic and amusing passage on p. 267 (English edition, p. 279): "It was not the gold standard *per se* that spread after 1871, but the English monetary system, which was the gold standard merely as it were by accident.

"In that case gold *per se* would be quite unimportant in the choosing of a standard? Was it only a question of historical circumstances, which were then (1875) favourable to gold? If the metallist puts this question, the chartalist can only answer Yes. All middle-sized and weaker States from exodromic considerations either have gone over to the gold standard or wish to do so. England is deaf to all suggestions of currency alteration, for she does not need to trouble herself with exodromic measures. It is the same with the system of military service. If the most victorious State has universal compulsory military service, its neighbours must have it too in so far as they share the same battle-ground. England stands out of it because she does not join in the continental battles. If, however, European States want to enter on a world-wide policy (*Weltpolitik*), they must imitate England's navy; and, if England chooses to build ships of iron, her rivals must also choose the 'iron standard' in shipbuilding." Knapp looks at the question from the standpoint of power; what he does not explain is why so many States want to be bound to the English standard; is it not precisely because of its stability and continuity, arising less from the power of England than from a certain conception of money?

discussion in the courts. Since they affect widespread interests currency changes excite heated controversies, but this is not the place to discuss the passions aroused by such events. The legal abolition of the gold clause in America in 1933 (a clause which had been in general use since the Civil War), the partial maintenance of this clause in certain countries (for example England and France) are events of great economic import. From the point of view of the history of theory, they merely reflect the intellectual confusion created by situations in which the interests of the State come into violent conflict with the interests of certain sections of the population. All currency devaluations represent a triumph for the State in a matter where its interests conflict with the interests of individuals, or where the interests of certain groups conflict with those of other groups. Devaluation is a method by which the State lightens the burden of its debts and the debts of certain economic groups (farmers in the U.S.A., the banks in Belgium, heavily indebted industries in France and England). It is a political act—an act of the sovereign—in which the State ranges itself on the side of certain interests in opposition to others which it considers less important. Most frequently it is regarded by the State as the only way of liquidating debts incurred in war. Devaluation, or a change in the monetary standard which is not accompanied by devaluation (for example the transition from the silver standard or bimetallism to the gold standard), can only be judged from the political standpoint, and according to the circumstances prevailing at the time;[1] on this point the reader cannot do better than refer to what Galiani wrote in the middle of the eighteenth century.

What is surprising is that an economist like Knapp should take one of the most characteristic manifestations of *raison d'Etat* as the foundation of his currency theory, that he should have conjured up a higher economic and juridical verity—the nominal character of the monetary unit—as the theoretical justification for a simple

[1] I would not say the same of the refusal of the courts to recognise the gold clause. When individuals have taken explicit precautions against devaluation, it is against the most elementary conception of equity to prohibit them from putting their own agreements into operation. It might be argued that the gold clause as it was used in the United States makes any devaluation impossible, and may be opposed to the most vital interests of the State. That is true; but it also means that the State will hesitate before embarking on political or financial adventures which are bound to lead to devaluation.

act of the sovereign power, so that the State, when it introduces currency changes, is in his opinion merely drawing a logical conclusion from this verity.

This verity, he argues, has up to now not been recognised. Is this really the case; or is it not rather that Knapp's verity is an idea which reappears from time to time and misleads certain writers? The eighteenth century adopted the idea of token money expressly rejected by Turgot. During the bimetallist controversy certain writers maintained that the public were in actual fact unaware whether they were using gold or silver francs, and thought merely in abstract francs. A little later a French jurist, Mongin, put forward the same contention in some articles in the *Revue d'Economie politique*, which created a mild sensation.[1] In 1855 a German, writing on the nature of money, remarked that the public never evaluate goods in relation to gold or silver, but consider their value in relation to the value of other goods, using for purposes of comparison a common unit (franc, mark or rouble), but never thinking of the value of the metal content of that unit. There is one answer to all these arguments:[2] the public do in fact base their calculations on goods and services with the price of which they are familiar, and on their income, without thinking of comparing them directly with the value of gold. But that is because age-old custom has made it unnecessary for them to verify the metal content of the money they use. But should any doubt arise as to the convertibility of that money into gold, they immediately hasten to reassure themselves.

Knapp is the most recent in a long line of economists who take only one aspect of money into consideration, who allow themselves

[1] *Des Changements de Valeur de la Monnaie*, 1887. Cf. in particular § 27.

[2] Carl Menger's reply to Oppenheimer, author of *Die Natur des Geldes*, runs as follows: "I agree that economic man is often completely unconscious of the character of money as metal, with a use of its own, and consequently is concerned only with its qualities as a medium of exchange. From this point of view it is the strength of custom alone which maintains the exchange value of money, even when its character as a useful metal is not itself directly appreciated. That is quite true. But it is obvious that the exchange value of money, like the custom on which it rests, would immediately vanish if the real value of the money metal were for any reason to vanish. I would not dispute that, where trade is highly developed, money often appears merely as a token; but there is no doubt at all that this illusion which can easily be explained, would immediately be dispelled if the money were to lose its character of representing a fixed weight of metal useful in itself" (*Grundsätze*, p. 335).

to be misled by the complexity of modern systems of payment and forget that in trade between individuals as between countries, there is always a balance which can only be settled by something that has a value in itself, and does not lose that value with time, which is also a reality.

The attitude of the State on currency questions, which Knapp believes it is possible to explain only by the "nominal" character of money, is in reality perfectly simple, and requires no economic metaphysics for its understanding.

The State does not merely change the monetary unit. From time to time it changes the units of weight and measure; but in these latter cases the *name* of the unit is also changed. When a new unit of weight or length is introduced, when the ell is dropped in favour of the meter, or the pound replaced by the kilogram, the new unit is introduced under a new name. Consequently no doubt can arise as to how much the seller has to give the buyer. If he has undertaken to supply ells he will supply ells even if in the meantime the unit of length has been changed. On the other hand, when the State changes the measure of value, that is to say the weight of the monetary unit, it usually refrains from changing the name. During the French Revolution an exception was made; the same principle was applied to money as to other units of measurement, and the word "livre" was replaced by the word "franc." But in the great majority of cases the name of the old standard is kept for the new, and the new monetary unit, because of this confusion of names, serves to discharge debts contracted in the old. This decision is made because the State itself hopes to benefit from the confusion; it is itself a debtor. Monetary changes have always been made with this object in view, and the public shew that they understand them in this light by adjusting the prices of goods more or less closely to the new unit. The State has never felt called upon to say to the public: "When you made an agreement in francs, your agreement, without your being aware of it, was made in *abstract francs*; you undertook in advance to receive *abstract francs*, and you were not concerned with what you could buy for those francs (gold or goods or foreign bills of exchange)." Had such a statement ever been made, it would have been received with more derision than conviction.

Anyway, what is an "abstract" monetary unit? What does the

monetary unit represent, if not a certain power of acquisition, the magnitude of which is determined by a number of factors which at any given moment make a certain weight of gold worth so much in goods? The unit cannot merely be a name; it is only a unit in relation to the sums expressed in multiples of that unit. From this point of view, the franc is the unit in which sums of francs are reckoned.[1] But to be a unit of value, the franc must represent a certain value for those who demand it.

It is true that the unit of value does not function like other units of measure, and that is why Leroy-Beaulieu's term "valorimeter" is defective. It is not used as the meter is used. It is not put on a scale, like weights, to measure the weight of the things on the other scale. Its purchasing power is fixed on the market, in exchange against goods, and this exchange presupposes that it is itself in demand, desired for its own sake, like all things having value. The different rates at which money exchanges against different goods enables a comparison to be made between the value of the different goods; it is in this sense that money is the measure of value.[2] But in no case can it be merely a name. Goods are not given in exchange for names.[3] They are given in exchange for goods with a value of their own, or for legal claims such as paper money which has a value like all legal claims; for the economic value of these claims is determined by the right thereby conferred on the holders to obtain certain goods or services. For Knapp, paper money, like all means of payment, has as such no value.[4]

Rightly understood, Knapp's theory is not an economic theory of money. It is a *juridical construction* designed, like all such constructions, to provide an explanation of a number of legal

[1] "First," says Knapp, "the unit of value is nothing but the unit in which the amount of the payment is expressed" (p. 7).

[2] There is an excellent account of money as a measure of value in Menger's *Grundsätze* (second edition, pp. 290 and 297).

[3] "We should not apply the concept 'value' to this means of payment, and therefore not to this money itself, but only to things which are not means of payment" (Knapp, *loc. cit.*, p. 25. English edition, p. 30). The reader is referred to the section dealing with the controversy between "metallists" and "anti-metallists," both of whom wrongly denied that paper money had any value.

[4] I find it impossible to agree with M. Nogaro, who asserts: "Thus in each country the true measure of value, and therefore the true 'standard' of values, is the national monetary unit, the *abstract unit of account* with which the precious metal is legally bought at a fixed rate, and not the metal itself" (*Modern Monetary Systems*, London, 1927, p. 176).

decisions. Even in this respect it is far from complete, for it is in direct contradiction with the principles adopted by certain States as the basis of their currency systems.

For example, the law passed in America on March 14, 1900, expressly laid it down that a contract in dollars was to mean the delivery of a certain weight of gold, the word dollar, in this context, having no other meaning but that of a certain weight of metal. "The dollar, consisting of 25·8 grains of gold, nine-tenths fine, shall be the standard unit of value, and the value of all moneys issued or coined by the United States shall be maintained at par with this standard unit." The dollar is thus a unit of value, defined by a weight of metal.

The definition of the franc given in the law of the seventeenth Germinal, Year XI, is of the same kind; it was drafted when the memory of the *assignats* was still fresh in men's minds: "Five grammes of silver, nine-tenths fine, constitute the monetary unit, which shall be called the franc."

Those who drafted the French Currency Law of 1928, which stabilised the franc after a long period of paper money, were guided by the same idea. They did not want the franc to be merely a name. They wanted the word franc to have no other possible meaning than that of a certain weight of gold, so that, when used in a contract, the word was to imply the delivery of a given weight of gold, and to imply nothing else.[1]

Granted that events have made these laws inoperative. New decisions by the State, inspired by new circumstances, have modified former decisions. Jurisprudence in France, otherwise faithful to an age-old tradition embodied in the Civil Code, has upheld, even against the clearly expressed wishes of the legislature, the nominalist conception of money. In the United States a special law was required to annul the gold clause inserted in the majority of contracts, and it was not without some opposition that the Supreme Court agreed that this law was constitutional.

But these decisions, to which the citizens have had to submit, have not changed the nature and characteristics of money; they have only had this effect, that individuals when agreeing on a price

[1] The present writer is the better able to give evidence on this point, since, after lively debates, he succeeded in getting the text of the 1928 law referred to above accepted.

in money, have not thereby assumed that they were to receive a certain weight of metal, or its equivalent in claims giving a purchasing power equal to that of the weight of metal. The movements of capital from one country to another, and the price changes which occur whenever there is a danger that the value of a currency will be altered, provide adequate proof on this point.

Knapp declares that he is not concerned with what economists call the value of money, since he denies that money has a value. Nor is he interested, at least at a first glance, in the problems arising in connexion with the value of money. Nevertheless in the course of his book he states his position in regard to a large number of these questions, without bothering to justify his answers; he gives them as though they were obvious and indisputable, although in fact as a rule they are not.

For example, he takes it for granted that money has only one function, to act as a means of circulation; he does not even mention its function of storing up value, although it complements the former. Money is merely a token; like John Law, he regards it as a "voucher to purchase." He is as unaware that paper money may have a value as the most inveterate "metallist."[1]

Since he refuses to credit money with a value of its own, Knapp finds it impossible to understand that a money can *lose* its value.

[1] Knapp puts paper money in the category of "proclamatory morphic means of payment." He writes: "When we give up our coats in the cloak-room of a theatre, we receive a tin disc of a given size bearing a sign, perhaps a number. There is nothing more on it, but this ticket or mark has legal significance; it is a proof that I am entitled to demand the return of my coat. When we send letters, we affix a stamp or ticket which proves that we have by payment of postage obtained the right to get the letter carried. The 'ticket' is then a good expression, which has long since been naturalised, for a movable, shaped object bearing signs, to which legal ordinance gives a use independent of its material. . . .

"Perhaps the Latin word 'Charta' can bear the sense of ticket or token, and we can form a new but intelligible adjective—'chartal.' Our means of payment have this token, or chartal, form. Among civilised peoples in our day, payments can only be made with pay-tickets or chartal pieces" (pp. 26–27. English edition, pp. 31–32). It is curious that Knapp, with his juristic outlook, should not have realised that paper money, unlike cloak-room tickets, is a claim on an *indeterminate object.* In exchange for his ticket, the holder knows that he will get a particular coat or umbrella, the one that belongs to him. In exchange for a hundred-franc note of forced currency nobody knows what he will be able to get in a day or two. It is true it can be used to settle a debt for a hundred francs. But if *the holder has no debts*, he can only use the paper money to buy goods, and the quantity of goods he can buy may vary from day to day. Knapp's comparison is wholly irrelevant.

He dismisses the quantity theory with a few disdainful words. He asserts that changes in the monetary standard are without importance, apart from economic relations with other countries. For, he argues, when the monetary unit is changed, everybody is equally affected. As creditors, everybody will receive the new units instead of the old, but as debtors they partake of the benefit of the change. He entirely ignores the fact that a change in the monetary standard, even though it affects all debts equally, has different results for the different sections of the population, favouring those who have large debts and injuring those with fixed incomes. Knapp no doubt is not thinking of currency inflation, but of less spectacular changes in the standard than those witnessed during the war. But it is difficult to believe that the indifference to inflation displayed by the currency authorities in Germany and Austria after the war was not in some measure due to passages such as the following:

"So we can assert, in more general terms than before, the proposition that for internal trade, excluding the bullion business, the choice of the standard hardly matters at all, since it only produces secondary effects which vanish in the general welter of continuous price changes. Daily there are a thousand kind of disturbances, from new routes or canals, customs tariffs, transport rates, the building of new ships, etc., which now in this direction and now in that change the course of trade little by little, and in the course of time completely alter the picture. In the midst of all this movement each person is seeking his own profit, and in a thousand instances this or that price falls or rises. But always the rise is due to the increased power of the seller, the fall to his diminishing power [Knapp pays no attention whatever to the influence on prices of the demand for money]; and since prices are not expressed in terms of quantities of metals, but of lytric units (marks, francs, roubles), and since ultimately the payment is in valuta [i.e. standard] money, it follows that the relation of this money to the metals has no significance, for it is always quite clear which kind of money is valuta. . . .

"The usual views of the effects of the change to another standard on internal trade are quite inadequate, so long as the amphitropic position of individuals [i.e. their position as both creditor and debtor] is overlooked, and so long as our liabilities (in the chartist sense) are left out of account. But, if both these are taken into consideration, it is immediately clear that the effects of the change in standard are quite negligible, whether the change is down or up, always bearing in mind that this refers to internal trade only, and leaves trade in the precious metals out of account."[1]

When at last Knapp does turn to international currency relations he is no less exclusive. He upholds the view, apparently without any thought of the possibility of contradiction, that the balance of payments is the only factor affecting exchange rates. Naturally, he does not for a moment think that the quantity of money can affect exchange rates. Finally, with the Indian system in mind, he asserts that a fixed rate of exchange can be maintained between several countries in the absence of metallic currency, which proves incontrovertibly that money has nothing to do with the precious metals:

"Theoretically it would be possible to stabilise the inter-valutary exchanges even without hylodromy [*i.e.* without the use of a metal in common]. It is only necessary that the two States concerned should decide on a parity, *e.g.* England and Germany might agree that—fractions neglected—the pound sterling was to be kept at a par of twenty marks. When this is done, the lytric administration of England decides always to give one pound sterling for twenty marks and that of Germany twenty marks for one pound sterling. Kindly observe that we are not speaking of handing over sovereigns or of double crowns, but of valuta money, which in our own case might be notal, *e.g.* might consist of inconvertible paper money. We are not proposing this; we only assert that it is conceivable, and that the inter-valutary exchange would be stable, so long as this arrangement was retained."

He continues:

"There is, moreover, the further consequence that the specie form of valuta money which can certainly be dispensed with for internal circulation can also be left out for foreign trade without affecting the stability of the inter-valutary exchange, on condition, of course, that the exodromic organisations of the kind indicated are established."

And his final conclusion follows:

"Currency is not bound up with the hylic use of metal, either at home or abroad. All metals might be as common as water or as rare as helium; in both cases it would still be possible to have a convenient currency, for hylogenic money, though highly desirable in practice, is not necessary in theory. Money is a creation of law, and, in the last resort, can continue

[1] Knapp, *loc. cit.*, pp. 197–198. English edition, pp. 209–211.

to exist even without hylic metal, because the unit of value is defined not technically but legally. The law indeed only runs within the boundary of the State which makes and maintains it. But States can make treaties and so do away with boundaries; and this they must do on the disappearance of hylogenic money, or there would be no possibility of a stable inter-valutary exchange."[1]

If Knapp had himself had to undertake the task of stabilising the exchanges, he would have soon discovered that, in the circumstances assumed, England's real difficulty would consist in having a sufficient quantity of marks to be sure of being able to provide them at the rate of twenty to the pound whenever necessary. For England *could not create one single mark*. Only Germany could do so; England would have to acquire marks, and consequently to pay for them. The advantage in having gold is that it constitutes a *general* reserve, that England can acquire from all countries and use to pay all countries, including Germany. From the moment that England can pay Germany in marks alone, she will have to build up a stock of marks (and of lira for Italy, francs for France, etc.), and *if that stock should prove inadequate*, not all the agreements in the world would prevent the mark from rising as against the pound. It is because metallic currency is everywhere accepted freely and willingly *without any previous arrangement* that it is so well adapted for use in international relations.

§ IV. *Can the Price Level be Stabilised?*

Knapp is the great heresiarch. In treating money as a purely nominal unit with no value of its own, he made a complete break with economic doctrine as it had been formed in the course of centuries; not only with German doctrine, as represented for example by Helfferich, but with the entire body of English doctrine, Austrian doctrine as represented by Menger, Wicksell in Sweden, Fisher in America, and all French and Italian economists.

In one respect, however, Knapp's theory fell in with a tendency that was becoming more strongly marked before the war, at least among speculative economists (for States themselves, indifferent as always to theoretical arguments, continued to build up as strong a

[1] Knapp, *loc. cit.*, pp. 280–282. English edition, pp. 294–295.

gold reserve as possible). Knapp closes his book with a profession of faith in the superiority, at least theoretically, of paper money. Paper money was also advocated by writers such as Wicksell and Cassel, the outstanding representatives of the quantity theory and therefore necessarily hostile to the nominalist conception of money. The Belgian economists of the Ernest Solvay school were of the same opinion; starting from a philosophy of history that was as fallacious as all such philosophies are bound to be, and on the analogy that, as a means of circulation, metallic currency was steadily being replaced by circulating credits, they conclude, by a rash extrapolation, that it will also lose its function of acting as a store of value. Irving Fisher, although he expresses no sympathy for paper money, advocates a system which, he believes, by varying the metallic content of the monetary unit, will liberate the price level from its "enslavement" to fluctuations in the output of the precious metals. Eminent thinkers in every country were debating the idea that a more stable price level, a level more closely controlled by the rational human will, would be of benefit to mankind. They were spurred on to these investigations by the marked rise in world prices at the beginning of the twentieth century, coming after the prolonged fall at the close of the nineteenth.

Sceptics to-day cannot refrain from a smile when they remember that these efforts were made on the eve of a world conflict which was to give rise to the most catastrophic monetary changes witnessed in the world since the *assignat* experiment, changes which were due to an unprecedented output of paper money. But history is full of such ironies. What is more curious is that, after such catastrophes, there should still be economists prepared to maintain the superiority of paper to metallic currency, and to attribute to gold variations in the price level which were the direct and immediate result of the war-time policy of governments.

Since the war a strange legend has grown up among certain English economists as to the behaviour of prices before 1914. This relates that in the fifty years before the outbreak of the war the London money market, and in particular the Bank of England, watched over price movements, and, with the intuitive sagacity of a wise guardian, succeeded, with consummate but still unconscious skill, in preventing violent fluctuations such as those to which we have grown accustomed in the last fifteen years. "It has been pointed out," remarks one of these writers, "that during the nineteenth century London's financial supremacy gave her a predominant voice in determining gold prices, and though she did not even try to secure a constant price level, gold prices were in practice kept fairly stable and fluctuations were moderate in comparison with recent experience."

Elsewhere he writes with still greater emphasis:

> "The Bank of England was able for nearly a century up to 1914 to keep sterling at parity with gold, and though it did not keep prices stable or envisage stability of the price level as its objective, the position of sterling in world finance was so dominant that in fact the Bank of England was regulating world gold prices."[1]

This legend, like all historical legends, is not without its purpose. It is meant to prove that the world will find it an improvement if its monetary fate is once again entrusted to London (or to London jointly with New York).

It has only one defect—that it does not in a single respect correspond to the truth. Before the war no English economist or banker would have dreamt of endowing the Bank of England with such virtues; the most eminent among them were always greatly preoccupied with variations in the gold price level. Men like Marshall, Jevons or Robert Giffen, who had been at such pains to investigate and explain the causes of variations in the price level, would have been highly amused at the statement that it was controlled by the Bank of England. If anything did moderate such fluctuations, it was rather bimetallism, which, as all are agreed, acted as a balancing and restraining force after the Californian gold discoveries. But, during the 1873–1895 depression, it was London which was most firmly opposed to any international effort to re-establish bimetallism. As to the maintenance of the gold standard (and consequently gold prices), countries such as Germany, France, the United States and Scandinavia, to mention only the most outstanding, were at least as important as England. Indeed, it is well known that the Bank of England, bound by the absurd regulations of the 1844 Act, would on certain occasions have found

[1] B. Blackett, *Planned Money*, pp. 112 and 132. Sir Basil Blackett was a Treasury official and at his death held an important financial post in India.

it difficult to maintain that standard were it not for the support forthcoming from continental banks, in particular the Bank of France. The inadequacy of the Bank of England's gold reserve, as we shall see in the next chapter, was the subject of lively debates in England itself in the first fifteen years of the twentieth century.[1]

England has rendered great enough economic and financial services to the world to have no need of claiming, after the event, credit that nobody until then would have dreamt of giving her. For indeed price fluctuations in the nineteenth century, and particularly from 1875 onwards, greatly engaged the minds of contemporary economists, as has been amply shewn in the preceding chapters. It was precisely the magnitude of these fluctuations which induced several outstanding economists to investigate ways and means of stabilising the price level. Their attempts have been frequently referred to in these pages, and we shall now examine them more closely, for they are a prominent feature of currency doctrines at the end of the nineteenth and the beginning of the twentieth centuries. Neither in France nor in England have they so far met with a sympathetic response.

[1] Basil Blackett's book is an extremely striking illustration of the mental disturbance caused among certain English experts by the sterling crisis of 1931. It says, for example, that barter is preferable to a régime in which money has a value of its own. It expresses the hope that German National Socialism, which is anxious to escape from 'enslavement' to gold, will assist England to pursue a similar policy. It advocates the use of paper money as a certain means of maintaining price stability, etc., etc. Above all, it expresses the deep desire to organise, in agreement with the United States, a monetary system to which other countries will subsequently adhere. It displays, together with a complete disregard of all past experience, utter ignorance of conditions in other countries. The old quantity theory in its crudest form is the only guide that the author follows in all his lucubrations. It would be too ingenuous for other countries to place the destiny of their currency in the hands of London. London has an excellent banking system but English ideas on monetary organisation have always been inspired by the immediate needs of the City. This can be shewn without going back far into the past, or reiterating our criticism of the Peel Act; it is only necessary to recall what happened after the war: England made a mistake in alone deciding to pay her debts to the United States, for this upset currency relations between the two countries; it was an error when in 1925, against the advice of her best experts, she decided to bring the pound back to its pre-war parity; it was an error to wait until 1925 to stabilise the pound, thus allowing gold to be accumulated in the U.S.A.; she was mistaken in the belief that the world supplies of gold were inadequate, and in getting this belief adopted by a Committee of the League of Nations, etc., etc. The fact that other countries made equally grave errors in their monetary and financial policy is no reason for attributing infallibility to England.

The idea of stabilising the price level is very old. John Law inveighed against the variability of the silver standard and urged the adoption of paper money; the result of the experiment by which he hoped to prove its superiority is well known. Hume rather diffidently suggested that the metallic content of money should be slowly and steadily reduced. At the end of the eighteenth century, in a book contemporary with the *Wealth of Nations* but almost completely overlooked because of the success of Adam Smith's great work, Sir James Steuart proposed that gold should be replaced by a price index as standard.

Ricardo criticised this proposal, which was to be renewed time and time again, in terms which deserve quotation in full. He too was anxious for the utmost possible stability of the monetary standard, and freely admitted that in this respect the precious metals left much to be desired. But he argues that they are still superior to any other commodity, and continues:

"During the late discussions on the bullion question, it was most justly contended, that a currency, to be perfect, should be absolutely invariable in value.

"But it was said, too, that ours had become such a currency, by the Bank restriction bill; for by that bill we had wisely discarded gold and silver as the standard of our money; and, in fact, that a pound note did not and ought not to vary with a given quantity of gold, more than with a given quantity of any other commodity. This idea of a currency without a specific standard was, I believe, first advanced by Sir James Steuart, but no one has yet been able to offer any test by which we could ascertain the uniformity in the value of a money so constituted. Those who supported this opinion did not see, that such a currency, instead of being invariable, was subject to the greatest variations—that the only use of a standard is to regulate the quantity, and by the quantity the value of the currency—and that without a standard it would be exposed to all the fluctuations to which the ignorance or the interests of the issuers might subject it.

"It has indeed been said that we might judge of its value by its relation, not to one, but to the mass of commodities. If it should be conceded, which it cannot be, that the issuers of paper money would be willing to regulate the amount of their circulation by such a test, they would have no means of so doing; for when we consider that commodities are continually varying in value, as compared with each other, and that when such variation takes place, it is impossible to ascertain which commodity has increased, which diminished in value, it must be allowed that such a test would be of no use whatever.

. . . . . .

"Commodities generally, then, can never become a standard to regulate the quantity and value of money; and although some inconveniences attend the standard which we have adopted, namely gold and silver, from the variations to which they are subject as commodities, these are trivial, indeed, compared to those which we should have to bear if we adopted the plan recommended.

"When gold, silver, and almost all other commodities were raised in price, during the last twenty years, instead of ascribing any part of this rise to the fall of the paper currency, the supporters of an abstract currency had always some good reason at hand for the alteration in price. Gold and silver rose because they were scarce, and were in great demand to pay the immense armies which were then embodied. All other commodities rose because they were taxed either directly or indirectly, or because, from a succession of bad seasons, and the difficulties of importation, corn had risen considerably in value, which, according to their theory, must necessarily raise the price of commodities. According to them, the only things which were unalterable in value were bank-notes, which were therefore eminently well calculated to measure the value of all other things.

"If the rise had been 100 per cent, it might equally have been denied that the currency had anything to do with it, and it might equally have been ascribed to the same causes. The argument is certainly a safe one, because it cannot be disproved. When two commodities vary in relative value, it is impossible with certainty to say whether the one rises or the other falls; so that, if we adopted a currency without a standard, there is no degree of depreciation to which it might not be carried. The depreciation could not admit of proof, as it might always be affirmed that commodities had risen in value, and that money had not fallen."[1]

In this passage Ricardo raises the two chief objections which can be made against any currency system based on a price index: one is of a technical character, the other psychological.

To deal with the first: when the rate at which two commodities exchange varies, how is it possible to say which has risen, or which fallen in value, unless there is a third commodity in relation to which such variations can be measured? This is of the utmost

[1] Ricardo, *Economic Essays*, Gonner edition, 1923, pp. 161 *et seq.*

importance, and applies to the exchange rates of national currencies as well as to the exchange of commodities against other commodities. If sterling, francs and dollars are all paper currencies, how will it be possible to determine which has risen or fallen when their rates change, in the absence of a fourth currency, variations in which are not caused by purely national factors, and in relation to which variations in the other three can be measured? Of course it may be agreed to take sterling, or francs, or dollars as the fixed currency serving as the basis for comparison, but can it seriously be believed that many countries would agree to take a foreign currency as the universal basis of comparison? This would mean their agreeing, if they were anxious to keep their own exchanges stable, to subordinate their national economy to the currency fluctuations of another country.

As to the psychological objection, Ricardo's eyes were opened by the twenty years' experience of and argument about the fluctuations of the paper pound in relation to gold. It is obvious, given the interests at stake and the influential position of the groups that profit from rising prices, that any rise in the index would always be attributed to commodities and any fall to an inadequate supply of money. There would therefore always be good reasons for increasing the quantity of money but good reasons would never be found for decreasing it or leaving it alone. What is true in the national sphere would be even more true on an international scale. If the nations were to agree to draw up an international price index, and to regulate their national currencies in accordance with changes in the index, is there a single country that would deliberately bring about a price fall on its own markets in order to comply with an international decision, if such a fall were to be injurious to its own economy?

The observations made by Ricardo are still true to-day. They are, we think, sufficient to condemn any monetary system based on anything but a real international standard. Only a precious metal, the fluctuations in which are independent of the political and financial vicissitudes of any given country however strong or wise, only a good representing, like other economic goods, labour and saving, and which has to be paid for to be acquired, has any chance of being permanently accepted by all independent countries as measure and store of value.

A hundred years after Ricardo, Carl Menger, an economist with a mind at least as able and perhaps more penetrating than the great English classicist's, discussed the same problem. He asks whether it is possible to hope that one day the purchasing power of money (which he calls its external exchange value, *aüsserer Tauschwert*) will be stabilised, and comes to the following conclusion:

> "The researches undertaken into this problem, that has often, and not without cause, been described as squaring the economic circle, have proved unavailing. The problem of establishing an absolutely stable measure of exchange value may be regarded as scientifically settled, and taken as insoluble."[1]

For, he argues, the desire to stabilise the purchasing power of money is in fact the desire to stabilise the exchange value of all products, since the purchasing power of money is established in exchange against products. To undertake to stabilise the purchasing power of money is to undertake to stabilise the conditions of production and marketing of all goods and services. There is no sense in talking of stabilising the exchange value of money without undertaking to stabilise the production of commodities.

But Menger admits that it is possible to try to stabilise what he calls the "internal value" of money, that is to say the conditions of production of the money metal.[2] There is, he believes, nothing utopian in such an undertaking, and if successful it might have the happiest results. This, of course does not mean that the price level would be stabilised; that, as he points out, depends as much on the production of goods as on the output of metal. But he believes that it might provide a standard with the least possible variation in time and space, against which to measure changes in the value of commodities.

Unfortunately for Menger the distinction between the internal and external value of money is illusory. The value of money depends not only on the conditions of its production, but also on the *demand* for it. It is extremely curious that an economist like Menger, who placed such great emphasis on the influence of demand on *prices*, should have believed it possible to make a theoretical

[1] Menger, *Grundsätze*, second edition, pp. 299–300.
[2] *Ibid.*, pp. 308–309.

distinction between an internal and an external value of money, although it might be argued, and this is probably what Menger meant, that if it were possible to establish a regular flow of the precious metals, any subsequent large scale price variations could rightly be attributed to the production of commodities.

However that may be, the problem of stabilising the price level has for a hundred years been regarded as insoluble by the finest thinkers, and the reasons they give are unanswerable. It is nevertheless constantly being raised by economists whenever a sudden shock to prices introduces confusion into world economy.

Why is it that this obviously utopian currency project is always cropping up? Just as socialist utopias are based on the hypothesis of the infallibility of the State, and anarchist utopias on the converse hypothesis of the infallibility and goodness of the individual, whereas in fact the life of States represents a continual compromise to maintain a balance between the only too obviously imperfect but undoubtedly necessary actions of the State and of individuals, so the utopia of stabilising the price level rests on a false conception; it is a conception encountered as early as the seventeenth century, and one which, expressed with greater or less lucidity, has even inspired many classical works, in particular those of Ricardo and J.-B. Say. It consists in regarding money as an *extrinsic factor in national economy*, a sort of artificial instrument which has its use in settling accounts, but which can be replaced by any other accounting mechanism. This is the *great currency illusion.* We have already dealt with it at the beginning of this chapter. In reality money is a good, chosen from among many goods by a sort of social selection, whose original function was to guard against the uncertainties of the future. The settlement of both national and international accounts by clearing and compensation, however highly this process is developed, is bound to leave some *balances* over, and since it is impossible to go on carrying them forward (which would require a degree of mutual confidence that is only found among persons who have long known each other, or who have never suffered from another's insolvency) these balances can only be paid in real wealth.[1]

[1] This is true in the first instance of balances in international payments, since no country has yet been persuaded that the currency of other countries, when it consists of mere paper, is a stable good protected from the financial or political fantasies of

Since this is so, and since money must necessarily be a good with a value, it is bound to be subject to those changes in value which are characteristic of all goods; it is subject to the hazards of wealth in all its forms, and in its turn, like all other goods, it exerts an influence on the price level. No currency contrivance, however ingenious, can bring about that immobility in economic conditions that a stable price level presupposes.

In fact, of course, the majority of the writers who have worked out proposals for price stabilisation have not deluded themselves as to their permanence, and confine their ambitions to *reducing the magnitude* of fluctuations when they go beyond a certain point. Plans of this kind may be divided into two main categories, those which advocate the introduction of a purely paper currency, and those which advocate the maintenance of a metallic currency but propose to adapt its volume to changes in economic conditions.

The mechanism suggested is always the same: increase or decrease in the quantity of money. The innovators always appeal to the old quantity theory, and usually in its crudest and most simplified form.

The plans based on a purely paper currency thereby reject an international currency; they advocate the purest nationalism in monetary matters. The State or the bank of issue will increase or diminish the quantity of money in accordance with the downward or upward movements of a price index, constructed on principles which, it is admitted, are difficult to define, and based on a selection of commodities requiring the utmost delicacy in adjustment. These are the chief features of the scheme put forward by Sir Basil Blackett in his book on *Planned Money*.

All plans of this kind presuppose that a certain number of

governments. (Similarly, no country has yet been convinced that the armies of other countries are exclusively defensive in character, although if all countries could be convinced of this the problem of peace would be solved.) It is equally true of balances in home accounts. Every individual requires a reserve for the future (the sum of which will vary according to price movements and to the greater or less political security, and which may of course be physically in the possession of others). But there is no country where confidence in the government's policy and in the administration of its finances is so great that the individual is satisfied to hold his reserves wholly in the form of legal claims whose realised value will depend on the actions of that administration.

questions have been satisfactorily answered; these questions are fundamental and touch the roots of any monetary system. They must be answered in any plan for a managed currency.

Firstly, what will be the relations of a system of this kind with price levels in other countries? As a rule the authors of such plans begin their argument by shewing that a paper money régime can function satisfactorily in a closed national system. It is rather as if a beginner at chess were taught to assume at the outset that he has no opponent, or as if an instructor in military strategy were in his first lecture to omit all mention of the enemy's army. For up to the present there has never been a closed economy, and it is we think highly improbable that there ever will be one in the future. But if there are relations with foreign countries, then the prices of foreign goods exert an influence on the national price level, an influence which varies with variations in the rate of exchange. How can the stability, or at least the comparative stability of that rate be assured in the absence of an international currency? No answer has yet been given to this question.

Supposing this difficulty were met, a second question arises. It is universally admitted that the domestic price level depends not only on the quantity of money, but also on its velocity of circulation. How would that be regulated? It is not merely a question of the volume of credit granted by the banks; it includes also the rapidity with which individuals make both money and credit instruments circulate. Nobody has yet been able to suggest a method of controlling this factor.

Finally, assuming that both these difficulties were overcome, a third problem would remain, to which reference has been made in an earlier chapter, and the terms of which have been very clearly defined by Cassel. Price stability, just as much as price instability, gives rise to inequalities as between the citizens of one and the same country. If prices remain stable while the volume of goods increases, the entire benefit of the greater production will go to the producers, and consumers will have no share in it. This jeopardises the very principle of stability and its beneficial consequences. Cassel, as we have seen, refrains from taking sides on this question. Blackett unhesitatingly decides in favour of price stability to the profit of producers. But is this stability (which can obviously only be attained by an increase in the quantity of money corresponding to the expansion of production) compatible with a rational organisation of production and with progress in manufacturing methods? These, too, are questions to which those who advocate price stabilisation by a paper currency have not yet given an answer.

The second group of writers, who wish to keep to a metallic currency, have tried to work out what measures should be taken when the output of the precious metals is either too small or too great. The group includes Wicksell, Fisher and Flux. Their problem is not that of stabilising prices, but of finding a way of counteracting excessively violent price movements due to an inadequate or a too plentiful output of gold.

The last section of Wicksell's *Lectures* is given up to this question. We have seen that he was in favour of using the discount rate to control the price level; but we have also seen that the manipulation of the discount rate must, in his opinion, be accompanied by a corresponding issue of money. But if the output of gold is not great enough to fill the gap in the currency that the desired price rise will create, this requirement will have to be met by the creation of paper money. We are thus back among the paper money systems of price stabilisation. In recent years governments have preferred to adopt another course; England did so in 1931 and the U.S.A. in 1933. It is the old method used by the *ancien régime* in France, currency devaluation. It consists in a sudden adjustment of the price level by reducing the weight of the currency unit to the exchange value of gold, without diminishing nominal incomes. It amounts to a reduction in the total gold value of all currency instruments in circulation. We have explained in an earlier chapter how this method restores to gold production the ability to influence prices which it had lost as a result of the excessive weight of the currency unit. But in the circumstances in which devaluation was carried out after 1930, the sudden and prolonged price fall was not, as we have seen, and despite the clamorous reiterations of well-known economists, the result of a shortage of gold. It was merely the rebound from the former rise that followed the large-scale issue of paper money. Devaluation, at least in England and the United States, was merely a far too tardy recognition of the decline in the value of the monetary unit due to the indebtedness incurred during the war.

Wicksell, however, also deals with the converse phenomenon,

which was in fact in full swing at the time he was writing: he takes as his hypothesis a marked rise in prices due to an unexpected influx of gold. He suggests as the one method of dealing with the disturbances thus created the suspension of the free coinage of gold and the limitation of coinage to a fixed sum in each country. He does not disguise the fact that this too means that all monetary systems will take on a national character, since gold, no longer having a fixed price in each country, will be imported and exported like an ordinary commodity at varying prices, and that consequently the fixed limits to the variations of gold currencies in relation to each other established on the exchange markets will disappear. He admits that the abandonment of an international standard will be extremely vexatious, but that is the price that has to be paid for a system of price stabilisation.

Certain considerations are bound to occur to the reader who ponders these proposals:

1. The composure with which these writers envisage the return to paper money, or the disappearance of the international monetary standard, gold, is truly disconcerting. It was so before the war, and it is still more so now, after the bitter experiences of such currency régimes. They do not ask whether it is worth while to seek to establish a price stability obtained by the abandonment of the international standard, even if it were possible (which we do not believe, since stability of prices presupposes exchange stability). The uncertainty in all international relations that would follow from such an action would more than offset the internal stability, which in any case would be far from absolute, that they hope would be achieved.

2. These writers also forget that an increase in the output of gold, even if it gives rise to difficulties by raising prices, has the advantage of *strengthening the monetary and financial position of States to a remarkable degree*. Tooke pointed this out, and it was a noteworthy feature of the period 1895 to 1914. Moreover it greatly encourages the expansion of trade. In the world to-day, where many countries have abandoned the gold standard, and many others have not yet introduced it, it should not be difficult to create a demand for gold large enough to counteract any rise in prices that is feared from a plentiful output of gold. As Newmarch said, there is no comparison between the effect on prices of an abundance

of gold, and the effect produced by paper money. It should be borne in mind that crises were never so short as in the period from 1895 to 1914. It should be borne in mind that the output of gold is not stopped suddenly, as is the issue of paper money, and that therefore the effects of a fall in prices consequent upon a diminished gold output are thereby greatly mitigated, just as the disturbances caused by a greater output and consequent price rise are offset by indisputable benefits.

3. Finally these writers seem to forget that in the present technical state of mining a fall in the price level encourages the production of gold, and conversely a rise in prices tends to slow down gold output. Thus there is a tendency evident in recent years for gold output, under the pressure of this compensating movement, to adapt itself to requirements.

It has also been suggested that the drawbacks of a too rapid rise in gold prices can be avoided either by regulating gold output (which would at least have the advantage of allowing free coinage to be maintained in each country), or by increasing the weight of the monetary unit. The latter idea is embodied in Irving Fisher's famous plan for the "compensated dollar." Wicksell is opposed to this proposal, and is sceptical as to its effects. To stand any chance of success, two conditions would have to be fulfilled: 1, the plan would have to be adopted on an international scale; 2, agreement would have to be reached as to the *extent* to which the weight of the different currencies would have to be increased in order to correspond with the anticipated price rise. Both conditions would be extremely difficult to fulfil.

Writers who work out proposals of this kind must have extremely great confidence in them, and great contempt for the risks that would attend their being put into operation. They appear to forget that mankind itself has always been the most disturbing factor in currency systems. Wars, revolutions, and crises are at the bottom of the disturbances for which, with touching zeal, governments and economists subsequently seek a remedy. If there is a sphere in which human foresight has proved unreliable it is in the sphere of currency. The idea that the nationalisation of currencies will bring international price stability nearer represents the last of the currency utopias. It is in harmony with the spirit of the century. It is, in the present writer's opinion, the most dangerous form of economic nationalism, which would create, in the majority of States that adopted it, the most intolerable tyranny.[1] [2]

[1] Irving Fisher's book *Stable Money* (New York, 1934) provides the most complete bibliography of projects for currency stabilisation and an analysis of their main features. The book is very instructive. The Kardex Company, of which Fisher was one of the founders, first issued bonds on which interest and repayment were to vary according to the price index. But these were soon replaced by gold bonds "to gain a wider market than was possible for an unfamiliar form of security" (p. 112). Fisher is in favour of local stabilisation (Sweden, the United States, the British Empire), after which "the secondary problem of foreign exchanges would be solved of itself" (p. 396). The present writer does not share his confidence. The stabilisation of the exchange rates between countries whose price levels had previously been stabilised by means of a managed currency would necessitate restrictions on foreign trade and on movements of capital.

[2] I should like to say a few words here about a school of thought that is little known but extremely interesting; following the lead of the German economist, Eugen Dühring, they advocate the return to a perfectly free metallic currency. Dühring regarded paper money as a "robber currency" (*Raubwährung*) and urged that coins should be named after their weight, and not by special names. He elaborated these ideas in his lectures and in the review, written almost entirely by himself, called *Personalist und Emancipator*. Proceeding from Dühring's ideas, an eminent Austrian, Dr. Herman Schwartzwald, has advocated in recent articles the return to the "parallel standard," in which gold and silver are both used, but each according to its real metallic value, and without a legally fixed relation. See his remarkable article *Das Silber und das Dühringsche Gewichtsgeld* in the *Sendbogen*, a periodical devoted to propagating Dühring's ideas, for July, 1937. Pierre Quesnay, Director of the Bank for International Settlements until his untimely death in a tragic accident, made great efforts to introduce the gold-gramme as the monetary unit in B.I.S. transactions. Many distinguished persons have noted the great danger to the currency future of the world represented by the ideas born of the prevalence of paper money systems during the war; the danger is one which threatens not only world economy, but the intellectual balance of many economists.

CHAPTER NINE

Theory of Central Banks of Issue

§ I. THORNTON, FIRST THEORIST OF THE CENTRAL BANK.—§ II. TRIUMPH OF NOTE ISSUE MONOPOLY AND FORMATION OF THE CLASSIC DOCTRINE OF THE FUNCTIONS OF A BANK OF ISSUE BETWEEN 1825 AND 1870.—§ III. THE BANK OF ISSUE AS THE COUNTRY'S SUPREME GOLD RESERVE. FROM BAGEHOT TO THE FEDERAL RESERVE BANKS.—§ IV. BANKS OF ISSUE. THE PRICE PROBLEM.

In the second half of the nineteenth century central banks of issue became so important as the *points d'appui* of the chief money markets that it is difficult for us to imagine a time when they did not exist.

But at the end of the eighteenth century, when the first credit theories were being formulated, there was only one bank of issue that acted as a central bank, in the sense in which that term is now used. This was the Bank of England. England alone possessed at that time a real money market in London. The country banks of issue, however important, were all dependent in a greater or less degree on London. The deposit Bank of Amsterdam was not in any respect comparable to the Bank of England. As to France, although Paris was the centre of financial transactions, and bills on Paris were in common use as means of payment, the issue of notes was confined to two or three Paris banks of wholly secondary importance.

Central banks of issue, and consequently theories concerning their functions and operations, really developed in the course of the nineteenth century. The Bank of France, with its large reserves of bullion, and the growing abundance of French capital, made France, in the period between 1850 and 1870, the second financial and money market of the world. Other continental money markets were either too small, or were situated in countries politically too split up to play a part comparable to that of London or Paris. The monetary and banking system of the United States was not centralised, although New York was steadily becoming the financial centre of the country, and bank-notes were of secondary importance only; in that country stock exchange centralisation preceded currency unification. It was therefore in England and France that the classical doctrine of central banks of issue was gradually elaborated; interesting discussions on the same subject also took place in Holland and Belgium.

After 1871 a new and important money market arose, the Berlin market. The Reichsbank immediately entered the front rank of European central banks. Later central banks, occupying in their own countries a position very similar to that of the Banks of France and England, were established or developed in Austria, Italy, Switzerland, the Scandinavian countries and, with the return to the gold standard, in Russia. Their establishment and operation naturally gave rise to serious theoretical discussions in the legislatures and in print. Statesmen and the public in general paid greater and greater attention to the duties and functions of the banks within the national economy, and books on the subject became more and more numerous.

A new impetus was given to these discussions when the United States, after the 1907 crisis, proposed in its turn to establish a central bank (or rather twelve large central banks under unified control). The principle of unifying the great national money markets by the unification of the note issue became as it were an elementary truth in currency policy.

As might have been expected, the war, with the need for money that it implied, and the concentration of national resources which was one of its immediate results, accelerated the movement towards the establishment of central banks, considered less as credit institutions than as instruments of State finance. After 1918 new banks were created, and the functions and influence of the old banks were extended. There was indeed a widespread tendency to attribute to them greater powers of action than they actually possessed; and certain central banks were tempted into efforts to gain international predominance which aroused anxiety in those countries jealous of their financial independence. Since it is often difficult to grasp the real driving forces and the methods used, the public as a whole regard these activities as mysterious, although they are in fact simple enough; they have given rise to such a vast quantity of literature that on this subject as on no other the historian must confine himself to the few most important writers and the main currents of thought only.

As early as 1802 Henry Thornton noted the centralising role of the bank of issue regarded as a "national" bank. The superiority of his ideas to Ricardo's is striking. In his book Thornton brings forward and in part answers all those questions which even to-day daily confront a bank of issue. Like Tooke, his grasp of these problems gives evidence of a breadth of mind and a practical common sense that are of far greater worth than the strict and narrow logic which Ricardo brought to bear on their solution.

Once the Napoleonic wars were over, England, like France, had a central bank which henceforth fulfilled all the functions that devolve on such an institution. These functions arise less from a preconceived plan than from an organic development out of the note issue monopoly conferred on a bank situated at the chief business centre of a country. There were, it is true, profound differences in the methods of the Bank of England and the Bank of France, the former displaying a more marked tendency to intervene on the market, and greater initiative than the latter. The important parliamentary enquiries which were held whenever the charter of the Bank of England came up for renewal, and the great 1864 enquiry in France, provided opportunities for working out a theory to fit the practice which events had step by step imposed on the central banks. Thus there arose what might be called the classical theory of central banks, summarised in the formula: "The central bank of issue is the banks' bank."

From 1871 onwards, with the growing severity of financial and monetary crises (the 1866 crisis which inspired Bagehot's great book gave, as it were, a warning of the difficulties of a prolonged depression), and the rapid expansion of the large commercial banks in England and France (by means of which the unused cash balances of the public were made available on the market instead of remaining split up among numberless private banks), it became increasingly obvious that it was imperative to strengthen the metallic reserves of the great central banks. It was as much a question of checking too frequent variations in the discount rate as of ensuring the convertibility into international currency no longer of bank-notes only, but of all circulating credits in the country. From Bagehot to Hartley Withers we can trace an unceasing effort to inculcate in all minds the idea of a cental bank conscious of its responsibilities as the country's supreme gold reserve. This idea found its embodiment in the establishment of the Federal Reserve Banks of the United States; the name alone is a sufficient indication of their character. To Paul Warburg, practical banker and theorist, is due the credit for formulating with incomparable lucidity the principles governing a bank of this kind.

After the war a new current of ideas set in. During hostilities the banks of issue ceased to be credit institutions and became government contractors for paper money. Then came the world crisis, inevitable after the orgies of "necessity moneys," as Galiani would have called them, and certain persons, misunderstanding the real origins of the crisis, exaggerating the influence of credit on prices, and overestimating the possibilities of international agreement, urged that the central banks should assume the function of controlling the world price level. Curiously enough, this proposal was, as a rule, made by the same writers and experts who advocated the return to paper money as being more easily "manageable," and the abandonment of the only international currency so far known to the world, gold. This current of thought is in fact in harmony with the tendency towards economic nationalism, apparent in so many States to-day; for the central banks of issue, since their normal operations result in the concentration of the country's currency reserves, have potentially become powerful instruments of nationalism in monetary affairs.

In the following pages we shall examine this development of ideas concerning the role of banks of issue.

§ 1. *Thornton, First Theorist of the Central Bank*

Adam Smith described the working of the Bank of England as if it were an ordinary bank of issue. Nowhere does he allude to its role as a central bank acting as the fulcrum of the entire English money market. Henry Thornton's description of this mechanism is the first of its kind in English economic literature; it was followed later by the famous descriptions given by Bagehot and Withers.

The oblivion into which Thornton's book has fallen can only be explained by the popularity gained by Ricardo's ideas after the Napoleonic wars. The recently published American Encyclopedia of the Social Sciences does not even mention his name. Nevertheless his ideas dominated the *Bullion Report* and he was as a man not lacking in distinction. Member of Parliament from 1783 until his death in 1815, and member of the Governing Board of the Bank of England, he followed its policy from close quarters; business man and philanthropist (he assisted Wilberforce in the anti-slavery campaign), and the author of some devotional works, he was one of the small group of economists gathered about William Pitt who exerted so great an influence on the political life of England in the first quarter of the nineteenth century. He favoured a progressive income tax, and paid his own taxes not at the legal rate, but on a higher scale fixed by himself, and more in harmony with what he regarded as fiscal equity.

Thornton lived through two severe banking crises, which occurred in 1793 and 1797; the latter resulting in the suspension of payments in specie. In both cases the crisis was reflected not in a run on the provincial banks for gold, but in an intense demand by these banks for Bank of England notes. Far from credit restriction alleviating the crisis (the remedy prescribed by Adam Smith) it was only the issue of supplementary notes which brought the crisis of 1793 to an end.[1] Four years later, in 1797, the panic assumed such proportions that it was decided to introduce forced currency

[1] This crisis occurred immediately after the outbreak of war with France; it took the form of suspension of payments by a large number of banks, particularly in Newcastle. The Bank of England restricted its note issue, leaving the country's economy without any safeguard. With credit restricted, there was a certain amount of hoarding of Bank of England notes (cf. Thornton, pp. 48–49). After a meeting of City bankers, the Government decided to alleviate the shortage of currency instruments by issuing Exchequer bills to the value of five million sterling; merchants could obtain these bills against the security of their goods. They could be sold, or used for obtaining credit at the Bank. "The very expectation of a supply of exchequer bills, that is, of a supply of an article which almost any trader might obtain, and which it was known that he might then sell, and thus turn into bank-notes, and after turning into bank-notes might also convert into guineas, created an idea of general solvency. This expectation cured, in the first instance, the distress of London, and it then lessened the demand for guineas in the country, through that punctuality in effecting the London payments which it produced, and the universal confidence which it thus inspired" (Thornton, pp. 50–51). The panic did in fact subside before even half the authorised issue was taken up.

rather than cut down banking advances, which would have precipitated bankruptcies and brought about a breakdown of trade.

Here are two cases which belied Smith's well-known thesis, according to which a demand for note redemption is certain proof of excessive note issue. To calm the market and avoid a catastrophe, it was necessary to issue additional notes to take the place of the Bank of England notes that were being hoarded.

The contradiction between the facts and the theory arises from the character of the Bank of England. It was not an ordinary bank but a "public" or "national" bank, as Thornton frequently remarked;[1] he may indeed be regarded as the inventor of the term. Private banks depend on the national bank. When they are in difficulties they want its notes, and not gold, for the notes are equivalent to gold. This means that the national bank's duties are different from those of an ordinary bank. Here, for the first time, the classical problem which confronts central banks of issue during a crisis is enunciated in its broadest terms: to what extent shall they restrict credit in order to safeguard their cash position; to what extent shall they expand credit in order to save a financial centre threatened by panic?

The distinguishing characteristic of a "public" or "national" bank, the feature in which it differs from private issuing banks, consists in this, that as a rule, and by a natural process of development, it becomes the country's gold reservoir. Thornton was the first to draw attention to this outstanding feature of countries with central banks:

> "The establishment of a great public bank has a tendency to promote the institution of private banks. The public bank, obliged to provide itself largely with money for its own payments, becomes a reservoir of gold to which private banks may resort with little difficulty, expence, or delay, for the supply of their several necessities." [2]

The great service that Thornton rendered was to emphasise this special feature of the Bank of England and to shew how it affected the organisation of credit; Adam Smith, with his attention focussed on the Scottish banks, does not mention it; it is true that it was probably not so marked at the time he was writing.

[1] Cf. pp. 93, 146 and 174.

[2] *Ibid.*, p. 50.

Of its effects on credit organisation, two are particularly important:

1. The notes of the central bank take the place of gold. In case of need, or in times of panic, it is these notes which are sought after. They serve the same purpose for the big business men of London as coin does for small traders: if they are agitated, if they fear that they will be short of ready cash to meet their commitments, they hoard their notes, as smaller men hoard coin. This is what happened during the panics of 1793 and 1797. As soon as they were given the means of obtaining bank-notes, the panic subsided. Thus, by meeting note requirements, the demand for coin was arrested.

"It also deserves notice, that though the failures had originated in an extraordinary demand for guineas, it was not any supply of gold which effected the cure. That fear of not being able to obtain guineas, which arose in the country, led, in its consequences, to an extraordinary demand for bank-notes in London; and the want of bank-notes in London became, after a time, the chief evil." [1]

The same happenings occurred in 1797. Thornton notes moreover that the total note circulation in London never exceeds what is strictly necessary for trade, so great is the economy which time and experience have made possible in the means of payment. Thus any reduction in their quantity, far from improving matters, may create difficulties, aggravate the crisis and encourage rather than stop the hoarding of gold.

"A reduction of them [Bank of England notes] which may seem moderate to men who have not reflected on this subject—a diminution, for instance, of one-third or two-fifths, might, perhaps, be sufficient to produce a very general insolvency in London, of which the effect would be the suspension of confidence, the derangement of commerce, and the stagnation of manufactures throughout the country. Gold, in such case, would unquestionably be hoarded through the great consternation which would be excited; and it would, probably, not again appear until confidence should be restored by the *previous* introduction of some additional or some new paper circulation." [2]

2. A second result of the establishment of a "public" or "national" bank of issue is that private banks, instead of keeping their own gold reserve, rely on the gold reserve of the Bank of England and

[1] Cf. p. 50. [2] *Ibid.*, pp. 75–76.

henceforth only keep either bills on London or Bank of England notes. Private banks of issue acted then in the same way as commercial banks act now. They trust the central bank to ensure their immediate solvency. Adam Smith, Thornton points out, was mistaken in believing that private banks keep their own gold reserve. They do no more than make sure that they have in London the wherewithal on which to draw in case of need.

"The country banker, in case of an alarm, turns a part of the government securities, bills of exchange, or other property which he has in London, into Bank of England notes, and those notes into money, and thus discharges many of his own circulating notes, as well as enlarges the fund of gold in his coffers. The Bank of England has, therefore, to supply these occasional wants of the country banker; and, in order to be fully prepared to do this, it has, ordinarily, to keep a quantity of gold equal to that of the notes liable to be extinguished, as well as a quantity which shall satisfy the other extraordinary demands which may be made at the same season of consternation either by banking houses, or by individuals. Thus the country banker by no means bears his own burthen, while the Bank of England sustains a burthen which is not its own, and which we may naturally suppose that it does not very cheerfully endure."[1]

Thus London became the centre for payments for the whole country, and in London the means of payment was Bank of England notes. Furthermore, *London became the centre where all payments due to England were made.* Thornton paints that picture of London as the Clearing House of the entire world which so many writers were to describe during the course of the nineteenth century, and which still remains its characteristic feature:

"Bills are drawn on London from every quarter of the Kingdom, and remittances are sent to the metropolis to provide for them, while London draws no bills, or next to none, upon the country. London is, in this respect, to the whole island, in some degree, what the centre of a city is to the suburbs. The traders may dwell in the suburbs, and lodge many goods there, and they may carry on at home a variety of smaller payments, while their chief cash account is with the banker, who fixes his residence among the other bankers, in the heart of the city. London also is become, especially of late, the trading metropolis of Europe, and, indeed, of the whole world; the foreign drafts, on account of merchants living in our outports and other trading towns, and carrying on business there, being

[1] Cf. pp. 173–174.

made, with scarcely any exceptions, payable in London. The metropolis, moreover, through the extent of its own commerce, and the greatness of its wealth and population, has immense receipts and payments on its own account; and the circumstance of its being the seat of government, and the place where the public dividends are paid, serves to increase its pecuniary transactions. . . . On the punctuality with which the accustomed payments of London are effected, depends, therefore, most essentially the whole commercial credit of Great Britain. The larger London payments are effected exclusively through the paper of the Bank of England; for the superiority of its credit is such, that, by common agreement among the bankers, whose practice, in this respect, almost invariably guides that of other persons, no note of a private house will pass in payment as a paper circulation in London."[1]

It should be noted in passing that even at that date Bank of England notes were no longer the only means used in London for settling English or continental debts and claims. At that time the bankers had organised the Clearing House among themselves (probably following the example set by the Dutch bankers); it developed very rapidly and the description of it given by Jevons sixty years later has become classical; clearing houses on the English model were founded throughout Europe and America. The relevant passage in Thornton is as follows:

"The following custom, now prevailing among the bankers within the city of London, may serve to illustrate this observation, and also to shew the strength of the disposition which exists in those who are not the issuers of bank-notes to spare the use both of paper and guineas. It is the practice of each of these bankers to send a clerk, at an agreed hour in the afternoon, to a room provided for their use. Each clerk there exchanges the drafts on other bankers received at his own house, for the drafts on his own house received at the houses of other bankers. The balances of the several bankers are transferred in the same room from one to another, in a manner which it is unnecessary to explain in detail, and the several balances are finally wound up by each clerk into one balance. The difference between the whole sum which each banker has to pay to all other city bankers, and the whole sum which he has to receive of all other city bankers, is, therefore, all that is discharged in bank notes or money; a difference much less in its amount than the *several* differences would be equal to. This device, which serves to spare the use of bank-notes, may suggest the practicability of a great variety of

[1] Cf. pp. 59–60.

contrivances for sparing the use of gold, to which men having confidence in each other would naturally resort, if we could suppose bank paper to be abolished." [1]

The originality of Thornton's book, as against the account of the English banking system to be found in Adam Smith, consists in his description of the specific part played by the central bank of issue. Its power, combined with the concentration of the country's commercial business in London, brought about the unification of the English money market, and its notes provided a general means of payment and enabled the country banks to dispense with a gold reserve of their own. But if this system was to work, both the private banks and the bank of issue had to carry out certain obligations. Thornton realises this very clearly; and there is no essential difference between his definition of these obligations and that which was to be given early in the twentieth century.

Private banks must keep in London assets easily convertible into bank-notes. Deposit banks to-day regard this liquidity as essential. Here again we see the similarity between our present-day commercial banks and the private banks of issue of earlier times, and note the identity of the function fulfilled by bank-notes and by current credit accounts.

The duties of the central bank are equally imperative. Its first and chief duty is to maintain exchangeability between paper and gold, and to accumulate reserves large enough to meet any sudden domestic and/or foreign demand for gold.

"In order to secure that this interchange [of notes for gold] shall at all times take place, it is important that, generally speaking, a considerable fund of gold should be kept in the country, and there is in this kingdom no other depository for it but the Bank of England. This fund should be a provision not only against the common and more trifling fluctuations in the demand for coin, but also against the two following contingencies. First, it should serve to counteract the effects of an unfavourable balance of trade, for this infallibility will sometimes occur, and it is what one or more bad harvest cannot fail to cause. It is also desirable, secondly, that the reserve of gold should be sufficient to meet any extraordinary demand at home, though a demand in this quarter, if it should arise from great and sudden fright, may undoubtedly be so unreasonable and indefinite as to defy all calculation. If, moreover, alarm should ever happen at a

[1] Cf. p. 55, footnote.

period in which the stock of gold should have been reduced by the other great cause of its reduction, namely, that of a call having been recently made for gold to discharge an unfavourable balance of trade, the powers of any bank, however ample its general provision should have been, may easily be supposed to prove insufficient for this double purpose. . . .

"For this reason, it may be the true policy and duty of the bank to permit, for a time, and to a certain extent, the continuance of that unfavourable exchange, which causes gold to leave the country, and to be drawn out of its own coffers: and it must, in that case, necessarily increase its loans to the same extent to which its gold is diminished. The bank, however, ought generally to be provided with a fund of gold so ample, as to enable it to pursue this line of conduct, with safety to itself, through the period of an unfavourable balance; a period, the duration of which may, to a certain degree, be estimated, though disappointment in a second harvest may cause much error in the calculation."[1]

Just as he emphasises the duty of the national bank to free the country banks from the necessity of keeping reserves, so Thornton regards it as the duty of a central bank to re-establish equilibrium in the balance of payments without the internal market being disturbed. Far from advocating economy in the use of gold, as Ricardo was to do later, he was in favour of a "very considerable" quantity of gold being in circulation or at the bank. "The possession, in ordinary times, of a very considerable quantity of gold, either in the bank or in general circulation, or both, seems necessary for our complete security in this respect."[2] He is thus the first in a long line of economists who, from Tooke to Withers and Palgrave in England, or Warburg in the United States, were to insist on the necessity for strong gold reserves. He goes even further, and asserts that this reserve can only be guaranteed by a *single* central bank; the arguments which Thornton uses are the same as Warburg was to use when he urged the establishment of a central reserve bank.

"It may be apprehended, also, that, if instead of one national bank two or more should be instituted, each having a small capital; each would then exercise a separate judgement; each would trust in some measure to the chance of getting a supply of guineas from the other, and each would allow itself to pursue its own particular interest, instead of taking upon

[1] Cf. pp. 71 and 133. [2] *Ibid.*, p. 189.

itself the superintendance of general credit, and seeking its own safety through the medium of the safety of the public; unless, indeed, we should suppose such a good understanding to subsist between them as to make them act as if they were one body, and resemble, in many respects, one single institution.

"The accident of a failure in the means of making the cash payments of a country, though it is one against which there can be no security which is complete, seems, therefore, to be best provided against by the establishment of one principal bank." [1]

Thornton, of course, does not mean that the country banks of issue should disappear; on the contrary! What he means is that *at London*, the national centre for the country's payments, there should be one single bank of issue, whose functions and duties cannot be compared with those of private banks; this bank, he adds, should not be judged on the same standards, nor, if it is unable to carry out its engagements, criticised in the way in which one would be justified in criticising private banks.

He believed that the bank should keep a strong cash reserve, and (what is no less remarkable, for it was the policy that Tooke was to advocate later) he was in favour of using the discount rate to regulate the volume of credit. He does not, of course, dispute the effect of credit restriction on domestic prices, or deny that it may help to re-establish equilibrium in the balance of trade. On the contrary, he fears that credit restriction may go too far in this direction and prove so drastic a remedy that it aggravates the ailment. As against the over-mechanical theories of Smith, he draws on his practical experience as a banker. His book may be taken as the first reaction of practical bankers against the too doctrinaire or even wholly erroneous conceptions of the theorists.[2] In this respect the difference between Thornton and Adam Smith was later paralleled between Tooke and the Ricardians in regard to the Act of 1844.

There is a middle road between the policy advocated by Smith

[1] Cf. p. 94.

[2] "One object of the present and succeeding chapter will be to shew that, however just may be the principle of Dr. Smith when properly limited and explained, the reduction of the quantity of Bank of England paper is by no means a measure which ought to be resorted to on the occasion of every demand upon the Bank for guineas arising from the high price of bullion, and that such reduction may even aggravate that sort of rise which is caused by an alarm in the country." *Loc. cit.*, pp. 58–59.

and an unlimited provision of credit—*that of raising the discount rate.*

At the time that Thornton was writing, the usury laws prohibited a higher rate than 5 per cent for commercial loans. These laws applied as much to the Bank of England as to any other institution; it was therefore compelled, when its rate stood at the maximum, to cut down the volume of discounting. This is a method still used to-day by certain banks of issue, but it has great drawbacks. It substitutes the arbitrary choice of the bank for the spontaneous distribution of credits that results when credit is made dearer, and induces banks to demand more than they actually require in fear that they may not get enough for their needs.

Thornton is opposed to this method and urges that the raising of the discount rate alone should be used to ration credit:

"The bank is prohibited, by the state of the law, from demanding even in time of war, an interest of more than 5 per cent, which is the same rate at which it discounts in a period of profound peace. It might, undoubtedly, at all seasons, sufficiently limit its paper by means of the price at which it lends, if the legislature did not interpose an obstacle to the constant adoption of this principle of restriction. . . . At some seasons an interest, perhaps, of 6 per cent per annum, at others of 5 or even 4 per cent may afford that degree of advantage to borrowers which shall be about sufficient to limit, in the due measure, the demand upon the bank for discounts. . . . The interest of the two parties is not the same in this respect. The borrowers, in consequence of that artificial state of things which is produced by the law against usury, obtain their loans too cheap. That which they obtain too cheap they demand in too great quantity. To trust to their moderation and forbearance under such circumstances, is to commit the safety of the bank to the discretion of those who . . . have in this respect an individual interest which is at variance with that of the Bank of England." [1]

Thornton's views as to the role of a central bank may be summarised as follows: it should maintain exchangeability between notes and gold; it should be the central gold reserve both for the internal demand for gold and for payments abroad; to provide against emergencies from either quarter it should build up a strong reserve; in times of crisis it should not suspend credit but merely sell it more dearly by raising its discount rate; it should have a

[1] *Loc. cit.*, pp. 287–289.

monopoly of the right to issue notes, at least in the capital where, in the nature of things, an overwhelming proportion of the country's payments is made. In these conditions its notes become the usual means of payment and provide the element of elasticity in the currency. The knowledge that they can obtain these notes allows local banks to keep as their reserve assets for which they can easily obtain the notes of the central bank, and compels them to keep the credits they grant (and for which notes are used) within the limits which make it possible for them to maintain solvency by an appeal to the central bank.

Here are all the ideas that Tooke was to develop in his controversy with the Currency School. Here are all the ideas which were to be regarded as the essential of what might be termed the classical theory of banks of issue as it developed in the course of the nineteenth century. They mark a notable advance over the ideas of Adam Smith and bear—particularly in comparison with those of Ricardo, for whom bank-notes were a money similar to metallic currency, differing only in that they cost less to produce—the stamp of realism which is entirely lacking in the theories of the arch doctrinaire.

One last observation, which is of interest mainly in relation to the widespread discussions which have taken place in the last twenty years concerning the method known as open market policy. We have seen that this method is by no means new. Cantillon describes it in detail and Ricardo advocates its use. Thornton, too, defends its use, but with a certain hesitation.

At the time that he was writing, the securities held by the Bank of England consisted more of Treasury bills than of commercial paper. This proportion was reversed during the Napoleonic wars, but on their conclusion the old position was re-established. The Treasury was the Bank of England's biggest client, while the Bank refrained from "direct" discounting. Thornton notes the "preference given by the Bank to the Government securities."[1] He rejects the idea that this may be due to the Bank's dependence on the government and tries to shew that, by discounting Treasury bills, the Bank is merely allowing the other banks to concentrate on commercial discounting, and that, in the absence of the Bank of England, the government's bills would be taken up by the market.

[1] *Loc. cit.*, p. 62.

We shall soon see what reply Gilbart made to this argument. Here we would note the utter difference between the French and the English attitude towards the note issue. Mollien believed that it was the requirements of commercial discounting which determined the volume of notes issued; in England an entirely different principle was invoked, with which we shall presently deal.

Mollien was working out his plans for reorganising the Bank of France at the same time that Thornton was writing his book. As we have seen, he took his ideas about bank-notes straight from Adam Smith, but there is no doubt whatever that he wanted the Bank of France to become the central bank for that country in the same sense that the Bank of England was for Britain; the position of the Bank of England as a central bank had become even more obvious since the establishment of forced currency.

In the first place, he urged that in Paris the Bank of France alone should have the right to issue notes. It was at his instigation that in 1802 Napoleon agreed to the fusion of the three banks of issue then operating in the capital.[1] On the other hand, he was opposed to a "general" bank, that is to say to a single bank for the whole of France on the lines of Law's disastrous institution. He took British banking organisation as his ideal: one bank having a monopoly in the capital, and provincial banks connected to it by reciprocal credits. Article 8 of the proposal contained in his second memorandum on banks is extremely significant: "The Bank of Paris (which under article 5 was to be given a monopoly of the note issue for the Paris district) may open credits with the chief banks of other towns and maintain with them such relations as promote their mutual interests." In a footnote Mollien adds:

> "The object of this arrangement is to confer on the Bank of Paris all the advantages of a general bank without exposing it to any of the disadvantages that a general bank as such may suffer or cause."

He elaborates the idea in another passage: what had been done in London should be done in Paris, neither more nor less:

> "I regard banks as a great instrument of prosperity, and in the present state of Europe I think that France should become the home of banks, and Paris the home of the greatest bank in the world, because it is the point at which the roads from the capitals of all countries meet and cross.

[1] Mollien, *Mémoires*, Vol. I, p. 339.

But can a real bank exist in Paris? Nothing of this kind need be created, or even improved upon. . . .[1]

"If we recall what London was like in 1694 [i.e. in the year the Bank of England was founded] we have an answer to this question; and the example of what the Bank of London did to strengthen the position of the new government that had been established [he is here drawing a parallel, which the First Consul did not overlook, between Napoleon's position and that of the English government in 1688] and to develop the industrial resources of the country shews, by a hundred and eight years of success, what may be expected from the establishment of a bank in London and in other English towns; advantages which Paris and the cities of France can in their turn appropriate to themselves, and with still greater success.

"The Bank of London is a tried and tested machine, like the spinning mills of Manchester; we have but to copy it, as the mills have been copied, and study with as much care its no doubt more complex mechanism." [2]

Mollien, a great admirer of England, proposed that the Emperor should set himself the task of making Paris the banking centre of the continent.

§ II. *Triumph of Note-Issue Monopoly and Formation of the Classic Doctrine of the Functions of a Bank of Issue Between* 1825 *and* 1870

At the end of the Napoleonic wars the resumption of cash payments in England and the convertibility of notes in France re-established a more normal functioning of the currency systems.

In England there was no banking monopoly except within the area allowed by law to the Bank of England; in France country banks of issue were gradually established, but without much success. In both countries events tended to emphasise the function of the two chartered banks to act as the country's central gold reserve. In England this represented the maintenance of an old tradition, which Thornton had described. In France it was a new but characteristic phenomenon. Bank of France notes became the means chiefly used by the big merchants of Paris in their transactions, while bills on Paris, as we have seen, served this purpose for the rest of the country.

[1] Quoted by Ramon, p. 44.

[2] *Mémoires*, Vol. I, p. 459.

In Paris the Bank's notes came to be used more and more instead of coin, and its branches became the reservoirs of coin to which, in case of need, both individuals and other banks of issue could turn for the hard cash they required.

It is not surprising that in these circumstances the banks of issue in both countries should try to obtain a monopoly of the note issue. In London as in Paris a new bank would be bound to prejudice the concentration of reserves. The two banks would either be rivals, which would hamper the operations of both, or they would tacitly co-operate, which would amount in fact to a monopoly. As to the country banks, it was quite natural, as Thornton and Mollien perceived, and as was shewn in the debates of 1840 and 1848 from which we have quoted in Chapter Five, that they should be content to rely on the central bank to keep their position liquid. It is a curious fact that the arguments used in the theoretical discussions for and against a monopoly of the note issue rarely take these realities into account, although they are in fact decisive. The controversies still go on with the aid of general principles, when the facts have already imposed the unitary solution on both countries. But the majority of those who take part in them fail to understand the structure and development of the money market. In France the dispute went on long after the legal decision was taken in 1848, and when the issuing monopoly was so deeply rooted in the currency structure of the country that there was no risk of any attempt to break it. The Péreires raised the question again when they took over the Bank of Savoy. To overcome the difficulties placed in their path by the Bank of France, they conceived the idea of competing against it. This was the origin of the *Enquiry into the Fiduciary Currency* which was held between 1864 and 1868, and contains much valuable material on the history of French thought on banking. The most interesting evidence was put in by business men rather than by economists. It shews how small was the number of men who realised that monopoly had become essential, for the public as a whole and the professional economists did not share this opinion.

In England the question was settled by the Peel Act of 1844. The evidence submitted by experts to the commissions appointed in 1832 and 1840, following the crises which shook the country, gives a comprehensive survey of the ideas of the time relating to central banks of issue and to the question of monopoly or plurality. As Professor Gregory has so well said: "The men of the period did not, as we are inclined to do, take a Central Bank for granted; whilst the paradoxical aspect of the situation lay in the fact that, in spite of indecision on the main point of principle, a Central Bank in the true sense did actually exist."[1] It is however true to say that from 1832 onwards it was the ideas of Thornton which inspired the action of the Governors of the Bank of England and the legislative measures which they advocated. In his evidence before the 1832 Commission Palmer, one of the Governors of the Bank, argues strongly that the Bank should protect its reserves in order to be able to undertake discounting on a large scale in times of crisis. He adds that to give the required support to the market it should be able to raise its discount rate above the legal maximum of 5 per cent still enforced for commercial loans. Unless it has that power, he says, it will have to ration credit. It will be in a better position to support the market in times of crisis if on the one hand it has a monopoly of the note issue and its administration is independent of the government, and, on the other, if it does not undertake commercial discounting in normal times. Palmer's evidence recapitulates Thornton's arguments. His ideas were those which the Bank applied in 1825, when it allowed its cash reserve to fall to a minimum while it continued to grant credit in order to support the market.

An extract from Palmer's evidence will illustrate the difference in the English and the French attitude towards a note issue. "My intention was to impress upon the Committee an opinion, that in ordinary times the leading functions of the Bank of England have been to furnish, upon a stated principle, an adequate supply of paper money convertible into coin and bullion upon demand, and to act as a bank for safe deposit of public and private money, and in so acting, that it is not deemed to be desirable to attempt to regulate the amount of issues of the Bank in London through commercial discounts."[2] Herein lies the fundamental difference between the English and the French conception of bank-notes. It is well to bear it in mind to-day.

[1] Cf. Gregory, *Select Statutes, Documents and Reports, relating to British Banking, 1832–1928*, 2 Vols., London, 1929. Introduction, p. xiv.

[2] *Ibid.*, p. 14, Sitting of June 5, 1832.

Two important steps, both inspired by Thornton's ideas, were taken as a result of the 1832 Commission of Enquiry. The first was that the Bank was given power to raise its discount rate above 5 per cent for bills of less than 90 days, that is to say for the very kind of bills which it was asked to rediscount in times of crisis. From then on the power to manipulate their discount rate at their own discretion became a standard feature of all banks of issue.

The second step was to give *legal* currency to Bank of England notes, that is to say to make them as much a legal means of discharging indebtedness as metallic currency itself. This step (which was also copied by almost all issuing banks) was taken with a wholly practical object in view, that of safeguarding the Bank from an internal drain of gold during times of crisis or panic; it made any demand for gold on the part of local banks unnecessary by providing them with the means of legally satisfying the demands either of their depositors, or of the bearers of their notes, without having to obtain gold. From one point of view the consequences of this step were unfortunate, for it created doubts as to the nature of the notes. It strengthened the idea that bank-notes are money in the same sense that coin is money. But bank-notes, whether legal tender or not, derive their value wholly from their convertibility. The holders of the notes always retain the right of converting them into gold if they wish to; notes remain merely circulating credits, and do not lose this character when they are made legal tender. When, in order to protect the cash reserves of the Bank from sudden demands for gold, they were made legal tender, the confusion between notes and money, which was later to take, as it were, concrete form in the 1844 Act, was strengthened. A further step in the same direction was taken, and further confusion created in 1925, when the law which re-established in England the convertibility of notes into gold laid it down that notes could only be exchanged for bullion and not for coin. The idea that the Bank's reserves should be kept for payments abroad—an idea that Thornton had already put forward—was embodied in these two measures, separated by nearly a hundred years.

The Currency School was not satisfied with Bank of England notes being made legal tender, nor probably was the Bank itself; they wanted a monopoly of the note issue. This demand was met by the 1844 Act, which laid it down that private banks of issue were not to increase the number of their notes beyond the point then reached. The arguments adduced at that time by Lord Overstone, the chief protagonist of the Currency Principle, shew that he had failed to understand the course of development taken by the banking system, and the role of central bank filled by the Bank of England. He criticised the private banks for not varying their note issue in accordance with gold movements, which, he said, is the duty of all issuing banks. The private bankers admitted that in fact they had not followed this rule, for the very good reason that they could safeguard their position by holding the credits necessary to obtain Bank of England notes. The position of the deposit banks to-day is exactly the same; they too, like the private banks of earlier times, may create difficulties for the central bank by a too sudden demand for rediscounting facilities, but they consider themselves entitled to rely upon getting them. Lord Overstone's arguments were invalid because they were based on the false assumption that banks of issue create money,[1] but his conclusion (which events themselves tended to bring about without the intervention of the law) was correct. Tooke came to the same conclusion by a wholly different process of argumentation.

It is extremely instructive, having read Loyd's evidence, to turn to Gilbart, the founder of the first large deposit bank and author of a famous treatise on banking. The only bank of issue which does not regulate the volume of its notes according to market needs, says Gilbart in reply to Lord Overstone, is the Bank of England. In fact, in normal times, the Bank of England refrains from discounting commercial paper and purchases government securities. It therefore puts on to the market a greater quantity of notes than is required for the purposes of trade. It is therefore not astonishing if, having forced up the note circulation and kept the discount rate artificially low, it is compelled to push that rate up to excessive heights in order to retain its gold. His statement is extremely interesting, for it shews that the Bank was still pursuing the policy of open market operations described by Cantillon and recommended by Ricardo

[1] Cf. on this point the evidence of Samuel Jones Loyd (Lord Overstone) before the 1840 Commission, reprinted on pp. 27–62 of Gregory's *Select Statutes, Documents and Reports*, 1929: "Issuing paper I always consider as the creation of money, and that is a duty or privilege which I think can be better exercised for the benefit of the Community by one body, acting under the control of the Legislature or Government, than by trusting it to the principle of competition" (p. 49).

and which, after the World War, it urged so strongly on the Bank of France, as if it were a wholly new device.

"The country circulation can be issued only in consequence of transactions which have taken place, and to the extent only required by the wants of the district; whereas it is obvious that the Bank of England has the power of increasing the circulation by the purchase of Exchequer bills or stock, or by purchasing bullion,[1] and throwing a mass of notes on the market when the state of trade does not require them." [2]

In fact, throughout this period, the Bank's policy was to maintain the note circulation at as constant a level as possible by buying Treasury bills when the volume of discounting declined and reselling them when the market brought in a larger volume of discounting.[3] One of the members of the Commission remarked to Gilbart that by buying government securities the Bank set free the capital of those who held the securities and that consequently "it comes to the same thing, whether the persons applying for discount obtain their discount through those parties whose capital is thus liberated, or whether they make direct application to the Bank of England, and obtain discount," to which Gilbart rightly replied: "But you are not warranted in assuming that those notes do go into channels of commerce afterwards; the probability is, that they remain upon the Stock Exchange, and make interest low, and excite speculation."[4] Gilbart's words were prophetic. When we remember the open market policy pursued by the American Federal Reserve Banks between 1926 and 1929, and its effects in facilitating stock exchange speculation in New York, it is impossible not to admire the accuracy of his judgment. No doubt the Governors of the Bank of England could justify their policy of buying Treasury bills on the ground that thereby they did not enter into competition with the private banks on the discount market; but there was perhaps another reason, the same reason which explains the purchase of securities

[1] It appears from this passage that Gilbart was also opposed to the purchase of gold by the Bank with the object of expanding the currency, at a time when there was no commercial demand for such an expansion. Gilbart wanted the note issue to be backed entirely by bills of exchange. He forgets that, in order to maintain the interchangeability of notes and gold and to retain contact with the international standard, the Bank must buy gold at a fixed price, or the foreign exchanges will fall.

[2] Gilbart's evidence in Gregory, *loc. cit.*, Vol. I, p. 83.

[3] Some extremely interesting data on this question are given in Professor Gregory's introduction to the *Select Statutes*, pp. xviii and xix.

[4] *Ibid.*, pp. 93 *et seq.*

on the market by the Federal Reserve Banks—that is, the Bank's desire to make profits. That policy is noteworthy in two other respects. In the first place it shews the Bank's confidence in the solvency of the State, in its punctual fulfilment of its obligations. In one of the two memoranda which we have already quoted from so often, Mollien pointed out to Napoleon the unfailing readiness of the Bank of England to act as banker to the State; this, he remarks, is due to the promptitude with which the State for its part carried out all its obligations as debtor to the Bank. Still later, when the 1864 Commission was holding its enquiry, this difference in the financial standing of the State in France and in England was noted by more than one witness, in particular by Baron Alphonse de Rothschild; the unwillingness of the Governing Board of the Bank of France to meet the State's requests for credit has been an unchanging feature of its history from the day of its establishment; such a state of affairs was unknown in England.

In the second place, the open market policy has a tendency to insulate the national money market by enabling the Bank to exert a direct influence on the market, either by increasing or by diminishing the funds available, apart from any inflow of gold from abroad and from any demand for credit. In the absence of such a policy, the issue of notes (or the creation of current accounts) depends on two factors only: the inflow of gold from abroad, and the extent of the internal demand for credit on the market. In respect to both these factors the Bank remains passive. It issues notes to the amount required. On the other hand an open market policy enables it, should the occasion arise, to increase or to diminish the currency media at the disposal of the market, in order either to offset the tendency towards restriction or expansion that normally follows from gold movements, or to avoid a rise in the discount rate if the market is short of cash, or on the other hand to force the market to raise its rate if the funds available are too abundant. This is what Warburg had in mind when, later, he said that in its open market policy the Bank plays the part not only of anvil but also of hammer. But it is obvious that a bank of issue, when it buys securities on the market in order to offset by the credits that it thus creates the monetary restriction that an outflow of gold normally produces, tends, at least for a time, to detach the national market from the international money market.

Peel's Act, by giving the Bank of England a practical monopoly of the note issue, apparently confirmed its position as the central bank. It recognised its character as the central money reservoir, as the mainstay of the private banks in times of crisis, as the supreme arbiter of credit. On the other hand, and without fully understanding its import, it tended to weaken the Bank's capacity for action as a central bank, by prompting the Banking Department to overlook the necessity for accumulating strong reserves. Lord Overstone, obsessed by the idea of "economising money" (as Ricardo was in his 1823 Plan), is of the opinion that the Issue Department does not need strong gold reserves, while the Banking Department is, in respect to this problem, in the same position as any other commercial bank.

In short, the establishment of a note monopoly in England weakened rather than strengthened the conception of the central bank as it had been formulated by Thornton and later by Tooke, for both of whom one of the essential features of such a bank was the creation of strong gold reserves. We shall return to this point later on.

In France, during the same period, the idea of a central bank gradually took root among the most farsighted men of the time. Underlying the discussions as to the advantages and disadvantages of a note-issuing monopoly, the idea of the importance to the national economy of a single bank concentrating the country's reserves of metal and supplying the other banks, in times of crisis or panic, with the credits they required, gradually took on a clearer outline and won an increasing number of adherents. The principle of monopoly itself had gained the field on the day when Napoleon wrote his famous letter to Mollien, asking him to amalgamate into one, the three banks of issue then operating in Paris. "I take up this standpoint: it is easier for the government and the public to supervise one bank than many; whatever the economists may say about it, competition cannot serve any useful purpose in this case."[1]

In an earlier chapter we have described how a unified note issue gradually became a necessity as the money market itself was unified. No practical man of affairs believed that it was possible to revoke the monopoly enjoyed by the Bank in law and in fact. While Michel Chevalier and Courcelle-Seneuil went on endlessly

[1] Mollien, Vol. I, p. 339.

discussing the general benefits of competition,[1] a small group of men, including Adolphe Thiers, Vuitry, President of the Council of State and author of some excellent works on French financial history, bankers like d'Eichthal, economists like Wolowski and Léon Faucher, extracted from events themselves arguments proving that the Bank of France really fulfilled the functions of a central bank (this is the name used by Léon Faucher), that is to say of a banks' bank, and that the existence of such an institution had become vitally necessary to the economic life of the country.

Their ideas are already familiar to us: the bank of issue is the credit reserve on which the private banks can draw in times of crisis; the concentration at one point of the country's metal reserves makes it possible to use them, in the best and quickest way, at whatever point they may be required; the chief method of protecting this central reserve is the manipulation of the discount rate. In short, the bank of issue represents the country's monetary reserve for internal and external payments.

Adolphe Thiers was the first to bring these arguments forward, and he did so with exceptional vigour in 1840, in a speech which has become famous, and again in 1864 in his evidence before the Commission of Enquiry into the Banks. Few statesmen have had as clear a grasp of the character and operation of the Bank of France.

[1] In his evidence Chevalier remarked: "We should remember that the principle of freedom for banks of issue is implicit in the fundamental principle of modern legislation, which is that industry is free." This was the kind of generalisation that appealed to the great rhetorician. He forgets that even Adam Smith was in favour of limiting the freedom of banks. Courcelle-Seneuil and his followers also appealed to general principles of freedom in their advocacy of competition among banks of issue, though in his book he does make an attempt, from which Chevalier carefully abstained, to give a theoretical justification of his position. Courcelle-Seneuil's argument rests solely on the idea that banks of issue can in no case issue more notes than are required for circulation. Consequently they must be acquitted of the charge made against them, that they help to provoke crises (cf. p. 229 of his *Traité des Banques*, 1889 edition). But although he believed that in this he was upholding the position of the Banking School, he does in fact, as regards banks of issue, take up the standpoint of the Currency School and of Adam Smith, that bank-notes replace coin, and that they can never exceed in quantity the coin which *would have been* in circulation if no notes existed. He had not caught up with Thornton, who had so clearly exposed Adam Smith's mistake; or with Mollien, who knew that notes took the place of discounted commercial paper and were therefore an *addition* to the existing metallic currency. Of course, it never occurred to Courcelle-Seneuil that notes are merely a means of putting hard cash into circulation without its being used in the physical sense.

Since writing his book on John Law, he had never lost interest in currency problems, and he had gained undisputed mastery in handling them. In 1840 he describes in the following words how, in times of crisis, the national bank comes to the rescue of the market:

"Let me say that I think the Bank behaved admirably when, during the crisis, it doubled its discounts. The Bank is accused of keeping reserves equal to the note circulation, but I make bold to say that if it had not performed this service in the time of crisis it would have acted unwisely. . . . A bank should be cautious when everybody is offering money, but in times of crisis it should have the courage to supply trade with money. I say that an institution which obeys this precept of being close-fisted during prosperity, and generous during crises, is fulfilling its true function. That was when the Bank demonstrated its great usefulness to the government. There was one thing in which people had not lost confidence when they distrusted everything else, and they proved this by bringing their money to the Bank. This Bank, which seemed to have been instituted for private credit, has become an instrument of public credit and has saved the country." [1]

If it was to fill this position the Bank had to be free of too rigid control. Its note issue had to be given the necessary elasticity. In his evidence before the 1866 Enquiry into the Fiduciary Note Circulation, Thiers makes a comparison between the Bank of France and the Bank of England, as governed under the Peel Act:

"Mr. Peel is a great political and historic figure, for whom I have the greatest respect; but it must be admitted that the Act which he sponsored has met with general disapproval. It was a mistake on his part to fix an absolute limit to the note circulation, and to tie the Bank down to an unvarying proportion between notes in circulation and the reserve of bullion. It is good to keep a certain proportion always in mind, in order to depart from it as little as possible; but to make that proportion compulsory is so excessively cautious as to be imprudent; it has been necessary to suspend this provision three or four times. In France, and practically everywhere, it has been decided that bullion reserves should be kept at one third the note issue. I think that is not a bad figure to have chosen, and it should always be borne in mind, but it is unwise to impose it as absolutely binding. It is bad enough when we get near the figure which denotes exhaustion of the bullion reserve; it is bad enough to have this terrifying vision ahead, without adding the terror of a fixed and absolute

[1] Quoted by Ramon, *La Banque de France*, pp. 190–191.

limit. When the figure falls below one third, this is and should be a matter of anxiety, but it is not predestined that it will be followed by insolvency. With courage, coolness, and timely action, that may still be averted. Money may flow in again, as it usually does. But to fix a precise and compulsory limit is to create insolvency beforehand, and to declare oneself bankrupt before one has actually reached bankruptcy. Whenever there has been a crisis the Peel Act has filled everybody in London with fear; they have clamoured for its suspension, and immediately it is suspended people calm down and gradually the panic subsides. Mr. Peel's very strict Act was the consequence of the mistakes made previously by the banks. There was an outcry against them, and everybody welcomed the severity displayed by Mr. Peel. . . . But you cannot resist evil by evil, and I think that in the end the 1844 Act will be abrogated. As far as their management is concerned, I think the Bank of France is the superior; and it is also superior in organisation, for it regards the proportion that it is desirable to maintain between note issue and cash reserve as a principle of prudence and not a compulsory rule." [1]

This statement was made at a time when deposit banks in France, unlike those in England, were still in their infancy. The concept of the banks' bank which Burdeau was to emphasise in his famous Report of 1892,[2] and Pallain in his reply to the 1910 Commission of Enquiry into the National Currency in the United States, was well understood long before the great commercial banks had covered France with their branches.[3] In 1870 these banks refused the offer of a moratorium, for the rediscounting undertaken by the

[1] Thier's evidence before the 1866 Enquiry; *Report*, Vol. III, pp. 436–437.

[2] Burdeau's report is dated June, 1892. It is very concise, and it is a pity that he did not at times elaborate his basic ideas somewhat more fully. Theoretically it does not differ from evidence submitted to the 1864–1868 enquiry. Below we give the statement of M. de Saint-Paul, more detailed than the brief phrase in which Burdeau remarks that "in times of difficulty private credit institutions have to rely on the Bank to take over a large part of their commercial bills" (p. 38).

[3] At the 1864 enquiry M. de Saint-Paul was practically the only witness to refer to the deposit banks and to the function of the Bank of France in relation to them. "I call your attention to the nature of the repayments which may be demanded. The deposit banks are as follows: The Société Générale de Credit Industriel, the Société de Depôts et Comptes Courants, the Société Générale pour le Développement du Commerce, and five other deposit banks. If the Bank cannot rediscount their bills, these banks would have to close their doors the day a panic started. They have to accept first-class bills, bills which the Bank will never refuse if it is accepting any paper at all; but if there is a crisis, a panic, and the Bank can no longer give cash, it will no longer rediscount even such bills. Then all deposit banks will be endangered." Vol. I, p. 432.

Bank of France made it unnecessary. On the outbreak of the war in 1914, the Bank of France, forgetting this principle, faintheartedly preferred a moratorium for the deposit banks, with all its disastrous consequences, to rediscounting on a large scale, although that would immediately have put an end to withdrawals by depositors. But the theory about the role of the central bank in times of crisis had been firmly established long before that date.

A further point was made by Vuitry at the 1864 Enquiry; he pointed out that, with the country's metal reserves concentrated, it was possible to send coin to the places where it was at any time most urgently required. The Bank is not merely the supreme reserve of credit; it is also a guarantee that coin or bullion will always be available if required. This essential fact, which was to be used by Warburg in the United States after the 1907 crisis to justify his proposal for the establishment of a central bank, was emphasised by Vuitry (as it had been by d'Eichthal in 1848[1]) in the following words:

"During the session on November 21, 1868, something very curious happened, which attracted little attention from the economists: I refer to the movements of the currency, the currents running in different directions which it follows. The Bank of France has branches all over the country. Some of these branches accumulate currency steadily; from others there is as constant an outflow, and the Bank frequently has to send money to the latter. The cause of such a movement is difficult to find, but the fact is indisputable; there are a certain number of branches in which a balance is achieved after fluctuations in their cash reserves; others, and they are always the same, have to have money sent to them at great cost in order to cover their transactions; in a third category of the Bank's branches the cash reserves accumulate to such an extent that sometimes cash has to be sent to Paris, to the Bank, which then distributes it throughout the country. These movements of the currency arising out of the commercial practices peculiar to different districts, I think it follows that it is inadvisable to have separate privileged institutions for each district, for those whose cash is constantly being drawn out would encounter grave difficulties because of the considerable costs with which they would be burdened, while in the areas where the reserves accumulated

[1] "What are the results of a single currency bank? Far from concentrating resources it divides them equally, distributes capital equally; it takes them from where they are not serving a useful purpose commensurate with the costs and risks, and brings them where they are lacking, where they can be useful" (G. d'Eichthal's speech of February 22, 1848).

the banks, not knowing what to do with them, would choke of surfeit. That is what happened before 1848. The inconveniences of the system have been amply demonstrated by experience."

The reserves which are concentrated at the Bank are drawn not merely from holdings within the country; gold, of which the Bank is the principal buyer, is also brought in from abroad. Thiers summarised the position in a felicitous phrase: "The Mint should be the manufacturer of coin; it is the Bank which fills the position of merchant, by obtaining the raw materials which the Mint requires."[1] That in fact was what the Bank was, the middleman through whom gold imported from abroad was transferred to the Mint. All the witnesses at the 1864 Enquiry agreed in recommending the Bank to buy all the gold offered to it and to do voluntarily what the Bank of England was by law compelled to do, buy the gold at a minimum price[2] so that all the available metal would be brought to it. That is what the Bank decided to do; it was in fact the only practical result of the Enquiry.[3]

From that time, it became a recognised maxim that the normal method by which a central bank protects its reserves, in the event of an outflow to foreign countries, or to prevent excessive credits on the market which might lead to the export of gold, is the raising of the discount rate. On this point unanimity reigned. The words which Bagehot used in his famous *Lombard Street* were accepted by all competent men:

"If the interest of money be raised, it is proved by experience that money *does* come to Lombard Street, and theory shows that it *ought* to come. To fully explain the matter I must go deep into the theory of the exchanges, but the general notion is plain enough. Loanable capital, like every other commodity, comes where there is most to be made of it. Continental bankers and others instantly send great sums here, as soon as the rate of interest shows that it can be done profitably. While English credit is good, a rise of the value of money in Lombard Street immediately by a banking operation brings money to Lombard Street. And

[1] *Inquiry*, Vol. III, p. 422.

[2] "The Bank of France," said Alphonse de Rothschild in his evidence in 1864, "is not compelled to accept gold always, but in fact it does so and has done so for a great many years. In certain circumstances it has bought gold at a premium, but usually it buys it at the Mint rate" (*Inquiry*, pp. 459 *et seq.*).

[3] The law passed in 1928 made it compulsory for the Bank to buy gold when offered.

there is also a slower mercantile operation. The rise in the rate of discount acts immediately on the trade of this country. Prices fall here; in consequence imports are diminished, exports are increased, and, therefore, there is more likelihood of a balance in bullion coming to this country after the rise in the rate than there was before.

"Whatever persons—one bank or many banks—in any country hold the banking reserve of that country, ought at the very beginning of an unfavourable foreign exchange at once to raise the rate of interest, so as to prevent their reserve from being diminished farther, and so as to replenish it by imports of bullion.

"This duty, up to about the year 1860, the Bank of England did not perform at all, as I shall show farther on."[1]

Bagehot was not the only one to express this idea; all the witnesses at the 1864 Enquiry were of the same opinion, and when in 1871 a third great bank was established on the continent, the Reichsbank, its entire legal structure was based on the use of the discount rate as the means of protecting the reserve and controlling credit.

There is practical unanimity as to the process by which the discount rate attracts short term foreign funds and eventually causes a fall in the price of stock exchange securities and then of commodities; it is described by Goschen in his *Theory of the Foreign Exchanges* (1861), by Bagehot in *Lombard Street*, by Marshall in his evidence before the 1887 Commission of Enquiry, and earlier by Tooke in his *History of Prices*. The theory which they formulated on this point remained practically unchanged, and was repeated in all standard textbooks and in Léon Say's preface to the French edition of Goschen.[2] It was not challenged until 1928, when Mr. Keynes published his *Treatise on Money*.[3]

On the other hand, objections to the too frequent variations in the discount rate became more and more numerous at this time, particularly in France; it was suggested in many quarters that the raising of the discount rate should be replaced by other methods which would not expose the market, and trade in general, to the

[1] W. Bagehot, *Lombard Street*, London, sixth edition, 1875, pp. 45–47.

[2] "There is only one legitimate way of attracting gold from abroad when the exchanges become unfavourable: that is the raising of the discount rate, and this method, with which Mr. Goschen deals, amply proves that it cannot be replaced by any other, however ingenious it may appear." Léon Say's *Preface* to the *Théorie des Changes*.

[3] Cf. Chap. XIII, which is given over to this question.

shocks arising from sudden rises and falls. Secondly, great differences of opinion began to emerge as to whether the bank of issue could control the discount rate, or whether it had itself to submit to it. These two elements in the classical theory of central banking require more detailed attention.

As early as 1840 Tooke had criticised the Bank of England for keeping its discount rate too low, in normal times, in order to attract more business. The bank of issue, he says, should always take care to maintain ample reserves, and should not let its rate fall below 4 per cent. By letting it fall too low, it is acting like an ordinary commercial bank which is anxious to attract clients, and it thus allows its reserves to be exhausted, whereas its position as the central bank should make it keep a greater reserve in order to meet possible crises.

At the 1864 enquiry in France many witnesses, of whom most were engaged in banking, accused the Bank of France of being too ready to raise its discount rate: it should, they argued, try to protect trade from too frequent and too great increases; it should regard it as one of its principal duties to maintain the utmost possible stability in its discount rate, and to be prepared to lose gold rather than follow, almost automatically, and to the great detriment of French trade, rises in the discount rate on the London market. Such criticism can be traced back to the working of the absurd clause in the Peel Act of 1844 under which the Bank of England was too frequently compelled to raise its discount rate; this naturally had an immediate repercussion on the French market. The argument was put forward with great vehemence by the Péreire brothers,[1] whereas bankers like d'Eichthal thought that the intimate connexion of the two markets in London and Paris made it necessary for the Bank of France to follow movements in the London rate.[2]

The two suggestions made to meet this point were designed to give the Bank of France alternative means of defending itself against changes in the London rate which would not react unfavourably on French trade. The first is no longer of interest except as a curiosity: the Péreire brothers proposed that the capital stock of the Bank of France should be sold and replaced by bullion.

[1] Cf. Isaac Péreire's book, *La Banque de France et l'organisation du Crédit en France*, 1864, which resulted in the appointment of the Commission of Enquiry into the currency.

[2] Cf. d'Eichthal's remarks on Péreire's evidence.

Their proposal was rejected at once on the ground that the sale of this stock would withdraw coin, or more probably notes, from the home market, and the Bank would be compelled to increase its discounting to an equal extent, in order to fill the gap in the currency created by this operation. The number of notes would therefore remain the same, or it might be increased, without the Bank having really strengthened its reserves. If, on the other hand, the Bank sought to obtain gold abroad, the foreign markets would be compelled, because of the loss of gold, to raise their discount rate and thus to recapture part of the gold which the Bank had tried to get. In neither case would the gold position of the Bank be strengthened.

The second suggestion is of interest because, although it was at that time rejected by the Bank (as Lord Overstone had rejected it at the Banking Enquiry of 1840 in England), it was, considerably later, adopted. This was the suggestion that the Bank should purchase foreign securities, not as a permanent investment, but in order to be able to use them in a temporary crisis and thus to avoid the disagreeable necessity of raising the discount rate in the event of temporary disequilibrium in the balance of payments. Many of the witnesses (in particular M. Pinard) supported this proposal.

This is in fact one of the methods used under the Gold Exchange Standard. It was employed freely by the Bank of Belgium. Later (in 1906 and 1907) it was adopted by the Bank of France in exceptional circumstances as a measure of assistance to London, and, on a much larger scale in 1927 and 1928, in order to avoid embarrassing London by the withdrawals of gold which the Bank of France's extensive deposits in London would have allowed her to make.

In 1864 the object of the proposal was to enable the Bank, if dollars or sterling rose, to supply the market for some time with bills on New York or London, without having to embarrass the money market by raising the discount rate. It was conceived as a way of meeting a temporary difficulty. The same object would have been served by the Bank's keeping a reserve of gold large enough to withstand a drain without taking any defensive measures. Those who supported this suggestion were fully aware that it would not prove effective against a steadily unfavourable balance of trade; in such cases the balance itself would have to be readjusted, which could only be done by changing the movements of capital or commodities.

The opponents of this proposal were chiefly the representatives of the large private money houses, who kept extensive holdings of foreign bills. The evidence of Baron Alfred André and Baron James de Rothschild is particularly illuminating on this point. At that time, and subsequently, the private houses kept a large portfolio of bills on London, firstly, in order to take advantage of differences, often considerable, in the rate of interest at the two centres, and secondly, to have at their disposal a reliable means of obtaining gold at all times (since Bank of England notes were always convertible into gold) in case the Bank of France, exercising its legal right, chose to give silver instead of gold in exchange for its notes (this practice was condemned by Léon Say in the Preface referred to above). In other words it was London and not Paris which to some extent served as the central bank for the French private banks.

The bills held by the private banks constituted an ever available reserve by which Paris could make certain that on the dates due gold would flow in. The situation was similar to that of London itself, which, by means of its acceptances covering world trade as a whole, was at all times in a position, merely by refusing to renew these credits, to make certain of a substantial access of specie, or to reduce in equal measure the volume of the demands which could be made on it for gold.

The arguments brought forward by the opponents of this measure were twofold: in the first place, if an institution as powerful as the Bank of France were to build up such a portfolio, foreign markets might regard this as a potential danger (and this in fact did happen in 1927 and 1928); secondly, foreign banks of issue, by constituting their own portfolios of bills on France, could easily counteract French policy.

During the course of the enquiry Alphonse de Rothschild outlined another method of influencing the market. This was for the Bank of England to compel the market to raise its discount rate if it differed too widely from the Bank rate. With the government bonds and Treasury bills which it held, it was in a position either to sell them on the market, or to borrow on their security, and thus to withdraw part of their cash reserves from the banks, which would then be compelled to raise their discount rate.

But Baron de Rothschild was careful to add that such action presupposes that the banks regard the government bonds as a perfectly safe investment that would not fluctuate, in short that the financial standing of the State is above all suspicion. He remarked that the financial standing of the French State was not so incontestable that methods of this kind could be used. The central factor in these proposals is the use of open market policy.

All witnesses however were agreed that the raising of the discount rate, the method *par excellence* of protecting cash reserves, should be used only as a last resource. On this point too Thiers merits quotation.

"I agree that as a brake, as a means of stopping speculation when it has become a matter for anxiety, the raising of the discount rate can be a good thing in itself, but only on condition that its use is timely, not during a crisis, but beforehand, when it is first anticipated. I admit that it is difficult to act in this way, and that it requires great courage and foresight, for the bank would certainly be attacked for slowing down business. The brake has always been put on too late; facilities having been granted when they should have been refused, they are withdrawn when they should be granted. The raising of the discount rate is not very useful as a brake; it is useful only as a means of preventing our cash reserves from draining away to our neighbours. The situation disclosed by the state of the exchanges shews that in many cases this danger has been illusory. But I repeat that the raising of the discount rate cannot be wholly condemned; it is even legitimate and indispensable if bullion has to be bought. The Bank has sometimes spent as much as 14 million for premium alone in order to get gold, and it is natural that the effect should be felt in the discount market. But it would be better if the Bank of France, instead of raising its rate to 10 per cent, as the English do, were to work within narrower limits, not going below 4 per cent and not rising above 6 per cent or 7 per cent at the most. But it is impossible to be dogmatic on this point; the best advice that can be given is that changes in the rate should be kept as small as possible." [1]

One further question, which we cannot overlook, was raised at the enquiry. What are the real powers of the central bank as regards discounting? Can it force the market to obey, or does bank rate merely reflect the state of affairs created by the supply of and demand for short-term capital?

According to the Governor of the Bank, M. Rouland, and to M. Thiers, whose evidence on this point is of great interest, the

[1] Thiers' evidence at the 1866 Enquiry, Vol. II, pp. 439–444.

Bank of France does not claim to do more than register the state of the market; it merely affirms a position that already exists. Later, in his famous report, Burdeau writes: "It would be a mistake to think that the Bank fixes its rate arbitrarily. It can only register the rate for money."[1]

Bagehot does not agree with this official theory. He very rightly points out that the Bank, which holds a large part of the resources of the market, is in the position of a merchant with a large stock of non-perishable goods; he can offer a larger or smaller quantity of these goods on the market, and thus make their price vary. This view is obviously more correct than the preceding one, but it should not be forgotten that the power of the Bank is not arbitrary and that very precise limits to its control are fixed by the resources of the market. Any attempt on the part of the Bank to raise the discount rate at a time when the open market has abundant resources at its disposal is bound to be ineffective. Indeed, the gap between what is called the market rate and the official rate is one of the best indexes to the demand and supply position.

But, these reservations made, the powers of a central bank in this respect are far greater than those which the Bank of France and M. Thiers would have us believe. It is enough to remember the influence it can exert on the market by open market operations. Nor should it be forgotten that in France, for example, commercial discounting is usually undertaken by all the banks at a rate slightly above Bank rate, so that in fact the Bank does control the discount rate prevailing throughout the country.

It is true that if the Bank is mistaken in its judgment of the rate to be fixed, the effects immediately produced on external gold movements, on credit operations within the country, or on stock exchange speculation, will compel it to change its policy.

It will be seen that while experts in France were at that time familiar with the essential features of the policy of a central bank of issue, and discussed the pros and cons of the case, to the majority of economists, even those like Courcelle-Seneuil who specialised in banking questions, the idea of a central bank and its functions remained unfamiliar.

[1] *Report*, p. 34.

§ III. *The Bank of Issue as the Country's Supreme Gold Reserve. From Bagehot to the Federal Reserve Banks of the U.S.A.*

Throughout the period we have been discussing the idea of a central bank and the idea of a bank of issue were closely associated in men's minds. It was generally believed that it was because they were banks of issue that the Bank of England and the Bank of France became central banks. That, however, was not in fact the only reason. Another, and more important reason was that these two banks operated in the capital cities of England and of France, where the greatest part of the payments of the country are made; in such centres bankers and business men naturally try to *simplify* methods of payment, and wherever possible to replace payment in coin, with all the attendant difficulties and costs of transport, by less cumbersome methods. In the eighteenth and nineteenth centuries the alternative open to them was to use bank-notes; hence the gold of the country was gradually concentrated in the hands of the bank of issue in the capital. But if, instead of bank-notes, the method employed had been cheques or transfers, central banks would still have grown up. Gold would have been deposited in the most important bank, the bank inspiring the greatest confidence, and its owners would have been credited with a corresponding sum in their bank accounts. A clearing bank instead of a bank of issue might have become (at least in theory, and if bank-notes had not been, historically, the forerunner of cheques) the central bank, concentrating the country's gold reserves.

The distinction between the process of note issue and the function of a central bank became clearer as the use of cheques, settled by a clearing arrangement between the banks, became more widespread. A few shrewd men realised (and stated in books that have become famous) that what was important for a country, if it was to be prepared for internal crises and assured of a supply of international currency for its payments abroad, was in the first place the concentration of its gold in a central reserve which would ensure the best use being made of it. Whether this gold could be drawn on by means of cheques on the central bank or by means of notes was a question of practical convenience, not of principle.

Thus, between 1870 and 1914, there gradually arose the idea that central banks of issue were and should be first and foremost "central reserve banks." This was the name adopted by the American banks of issue when they were established in 1913.

In France Vuitry had given an admirable account of the way in which the concentration of gold in a single reserve ensures its rapid despatch to any centre where there is a shortage. He considered this concentration the chief advantage of a single bank of issue; bank-notes were useful to the extent to which they facilitated the concentration of gold.

In England the Act of 1844 and the ideas which inspired it deflected and retarded the natural evolution of ideas. Those who supported the Act thought that, once the administration of the special money represented by bank-notes was determined (which was the work of the Currency Department), the Bank of England, in so far as it was a deposit bank, was no longer in a special position. It was just one deposit bank among many; it had no specific responsibilities or obligations. Like any other business undertaking, it did its duty if it made a profit. Far from desiring the accumulation of a strong reserve, the promoters of the Act, and in particular Lord Overstone,[1] obsessed by the idea of economising money, and disdaining Tooke's precepts, were anxious to have the gold reserve reduced to the minimum.

In a work which is one of the most brilliant and most profound that have ever been written on this subject, Bagehot directed attention to the role of the banks as the country's supreme reserve, and to the duties which that position involves; in so doing he brought English credit and banking theory back to the road marked out by Thornton and Tooke, from which it had been turned aside by Ricardo.

Bagehot's book was written in 1866, on the occasion of the failure of the house of Overend and Gurney, when the Bank of England was once more compelled to ask for the suspension of the Peel Act in order to save the City of London from disaster. Bagehot seized the opportunity of formulating once more the doctrine that

[1] "I should have no hesitation whatever in saying, that whatever reserve of bullion has under the existing system been found to be sufficient, would be found to be amply sufficient under the new system proposed; and I should fully anticipate that our experience would soon justify us in reducing that amount." Cf. Gregory, *Select Statutes*, Vol. I, p. 59.

the Bank of England—even if it is regarded merely as a deposit bank—is a central bank with all the responsibilities implied by that position.

The fact that it was necessary, in England, to devote an entire work to defending a principle which was widely recognised by all competent men, economists or financiers, can only be explained by the curious organisation imposed on the Bank of England by the Act of 1844. Bagehot's book can only be understood if that organisation is borne in mind. Whereas in all other countries the cash reserves of the Bank and its unissued note reserve are spoken of as the supreme resource in times of crisis, Bagehot only speaks of *the reserves* of the Banking Department. It is this reserve, he says, which constitutes the country's supreme resource. Bagehot refuses to discuss the merits and demerits of the Peel Act; he takes it as it is, and is not concerned with the issue of notes, but only with the working of the Banking Department. Through its Banking Department, the Bank of England had become the cashier of all the English banks which kept their reserves there. On the other hand the cash reserves of the country banks and deposit banks did not exceed 12 to 15 per cent of their deposit liabilities (the rest being used to grant credits). Thus, apart from the Bank of England's reserves, that is to say the cash reserves of the Banking Department, there were no resources available for meeting any sudden demand for means of payment.

The Banking Department's reserve was made up entirely of the unissued note reserve of the Issue Department, which was prohibited from issuing notes in excess of a certain sum, fixed once and for all, except against new gold. The Banking Department's reserve was thus completely inelastic. It could only be increased by appealing to the government to authorise a supplementary issue.

Bagehot comes to the conclusion that the Bank—more particularly the Banking Department—is not entitled to conduct its business on the lines of an ordinary commercial bank. It should not be satisfied with a reserve of 10 or 12 per cent of its deposit liabilities, which represent the cash reserves of all the English banks. It should maintain a credit margin, that is to say a margin of note issue, which will enable it to meet and withstand any panic. Consequently in normal times it should restrict its discounting and keep a large part of its deposits inactive. It is true that the Bank of England admits this obligation in practice; but in theory it disputes it. Bagehot wants it to be openly and publicly acknowledged, and made the basis of the Bank of England's credit policy.

This is Bagehot's thesis. He was the first to propound the theory of a central bank *in relation to a bank which claims to be nothing but a deposit bank*. In fact his theory is applicable to all banks of issue and, although the Banking Department's reserve is the only one mentioned, to the gold reserve and the issuing powers of all central banks. Similarly, his concern extends beyond a panic at home, to the possibility of a drain from abroad.

"Of late there has been a still further increase in our liabilities. Since the Franco-German war, we may be said to keep the European reserve also [America was not yet important]. Deposit banking is indeed so small on the Continent, that no large reserve need be held on account of it. A reserve of the same sort which is needed in England and Scotland is not needed abroad. But all great communities have at times to pay large sums in cash, and of that cash a great store must be kept somewhere. Formerly there were two such stores in Europe, one was the Bank of France, and the other the Bank of England. But since the suspension of specie payments by the Bank of France [the Bank of France had established forced currency during the war of 1870–1871, and it was retained until 1876], its use as a reservoir of specie is at an end. No one can draw a cheque on it and be sure of getting gold or silver for that cheque. Accordingly the whole liability for such international payments in cash is thrown on the Bank of England." [1]

Having thus indicated the special responsibilities incumbent on the Bank of England, he concludes with a trace of bitterness:

"It might be expected that as this great public duty was cast upon the Banking Department of the Bank, the principal statesmen (if not Parliament itself) would have enjoined on them to perform it. But no distinct resolution of Parliament has ever enjoined it; scarcely any stray word of any influential statesman. And, on the contrary, there is a whole *catena* of authorities, beginning with Sir Robert Peel and ending with Mr. Lowe [Chancellor of the Exchequer], which say that the Banking Department of the Bank of England is only a Bank like any other bank—a Company like any other companies; that in this capacity it has no peculiar position, and no public duties at all. Nine-tenths of English statesmen, if they were asked as to the management of the Banking

[1] *Lombard Street*, pp. 31–32.

Department of the Bank of England, would reply that it was no business of theirs or of Parliament at all; that the Banking Department alone must look to it.

"The result is that we have placed the exclusive custody of our entire banking reserve in the hands of a single board of directors not particularly trained for the duty—who might be called 'amateurs,'—who have no particular interest above other people in keeping it undiminished—who acknowledge no obligation to keep it undiminished—who have never been told by any great statesman or public authority that they are so to keep it or that they have anything to do with it—who are named by and are agents for a proprietary which would have a greater income if it *was* diminished,—who do not fear, and who need not fear, ruin, even if it were all gone and wasted.

"That such an arrangement is strange must be plain." [1]

Bagehot concludes that the organisation of the Bank of France is better than that of the Bank of England, and proposes that a permanent vice-governor should be appointed whose duty it would be to keep before the elected governors the special duties and functions of the Bank.

His book—which, after an interval of seventy years, comes, as it were, as a direct sequel to Thornton's—is for economists not merely an eloquent plea in a just cause, but the perfect model of the analysis of a money market. His account of the minute division of labour on the London market, with its deposit banks, its discount brokers, its acceptance houses, and their dependence on the Bank of England, is as interesting to the sociologist as to the economist, as important for the statesman as for the banker.[2]

The problem of strengthening the Bank of England's reserve was not however solved. It was to go on engaging the minds of experts and economists up to the eve of the world war. Twenty years after the publication of *Lombard Street* another crisis occurred in connection with the house of Baring. The Bank of England turned to the Bank of France and the Bank of Russia for assistance in strengthening its reserve and enabling it to issue more notes. This appeal to foreign countries made a deep impression on public opinion. The inadequacy of the gold reserve was commented on by all the important papers. *The Times* wrote that the gold reserve

[1] *Lombard Street*, pp. 41–42.

[2] For an account of the same market to-day see R. J. Truptil's excellent book *British Banks and the London Money Market*, 1936.

had for a number of years been too small. It suggested that the government should repay its debt to the Bank, which appeared in its balance sheet as capital; the Bank would then "be in a position to hold a large number of bills of exchange, as the Bank of France does, and could by that means exercise a more effectual command over the discount market, and consequently over the imports and exports of gold;" the article goes on: "Too large a proportion of the Bank's assets is in the form of fixed investments. If it transacted a much larger discount business it could afford to pay for a larger idle bullion reserve than at present."[1]

Once again it is suggested that the Bank should be reorganised on the lines of the Bank of France, but, the danger having passed, things remained unchanged. The proposal put forward by Lord Goschen, Chancellor of the Exchequer, that notes of small denomination should be issued to strengthen the Bank's reserve was not acted upon; it is an interesting indication of the trend of ideas, and from that time on was constantly under discussion, the more so as the mining of gold in the Transvaal and the consequent increase in the gold holdings of the majority of banks of issue after 1890 greatly strengthened the world monetary position, and made the acquisition of a large reserve an achievement coveted by all countries.

In Germany and France imports of gold were encouraged. Although long term international loans were made from Paris, the French balance of payments shewed a substantial bullion import each year. The only country where, notwithstanding the increase in the world's gold, the Bank's reserve remained more or less stationary, was England. The position was curious, since London was the chief gold market, and the volume of international credits granted by the English banks was far greater than that made by any other banking system in the world. Criticism arose from all sides. Clare pointed out[2] that the Bank of England's reserve served not only the English money market, but, in times of widespread crisis, the entire world. Inglis Palgrave[3] drew attention to the anomaly of a reserve growing steadily smaller in relation to the obligations not merely of the Bank of England itself, but of all the

[1] *The Times*, November 24, 1890, reproduced in Gregory, *Select Statutes*, Vol. 2, p. 193.

[2] *A Money Market Primer*, 1891, pp. 112–113.

[3] I. Palgrave, *Bank Rate and the Money Market*, 1903.

banks in the United Kingdom, and to the impossibility, in such conditions, of keeping the discount rate as stable in London as it was on the chief foreign markets. He urges the banks to come to an understanding about the maintenance of adequate reserves. Shortly before the war he returns to the same point in an article in the *Bankers' Magazine* for 1912, in which he compares the amount of gold acquired by the Bank of England with that acquired by other continental banks, and shews how inadequate it is.

It was, however, the 1907 crisis which brought home the weakness of the London market's reserves in relation to its international liabilities. A sudden loss of confidence led to enormous withdrawals from the banks in New York and throughout the United States. In the absence of a central bank where the American banks could rediscount their bills, the American market was for a short time in a state of bankruptcy. Gold stood at a premium over cheques and even over notes. This premium served to attract gold from Europe, and London was called on to provide the gold. London in its turn was unable to cope with the sudden demand; the discount rate was raised to attract gold from the continent. The Bank of France sent gold to the Bank of England and agreed to rediscount English bills.

These events provided a further demonstration of the necessity of having strong gold reserves at the central banks, and the advisability of establishing a central bank where no such institution existed. In England the occasion called forth Hartley Withers' *Meaning of Money* (1909) a worthy sequel to Bagehot's masterpiece, and in the United States it led somewhat later to the establishment of the Federal Reserve Banks, and to an enormous output of literature on banking questions.

In his really great book which, after a lapse of forty years, carries on Bagehot's penetrating analysis of the London money market, Withers brings home the contrast between the Bank of England's gold reserve and the enormous liabilities of the banks, emphasising the weakness of the first in relation to the second. He is disturbed not so much by the Bank of England's responsibilities in regard to the home market, as by its obligations abroad, which had become much greater since Bagehot's days as a result of the increase in the volume of international loans.

Withers then examines the various proposals made for strengthening the Bank's reserves: the creation of a special Treasury reserve to guarantee the deposits of the savings banks; repayment in gold of the state debt to the Bank of England; the issue of one pound notes against gold; the creation of a special reserve by the banks to be held by the Bank. He concludes that all these methods amount to no more than taking gold out of one pocket and putting it in another.

The Bank's reserves might also be strengthened by its keeping the gold imported into England, but that would mean a high discount rate, and a high discount rate means credit restriction. The desired object might perhaps be attained by making all the important banks publish a weekly return, shewing the proportion maintained by each between its reserves and its advances. The publication of these figures would necessarily reveal any tendency to grant excessive credits, and the banks would consequently practise greater caution; "its immediate effect would be the blotting out of a certain amount of credit which ought not to be in existence." The result, it must be admitted, would not be startling.[1]

The most important outcome of the 1907 crisis was the establishment of the Federal Reserve Banks in the United States, and the unequalled clarity with which on this occasion the concept of a central bank emerged. For the first time in the history of economic thought the concept of a central bank was linked up, not with the issue of notes, but with the concentration of the country's gold reserves. In England and France the spontaneous development of the money market had made of the bank of issue the country's gold reserve; from now on this is regarded as the purpose for which a central bank exists, the issue of notes being merely *one* of the methods that a central bank may use to fulfil its main function.

The evolution of ideas along these lines is particularly noticeable in the writings of Paul Warburg, an American banker of German origin, who from 1907 on took an active part in the campaign for an American central reserve bank. In articles and speeches he explained with truly admirable lucidity and comprehensiveness the role and functions of central banks of issue; at the same time he helped to draft bills for submission to Congress; the law establishing the Federal Reserve Banks was finally passed in 1913. In these articles

[1] *Meaning of Money*, p. 280.

and speeches, which were published in two volumes in 1930,[1] the role and functions of a central bank are formulated with the matured elaboration gradually achieved by a century of experience.

The essential ideas may be briefly summarised as follows:

1. The violent crisis experienced in the United States in 1907, which shook the whole of Europe, was the result not of a shortage of gold in the United States, for the bullion reserves of the banks were in themselves equal to if not greater than the reserves of all the European banks put together, but of the dissipation of these reserves among a very large number of banks. Since gold was scattered in this way, the banks, when the panic started, all hoarded gold, and thus brought about both a shortage of gold and a prolonged crisis. "The net result of our system is that immense amounts of gold and currency are wastefully locked up, and that, in spite of our immense gold treasure, which is four times as large as that of England, and notwithstanding our enormous *per capita* circulation of thirty-five dollars, we suffer almost annually from acute scarcity of money."[2]

In one passage he makes a striking comparison between the position in the United States in regard to the gold reserve, and an Eastern town where each household is given a few buckets of water for protection against fire at a moment when a violent storm is about to break. If the United States had had a central reserve on which all banks could have drawn by rediscounting their bills, the panic would not have spread and the crisis would have been avoided.[3]

Burgess makes another illuminating comparison in his *Federal Reserve System*. He says that the system under which it is necessary for each American bank to keep its own reserve brings about a position similar to that which would exist in a town where every taxi rank is compelled to keep three or four taxis in readiness all the time; for the town as a whole there would be an enormous waste of taxis. It might be claimed for such a system that it guaranteed the services of taxis whenever required, but in fact its introduction would greatly diminish the supply of taxis in relation to the demand.

Warburg is of the opinion, held earlier by Thiers, Vuitry and

[1] *The Federal Reserve System, its Origin and Growth. Reflections and Recollections* by Paul Warburg. [2] *Ibid.*, Vol. II, pp. 55–56. [3] *Ibid.*, Vol. II, p. 125.

d'Eichthal, that the main purpose served by a bank of issue is the concentration of reserves; this was achieved by its having a monopoly of the note issue;

2. The issue of notes is a secondary function of central banks. Notes, says Warburg, represent an "auxiliary" reserve, an addition to the main reserve which consists of gold. The object to be kept in mind in the organisation of a banking system is less the issue of notes, and the conditions of their issue, than the centralisation of reserves.[1] Thus the idea of a *reserve bank* clearly takes precedence over the earlier idea of a bank of issue;

3. Once a central reserve is formed, it is essential that the subsidiary banks should at all times be able to obtain credits at the central bank for which, should the need arise, they can get gold. The necessity to draw on these credits in gold will arise less frequently when the banks themselves are in a position to supply their clients, in the form of notes, with claims convertible into gold at the central bank.

Europeans did not find it difficult to grasp this concept, which had been clearly explained by Thornton; it was not so readily comprehensible to Americans, for they were not accustomed to the use of internal bills of exchange; merchants obtained funds from their bankers by giving them promissory notes, which it was difficult for an issuing bank to rediscount. These notes were held by the banks against advances, but they did not represent assets that could be always and easily realised. In the United States the banks' loanable funds were employed largely in forward operations on the New York Stock Exchange, so that the surplus funds of the country, instead of being used in trade, were employed to finance stock exchange speculation.[2] Warburg also makes great efforts to convince the Americans of the usefulness of a rediscounting system which would ensure the safety of the funds used for financing commercial bills and provide merchants with a constant reservoir of short term capital;

4. In his vivid account of the rediscounting system operated by

[1] *The Federal Reserve System, its Origin and Growth.* Vol. I, pp. 123–128.

[2] Apparently this still holds good; writing in 1937 Mr. M. Palyi says: "The introduction of the Federal Reserve System did not succeed at all in altering this characteristic feature of the American money market: the extraordinary concentration of surplus liquid funds in the field of financing security speculation." *The Chicago Credit Market*, p. 83.

European central banks, the advantages of which he constantly brings to the attention of American bankers, Warburg takes the Reichsbank and the Bank of France, not the Bank of England, as the model on which the system which he advocates should be based.

Without directly criticising the Bank of England, he makes it clear that he is no admirer of its hybrid and complicated organisation; he is, however, explicit in his praise of the English deposit banks which are, in his opinion, the best commercial banks in the world;

5. In regard, however, to direct intervention on the market by the purchase of relatively short term government securities, Warburg supports the Bank of England; the majority of continental banks have always rejected this method as dangerous; both in his draft constitution for the Federal Reserve Banks, and in his articles, Warburg explicitly favours this practice; he also advocates the purchase of international bills; he hopes that New York will become as important a centre for such operations as London.

In advocating the adoption of this twofold method he uses a striking phrase: "The bank of issue," he says, "should be able to act both as anvil and hammer." That is to say, in providing the money market with funds, it should at times assume a passive role, awaiting the demands for rediscounting that come to it as and when the market requires funds, and at times take the initiative by itself entering the market, either to increase the funds available on the market, or to diminish them, by the purchase or sale of government securities.

At first the primary object of the purchase of government securities in periods of stagnation, when the commercial bill holdings of the bank of issue tend to decline, was to enable the Federal Reserve Banks to earn some income (since the Government paid interest on these securities) during the lean years. It was only later that this method was employed as a means of maintaining business activity by making fresh funds available whenever the withdrawal of gold by foreign holders, by compelling the bank to raise its discount rate, might have caused a setback.

This open market policy, when conducted on a large scale, means that the bank of issue's judgment as to the *real* needs of the money market takes the place of ordinary gold movements as the controlling agency on that market. The dubious results achieved by this policy on the American money market are well enough known. We have already shewn that it tends to isolate the different money markets, since the bond established between them by gold movements is no longer effective. Furthermore, it deprives the national money market of the one effective check that can correct an exaggerated rise in relation to other markets, that is, the withdrawal of bullion.

It was not until after the war that the full consequences of this policy became apparent. The central banks of issue had departed further and further from the position of distributors of gold among the world's money markets, and had become purely national instruments for the creation of money. This change represents the last stage in the development of ideas relating to central banks.

At the time when Warburg was writing, that is to say in the period following the 1907 crisis, the dominant idea, as we said at the beginning, was that of the central bank acting as the country's gold reserve; and it was on these lines that the Federal Reserve Banks were organised. From the moment of their establishment they were taken as the model *par excellence* of the central bank, and the new banks of issue in different countries were founded on the same principle and usually bore the same name.

Thus the concept of the central bank, originating in the functioning of the Bank of England at the end of the eighteenth century, taken up by the continent, and for a time obscured in England by the disastrous ideas introduced by Ricardo, found its fulfilment in the United States in the early years of the twentieth century. It was elucidated in a comprehensive and brilliant fashion by a banker with a thorough knowledge of European banking practice. The theory of central banks might then appear to have been definitely established; it was however at this moment that a wider ambition was expressed. A few hardy spirits, shaken by the 1930 crisis, wished to give a new function to central banks, that of regulating world prices.

§ IV. *Banks of Issue and Price Stabilisation*

In the years which followed the war it occurred to certain economists that banks of issue might be entrusted with the task of stabilising prices; an attempt should be made on an international scale to keep the volume of loans within the limits commensurate with the price level that it was desired to maintain.

The banks of issue themselves shewed no disposition to take up the proposal. In the United States (still haunted by memories of the severe crisis of 1922) a Senate Committee was set up in 1928 to investigate the question whether the Federal Reserve Banks should adopt as part of their policy the stabilisation of prices. The most eminent authorities consulted, including Benjamin Strong, Governor of the New York Federal Reserve Bank, were emphatically opposed to the suggestion; they believed that a central bank of issue should in no circumstances assume such a responsibility.[1]

More imaginative men, like Mr. Hawtrey (in his *Art of Central Banking*) and Mr. Keynes (in the last chapters of his *Treatise on Money*) proposed that a joint effort should be made by the central banks of issue to achieve, by deliberate credit policy, the object which Benjamin Strong thought it impossible to reach.

"If the central banks of the world, acting in concert, aim at stabilising the wealth value of their currency units and therefore of gold . . . the gold standard would be maintained, but gold would be tied to the currency units, instead of the currency units to gold."[2]

In another passage Hawtrey puts it this way:

"The central banks are the source of the world's supply of money. It is their essential duty to adjust the supply to the world's needs. The supply of money is made dependent on the supply of gold, but the relation between the two is determined by the central banks and legislatures. The legislatures limit the freedom of the central banks. The residue of freedom remaining to the central banks was quite sufficient to enable them to prevent the depression and crisis of the past three years. That it was not so used was the result partly of divided responsibility and partly of a want of far-sightedness."[3]

The idea of regulating the price level by the restriction or expansion of credit has attracted a great number of people. It has, of course, always been recognised that a bank of issue, if its inter-

[1] Cf. *Hearings before the Committee on Banking and Currency: House of Representatives*. 69th Congress. Washington, 1927, 2 vols.

[2] Hawtrey, *The Art of Central Banking*, p. 194.

[3] *Ibid.*, pp. 245–246.

vention is *timely* (the entire difficulty lies in that one small word) can prevent a crisis from being extremely severe; the restriction of credit serves as a warning and checks the violence of a speculative boom. What is new in the recent suggestions is the proposal, firstly, that such action should be taken simultaneously on all markets, and, secondly, that while credit restriction should be employed to mitigate an impending crisis, *credit expansion* should be used to maintain a given price level, or to overcome a prolonged depression.

Nobody will deny that in *certain clearly defined circumstances* the co-operation of the chief central banks could mitigate certain price fluctuations, particularly those which arise from excessive credit. But to contend that by such action it is possible to maintain a given price level over a long period seems to the present writer to rest on a failure to discriminate between the action of credit, which can only cure the ills created by credit, and the action of the fundamental and permanent factors which determine long term price movements.

This confusion touches the very concept of credit and of money. It requires a brief examination here, although in a theoretical work of this kind it is, of course, impossible to examine the wholly practical and ever changing problem of co-operation between the great issuing banks.

The real question at issue is the extent to which credit can affect prices; it is one which in the last few years has been the occasion of a great deal of subtle and complex discussions on the interaction of saving and credit. It is the same problem, in slightly different guise, as the one that Tooke examined when dealing with the relations between short term price fluctuations and what he called *general* price movements.

The central banks are asked to increase the credits they grant, or to make it possible for the commercial banks to increase their credits, in order that world prices may be maintained at a certain level. We think that this proposal rests on a delusion. They are asked to bring about the result that would be brought about by inconvertible paper money (assuming that this paper money did not depreciate because of lack of confidence).

What can the central banks do? They can only make *advances*, and short term advances at that. These advances are necessarily *repayable*. The additional purchasing power put into circulation by the banks is to be returned to them (if not wholly then at least in large part) in the future, and indeed in the near future, unless it is assumed that the banks of issue no longer regard it as their duty to grant *credit*, but to create definitive purchasing power.

How can the purchasing power which they lend be returned? Only by deductions from the final income of those to whom the credit was granted. In other words, *if credits are repayable* (and it cannot be assumed that they are not) they take the place of sums which, though not in existence at the moment, *have to be deducted a little later from the final income of those who enjoyed the credits.* This means that the present increase in expenditure (with the action on the price level that it involves) will subsequently be offset by a diminution of the expenditure that *would have* been made if there were no credits to be repaid; and this diminution tends to lower prices.

Three examples may be given to make this clear.

If the advances made by the banks are purely commercial advances intended for the purchase of commodities already in existence, the anticipated sale of which will automatically provide funds, it is obvious that the advances are repaid from the gross proceeds of the sale, which are part of the normal income of the community.

If the advances represent loans to provide working capital, the problem is more complicated, for in this instance the advance made by the bank takes for the time being the place of *long term savings* which have not yet been accumulated. When a bank lends an industrialist the funds to pay for the labour and raw materials which he requires, it replaces by a bank credit a sum which as a rule the business man should have saved, before starting the undertaking, out of income, and which should have provided him with his working capital. The bank lends him these savings in advance. It follows that in subsequent years the business man, in order to repay his obligations to the bank, and to regain "the freedom of his treasury" will have to deduct *from his net income*, that is from his profits, savings *equal to the entire loan made to him by the bank.* Thus the *present* demand for goods is increased at the cost of a *reduction in the demand for goods and services exactly equal to the advance originally made by the bank*, this reduction being made at a later period. Unless it is contended that the banks need pay no heed to their *credit margin*, and that they can prolong their loans indefinitely, the initial action on the price level *will be offset by an exactly equivalent action in the opposite direction* in the period following the advance.

This argument is even stronger when the banks grant credits, not to provide working capital, but for investment, that is to say when they render their funds immobile by granting long term loans with short term capital. The history of every crisis demonstrates that it is impossible to maintain the price level by bank credit.

But, it will be asked, do not bank loans themselves create the income with which they can later on be repaid? Nothing of the kind! It is true that bank loans create incomes (wages and profits) which increase the general demand for goods and consequently the *gross* income devoted to their production. But these loans (which represent, at least in the two last examples, anticipated savings) can only be repaid out of *actual savings*, that is to say with funds deducted from the net proceeds of industry. Now there is no reason to believe that in the usual term for which a bank credit is granted, savings will increase by a sum equal to the advance. On the contrary, the advance is as a rule greater than the sum usually saved in the same period. Consequently the demand for goods in the period following the advance will be smaller than it *would have been* if the advance had not been made. That will exert downward pressure on prices.

Thus, the rise of prices resulting from the granting of loans is subsequently offset by the deductions that have to be made from net income to meet the repayment of the loans.

This process is entirely different from that set in motion by the issue of paper money—except of course when a State decides to redeem the paper money, that is to say to start deliberately the process of deflation, which is automatically set going in the case of bank credits.

The only way in which the pressure exerted on prices by the repayment of bank advances can be counteracted is by an inflow of gold; *this increases the banks' credit margin*, and thus enables them either to grant further credits, or to put up with delays in the repayment of loans without suffering any ill effects.

This being so, it seems to the present writer wholly mistaken to believe that a world price level can for any length of time be maintained by means of credits granted by the central banks, or through the banking system in general.

If the discussion of this problem is to serve any useful purpose, it must be based upon a thoroughly clear understanding of the way in which credit and savings affect income. This is not the place in which to discuss this process, which has in recent years exercised the ingenuity of many economists. This question is part of the general problem of savings and crises, which lies outside the field covered by a general history of credit theories, and requires separate investigation. But I would say that the way in which this problem has in recent years been treated has often been far from satisfactory. The mechanism of saving is complex. Its effects vary according to whether the savings are made out of consumption or out of increased income (consumption, in the latter case, shewing no decline); whether they are made in a country where population is stationary or growing; whether they are invested entirely at home, or partly in other countries, etc., etc. The majority of economists who have studied the effects of saving on the national economy have not taken these possible alternatives into account. They have examined the effects of saving as though it were a simple phenomenon, whose consequences in regard to consumption and production develop in strict accordance with a single uniform pattern. Nothing is further from the truth. What we unquestionably know is that savings, in so far as they are used to increase agricultural or industrial productivity, tend to bring world prices down. There is no reason to believe that this profound and permanent effect can be counteracted by credit expansion. On the other hand an increase in gold output (provided, of course, that Governments do not sterilise the new gold) and the issue of paper money can be relied on (though the two have very different results) to bring about a rise in prices or to check a fall.[1]

[1] It is impossible to mention all the writers who in the last few years have, with greater or less success, tackled this problem. A complete bibliography, as well as a notable analysis and examination of the different theories put forward, is to be found in Gottfried von Haberler's *Prosperity and Depression* (Geneva, 1937). For the theory of savings the reader will find M. Divisia's *L'Epargne et la Richesse Collective* (Paris, 1928) particularly useful.

CONCLUSION

The question of currency organisation is one which is constantly coming to the forefront. If the history of monetary doctrine shews anything, it is that money (whether of metal or paper) is a "social reality," as François Simiand said. It is not a book-keeping process superimposed on an economic system which could function equally well in its absence; this assumption is constantly being made, and explains many of the mistakes of the classical school. Since it is an economic reality, it is influenced by economic evolution, and itself exerts an influence on that evolution. It is both "anvil and hammer," as Warburg said of central banks of issue. The instrument which serves as a store of value, which enables the proceeds of labour and of saving to be safeguarded until they are transformed into objects of direct utility, itself has a value, fluctuations in which necessarily exert an influence on the economic system. "Neutral" money is an impossibility. The reactions to such fluctuations are varied and conflicting.

Theorists have always been interested in the prolonged upward and downward movements of world prices. As soon as they are observed, efforts are made to find a way of checking them or of avoiding them. We have examined the various remedies proposed for escaping these powerful movements. All of them boil down to the creation of national currencies, of which paper money is the chief example.

But no sooner is this road taken than a new problem is engendered, for the break with the international gold standard immediately gives rise to variations in the foreign exchanges, to internal price movements, to divergences between domestic and foreign price levels, followed by disturbing movements of capital, and finally to all round instability as a result of the "currency war"[1] that inevitably breaks out when there is a variety of standards, and to growing economic nationalism. Those who would reform monetary systems must first of all choose between these two alternatives—an international standard with the attendant risk of prolonged upward or downward price movements throughout the world, and national

[1] This is the title of M. Mario Alberti's book, *La Guerra della Monete*, Como, 1937.

standards with all the instability and all the constraints and fetters that they imply. The greater number prefer to fix their attention only on the advantages of the one system or the other. This makes their propaganda easier, but adds nothing to truth. The sacrifices involved by choosing one rather than another must also be measured. Those which are made when the international standard is abandoned are, in the opinion of the present writer, so great, that a country which takes this course is exposing its economy and its political security to the utmost danger.

Monetary systems, however, are subject to other influences than those of normal economic development; they are profoundly affected by wars and crises. Wars and crises, as has been amply shewn in this book, have been of tremendous importance in shaping currency systems and currency theories.

In time of war, money is a purely national instrument. It ceases to be "anvil" and becomes "hammer." By issuing paper money to cover their financial requirements, governments do away with the function of money to serve as a store of value and use it exclusively as purchasing power, making its acceptance as means of payment compulsory. Since the war there is little need to describe the confusion and disorder thereby created in prices, incomes, and exchanges.

In times of crisis it is not the state but the economic community itself that seems to change at will the value of the money standard, creating those alternations of rising and falling prices which result from the greater rapidity given to the circulation of money and the subsequent slowing down in its movement. The process by which excessive credits are wiped out is almost as painful (though less prolonged) as the return to normal gold prices after a period of paper money.

Currency cranks dream of making these transitions painless. They believe it possible to establish a currency system adapted to all occasions; capable of shielding the community from the consequences of misuse and error in the management of the currency, whether on the part of individuals, governments or peoples. Their dream is more mischievous than fruitful, for as a rule the system they propose is one of curing the ill by the ill, and the abuse of currency by a still greater abuse, just as, in medicine, certain charlatans drug their patients until it is difficult to say whether the malady or the treatment constitutes a greater danger to their health.

Fortunately, the problem which civilised states have to meet is more simple: it is the problem of organising the return to an international standard, of re-establishing between politically independent states a common standard on the basis of which stable commercial relations can be resumed. The gold standard alone can serve this purpose.

The first requirement is to abandon the incorrect diagnosis with which for the last six or seven years the patient has been deluded. It is no longer possible to maintain that the gold standard is the cause of all our ills, and that it is the rise in the value of gold that has thrown world economy into disorder. It is no longer possible to believe that the 1929 crisis was an ordinary crisis, or that the remedy is of the kind suitable for ordinary crises.[1] We must recognise this one very simple fact, frequently stated in the course of the present work, that the issue of paper money during the World War made all prices rise to a level incompatible with normal conditions of gold output on the one hand, and of the production of commodities on the other. The continuity of the gold price level had been seriously disturbed. At the present time it seems to be almost re-established. To reach this stage it was necessary to go through painful but unavoidable processes, the most important of which was devaluation. Failing a new world war we may hope that this continuity will be maintained for some time. After violent disturbance the price level seems liable in times of peace only to those fluctuations which accompany the usual alternation of periods of boom and depression, and to those which arise from the more or less rapid increase in the output of commodities and of gold. (Improvements in the methods of payment have of course also to be taken into account, but so far nobody has succeeded in measuring the progress of this factor). Failing new world wars there is no likelihood of a price collapse such as that which occurred between 1930 and 1935. The President of the United States has often proclaimed the desirability of a dollar whose purchasing power will remain stable for at least a generation. *Assuming that new gold will be allowed to produce its normal effects on world economy*, we may

[1] I should like to refer to my pamphlet, accompanied by a chart which is, I think, conclusive: *Interprétation de la chute des Prix depuis 1925* (Paris, Sirey, 1936).

look forward without anxiety to a period in which the purchasing power of the dollar will fall very slowly and slightly, a course which will give nobody cause for complaint.

Secondly, it must be recognised that the belief in gold arises not from age old superstitions of a more or less magical character, but from age old experience. A claim on gold—a cheque or a bank-note—is something clear and precise that everybody understands, just as everybody understands a mortgage on a piece of land or a house that he knows. Paper money is a claim on something unknown, on a country or a government, whose political, social or financial escapades and arbitrary decisions nobody can be sure of beforehand. Certain theorists make the mistake of believing men to be more dull witted than in fact they are. After the events of the last twenty-five years it is obvious to all that a man who in 1913 put all his fortune into bullion, which he kept buried until 1937, would have made the finest possible speculative investment. The poorest and most ignorant villager cannot but realise that in the course of these twenty-five years the only commodity whose value has, without any possibility of doubt, risen, is gold. The stability of the value of gold is a fact which survives all paper currencies. It seems to me wholly false to believe that by demonetising gold it will lose its value, although that belief is held by so many serious minded men. The demonetisation of gold is easy enough. The difficult thing is to find something to take its place; so far nobody has found that. At the present time no credit system is conceivable without a gold basis, whether direct or indirect.[1] The more complex and highly developed the credit system, the more necessary is the gold basis. It is surely not an accident that London has never held such large gold reserves as since the time when it professedly abandoned gold.

There would be more readiness to listen to the advocates of currency systems not bound to gold if they were more disinterested. But these benevolent reformers have as a rule been aware that the gold standard is a powerful means of guarding against the arbitrary actions of governments in the sphere of currency and finance. The majority of men are anxious to have a stable money standard and

[1] In London, for example, although notes are not convertible, holders of paper money know that they can get all the gold they need, at a more or less unvarying price, by the purchase of stable gold dollars.

the comparative stability of prices which that represents. They are disturbed by any action which threatens that stability. Although the interests of farmers, manufacturers, and merchants, of labourers and working men, frequently clash, there are some matters in which their interests are the same—as savers and as consumers they all derive great benefit from a stable money standard and from the resulting relative stability of prices. Consequently the reactions to any step that may affect this stability are widespread and general—flight from money, withdrawal of bank deposits, purchase of real values, etc.

There is a singularly instructive similarity between the greater or less political liberty which governments to-day permit their subjects, and the greater or less liberty which they allow in currency operations.

We are willing to admit that improvements could be made in the international organisation of the gold standard, that a better understanding between the central banks of issue, that certain agreements reached by them might make it possible to avoid minor fluctuations in credit and even in prices. But these reforms are possible only on the assumption that all the countries where the central banks have both the desire and the power to co-operate for the common good shall first of all return openly and publicly to the gold standard. Which is more easy to organise? Co-operation between banks having the common bond of union represented by the gold standard, or co-operation between countries whose standards are all independent and lack a common foundation? There can be no doubt as to the answer.

It would, of course, be a great illusion to believe in the eternal stability of a given gold standard, and a still greater mistake to desire it. It is quite likely that the progress of European civilisation has been tremendously facilitated by the slow and gradual fall in the value of gold and by the universal rise in prices which was the result. This was Hume's opinion, and provides additional proof of the shrewdness of that extraordinarily intelligent man. Great industrial and commercial changes are made much more easy by a slight rise in prices which facilitates all transactions and gradually lightens the burden of debt. It mitigates the effects of the rashness inherent in all economic initiative. The modernisation of Europe after the discovery of America was rendered possible only by the universal fall in the value of gold. The war of 1914 made a profound reorganisation of the industrial structure necessary in all countries; this could never have been accomplished without the rise in prices resulting from the creation of money. But war excuses many things which become criminal in times of peace.

That is why the attempt made after the war to return to pre-war parities was one of the most disastrous that have ever been made. Countries which pursued this course assumed a heavy responsibility. The present writer has always been of the opinion that currency devaluation was a necessity for the world after the World War and the gaping differences in price levels to which it led.

No less heavy was the responsibility of those countries which, after the war, tried to use currency depreciation as an easy means of concealing their financial extravagance and of indulging in chronic budget deficits. Just as the gradual and widespread rise in prices due to abundant gold output encourages economic development *because it takes place on an international scale*, so the deliberate or unconscious organisation of price instability and of financial disorder in the national field weakens the economic forces of a country and puts a scandalous premium on speculation to the detriment of labour and of saving.

Of the two mistakes made by the belligerent states after the war—the return at any cost to pre-war parity, and the disregard for financial equilibrium which was bound to lead to further currency depreciation—it is difficult to say which was more disastrous.

To-day, in any case, when the return to an international standard has become an obvious necessity, it is unmistakably clear that this return is possible only on condition that the financial discipline which it implies is respected by all the countries which wish to pursue this policy. Now that gold prices have returned to a level which may be regarded as normal, the only danger to currencies arises from bad financial administration on the part of governments, and from the pursuit by group interests of advantages which can only be obtained by thwarting the legitimate activities of the country as a whole.

As to the policy of sterilising gold because of the fear of a too rapid price rise, that seems to me no less disastrous. The readers of this book will without difficulty find the origin of that policy in the ancient theories which, backed by Ricardo's authority, dominated England's monetary policy. The rebirth of these ideas a century later is for the historian peculiarly instructive. The effects of gold on the economic and financial structure of the world have always been beneficial. Given the vast monetary requirements of the world, an abundance of gold would not to-day give rise to any disquieting price rise. In any case, it would not be very difficult, if anxiety on this score were felt, to regulate the entry into circulation of the new purchasing power represented by newly mined gold. The hoarding policy now pursued by England and America obviously derives from the theories in which metallic money is regarded merely as a "voucher to purchase," and flouts those according to which money is primarily a "store of value." Thus the old conflict of ideas which we noted in the first chapter of this book reappears in a new guise. This book will not have been wholly useless if, in however small a degree, it helps to settle the dispute in the only sense in conformity with social and scientific truth.

INDEX